READING DIFFICULTIES
their diagnosis
and
correction

READING

PRENTICE-HALL, INC., *Englewood Cliffs, New Jersey 07632*

DIFFICULTIES

their diagnosis
and
correction

GUY L. BOND
University of Minnesota

MILES A. TINKER
University of Minnesota

BARBARA B. WASSON
Moorhead State University

fourth edition

Library of Congress Cataloging in Publication Data

Bond, Guy Loraine,
   Reading difficulties—their diagnosis and correction.

   Includes bibliographies and index.
   1. Reading—Remedial teaching   I. Tinker, Miles
Albert,   joint author.   II.   Wasson, Barbara B.,
joint author.   III.   Title.
LB1050.5.B6 1979   372.4'3   78-23807
ISBN 0-13-754978-4

©1979, 1973, 1967, 1957 by PRENTICE-HALL, INC. *Englewood Cliffs, N.J. 07632*

READING DIFFICULTIES: Their Diagnosis and Correction, 4th edition
Guy L. Bond, Miles A. Tinker, Barbara B. Wasson

Printed in the United States of America

10   9   8   7   6   5   4   3   2

editorial/production supervision and interior design: CATHIE MICK MAHAR
cover design: JORGE HERNANDEZ
manufacturing buyer: JOHN HALL

PRENTICE-HALL INTERNATIONAL, INC., *London*
PRENTICE-HALL OF AUSTRALIA PTY. LIMITED, *Sydney*
PRENTICE-HALL OF CANADA, LTD., *Toronto*
PRENTICE-HALL OF INDIA PRIVATE LIMITED, *New Delhi*
PRENTICE-HALL OF JAPAN, INC., *Tokyo*
PRENTICE-HALL OF SOUTHEAST ASIA PTE. LTD., *Singapore*
WHITEHALL BOOKS LIMITED, *Wellington, New Zealand*

Contents

eight

nine

ten

eleven

sixteen

Preface

Deficiencies in reading ability among both children and adults have become of increasing concern. Capable young adults severely retarded in reading are unlikely to find suitable employment, for at least moderate reading ability is needed even to apply for most jobs. But even if employment is found, advancement for the severely retarded reader is usually difficult or impossible.

This fourth edition of *Reading Difficulties: Their Diagnosis and Correction* has been extensively revised, reorganized and modified. There are three recent trends, based on research findings, which have made these changes desirable.

First, recent studies have shown that a combination of methods develop reading capabilities better than does any one method alone. Such combinations of methods should include teaching skills and abilities systematically, as is done in *basic readers;* coordinating of reading skills with the other language arts, through *language experience* approaches; and using extensive independent reading, as suggested by *individualized reading* approaches.

Second, the recent contributions made by the fields of linguistics, psycholinguistics, and sociolinguistics have shown the importance of differing language patterns among children of various environments; the need for closer coordination between the written and spoken language in teaching reading; and the necessity of teaching the perceptual and decoding skills in such content that meaning clues, including syntax clues, semantic clues, and expectancy clues, may be utilized fully.

Third, the *learning disability* movement in special education has changed the roles of both classroom teachers and special resource teachers. With the current emphasis upon educating handicapped children in the least restrictive environment (mainstreaming), handicapped children have been placed in regular classrooms for regular instruction, and are aided as needed by resource teachers. Thus classroom teachers have had to become diagnostic reading teachers, and resource teachers have had to become reading specialists and consultants. There needs to be close cooperation established between the two.

The aim of this book is to help the classroom teachers, resource teachers, and reading specialists to diagnose and to correct the various kinds of problems involved in preventing and correcting reading disabilities. The authors are keenly aware of the fact that learning to read is complex and that there are many possible confusions along the route. If the classroom teacher can detect and correct these difficulties early many minor problems that may lead to a major reading disability may be prevented. This book is designed to give the teacher specific help by describing how to diagnose and correct reading difficulties in the formative stages.

Certain children will persist in their reading difficulties to the point that they will need more detailed diagnosis and individualized remedial training. The classroom teacher cannot be expected to make these more detailed and complex analyses, but this book discusses the various reading disabilities in a sufficiently detailed and direct manner so that a thorough understanding of the most complex cases is possible. Finally, there are specific suggestions for diagnosing and correcting even the most stubborn kinds of problems of disabled readers so that all who are concerned with disabled readers will have the information necessary to understand the adjustments required.

For the sake of convenience and brevity in this book, we refer to the child as "he" and to the teachers as "she." This does not mean that we do not recognize the equal importance and needs of "she," and we regret that there is no neutral term which would reflect our feelings.

The authors have used extensively the results of research on reading instruction and reading disability. We wish to thank all of the research workers who have made this book possible. We have drawn heavily on our own and many coworkers' clinical experience at the University of Minnesota Psycho-Educational Clinic and the Moorhead State University Reading Clinic. For their many suggestions, we wish to thank specifically Bruce Balow, Theodore Clymer, Robert Dykstra, Leo Fay, Bjorn Karlsen, Virginia McKinnon, and Maynard Reynolds, associates of the authors on the faculties of the University of Minnesota and Moorhead State University. We also wish to thank the many teachers-in-service for their insights, which they presented when discussing the problems of reading instruction while they were taking advanced courses and seminars. Finally, the authors wish to give special thanks to Fredericka H. Bond for her extensive editorial and other help in the preparation of this book.

GUY L. BOND
MILES A. TINKER
BARBARA B. WASSON

Introduction

one

The ability to read well is one of a person's most valuable achievements. Our world is a reading world. It would be difficult to find any activity, whether in school, in the home, on the farm, in business, in the professions, or even in recreational pursuits, that does not require at least some reading ability. Often reading is an indispensable channel of communication with an ever-widening world.

Even a casual observation of people's activities reveals the prominent role of reading in their lives. What they do is made possible or is expedited by tremendous quantities of reading matter in the form of magazines, newspapers, books, directories, pamphlets, and catalogues. People read to obtain information, to buy economically, to arrive at a decision, to provide pleasure, and for many other reasons. More people read today than ever before.

NATURE OF READING GROWTH

Preparation for reading begins long before the child enters school. Even before an infant talks, there are rudimentary forms of communication between him and his parents and others around him. From this time until he enters school, preparation for his reading is many-sided and elaborate. In a few short years, a child progresses from when he could only pat the pictures in his first book to learning to point out and name familiar objects in the pictures. It then is not long before he listens when read to, and soon he will recite little rhymes and talk about the stories in his books. These steps are gains in verbalization and in recognition of form and meaning. The processes of communication have begun. Thus we find that progress in *readiness* for reading can be extensive and significant during the preschool years.

Following the usual approaches in learning to read, the child must understand the relationship of printed language to oral language; he must understand that a printed word stands for a spoken word and has the same meaning as the spoken word. In beginning reading, the printed word should always be in the child's spoken and meaning vocabulary, as he will associate the printed word with the sound of the spoken word and with the meaning of the spoken word.

The printed words in any writing are merely symbols for the meanings intended by the author. These symbols serve as cues to the reader who must organize an understanding of what is meant. The ease with which a child can do this depends largely upon his past experiences. For a beginning reader, these meanings are acquired through his experience background and his previously acquired facility in understanding and using speech. The child reads using his experience and verbal capacity, interrelating them "behind his eyes," as it were.

To a large degree, a child's thinking uses verbal manipulations. When he begins to read, this is important, for thinking is essential to reading at all stages of development. In fact, reading as a tool for learning may be ineffective unless it is accompanied by thinking. Learning to read and reading to learn should develop hand in hand throughout the school years.

Reading is both a subject of instruction and a tool for studying. During recent years, there has been more emphasis on reading to learn. The writers of this book, however, do not want to emphasize either learning to read or reading to learn. Both views have a place and should be coordinated in the balanced program of instruction. Though we know that the skillful teaching of reading is of the highest importance in the primary grades, we recognize that it is still important in the upper grades and in high school in which additional skills and abilities are required to cope successfully with new reading situations. At all grade levels, there should be proper instruction for adapting the acquired skills to the reading of subject-matter material.

The special skills should be taught as they are needed. They should be taught in the appropriate context. For example, the special skills needed for reading in science should be taught with material similar to that used in science instruction. Even though this emphasizes reading as a tool, it also teaches reading.

Growth in reading abilities is developmental in nature. Each new learning is an addition to or an expansion or refinement of previous attainments. This growth involves the gradual acquisition of skills which together enable the learner to interpret printed symbols correctly and so to enter into meaningful language experiences. These skills are developed concurrently with their use as part of the reading act itself. Reading development is the result of tasks which are neither easy nor simple. Each new learning, for the child, rests upon his previously acquired achievements and requires that he apply his newly developing ones to increasingly more complex reading materials. Instruction must maintain balances among the various skills and abilities essential to growth, geared to the needs and characteristics of the children being taught.

Definition of Reading

Because of its complexity and the many successive stages of its development, Spache and Spache (187) consider that one simple definition of reading will not suffice. So they proceed to describe and define reading under a variety of headings: reading as skill development, as a visual act, as a perceptual act, as a thinking process, and reading as related to cultural background. Although it will be helpful to many readers to have these detailed aspects of reading called to their attention as Spache has done, it is surely also useful to have one overall definition, provided that it supplies a clear description of normal reading growth such as we have attempted to give in the following section.

Our definition of reading is as follows: Reading is the recognition of printed or written symbols which serve as stimuli to the recall of meanings built up through the reader's past experience. New meanings are derived through manipulation of concepts already in his possession. The organization of these meanings is governed by purposes clearly defined by the reader. In short, the reading process involves both the acquisition of meanings intended by the writer and the reader's own contributions in the form of interpretation, evaluation, and reflection of these meanings.

Description of Normal Reading Growth

To detect those children who have failed to make satisfactory progress in reading, it is necessary to have in mind some norms of reading growth. There are marked individual differences in rate of progress in learning to read. Some children will begin to read early and progress rapidly. Others will start late and move forward slowly. Between these are the average learners. It should be noted also that a child may progress at different rates at different stages in his development of reading abilities. In general, however, normal growth in reading tends to be fairly continuous and developmental in nature. At each stage, the abilities essential to success at the next level are acquired. When this progress is continued without serious interruption, the child eventually becomes a fairly mature reader.

THE PREREADING PERIOD. Soon after birth, the child begins to acquire experience essential to learning to read. With further growth in mental ability, in emotional adjustment, in acquiring interests and in all sorts of experience with objects and people, the child is ready to begin reading. An understanding and speaking vocabulary develops gradually. In time, sentences are comprehended and properly used. As this is going on, the child develops skill in auditory and visual discrimination. Varieties of concepts are formed. Under favorable circumstances, the child develops attentive attitudes which permit listening to and comprehending of stories. If experience is extensive, if many clear concepts have been acquired, and if adequate facility in the understanding and use of language has been achieved, the child will have a distinct advantage in getting ready for reading (Tinker, 209).

Many environmental factors condition the rate of development up to the time when the child is ready to read. To acquire auditory and visual skills together with language facility, there must be opportunity and guidance. Besides having a broad range of experiences, the child must be stimulated to discriminate sounds and objects, and to listen to and use words. It is important for older persons to talk to and with the child. Stories should be told and they should be read with the child while he looks at pictures and talks about them. The child's own extensive experience with picture books, crayons, paper, scissors, paint brushes, and the like, also prepare him for reading.

Under favorable circumstances, and provided that mental growth, emotional adjustment, and physical status are normal, the child not only will be ready to read but also will be eager to read. Obviously, there are marked differences in the rate in which children acquire reading readiness. A few may be ready even before reaching kindergarten, others by the time they enter first grade; many become ready soon after beginning first grade, but a few are not ready until later.

PROGRESS IN READING READINESS. The child is ready to begin a reading program only when he has reached a certain stage of mental maturity, has a satisfactory emotional adjustment, and has acquired an adequate background of experiences and attitudes. Mental maturity comes only through natural growth, at its own pace. As already noted, there are many degrees of readiness among children at the beginning of grade one. After an evaluation of each child's background, the teacher provides a program to offset whatever deficiencies in reading readiness she discovers. With proper guidance and instructional procedures, each child will, sooner or later, be ready to read.

Some authors imply that the readiness program is completed when the child has acquired those experiences and skills which assure success in beginning reading. Many teachers have the same unfortunate view. The concept of reading readiness is basic to the development of reading ability at all levels, from kindergarten on. With each new unit of instruction, the child should be prepared to carry out the reading and thinking activities involved in the unit. For success in any specific reading task, the pupil must possess the necessary concepts, vocabulary knowledge, and ability to handle the language relationships involved. He also must select and organize those meanings which are in line with his purpose. All this implies instruction and guidance so that the pupil will be *ready to read* each new unit proficiently.

INTRODUCTION TO READING. After proper preparation, the child is introduced to reading in grade one. He begins to accumulate a sight vocabulary and at the same time learns that printed and written symbols stand for meanings in a variety of situations. Training in auditory and visual discrimination continues. New word meanings are acquired. His teacher helps him in using elementary techniques and clues for word identification. In the meantime he is progressing naturally from reading labels, words standing for actions, short signs and notices to reading a book, the pre-primer. Systematic training in reading a book then becomes a reality with progress to the primer level and so on to the first reader. All along, learnings are reinforced through exercises suggested in manuals, through workbooks and other supplementary materials.

There will be marked individual differences in the reading progress made by first-grade pupils. By the end of the first grade, the average learners will have acquired a considerable stock of sight words, some independence in using techniques of word recognition, and considerable skill in both the oral and silent reading of easy materials. The children also will have developed desirable attitudes toward reading through their newly acquired skill in the use of books, and will, it is hoped, find interest and enjoyment in independent reading of other books outside the basic materials, including those in the public library.

PROGRESS IN THE PRIMARY GRADES. To a large degree, the reading instruction in grades two and three consists of an extension, refinement, and amplification of the program begun in grade one. New techniques are introduced, and the child begins to learn them at whatever time he is ready and at just the proper stage of development. Throughout the primary grades, there are no abrupt distinctions in progressing from one part of the program to the next. Under favorable circumstances, the average child will have achieved the following goals by the end of grade three: he will have made marked progress toward mastering techniques of word recognition and the other fundamentals of reading, developed considerable independence in reading, acquired a degree of flexibility in the use of reading skills, laid a sound foundation for the study-type of reading needed for the special sorts of reading ability and study, achieved greater speed in silent than oral reading, and acquired positive attitudes toward books and reading. With normal progress, by the end of grade three, the child will have acquired a sound foundation for all future reading, although there still are many basic skills in word recognition, comprehension, and techniques of study to be developed later.

Reading instruction in grades four through six is an extension of the developmental program begun in the primary grades. Besides perfecting the basic abilities, it concentrates on developing the specialized abilities and study skills required for reading subject matter in content fields and other work-type materials. Beginning with grade four, children move into a period of ever-increasing diversification of learning in which reading is the essential tool. To an accelerating degree, reading becomes a means of achieving information and pleasure. When there has been normal progress in the earlier grades, the consolidation of basic reading abilities and the extension of these abilities in specialized directions in the intermediate grades will proceed at a relatively rapid pace. The child becomes a more independent and extensive reader. Although the relative emphasis upon silent reading increases, oral reading should not be neglected. By the time the sixth grade is finished, the child who has made normal progress will have acquired a solid foundation for reading in later years. Additional instruction in reading in the junior and senior high school years is necessary to assure proficiency. This is particularly true with regard to perfecting the special abilities and skills needed for serious study and for the comprehension of difficult materials.

PROGRESS IN THE BASIC READING ABILITIES. Throughout the successive grades, there is more or less steady growth in the acquisition of word knowledge, skill in word recognition, and ability to comprehend printed matter. Progress is developmental or sequential, and each feature provides a basis for subsequent growth in features similar to it. Reading readiness plays an important role. A child is ready to advance to a succeeding level of a learning sequence only when his mastery of previously taught skills is sufficient to ensure success in more mature learning. In word recognition, for example, he learns letter and phonogram sounds in the early years. This equips him for the more mature features of word recognition which include syllabication, prefixes, suffixes, and word roots taught in the intermediate grades.

It can be demonstrated that many qualities of a mature reader can be detected in the early reading responses of the beginner. They even can be detected in the prereading program. Each succeeding learning builds on and utilizes the skill acquired earlier. These basic reading abilities are not acquired in isolation but as part of a well-integrated sequential reading program.

PROGRESS IN THE SPECIAL READING ABILITIES. The acquisition of the special abilities necessary for proficient reading in the content areas begins early and progresses at a gradual pace for most pupils. Since the reading of some content material is introduced in grade one in the better reading programs, it is necessary to teach the elementary features of the special abilities during the primary grades. By grade three, such guidance should become fairly prominent. If it is, the progress of the average pupil in reading to learn will have advanced far enough by the end of the primary grades so that the transition to the major reading tasks in the intermediate grades will be smooth and effective rather than abrupt and difficult.

As the child moves through grade three and into and through the intermediate grades, the study skills are added to the special reading abilities. Mastery of the basic reading abilities together with continuing improvement in the special reading abilities and study skills are coordinated into proficient reading habits. With normal progress, the child will have acquired considerable flexibility in adapting these abilities and skills to the purposes and subject-matter requirements for each of the content areas. He also will have learned the supplementary skills necessary for the reading problems which are unique to a particular subject. Although complete mastery of the special reading abilities cannot be achieved by the end of grade six, there will have been good progress in this direction. The child will have a sound foundation for further progress in the reading tasks in the junior and senior high school years. It is justified at any grade level to assume that the reading growth required for effective learning can be completed by an earlier grade only when the reading materials used are not more advanced than those the child had in the earlier grade. This is rarely the case. The materials read in high school are obviously more mature than those used in elementary school. Consequently, the child must be taught to meet these new demands.

Goals of Reading Instruction

An effective reading program does more than develop the abilities and skills, both basic and special, outlined in the preceding section. Nevertheless, the broader goals of the reading program are built upon these foundations. Reading is more than ability to identify and recognize words, to group words into thought units, to note details and follow directions, and is more than ability in all the skills and techniques. The reading program must offer every child a number of specific goals.

The overall goal of reading instruction is to help each pupil to become as able and as diversified a reader as his capabilities, the available facilities, and the instructional program permit. To achieve this, certain subgoals must be considered. These goals are present during early reading experiences and grow more apparent as reading matures up through the grades. It should be recognized that there is interdependence among the goals of reading instruction. One goal is not necessarily more important than another. These goals will be discussed in the paragraphs that follow:

BASIC UNDERSTANDING OF WORDS, SENTENCES, PARAGRAPHS, AND STORIES. Growth in these understandings is essential if the pupil is to progress into a mature reader. Word meanings are derived from experience. As language facility increases and words are used with newly experienced objects, situations, and events, concepts are clarified and enriched. Growth is continuous but slow. The instructional program for developing a child's vocabulary to express meanings will provide varied and rich experiences both firsthand and vicarious, wide and extensive reading, and study of words in context. It also will develop the habit of attending to the meaning of words so that if an unusual or expressive word is used, the child will note it and its meaning. An understanding of words is basic to understanding sentences, paragraphs, and stories.

The understanding of sentence structure affects reading comprehension. Besides knowing the meaning of words in a sentence, the reader must grasp the relations between words and groups of words. The kind and amount of instruction is determined by individual needs. With one child, the instruction may be guidance in proper phrasing, interpretation of punctuation, interpretation of figures of speech, use of a word whose meaning fits the verbal context, and sorting out and properly relating several ideas incorporated in one sentence.

Along with understanding words and sentences, comprehending a paragraph requires understanding the relationship among sentences in that paragraph. The instructional task involves guidance in identifying the topical sentence containing the key idea and in interpreting its relation to the explanatory or amplifying sentences. In a similar manner, some attention should be devoted to the relation between paragraphs in longer selections.

One set of learnings involved in comprehending a story consists of word, sentence, and paragraph understanding. Also involved is the degree to which a child has the ability to listen to and follow the sense of the story. Some children, when they begin school, have made considerable progress along this line. Others have acquired little or no story sense at that time. These will need preliminary guidance in learning, before formal reading instruction, how to listen carefully to what is said and how to follow a sequence of events in stories. The story sense cannot be developed to its maximum efficiency for any child by the time reading is begun. Since the acquisition of several important reading techniques is facilitated by ability to comprehend stories, continued instruction is needed. Guidance in listening attentively and in following sequences of events should be an integral part of reading instruction at least through the primary grades. After the primary grades, because of the more complex plots and more complicated organization of ideas encountered, the child must learn to sense the author's organization in order to grasp the meanings of the longer selections.

MATURITY IN READING HABITS AND ATTITUDES. Development of reading habits and attitudes begins early and continues as long as the child is growing in reading capability. The child learns to appreciate and to care for books. He develops intellectual curiosity and the realization that books can help him to satisfy this curiosity as he uses them to solve his own problems and to contribute to group enterprises. As he gradually learns that reading is a part of written communication, he will want to share in what the author has to say. The habit of attending to words and of demanding an understanding of their meanings should be encouraged at all levels. Finally, the habit of relying on one's own resources and of energetically attacking reading material should be encouraged early in the hope that it will be strengthened throughout the instructional program.

INDEPENDENCE IN READING. To begin to read well and to be able to continue his intellectual growth after formal education is finished, the child must develop independence in reading. There are several features in achieving this independence. The child must be able to recognize words rapidly and with a minimum of effort if he is to grasp and think over content. Growth in reading ability depends on the ability to work out the pronunciation and understanding of new words. The independent reader also will know sources where he can search out new material, he will know how to select relevant subject matter from these sources, and he will know how to judge the suitability of that subject matter. Independence in reading also is manifested by the ability to initiate one's own reading activities, to appreciate reading problems, and to set one's own reading purposes. Reading programs organized into important experience units that require related reading and activities encourages growth in independence. The teacher's guidance plays an important role in the development of independence in reading.

EFFICIENCY IN THE USE OF THE BASIC STUDY SKILLS. A number of skills are needed for attaining this goal. Efficiency in locating information through such aids as tables of contents, indexes, and card catalogues is one group of these skills. Instruction in the elementary techniques of finding information begins early. The more complex features are taught in sequential order.

Proficiency in the use of general reference material is a second group of study skills. Beginning with simple alphabetizing, the child goes on to use dictionaries, encyclopedias, and the like.

A third group of these skills is the interpretation of pictures, maps, graphs, and charts. Teaching this begins in kindergarten and progresses in a developmental manner through the school years. These skills are important, though frequently they receive little emphasis.

A final group of skills is especially important. It is the technique of organizing materials, including outlining, classifying materials under main and subheadings, organizing sentences in experience charts in sequential order, and ordering selected materials in sequence for a report to the class. Constructing time lines, two-way charts, and classification tables are other examples. The ability to organize materials is essential to well-rounded growth in reading proficiency.

MATURITY IN FIVE MAJOR CLASSES OF COMPREHENSION ABILITIES. The development of five interrelated types of comprehension, each corresponding to a different, though related, ability, is a major goal of reading instruction. They are as follows: (*a*) reading for specific information, (*b*) reading to organize, (*c*) reading to evaluate, (*d*) reading to interpret, and (*e*) reading to appreciate. These varieties of comprehension are the ever-present goals of reading instruction. They should not be postponed so that they have to be initiated at more advanced school levels.

MATURITY IN ADJUSTING TO THE READING DEMANDS OF EACH DISCIPLINE OF HUMAN EXPERIENCE. To impart their ideas to readers, authors write in ways appropriate to their purpose. To grow in reading proficiency, a child must learn to adjust his reading to the requirements of the specific type of material he is reading. An example is the contrast between the adjustment needed for reading and solving a verbal arithmetic problem and that for reading an easy short story. Such adjustments are made through coordination of the basic reading proficiencies, the different abilities involved in comprehension and the study skills. The reader must choose from his repertory of abilities and skills those best for reading effectively a particular selection for a specific purpose. Since the adjustment must be taught, it is a goal of reading instruction. A young child starts to develop a differential attack upon various types of reading material as soon as he reads a science unit in his basic reader or in a supplementary book. Versatility in this sort of adjustment improves from grade to grade. The teacher should help in making these adjustments. The achievement of facility in this differential attack becomes a goal of reading instruction at all instructional levels.

BREADTH OF INTEREST IN READING AND MATURITY OF TASTE IN ALL FIELDS OF HUMAN EXPERIENCE. This objective will seem obvious to teachers. To be successful, a reading program must go beyond development of the basic and special abilities and the study skills. The child also must want to read widely for enjoyment and profit. The amount, the variety, and the quality of what is read is the truest test of the quality of the teaching program. Guidance, beginning early and continuing through the instructional levels, should provide the child with broad, permanent interests and good taste.

POINT OF VIEW

The authors believe that a reading problem develops because one or more factors in a child himself or his environment, or both, prevent him from reaching his learning capacity. This reading difficulty may occur at any stage of a child's school career from first grade up through higher levels. The writers believe that a reading disability can be corrected through proper diagnosis and remedial instruction. Nothing is accomplished by blaming the disability on low intelligence, lack of interest or laziness, or home environment. For one reason or another, school instruction, in these cases, has not capitalized on the child's mental ability nor developed motivation by appealing to his interests.

If all the skills and abilities necessary for growth toward reading maturity are to be acquired, the learner must be motivated and energetic; one who works smoothly at his own level of accomplishment and is also a comfortable learner. Each child must be able to sense that his proficiency in reading is increasing and that the enterprise is worth his effort.

In recent years, the teaching of reading has gained an important position in our schools. Research has progressed, teachers are better trained, reading materials have multiplied, and techniques and devices for teaching have improved. As a result, pupils tend to be better readers than their predecessors. Nevertheless, a surprising number of pupils fail to make the progress in reading expected from their capacities. This is recognized especially by the importance given today to remedial reading and the widespread establishment of reading clinics.

The presence of reading disability cases in our schools is a serious problem at all levels of the academic ladder. Many reading difficulties can be prevented. The classroom teacher can correct others in their initial stages when correction is relatively easy. The preventive program stresses at least three kinds of instruction: (a) a thoroughgoing reading readiness program to prepare the child for beginning reading and for reading at successively higher levels; (*b*) proper adjustment of instruction to individual differences; and (*c*) systematic developmental programs at all levels.

A well-organized instructional program will try to prevent reading disabilities. If it were possible in day-to-day teaching to teach each pupil according to his capabilities, there would be less need for remedial work. Even with the best teaching and the best organized, systematic program, certain children will have difficulties serious enough to require remedial instruction beyond the capabilities of the classroom teacher. With less than the best teaching, the incidence of disability cases will increase. In any case, there will be an appreciable number of pupils who have serious difficulty with their reading, and there must be a remedial program to correct these difficulties.

View on Causes

The writers know that the causes of reading disability are multiple and tend to be complex. In the more difficult cases, there usually is a pattern of interacting factors operating, each factor contributing its part to the disability and each impeding future growth. The reading specialist must search out as many as possible of these limiting conditions, operating in a particular case, and apply the proper corrective measures.

In general, the writers believe that most disability cases are created and are not inherent. Reading disabilities are sometimes the result of unrecognized, predisposing conditions within the child, but for the most part, they are caused by elements of the child's environment at home, at play, and in school. Without appropriate guidance or without proper instruction given at the right time, the child will fail to acquire the skills needed to develop normal reading ability.

Reading difficulties vary from minor to very severe. When minor difficulties occur and are not recognized and promptly corrected, their deleterious effects become cumulative and frequently result in a severe disability.

Although the writers emphasize educational factors as causes of reading disability, they also recognize that there are others, which may and often do contribute as parts of a complex pattern of causes. These may include immaturity in various aspects of reading readiness, associated sometimes with low socioeconomic status, emotional instability, physical deficiencies, social pressures at home or at school, as well as other factors. There seldom is a single factor that causes reading disability, but one factor may be relatively more important than others.

The writers are aware that failure to recognize a child's handicaps and failure to adjust instruction in order to lessen their effects upon learning, may contribute to a reading disability. Unless all educational, physical, and emotional factors which may hinder normal progress in learning to read are identified early, are corrected if possible, and proper instructional adjustments are made, a disability case is apt to develop.

View on Remedial Instruction

The writers maintain that remedial instruction in reading is essentially the same as good classroom teaching, but it is more individualized. The teacher works with the child, using regular teaching methods but concentrates on the skill in which the child is deficient. Effort is concentrated on the pupil's needs, assuming that there has been a thorough diagnosis of his abilities and difficulties.

The authors believe the best results in remedial instruction are attained by designing *an individual instructional plan* that utilizes a combination of approaches, which usually has a basic reading series as its core. The remedial plan, however, should include any one or any combination of approaches that is suggested by the results of the diagnosis. When used as a framework, the basic reader should present a well-balanced program rather than an extreme approach. In selecting the basic reading series, these features should be considered: emphasis on reading for meaning rather than on isolated drill, controlled introduction of a utility vocabulary with adequate repetition to develop it into a sight vocabulary, natural sentence structure rather than mere repetition, a well-planned sequence of skill development with meaning clues and checks, and interesting content.

Four contemporary teaching procedures used in remedial reading instruction will be presented briefly. What we hope to accomplish in this book is to show which combinations of approaches will fulfill best each of the many diagnosed instructional needs of disabled readers.

The language experience approach capitalizes on the relationship between the child's reading and other language developments. To this end, reading is integrated with the teaching of other language skills. The trend in development advances from listening and speaking to writing and reading and then, with more mature abilities and skills, to total language development.

The child's language experience is the result of a stimulating class in which pupils have many opportunities to produce and share ideas through language. Reading begins when the pupils tell their experiences and ideas, and describe their interests so that the teacher can write them down for all to see, either on the chalkboard or in experience charts. Soon the children discover that material for reading is just talk written down.

Writing is introduced early, when the teacher begins instruction in word-recognition techniques, vocabulary development, and other reading skills. From the accumulated word lists, exercises planned for reading and illustrating word-recognition principles are organized by the teacher. A sight vocabulary is built by reading dictated material and doing classbook exercises so that the children are not restricted to high frequency words.

Van Allen (214) has outlined a language-experience program. Some of his points are: (*a*) All experiences which a child can express in oral language are raw materials from which reading develops. The child's oral language is a basic ingredient of word recognition. (*b*) Children's oral expression is based on their sensitivity to environment, especially language environment. (*c*) Many activities, experiences, and devices cultivate a child's communication skills, including what the teacher provides and what the child does in verbalizing and writing. (*d*) An advantage of a language-experience approach is that it allows great flexibility in organizing school activities—the teacher can work with the entire class, small groups, or individuals. (*e*) Other advantages are that it does not require standard English in beginning stages; available materials can be used effectively, children begin reading with a vocabulary already acquired, team teaching works well, the approach is ungraded, phonics becomes an integral part of the daily activities, independence is developed, and all children participate.

The language experience method can be valuable to reading growth. Most successful teachers daily use various elements of this approach while also relating reading to the other language arts. It is desirable throughout reading instruction to emphasize the relationship among listening, speaking, writing, and reading. In the diversified teaching program, the language experience approach decidedly is useful.

The linguistic approach is not yet fully developed, but is promising in helping to solve some of the disabled readers' problems. Some teachers are now trying linguistic approaches and procedures in their classroom teaching. Many others have expressed views on the effects of linguistics on reading instruction. Linguistics involves the origin, nature, modification, and structure of language. Upon examination, linguistics is found to emphasize patterns of speech, vocal habits, and systems of sound symbols.

One concern of linguistic scholars is the study of patterns of speech, such as the arrangement of words in sentences and the variation in function and meaning when the same word occurs in different locations in a sentence. According to Smith (181), many linguists stress being able to recognize other structural principles in word order, because they are fundamental to understanding the reading process. They contend that children at age six are using complex sentences and have recourse to sentence patterns already learned. The linguist notes that many books for children descend to a line of "baby talk" which is as unreal to the children themselves as it is to adults. They urge that when teaching reading it is best to utilize, for beginning reading material, sentence patterns that are more natural, and indeed are those already used by the children in conversation. It is Gliessman's (92) opinion that the development of sentence sense through linguistics would contribute to better comprehension in reading and would improve both fluency and speed.

It appears that linguists already have made many important contributions to reading instruction. One, helpful to the reading specialist, is the refinement of diagnostic and remedial reading practices. For example, the role of context clues and other meaning aids to basic word-recognition skills and basic comprehension abilities have long been considered essential elements in diagnostic and remedial reading programs. The linguists have expanded this concept. Goodman (94) has indicated that the reader has three types of information available in the act of reading. The first two are semantic and syntactic clues, which the reader uses in anticipating the content. He then uses the third type of information, graphic representation. The reader uses whatever perceptual (graphic) clues he needs for meaning, and he then checks the accuracy of his reading by the sense it makes. There is no question that the emphasis on the role of semantic and syntactic clues is an important adjunct to developmental reading programs. The skill the disabled reader has in using these specific meaning aids should be noted in diagnosing certain types of reading difficulties.

The authors of this book support the importance of the role of these meaningful reading clues. Therefore, throughout the book, all of the reenforcement exercises designed to overcome specific decoding and perceptual problems have been presented in content rather than in isolated drills. We agree with the pragmatic concept that the child anticipates what is to follow from what he has just read, as an aid in reading the specific sentences to come. We even go somewhat further by including the fact that in any reading act, the child anticipates words and concepts from the complete communicative situation and from his knowledge of the specific topic being read. Moreover, it is our point of view that all of these meaning clues, including syntactic and semantic, are used in concert in reading. Therefore, we will use the terms *meaning clues* for this group of reading aids, *context clues* for those derived from a specific sentence, and *expectancy clues* for those gained from the larger use of language and knowledge. We will break down *meaning clues* into separate segments only when the diagnosis or correction of the specific elements is involved.

The individualized reading approach is used enthusiastically in some schools both by teachers and pupils. Each child selects his own reading material, paces himself, and keeps records of his progress [Lazar and others (131), Putnam (158), Sartain (171), Veatch (216)]. With this method, used even in grade one, each pupil reads widely materials of his own choice, even if his teacher thinks his choice is unsuitable. The child is allowed to set his own pace, even if it means that he reads relatively little over a period of time. Once or twice a week, the teacher meets with the child in a pupil-teacher conference for five or ten minutes. The teacher uses the time to find out what the child has read since the last conference; to evaluate through questions the degree of comprehension; to note special needs and difficulties and to give specific help with these; and to keep a careful record of the child's reading capabilities, needs, and progress. The teacher guides the child, to some extent, in his choice of future material [Witty (229)]. Occasionally, the teacher groups children with the same reading need into a temporary group to teach them a reading skill or to provide classroom remediation. Also, there often are small-group or whole-class periods during which one or more children share with the others material selected for that purpose [Darrow and Hawes (50)].

The individual approach to reading has focused attention on the need for extensive independent reading. This need is pertinent to all remedial programs, but it is especially important to those building sight vocabulary, word meanings, and reading fluency.

The programmed learning approach is one in which the materials break the subject matter or skills into small units. After the subject or reader has responded to each unit, he immediately refers to the answer to see if he is correct. The material may be workbooks, textbooks, worksheets, or cards. Or, a teaching machine may be used to present the units. After each response, the student checks his answer by pushing a button or lever, or by working some other device. Thus the pupil is given a chance to correct his errors as soon as he makes them. In programmed instruction, the information to be taught is organized into units and then programmed in a logical, progressive order.

Programs may be a desirable adjunct to other materials under certain circumstances. Choice of the materials for a particular child should be guided by the observation that he can and will work independently, will profit from such application, shows a need for the particular ideas and skills offered, and does not have a highly dependent personality.

In reading instruction, programmed materials are perhaps most frequently put in the form of true-false or multiple-choice questions which cover the content that the child has read. After each response, he immediately checks his answer against the one provided him. In addition to testing literal comprehension and phonics, other areas in reading instruction in which programmed procedures might be used include critical reading, interpretation, study skills, and possibly word-identification techniques. But, in general, programmed instruction is best adapted to teaching facts that need to be memorized and to those processes that need to become automatic. It cannot be used for all teaching. As stated by Smith (181), proponents "think of programming as an effective learning device to free the teacher of repetitious tasks which take little advantage of her teaching skills and leave to her the aspects of teaching which require explanations, guided thinking, and intelligent discussion" (pp. 83–84). Since much repetition is frequently necessary in remedial instruction, it is likely that programmed teaching will be used.

In a critical review of programmed reading in the elementary school, Fry (79) concludes that there is plenty of evidence that programmed materials with computer instruction and talking typewriters can teach beginning reading. He states that "There is no proof, however, that programmed instruction can do any more for beginning reading than regular classroom teaching or human tutoring" (p. 410). He points out that in the only well controlled study available, "programmed learning and basal texts came out in a dead heat" (p. 410). It seems that the classroom teacher may use as much programmed instruction or as many automated procedures as she wishes and that the budget will allow.

Effective remedial instruction is given by a good reading teacher. She must be familiar with the principles and practices of sound reading instruction. Above all, she must be versatile in adapting materials and techniques to specific needs, and she must apply them with patience, understanding, and empathy. Successful remedial work can be achieved only when there is a good rapport between pupil and teacher.

The writers are convinced that well-conceived, remedial instruction will result in improved reading ability. Theoretically, the instruction should bring the child up to the reading grade that is in line with his learning capacity. This should be possible except in the small number of cases that are complicated by factors beyond the ability of the teacher to correct. It is, however, a rare case in which a skilled teacher is not able to bring about a significant improvement in reading, given a reasonable amount of time.

PLAN OF THIS BOOK

This book discusses a practical program to reading which is based on research findings and sound instructional procedures. Our chief concern will be the individual child who is in difficulty in his attempts to learn to read. We are convinced that both the classroom teacher and the reading specialist must be equipped to diagnose and correct reading deficiencies whenever they arise.

We will present the treatment of learning problems in ways that apply both to the classroom teacher and the reading specialist, the difference being only in the complexity of the disabled reader's difficulty and the amount of personal attention needed. Chapter 2 is concerned with the extent of individual differences and the problems of adjusting to the instructional needs of these differences.

The next three chapters are devoted to the identification and classification of disabled readers and the causes of their reading disabilities. Chapter 3 discusses the criteria used in identifying the disabled reader and then suggests descriptive categories for them. Chapters 4 and 5 cover the causes of reading deficiencies. The roles of physical, emotional, and educational factors are described and evaluated.

The next three chapters deal with diagnosis of reading disabilities. Chapter 6 discusses the principles and levels of diagnosis and deals with questions to be answered by the diagnostician in analyzing reading difficulties. Chapter 7 describes specific standardized and informal diagnostic procedures. Chapter 8 discusses the principles involved in using the diagnostic findings in order to formulate an *appropriate educational plan of remediation.*

The techniques used in the treatment of word-recognition difficulties are described in the next four chapters. The techniques used to overcome deficiencies in basic meaning clues necessary for successful word recognition are discussed in chapter 9. The remedial techniques used in faulty decoding skills in word recognition are presented in the following chapter. Chapter 11 describes the remedial teaching necessary for the complex reading problems of extremely disabled readers, and Chapter 12 presents the adjustments needed to solve the problems of the disabled reader handicapped physically, emotionally, intellectually, or environmentally.

The last four chapters are concerned with the problems of basic comprehension abilities and more specific types of disabilities related to comprehension. Chapter 13 describes remedial techniques for correcting basic comprehension difficulties. Chapter 14 deals with remedial treatment for weaknesses in specific comprehension abilities, basic study skills, and in various reading materials of the content fields. Chapter 15 is concerned with improving inefficient rates of comprehension and overcoming ineffective oral reading and chapter 16 covers ways to encourage continuous growth in reading by expanding interests in reading, increasing independence, and providing follow-up help.

To help the readers of this book identify antecedents, we have chosen to use "he" for the disabled reader, and "she" for the teacher. We also have used the labels, remedial teacher, diagnostician, reading specialist, or clinician, according to the phase of work being done, whether it be by resource teachers, reading specialists, or classroom teachers. Although the suggestions given for diagnosis and remediation are applicable to disabled readers at any age, we have used the word "child" in our writing. The principles are equally applicable to all disabled readers from the early grades to adult.

SELECTED READINGS

BOND, GUY L. and ROBERT DYKSTRA, "The Cooperative Research Program in First-Grade Reading Instruction," *Reading Research Quarterly,* no. 2 (summer 1967), 5–142.

GUTHRIE, JOHN T., ed., *Cognition, Curriculum, and Comprehension.* Newark, Del.: International Reading Association, 1977.

HARRIS, ALBERT J., and E. R. SIPAY, *How to Increase Reading Ability* (6th ed.), chaps. 3, 5, New York: David McKay, 1975.

LEE, DORRIS M., and R. V. ALLEN, *Learning to Read through Experience* (2nd ed.), New York: Appleton-Century-Crofts, 1963.

RUDDELL, R. B., E. J. AHERN, E. K. HARTSON, and J. TAYLOR, eds., *Resources in Reading-Language Instruction.* Englewood Cliffs, N.J.: Prentice-Hall, 1974.

SHUY, ROGER W., ed., *Linguistic Theory: What Can It Say about Reading?* Newark, Del.: International Reading Association, 1977.

STAUFFER, RUSSELL G., *The Language-Experience Approach to the Teaching of Reading.* New York: Harper & Row, 1970.

Adjusting Instruction to Individual Differences

two

The teacher's goal is to provide instruction and learning opportunities in her classroom which will encourage maximal growth in reading development and in achievement in all the other outcomes of the curriculum, for each child she instructs. The organization of classroom activities and the adjustment of methods and materials to the wide variations found among the children is one of the most crucial and complex problems which education must solve.

In any plan of school organization, the teacher is the main contributor to adjusting instruction in reading to the individual differences among the children she teaches. Each administrative plan is designed to give good teachers a better opportunity to adjust to the various rates of reading growth and to the learning characteristics among the children. The teacher must know the nature of reading growth, the types of reading difficulties that might impede the growth, and the characteristics of each child that might predispose him to getting into these difficulties.

NATURE OF THE TEACHER'S PROBLEM

The classroom teacher needs to be a keen observer and student to follow the reading growth of all the children. The knowledge she has of each child's general level of reading capability, while important, is not sufficient for maximum accomplishment nor for prevention of serious reading problems. The teacher also must study the attainment of specific skills and abilities, so that any faulty learning can be detected and corrected early and so that any omissions or overemphases can be avoided.

A class made up of twenty-five to thirty children cannot be taught as though all members of the class had the same interests, desires, intellectual capabilities, or physical characteristics; nor can they be taught as though they had reached the same levels of attainment in reading or possess identical instructional needs. Any one child must be given material that is as nearly suitable to his level of reading growth as is possible. He must be taught by methods compatible with his characteristics and capabilities. For him, those phases of reading instruction that demand immediate attention must be emphasized. Reading instruction, to be effective, must proceed on an individual basis.

The teacher, however, is teaching a class and not just one child. Her problem is one of organizing instruction so that a class may be taught as a community with all members doing educationally worthwhile things. At the same time, instruction must be adjusted to meet the needs and characteristics of individuals. Instruction must be organized so that, for at least part of the time, the teacher is free to devote attention to those children needing special guidance. The problem of adjusting instruction to individual differences in large classes is probably the most difficult faced by the teacher.

Improved Methods and Materials

Fortunately, today's teachers are better prepared to adjust instruction to individual differences in reading than were teachers in the past. As a result of laboratory research and classroom practice, the teacher is equipped with teaching techniques far superior and more diversified than was the teacher just a few years ago. The teacher knows that reading skills and abilities are developed gradually over the years in an orderly, systematic sequence. She also knows that a basic program of skill development is needed. The study of practices and procedures in classrooms in recent years has shown that progress in reading cannot be nurtured in an opportunistic or haphazard manner. The teacher of today is aware that reading growth is developed best in a classroom which is businesslike, energetic, and organized. Learning situations which are based on recognition of the complexity of reading and which develops systematically the skills needed, is the rule in today's classrooms.

Teachers of today are more aware of the individual instructional needs of children than were the teachers of the past. It was not unusual, in the past, to label a child as dull or mentally incompetent when really he had a learning difficulty. Today teachers have better means of diagnosing individual needs than were formerly available. They are far better trained in the use of diagnostic procedures and can, as a result, prevent many serious reading problems from occurring. Teachers can better diagnose and correct those learning difficulties that do develop. Because teachers who have been trained recently have more refined measures of reading growth available than did the teachers of the past, they have more accurate information with which to adjust the materials of instruction to whatever levels of competence exist in their classes. The results of testing programs are being made more available to teachers so that instructional programs can be adjusted to meet the known needs of a class.

Basic reading materials have improved markedly over the last few years. They are much broader in types of reading experiences used to develop skills and abilities. Programs designed a few years ago, for example, were composed entirely of narrative content. More modern books show the child how to read what he is actually expected to read in other phases of the curriculum. They give him instruction in reading both narrative content and factual materials in science, social studies, and mathematics. The newer basic reading programs train the child in the study skills, and they help him plan his own reading in all areas. In addition, more basic and supplementary materials, written at varying levels of reading difficulty, interesting to children of a given age, are available in recent publications.

The manuals and workbooks accompanying basic reading programs have more carefully planned exercises for developing skills and abilities than did those of just a few years ago. Not so long ago, it was assumed that the child could discover by himself the most effective ways of identifying new words and of organizing the material he was reading. Writers of modern manuals and workbooks are aware that few, if any, children develop well-balanced skills and abilities in reading, unaided. The modern teacher not only has better materials but also is encouraged to use them to meet individual needs of the children in her class.

Teachers of today have a greater supply of supplementary reading materials than did their predecessors. Classrooms, central libraries, and media centers are well stocked with both narrative and factual materials dealing with the topics introduced in basic readers. This is increasingly apparent at the more advanced levels. The teacher in grade one, for the most part, must depend upon carefully controlled basal readers for both her basic and supplemental materials. But as the children mature in reading, there is an increasing number of related books and materials available to supplement the basic reading program.

Reasons for Increased Attention to Differences in Reading

It is fortunate indeed that the contemporary teacher is better equipped to adjust instruction to individual differences than was the teacher of the past. There are several reasons why this is good. First, awareness of the importance of education and of reading ability in modern society has caused a greater concern for the reading capability of the growing child than there has ever been before. Second, children who have difficulty in reading are no longer allowed to drop out of school. Every child who enters the first grade is expected to go on developing reading proficiency up to the level of his capabilities as he progresses through the elementary and secondary schools. Third, because practically all children are retained in the school, reading ability is no longer used as the sole criterion for promotion. Children now, for the most part, are promoted in school so that they will be with other children of their own age, interests, and stage of development. This policy, in some respects, makes the problem of adjusting reading instruction to individual differences more difficult. Fourth, improved instruction has increased the need for adjusting instruction to individual rates of growth. The only way to make children equal in reading ability is not to teach any of them. Then they would all have the same stature in reading—none of them would be able to read. But instruction that allows each child to grow as rapidly as he is able, encourages differences in reading capability. Under improved instruction, a wide range in reading ability can be expected at any grade level. It would be unrealistic to expect children with divergent interests, with different backgrounds, and with unequal linguistic ability, physical stamina, hearing ability, vision, and intellect to grow at the same rate in a complicated set of skills and abilities such as those in learning to read.

Range in Reading Ability to Be Expected

At any grade level, then, it is reasonable to expect that there will be a wide range in reading ability. In the fifth grade, for example, it is quite normal to find a six- or seven-year difference between the least and the most competent reader. This range of reading ability within a fifth-grade class cannot and should not be prevented, but it must be recognized and adjustments must be made.

Failure to adjust the material and the instruction to the range of reading capability found within the classroom is a major cause of reading disability. This failure limits the usefulness of the printed page as a tool of learning throughout the curriculum. The teacher must know the reading capability and the varying instructional needs of each child. She must know how to make appropriate adjustments in class organization and in instruction to meet the range of reading talent and the variety of instructional needs.

Every teacher is aware that children grow in reading capability at different rates and that in any class there is a wide range of reading capabilities. She knows that there is a vast difference in the difficulty of a paragraph that can be read and understood by the most able and the least able within the class. Teachers know that some children read extensively and that others read very little. They know that many children initiate their own reading activities and that others must be urged to read. They know that some read books of high quality and others appear to be satisfied with relatively immature writing. They are aware that some children read broadly and others confine themselves to a single type or what satisfies a single interest.

It is little wonder that children grow at different rates. A child learns to read with his eyes, ears, energy, background of experience, interests, drives, emotional stamina, and intelligence. Any differences found within the children in any of these traits will make for differences in the rate at which they learn to read. The teachers know that it is quite normal for children to have differences in auditory acuity, in physical stamina, and in intelligence. The problem of adjusting to individual differences is one of recognizing these differences and the varying rates of growth, and thus of adjusting materials and instruction so that the child may be an energetic, comfortable learner, absorbed in the learning situation. The instructional program should allow the child neither to dawdle nor to be placed in situations that are so difficult that he may become confused and discouraged.

Most teachers quickly recognize that individual differences in reading exist within their classrooms. Teachers also are aware that each child varies in his own reading capabilities. They know that a certain boy, for example, is able to read and understand science at a relatively high level but that his oral reading of poetry is uninspired, to say the least. It often is evident that a child, by grasping the overall meaning of a sentence, is able to recognize unfamiliar words, even though his knowledge of phonics remains limited. Another child may have a high degree of independence in working out words but is unable to group them into thought units. The extent of these variations, the ways of diagnosing them, and the importance of making adjustments for individual differences frequently is not fully understood.

Figure 1 on page 30 illustrates the normal range of reading ability found within typical classrooms at the various grade levels indicated.

As shown in figure 1, the range of reading capability increases as pupils progress through school. The total range between the best and the poorest reader in a typical second-grade class is two years and five months; in the third grade, the range is three years and six months; in the fourth grade, four years and eight months; in the fifth grade, six years and one month; in the sixth grade, seven years; and at the secondary school level, the range of reading becomes very large indeed. These data approximate the range in reading ability that is usually found and that the teacher must be prepared to handle at the various grade levels.

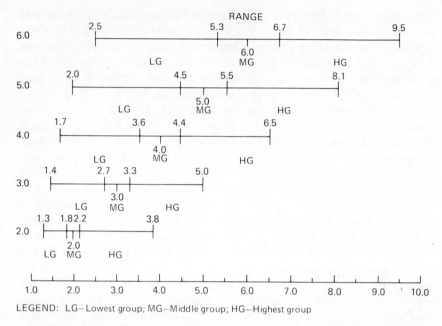

LEGEND: LG—Lowest group; MG—Middle group; HG—Highest group

Fig. 1 *NORMAL RANGE OF READING ABILITY FOUND IN TYPICAL CLASSROOMS OF GRADES TWO THROUGH SIX AT THE BEGINNING OF THE SCHOOL YEAR.*

Probably the most important information about a typical class is *the great range in reading talent that is to be found in the upper and lower third of the class.* Also, the fact that the middle third is relatively homogeneous in reading capability is important. In grade five, for example, the difference between the best and the poorest reader in the upper third of the distribution is spread over about two years and six months. Some members of this upper third will find themselves comfortable with books suited to typical students half-way through the fifth grade, while others can read profitably books appropriate to the early months of grade eight.

The problem of adjusting to this wide range of reading capability makes it important for the teacher to diversify instruction for the superior readers. Likewise, the lower third of a fifth-grade class has a great range in reading ability—a range of about two years and five months. A few of these pupils will find material suited to the typical beginning second-grader somewhat difficult. There are others within this same lowest third who can read profitably material suited to pupils halfway through the fourth grade. The lowest group also needs diversification of instruction to meet the wide range of reading capability.

The problem of adjusting instruction to fit the large range of reading capability found in the upper third and in the lower third of a fifth-grade class is, however, quite different. The pupils in the upper third of the distribution are competent, independent readers, and the teacher, in adjusting to their individual differences, can depend upon their proficiency and their independence. The adjustment to the large range found in the lower third of the distribution is complicated by the fact that these pupils are somewhat less than competent and are not independent readers at all. The problem is still more difficult in planning for the poorer readers, because there are not as many reading materials suitable to their age level and their interest level, and also to their reading level. The teacher is fortunate that the superior reader has little difficulty in selecting materials suitable to his reading ability, interests, and intellectual capacity.

Consider adjustment to the lower third of a typical fifth-grade class. If we use a textbook of fourth-grade difficulty in the basic reading instruction, it would be as suitable to the vast majority of the lower third of the class as the typical fifth-grade book is to the middle reading group.

Most of the pupils in the lower group read at between the 3.5 and 4.5 grade levels, whereas the pupils in the middle group are between the 4.5 and 5.5 levels. There are only one or two pupils within a typical fifth-grade class who are reading at a level lower than 3.5. With proper instruction, suitable introduction of words, development of readiness, and establishment of purposes, the pupil with a 3.5 reading ability can read a book suitable to the typical student with a fourth-grade reading ability. There will be one or two at the bottom of the distribution in the fifth-grade class who will require even more adjustments in their material and instruction.

For these reasons, most teachers who use grouping to adjust to individual differences will vary the number of pupils in the reading groups. She might make the middle group the largest because they are more homogeneous; the advanced group next, because they are more independent; and the lowest group quite small, because they need closer diagnosis and more help.

BASIC CONSIDERATIONS IN ADJUSTING
TO INDIVIDUAL DIFFERENCES IN READING

The problem of adjusting to the wide range of reading capability, resulting from the different rates of growth found in any classroom, has many dimensions. Each of these dimensions must be considered in formulating programs for adjusting to individual differences in reading. Some of the current approaches fail to take into account one or more of these dimensions and are to some degree inadequate or incomplete. Among the more important facts to be considered when formulating an instructional approach are:

1. Children are alike in many ways.

2. Children grow in many ways other than in reading capability.

3. A child's general growth curve in reading is not necessarily uniform.

4. Reading is a complex learning with many dimensions.

5. The problem and its solution change with advancement through the curriculum.

6. The problem changes according to the phase of the reading curriculum considered.

7. The problem changes with changes in school organization.

8. The solution must be realistic for the time it requires.

9. The adjustment must recognize that the teacher's energy and time for preparation are not unlimited.

These facts must be recognized in formulating classroom organization and procedures to adjust to individual differences in reading. They are so crucial that neglecting any one of them will limit seriously the adequacy of the adjustment. Quite obviously, an adjustment which so dissociates one child from another that the interplay of learning is impossible, is unfortunate; or an approach that takes more of the teacher's time in preparation than is reasonable, must be rejected; or a method that freezes a child in a less advanced group so that he cannot advance if his rate of learning accelerates, cannot be recommended. Adjustments to individual differences in reading, then, must recognize and provide for the many dimensions of the problem.

Children Are Alike in Many Ways

A program of adjustment to individual differences in reading must recognize the similarities as well as the differences among children. Each child in the classroom is an important individual. He has many drives, motives, and desires. Children of any given age, for example, are likely to be interested in much the same things. Each child in a class needs to be recognized as an important member of this little community in which he spends a large portion of his day. The poor reader as well as the good one must have friends and feel that he is an integral part of the class, that he has contributions to make to the class, and that he is not forced aside into any position of inferiority. Every child, then, should be helped to preserve his feelings of his own personal worth. Every child needs to feel that he is progressing. He needs to feel that he is becoming, day by day, a better reader even though he may recognize that his rate of growth in reading is somewhat slower than that of other children. Because the adjustment recognizes the personal worth of each child, allows him to participate in important enterprises within the class, gives him a feeling of confidence, security, and well-being, and because it avoids stigmatizing the child, it will encourage comfortable, efficient growth in reading for all children.

Children Grow in Many Ways Other Than in Reading Capability

Children grow in many ways other than in reading, and any adjustments must take into account the many characteristics of child growth and development besides level of attainment in reading. The child is changing in physical size, in social adaptability, and in interests. He is developing proficiencies in many skills and abilities.

It is sometimes asserted that the school system could regroup children so as to house all those with the same reading needs in the same classroom. The teacher then could use fairly uniform approaches in teaching them. This would not be a workable solution. The problem of adjusting to individual capabilities in reading soon would develop. Children might be equal in reading capability at the onset of instruction, but they soon would become heterogeneous. The differences in rates of reading growth would show up almost immediately. Moreover, children grouped this way would not be similar in any other characteristic, if they were grouped according to reading ability. For example, in a class of children with fifth-grade reading ability, there would be great variation in their arithmetic ability; their interests would range from those of second- to ninth-grade age; the size of the chairs would need to range from those small enough for second-graders to those big enough for ninth-graders. There would be almost as great a range in chronological age within a group classified according to reading ability as there is now in reading ability for children classified according to chronological age. They would not even be able to play together because of differences in age, size, and interests. Methods of adjustment, then, which place children of different ages and different interest levels within the same classroom are indeed unfortunate. Programs of adjustment that keep children, as nearly as possible, with others of their own levels of overall development are the ones that are most likely to succeed. Adjustment to individual differences in reading will have to be done in ways other than homogeneous grouping according to reading ability at any level of instruction.

A Child's General Growth Curve
in Reading Is Not Necessarily Uniform

A child's general growth curve in reading is not necessarily uniform, and any adjustment which does not provide for moving the child from one group to another is unfortunate. One child, for example, may find reading a very difficult undertaking at the outset, but as he progresses he may accelerate his rate of growth. This child may have high general intelligence but be limited in auditory acuity. The child, at the beginning, would find establishment of word-recognition techniques somewhat difficult. As a result, his growth in reading would be slow. But as the program advanced and as the role of reasoning became increasingly important, his rate of growth in reading would accelerate. Another child might start out being relatively good in the reading program as long as the building of basic sight vocabulary and word-recognition techniques were the important determinants of success. But were this child somewhat limited in the more complex reasoning abilities, such as ability to make accurate judgments and to visualize what is read, his rate of growth would taper off as the program, at more mature levels, began to emphasize these capabilities.

The correlation between intelligence and reading ability at the end of the first grade is relatively low, approximately .35. At the sixth-grade level, studies show this relationship has risen to about .65, and at the high-school level, the correlation is .80. The difference between these correlations shows that the rate at which many children attain competence in reading is changing. To the extent that the organization within the classroom allows the child to grow in reading capacity comfortably and energetically, and remains flexible enough to adjust to these varying rates of growth, progress can be expected.

Reading Is a Complex Learning with Many Dimensions

Reading ability is not a specific or single attribute. It is made up of a hierarchy of many skills and abilities, attitudes, and tastes. A well-rounded basic reading program encourages relatively uniform growth in the many components of reading ability. Nonetheless, a study of reading profiles indicates that no child develops the skills, abilities, attitudes, interests, and tastes in the same manner. There will be marked differences in degree of maturity of reading development in the various outcomes of reading instruction.

A fifth-grade child, for example, may show as great a difference as three or four years between his most mature reading capability and his least mature one. He may have a high degree of proficiency in using word-recognition techniques, but his ability to read to understand the fundamental idea in a selection may be relatively immature. Or he may, given an unlimited time, be able to work out words independently as well as the usual seventh-grader, while his fluency in understanding what the passage is about may be equal only to that of the beginning third-grader. Another child may be relatively efficient in reading material of the narrative type, but he may be relatively ineffective in reading materials in the content fields. Uneven profiles of reading, produced by the complex nature of learning, are unfortunate and indicate the need for corrective work.

That child would be rare indeed whose areas of best and worst performances in the complex task of learning to read is separated by less than a year. The reading program must be flexible enough to adjust to the differences in reading capabilities found in the individual child. The program cannot be so formalized that the adjustments cannot vary according to the type of reading done at a given time. The child with poor ability to understand the general idea of a passage should get considerably more exposure to that type of reading than he does to the word-recognition exercises in the basic program. The child who reads narrative material satisfactorily but is poor at reading material of a content field must have the level of difficulty of the latter material adjusted to the development of his comprehension abilities and to the application of these to reading content material.

A reading program designed to meet the individual needs of children must take into account not only the range of general reading capability found within a classroom but also the characteristics of each child's reading growth pattern. Measurement programs should be able to detect such differences and adjustment programs should allow for these differences. Undoubtedly, the complex nature of reading and the resultant unevenness in the growth patterns make adjusting to individual differences in reading difficult. The teacher can hope for success only by knowing the reading profiles of the students she is teaching and by utilizing materials and methods which facilitate individual adjustments.

The Problem and Its Solution Change with Advancement through the Curriculum

The problem of adjusting to individual differences changes in at least three ways during the school years. First, the range of reading capability found within any classroom increases as the pupils become more and more proficient in reading. You will recall that a beginning second-grade class usually has a range of reading capability of two and a half years, while a beginning sixth-grade class has a range of approximately seven years. The range is even greater at each higher grade level through high school and beyond. This difference in range does not mean necessarily that the teacher at higher grade levels has more difficult problems of adjusting to individual differences than do teachers at lower grade levels. It does mean, however, that there will have to be a greater difference between the level of difficulty in the materials used. An inspection of the difference between the material that the average fourth-grader can read and the material that the average sixth-grader can read will not be as apparent as the difference between material that an average second-grade child can read and the material that a child approximately halfway through the first grade can read. The rate of reading growth during the early grades is startling indeed, and the fineness of adjustment required to meet the reading capabilities within a second-grade class is more demanding than the adjustment needed to meet the range of reading capabilities in the sixth grade or beyond.

The second way in which adjustment to individual differences changes through the grades is found in the relative independence of students at the higher levels as contrasted with children in the second grade. The teachers in the first and second grades have very few who can be called independent readers, while the teacher at higher grade levels will find an increasing proportion of independent readers. Although there are many independent readers at upper grade levels, this does not mean that adjustment to individual needs is not necessary, but it does mean that teachers can rely more upon individual assignments that can be done independently. In the basic reading program, in which skills and abilities are developed, the problem of the sixth-grade teacher, for example, is similar to that of the second-grade teacher.

The need for basic reading instruction is not diminished as the child advances. The teacher of the intermediate grades must be alert to the need for adjusting to the level of development in each child's reading skills and abilities. She must be aware of the need for adjusting to the child's range of capabilities, of the importance of identifying his reading needs, and of giving systematic instruction to ensure balanced growth. It cannot be overemphasized that a systematic, well-organized basic program of instruction in reading is essential to the intermediate grades, and that the teacher will cause reading disabilities if this systematic reading instruction is not given. Incidental reading instruction with social studies material, for example, will not suffice.

Another way in which adjustment to individual differences changes as students progress is in the amount of available and suitable reading material. The teacher in the intermediate grades has more material, at various levels, for the range of reading talent found within these grades than does the primary teacher. The secondary teacher has an even wider range of materials from which to choose. It must be remembered that even the poorest group of readers in a sixth-grade class are as mature readers as the most competent readers in a beginning second-grade class.

In formulating programs for adjusting to individual differences, it is essential to recognize the changes that occur throughout the school years. It is fortunate that as the range of reading capability increases, the independence of the children in the class is increasing and that there is a wider selection of suitable materials available. It also should be remembered that at all levels of instruction there is an abundance of materials suitable for the capable readers. The problem is difficult only for the poor readers. Fortunately, the number of materials suitable for poor readers increases in the higher grades.

The Problem Changes According to the Phase of the Reading Curriculum Considered

The child, at all levels of advancement, must have at least four types of reading experiences if he is to become a proficient reader. First, he must progress through a carefully controlled set of reading experiences and exercises designed to show him how to read. This is the basic program of reading instruction, and is composed of a set of well-organized materials with suggested exercises that enable a competent teacher to develop in her pupils the essential skills and abilities. Second, the child must participate in those reading experiences in which he is using reading as an aid in gaining understandings and knowledges within subject-matter areas. Third, he must have reading experiences designed to enhance his own personal development, interests and tastes. These are experiences giving him broad contacts with children's literature, enhancing his understanding of himself, enlarging his awareness of social relationships, and developing his aesthetic appreciations. Fourth, he must have experiences designed to correct reading faults he may have established. This phase of the program can be described as reeducative or corrective. There is probably no child who, from time to time, does not have reading faults, or who does not need more practice in some reading skill or ability.

The adjustment to individual needs and capabilities in each of these phases of the reading program is a different problem. Adjustments suitable for one phase of the reading curriculum are not necessarily good for another. If the child's reading is to develop skills and abilities in reading, the adjustment to individual differences in reading is different from reading to understand the content. The goals set by the teacher in these two situations are different. When the teacher is teaching social studies, her primary concern is developing the outcomes of social studies instruction, even though the children are using books for this purpose. When the teacher is teaching reading, her primary concern must be the development of skills and abilities in reading even though the children may be reading in their basic readers material of the social studies type. It would be unfortunate if teachers thought that reading skills and abilities could be learned incidentally if the basic purpose was learning the subject matter of any of the content fields. It would be equally unfortunate if the basic reading program failed to give systematic instruction in the skills and abilities necessary to read materials of the content areas.

In summary, adjustment in the four types of reading experience is dictated by the results expected and the use of the reading. In the basic reading program, some form of group instruction is advisable. In the second type, reading in other branches of the curriculum, it is likely that the experience curriculum or topical unit approach is desirable. In reading for personal development, a highly individualized approach emphasizing the "right book for the right child" is most feasible.

In the reeducation or remedial phase of the program, the skill that needs attention prescribes the type of instruction needed and who among the children should work together. Much of the controversy over the most effective way to adjust to individual differences stems from the fact that proponents of one type of adjustment over another actually are concerned with one particular phase of the reading program which especially interests them. It should be remembered that these phases are not completely discrete. For example, when the children have a social studies lesson, the teacher may discern that certain ones are having difficulty in finding places on a map, and she may surmise that the cause of their difficulty is that they are ineffective in interpreting the marginal key numbers and letters. The teacher then would call these children aside and reeducate them in the skill needed in map reading. Although this skill was covered in the basic reading program, these children failed to learn it.

The Problem Changes with Changes in School Organization

As the child progresses through the grades, the school organization changes. The usual type of organization in the primary grades is a self-contained classroom. The teacher is responsible for all of the learning activities of the primary classes. This changes in the intermediate grades. In most school systems, there are special teachers for music, art, physical education, or other specialized areas. In some school systems, there are platoon arrangements in which teachers devote their entire day to teaching arithmetic, reading, or some other subject. In most secondary schools, the students have different teachers for each subject.

The problem of adjusting to individual differences in reading is different, depending on the school's organization. The task in a graded elementary school is somewhat different from that in the old, one-room school. It may be that the teacher in a one-room school was forced to face the problem of adjusting to individual differences more realistically than is, for example, the teacher in a fifth-grade classroom, even though the fifth-grade class will encompass practically all the levels of reading growth that are found in the typical one-room school. The graded classroom teacher has one advantage, however, and that is that the interests of the children, their sizes, and ages are more alike.

In the secondary school, the problem of understanding a student as fully as is necessary for adjusting to his reading needs is more difficult than it is in the primary grades. This is so because the secondary school teacher may be teaching as many as 150 different students in five classes for an hour a day, while the primary teacher lives rather closely with some twenty-five or more children during the day. It is fortunate, indeed, that reading growth begins when the teacher and children live and work together throughout the entire day, because a detailed understanding of the child's interests, his needs, drives, and levels of reading competency is necessary if proper provision for his reading needs is to be made. The application of this detailed information is crucial when the child is a relatively immature and dependent learner.

The problem of adjusting to individual differences in the graded elementary school is somewhat complicated by the fact that the teacher has the children for only one year, and each succeeding teacher must learn the needs of each child. The teacher in a one-room school did have the advantage of developing the child's educational growth over a period of years.

As stated, differences in school organization can complicate the problem of recommending adjustments to individual differences. In the secondary school, the need for guidance programs to collect information about the students and to see that it reaches the teachers who must make the adjustments must be fulfilled. This is not so essential a recommendation in the primary grades, for the teacher in this case can observe her children throughout the year. The recommendation for collecting and disseminating cumulative information in the graded elementary school is probably more pertinent than it was in the one-room elementary school.

The Solution Must Be Realistic for the Time It Requires

In considering suitable methods of adjusting to individual differences in reading, the time it requires becomes exceedingly important. The time that can be devoted to basic instruction in reading, for example, is limited. At all levels of instruction, other learning is taking place during the school day, and the efficient use of time in all of the school activities is serious business. Reading is no exception. Those methods of adjustment, then, that make undue demands either on the teacher's instructional time or the class's working time must be rejected. A teacher must organize her class in the most efficient way. She cannot, for example, devote her entire time to developing reading skills and abilities for just one child at the expense of the other members of the class, no matter how urgent the child's need.

Programs that recommend that each child have a different book for his individual needs for basic instruction are unrealistic. It is necessary for the teacher, in developing reading skills and abilities, to introduce the material, to establish purposes, to develop background, to introduce new vocabulary, to guide reading through asking pertinent questions, to discuss the selection after it is read, and to give comprehension exercises related to the selection read. The new words must be related to previously learned words in order to develop word-recognition techniques, and the selection must be used creatively so that the children feel they have completed the experience. Faced with such instructional demands, it is apparent that the teacher cannot have each child reading a different book while she is teaching the class to develop the skills and abilities in reading. There simply would not be enough time. If we were to assume that the teacher devoted an hour a day to systematic instruction in reading development, she would have somewhat less than two minutes in which to accomplish the fundamentals of reading instruction for each different selection that some twenty-five children were reading.

Because of the time factor, some form of grouping for basic reading instruction is recommended. It must be recognized that even if the class is divided into three groups, each reading a different topic, the teacher who devotes an hour a day to basic reading instruction must divide her time among each of the three groups. Whatever method of adjusting to individual differences in reading is adopted, the efficient use of the teacher's and class time must receive careful consideration.

The Adjustment Must Recognize that the Teacher's Energy and Time for Preparation Are Not Unlimited

The methods of adjusting to individual differences and of adopting a class organization must be realistic in its demands on the teacher. Sometimes it is suggested, for example, that teachers prepare the exercises to correct a faulty learning or to reinforce skills and abilities that the children have learned only partially. These recommendations are justified. But if the teacher were to prepare materials to meet all of the reeducative or reinforcing needs of a class of twenty-five pupils, she would need more than a twenty-four hour day. The use of workbooks accompanying basic readers, suitable to the child's level of development, is recommended as one means of saving the teacher's energy and preparation time.

In certain methods of group instruction in the basic reading program, the teacher is expected to teach three discrete sections in reading and therefore is expected to make three preparations. These involve the collection of pictures and other means of developing readiness, background, interest, and understanding of word meanings. They also include analysis of the stories or selections to be read by each group, the preparation necessary to develop the specific comprehension abilities and word-recognition techniques for three separate lessons. They entail finding three separate sets of related reading materials and planning three separate activities related to what is being read.

Though there are many plans for adjusting to individual differences in reading, whichever is used, the fact that the teacher is a person whose time and energy are not unlimited must be taken into account. The fact that children like to work and do things together also must be recognized. It must be remembered when formulating the approach to basic reading instruction that they are growing in many ways other than in reading capability; that their growth curves are not necessarily uniform; that reading is a very complex learning; and that class time is limited. All these considerations have to be taken into account when planning adjustments to individual rates of growth in reading.

MEETING INDIVIDUAL DIFFERENCES IN READING

A major responsibility of the school is to develop each child to the limit of his own capability. Any failure in the instructional program to adjust to individual differences in reading has two effects: first, failure to adjust materials and methods in reading instruction to the range of reading capability found within any classroom will impede growth in reading; second, failure to adjust the difficulty of reading material to the known reading capabilities of the individual pupils in the classroom reduces the usefulness of printed material as an aid to learning in all areas. In addition, material which does not challenge the capable learners in the various content areas limits the possibility of superior achievement in those areas for the brighter children and also limits their growth in reading. Exposing the less able readers to materials that are too difficult reduces for them the usefulness of printed material as an aid to learning and it can cause serious confusions and rejection of reading, thereby causing reading disabilities.

The entire reading curriculum of the children in a classroom must be adjusted to their individual reading capabilities, if the printed page is to become an effective tool of learning, and if reading disability is to be prevented. A fifth-grade child, for example, who can read material of seventh-grade difficulty with ease and profit, should have many reading experiences at that level of difficulty. A fifth-grade child who is unable to read third-grade material comfortably will not profit much from holding a fifth-grade book in his hands and staring at it. He would profit from reading a book more in keeping with his reading capabilities.

Individual differences in reading must be provided for throughout the curriculum if printed material is to become an effective aid to learning for all the members of the class and if maximum growth in reading is to be achieved. The adjustment of instruction to individual differences in reading is more than just an approach. It is a combination of approaches and adaptations of methods of instruction that encourages individual rates of growth.

The various approaches to meeting individual differences in teaching reading are difficult to discuss and to evaluate, because each phase of the reading curriculum has special problems. The basic program in reading is probably the most complex in the curriculum in the matter of adjusting to individual differences. This phase of the curriculum must assume responsibility for developing in an orderly, sequential manner, the skills and abilities needed for success in all other reading activities. The adjustment to individual differences in the basic reading program must be such that there is little chance for gaps in learning, for overemphases resulting in loss of balance among the skills and abilities, and for the persistence of faulty habits with consequent confusion and deterioration of reading progress. When reading is used as an aid to learning, adjusting to individual differences is considerably less complex and resolves itself into bringing children and books realistically together so that the topics under consideration can be effectively studied. In personal development reading, the problem is still less complex. This phase of the reading curriculum can be individual with guided reading programs in which children and books are brought together according to each child's level of reading maturity, interest, personal growth, needs, and the like. Neither an orderly sequence of skill development nor the knowledges and understandings of a curricular field need to be considered. The sole problem here is that of guiding each child into books that he can read comfortably and with pleasure and that develop him as a person.

The importance of finding suitable material for every situation cannot be overemphasized. In all of his reading, the child must have material that he can read effectively. At times, there should be material with which he must struggle, but he must be able to win. In this way he will increase his stature in reading. More often, he must read material which causes him little or no difficulty. It is through such reading that he gains fluency and the ability to understand the ideas of the author.

In the basic reading program, the difficulty of the material is ever increasing, and as soon as the child is really comfortable, the difficulty is increased so that the learner is challenged to grow. Fortunately, this material is well introduced, the difficulties are anticipated, and instruction on how to proceed is given.

Materials that the child reads independently in other phases of the curriculum should be somewhat less difficult than those in his basic reading program. This is especially true of the guided reading program. The teacher does not have time to give the necessary instruction in reading for twenty-five different references. The materials for both the content fields and for personal development should be at such a level of difficulty that they can be studied and read independently without faulty reading.

There are many ways in which the problem of adjusting to individual differences in the program of basic instruction in reading can be attacked. Many administrative and curricular plans involving school-wide adjustments have been tried. Some of the better known are: *ability grouping* among the classes according to intelligence, reading capability, or average achievement; yearly *retardation or acceleration* based upon overall educational advancement or reading achievement; *continuous growth* or *ungraded primary* plans in which the child is advanced to a higher reading level as soon as he completes the current reading program; *team teaching,* a large group of children taught together by several teachers in one large room for many lessons, and separated for reading instruction according to level of advancement; and *special rooms* where children of like reading maturity are taught reading, but for the rest of the day are in the regular classroom with other children of their own ages. As yet an adequate solution to the problem has not been found and maybe never will be.

Flexible grouping plans are very likely the best and most widely used approaches in adjusting to individual differences in reading. In the basic reading program, in which an orderly introduction of reading skills and abilities is essential and a gradual expansion of vocabulary load is demanded, it is likely that for certain parts of the instruction, three reading groups are desirable. There can be no method of promotion nor any static method of grouping that will solve the problem. When grouping is flexible, many of the difficulties are avoided, and grouping becomes one of the best single means of individualizing instruction in reading.

Grouping procedures must be flexible in three ways. First, the group formed for basic reading instruction should be used for that phase of the curriculum only, and the children should be regrouped according to need in other phases of the curriculum. Second, the children who need instruction in a certain reading skill or ability should form a temporary instructional group even if they come from different basic reading groups. Third, a child should be able to move readily from one group to another if he improves in reading ability enough to be better suited to a more advanced group. He also should be able to move to a less advanced group without stigma if he has been absent, or if he, for any other reason, needs to be with a less mature reading group. He may even meet with two groups for a time.

When the children use reading as an aid to learning in the content fields, the class will sometimes profit from working together as well as in groups. There is a great need for material, differentiated in difficulty, in the content fields so that the individual differences in reading can be met realistically and practically. When reading children's literature, it often is wise to have the entire class working together. When a book is shared through reading aloud parts of favorite stories would be one such time; showing new books added to the room library would be another. In the reeducative phase of the reading program, the entire class might profit from a demonstration of a word-recognition technique and could be taught together.

Instruction with its multiple, flexible grouping and with materials that allow the whole class to participate while each child is working with material he can read, will do much to allow children to grow in reading at the rate best for each. When adjustments to levels of reading capability are combined with attention to individual needs, the teaching of reading can be adjusted to individual differences. This instruction will do much to prevent minor misunderstandings from accumulating to the point at which the child becomes confused and becomes a complex reading disability case.

This administrative plan for meeting individual differences is designed to give a good teacher a more reasonable chance of making these adjustments. But no matter what arrangement is adopted, the crux of the adjustment lies in the ability of the teacher to diagnose the needs of the children and to be ready to provide whatever corrective help is needed.

DIAGNOSTIC TEACHING IN THE CLASSROOM

The effectiveness of diagnostic teaching is based on the extent to which the teacher knows each child within the classroom. In order to attain maximum growth in reading and to avoid confusions in learning, the teacher must be aware of and adjust to each child's capacities, physiological condition, emotional and social adjustments, interests, attitudes, drives and general level of reading ability.

Besides these personal, intellectual, and physical characteristics, the teacher must know his reading development. It is to the child's growth in the specific skills and abilities in reading, above all else, that the instructional program must be geared. Diagnostic teaching is based on an understanding of the *reading* strengths and needs of each child. This knowledge must be used to modify instructional procedures so that teaching, adjusted to the changing needs of the children, can be maintained. This teaching centers on continuous diagnosis of the skill development of each child, and on flexibility in instruction so that the teacher can alter the general procedures or methods, whatever they might be, to meet the specific needs of the individual.

One child may find most of the learnings relatively easy but some difficult and time-consuming. One, for example, may find the knowledge of sound-symbol relationships relatively easy to learn, whereas he may acquire only little skill in using meaning clues to word recognition. In the same class with the same instruction, another child may develop quickly too much dependence upon meaning clues and too little skill in sound-symbol relationships. Fortunately, most children maintain a rather consistent balance among the essential skills and abilities of reading, and need only a small and infrequent amount of reinforcement to maintain growth. Even for these children, the teacher should be alert to neglected skills or knowledges, so that there is no accumulation of minor problems. Many serious disabilities are simply the result of minor confusions which have been allowed to continue.

Most children get along remarkably well in reading. They learn to read according to their capacities. These children are helped if the teacher recognizes their minor deviations from effective, balanced reading growth, and gives added or modified instruction to overcome any faulty or inadequate learning. Some children require more careful and continuous diagnosis than do others. Children who have more complex problems in learning to read make up only a small percentage of those being taught. Usually there are no more than two or three in a classroom of twenty-five children. In these instances, more thorough and time-consuming appraisals may be needed. These children also may require a more intensive program of remediation. Some of their problems may be too time-consuming or too complex to be diagnosed and corrected by the classroom teacher. However, a thorough diagnosis of a particular child's reading problem accompanied by an *appropriate individual educational plan of remediation,* made by a reading specialist, will enable the classroom teacher to correct the difficulty without interfering with the progress of the rest of the class. In other cases, the child can be served best in a reading center or at a remedial clinic. These are decisions that must be made cooperatively by the classroom teacher and the reading specialist.

Every child's reading growth must be appraised continuously if his progress is to be at a high level, and if any confusion is to be detected before the more stubborn problems develop. Work samples, always present in the day-by-day teaching and learning activities of a class, enable the expert teacher to gain familiarity with each child's needs. More systematic observations may be made through informal diagnosis or standardized testing. In studying the children's reading patterns, the teacher uses many sources of information available to decide on the instructional modifications. These sources will be discussed later in this book.

Many teachers keep a diagnostic notebook in which they list the children within each instructional group. As the teacher studies each child's reading pattern, she makes a notation of any reading characteristic that might limit his reading growth, and any indication of visual difficulty, auditory limitations, bad attitudes, interests, tendencies toward fatigue, or anything else she observes. For example, a teacher might notice that one child, poor in comprehension, is a word-by-word reader; another child, good in using analytical skills, is ineffective in using context clues as an aid to word recognition; a third child has a limited meaning vocabulary; another reads rapidly, but with many inaccuracies, because he is uncertain about initial blends and digraphs; still another child reads slowly because he overarticulates as he reads; another has excellent word-recognition capabilities, is able to comprehend all the details in a passage, but is relatively ineffective in organizing, evaluating, and reflecting on what he has read. The teacher rightly feels that all of these types of problems can be corrected while teaching the group as a whole.

The expert teacher makes individual adjustments in the regular reading lessons. As the children progress through the reading lesson, the teacher has many opportunities to give each one the necessary experiences he needs to overcome his particular problems.

Knowing the results of all the appraisals, including her daily observations, the teacher is able to modify the general approach to reading so as to adjust instruction. The more diversified the approach, the greater the opportunity is for the teacher to make such adjustments. This may be one reason why combined approaches to reading prove more effective than do more narrow programs.

Most reading lessons can be separated into introductory, guided reading, and follow-up phases. During the introductory phase, which includes introducing the lesson, developing concept and word meaning, introducing unknown word patterns, and setting purposes for reading a selection, instructional adjustments can be made to help children with certain types of reading problems. In the guided silent reading and discussion phase, other types of instructional modifications are possible. During the follow-up phase of teaching the lesson, which includes exercises to develop specific skills and abilities, and related recreational and self-selective reading, there are many other opportunities for fulfilling individual needs.

During the introductory phase of teaching a selection, the teacher gives the child who is weak in the use of context clues more opportunities to select from among the new words being introduced those that fit the context of either oral sentences or those presented on the chalkboard. The teacher gives the child having difficulty with initial blends more opportunities to work on those presentations that emphasize similarity of initial blends in known and unknown words. The one with a limited meaning vocabulary should discuss the pictures and concepts for clarification of word meanings. He should be encouraged to attend to the meanings of all words introduced so that the habit of attending to words and their meanings is fostered. When the purposes for reading are being developed, children limited in specific types of comprehension should be given more opportunities to discuss how to read for a specific purpose. The teacher might even adjust the purpose for reading. For example, the child who reads to note the details but is poor in reflecting on what is read, might be asked to read the selection in order to tell in one sentence what the selection was about, or to write a title for the selection.

During the guided reading and discussion phase, the teacher might call upon the children to relate some of the content of the selection. If there is a misconception, the teacher should use this as an instructional opportunity to correct the faulty reading instead of calling upon another child for the correct response. The teacher should have the child who made the mistake find the place where the idea was presented, and then determine with him how the error came about. In this way, the reading difficulty would be called to his attention and help him to overcome his problem.

In the follow-up phase, the teacher has unlimited scope in adapting to individual needs. In the skill and ability exercises prepared by the teacher, emphasis can be placed where it is needed. In the skill development workbooks, the teacher may excuse a child who depends too much on context clues from those exercises emphasizing their use. Or the word-by-word reader may be excused from word-drill exercises and be encouraged to prepare a conversational selection for reading aloud, stressing reading the selection in the way people talk.

Most of these adjustments are made by the classroom teacher who is sensitive to the needs of each child and who makes modifications to correct any confusion before it becomes seriously limiting to his future growth. Such a teacher is a *diagnostic teacher.* If this teaching is coupled with a flexible grouping plan, the broad use of children's literature, and a stimulating learning environment in which children feel free to participate and express themselves, the reading program will provide maximum growth for all and will limit the frequency of reading disability because *it is the teacher who makes the difference* in adjusting to individual differences. The classroom teacher, however, cannot be expected to solve all problems in reading instruction. Her work must be supplemented, for each child who needs it, with a diagnostic and remedial program. The classroom teacher cannot spend the time necessary to correct the more complex reading problems.

Therefore, every school should have the services of a reading specialist. The reading specialist has three responsibilities, those of a consultant, a diagnostician, and a remedial teacher. The classroom teacher's responsibilities are to prevent disabilities, to aid in their early detection, and to carry out those corrective and remedial procedures appropriate to the classroom. It is the hope of the authors that this book will aid both the classroom teacher and the reading specialist in helping all pupils to become more effective readers.

SUMMARY

One of the most complex problems confronting the teacher is that of adjusting instruction to individual differences in reading. The children within any classroom vary greatly in reading maturity, reading habits, intellectual capabilities, and physical characteristics. The teacher must organize the class and the instruction so that each child can work up to his capacity. The teachers of today are better equipped with better professional training, improved materials and more penetrating measurements necessary for making these adjustments than were the teachers of the past.

The range of reading ability found in any classroom is large. The better the instruction and the longer it continues, the greater will be the range in reading ability. If instruction is excellent, not only will the average reading performance of the class be raised, but also the range of reading ability within the class will become greater. Each succeeding year of instruction increases the range of reading ability within the class. There will be extensive overlapping in the reading capabilities found in the various grades. Indeed, there is so much that the teacher, at any grade level, must be able to fulfill the reading needs of the children for grades above and below the one she is teaching. If the teacher organizes the class into three instructional groups, the range within the upper and lower groups still will be so great that further grouping is required. The problem of adjustment to the upper group is somewhat easier than it is to the lower group because of the reading competence and independence of the children and the greater availability of appropriate materials.

Among the more important considerations in meeting individual differences in reading are the similarities and differences in children, the nature of individual learning curves, the complexities in learning to read, the changes of approaches due to differences in curriculum and school organization, the differences at the various grade levels, and the need for realistic use of class time and teachers' energies.

The need for adjusting to individual differences in reading throughout the entire curriculum makes the problem somewhat more complicated than the problem of adjusting to the basic reading program alone. The methods and class organization effective for one type of reading will not always be good for another. The types of reading may be classified roughly as: basic instruction in reading, reading and study in other phases of the curriculum, independent personal development or recreational reading, and reeducative or remedial reading. These phases of reading are not completely separate. In general, the approaches to individual differences used in these phases are different and much of the controversy on methods stems from the fact that the proponents of one approach over another are emphasizing different phases of reading instruction.

Some approaches that have been tried include retardation and acceleration, curriculum adjustment plans, fixed grouping plans, and flexible grouping plans. Among these, the flexible grouping plans, reinforced by materials written on many levels of difficulty, seem to have the most promise. Whatever approach is used, the teacher should be sure that groups are not fixed but are adjustable to the outcomes expected from the instruction and also that the number and size of the groups are compatible with the maturity and independence of the children. In many instances, the groups should be reading about a topic of concern to the entire class, and the best and the poorest readers should have opportunities to work together.

Despite the type of school and classroom organization used to aid the teacher in adjusting to differences in reading growth, the skill of the teacher is the most important factor. The crux of meeting the individual differences found among children lies in the ability of the teacher to diagnose the needs of the children and to correct their minor confusions in reading before these confusions become major disabilities. Even under the best classroom instruction, a limited number of pupils will develop reading difficulties that can be solved only by special diagnostic and remedial procedures.

SELECTED READINGS

BOND, GUY L., "Employ More Diagnostic Teaching in the Classroom," pp. 35–39, in *Reading Improvement*, 14, no. 1, ed. Helen M. Robinson. Chula Vista, Calif.: Project Innovation, 1976.

BOND, G. L., and B. HANDLAN, *Adapting Instruction in Reading to Individual Differences*. Minneapolis: University of Minnesota Press, 1948.

BURMEISTER, LOU E., *Reading Strategies for Secondary School Teachers*, chaps. 1–4. Reading, Mass.: Addison-Wesley Publishing Co., 1974.

HARRIS, A. J., and E. R. SIPAY, *How to Increase Reading Ability* (6th ed.), chap. 5. New York: David McKay, 1975.

HEILMAN, A. W., *Principles and Practices of Teaching Reading* (3rd ed.), chap. 5. Columbus, Ohio: Charles E. Merrill, 1972.

STRANG, RUTH, CONSTANCE M. MCCULLOUGH, and A. E. TRAXLER, *The Improvement of Reading* (4th ed.) chaps. 14, 15. New York: McGraw-Hill, 1967.

TINKER, M. A., and CONSTANCE M. MCCULLOUGH, *Teaching Elementary Reading* (4th ed.), chap. 18. Englewood Cliffs, N.J.: Prentice-Hall, 1975.

Description
of
Disabled
Readers

three

Most children grow in reading with relatively desirable and consistent patterns of proficiencies. They develop reading capacities consistent with their general learning capability. The children's instructional needs can be met effectively by the classroom teacher using the approaches suggested for adjusting to individual differences in reading. There are some children, however, whose reading growth is so atypical, so different from that of the usual child, that they constitute a troublesome instructional problem. Often the classroom teacher can diagnose these difficulties and give these children the corrective or reeducative help that they need, so that they can continue to progress in reading growth. At other times, these disabled readers become so confused that they require more time for individual help than the classroom teacher can devote to them. In both instances, the child is a disabled reader, but the nature and severity of the disability makes one approach better than another.

In considering the nature of reading disability, it is necessary to isolate the group of children to be discussed, define the disabled reader, explain the characteristics that set him apart from the general population, and describe the categories into which disabled readers fall.

The child who is a disabled reader cannot be described as one whose reading ability is below his achievement in other school subjects. Although some disabled readers can be so described, the majority will be low both in reading and in general achievement. This is true because poor reading ability so limits other achievement that it is the rare child who can attain success in school in spite of having a reading disability. It also is important to note that the child who is low in both reading and in general achievement may or may not be a disabled reader. A child may be poor in reading and the other school subjects for reasons other than disability in reading.

The disabled reader is the child who is so handicapped in reading that his educational career is in jeopardy. Not only is his educational growth impeded, but frequently his reading patterns are so confused that future growth in reading becomes improbable. He is ineffective in using print as an aid to learning. He often is a discouraged student who thoroughly dislikes reading. In many cases, the child becomes so frustrated over his inability to read that his personal adjustment suffers a severe shock. He is, therefore, quite apt to show emotional tensions while reading. Sometimes these tensions upset him completely, and he demonstrates unfortunate adjustment patterns in general. These may vary from unfounded excuses for his trouble with reading to severe emotional disorders.

George illustrated the former type of poor adjustment when he said, "I don't want to learn to read because it is all make-believe. I don't want to read about a boy that has a boat. I want to have one myself." Many children who get into trouble with reading complain about the material not meeting their needs, but when they can read that same material, they find a new interest.

Henry displayed a functional disorder when it became apparent that he could not read even for two or three minutes without developing a headache and an upset stomach. He claimed to have eye trouble, although this could not be detected by thorough examination. He would work on puzzle-type material and numbers for long periods of time with no sign of visual discomfort or stomach unrest. After he attained success in reading by careful, individually planned work based on a complete diagnosis, he showed no signs of his former disorders. Not all children who have both poor reading and poor personal adjustment can be said to have them as a result of poor growth in reading. Sometimes the child is disturbed for other reasons and his reading suffers along with his other achievements.

Typically, the disabled reader is a child of intellectual capability who has for reasons discussed in the following chapters, failed to grow in reading. He is not living up to his potential as a learner, at least in reading. He is likely to be ineffective in all that is expected of him in school. He may reject reading, become discouraged, acquire unfortunate adjustment patterns, and become increasingly less able to learn. He is in need of educational help.

IDENTIFYING THE DISABLED READER

The problem now confronting us is different from the one discussed in the preceding chapter. The identification of reading disability cases is much more complicated than sectioning a class into reading groups or even finding the right level at which to start instruction for each child in a class. A reading test alone will not be enough to find the reading disability cases in a school. There are many poor readers in every class who cannot be classified as disabled readers, and there are some seemingly adequate readers who are truly disabled. Therefore we must discuss the factors that need to be considered in order to determine whether a pupil is disabled in reading or whether he is just a poor reader.

Opportunity to Learn

The child who is classified as disabled in reading must be distinguished from the child who has not had an opportunity to learn. If we did not take into account the opportunity of a child to learn, we would have to say that nearly all children are disabled readers before they entered the first grade. Although it is true that their ability to find meaning in the printed page is negligible and in no way in keeping with their ability to listen, they cannot be disabled because they have not yet been taught. They have had no opportunity to learn. They may have a relatively large listening vocabulary, but the typical child entering the first grade cannot read many more words than his own name. Most children, for example, cannot read the word STOP if it is taken off the octagonal sign on which they are accustomed to seeing it. In a way, they have had the opportunity to learn, because there has always been printed matter before them. But they did not receive systematic organized instruction, so, in reality, they have not had the opportunity to learn. Even though the child entering the first grade is not able to read as well as he can listen, he is not disabled because he is doing as well as could be expected of him.

The older child who has come from a non-English-speaking country to the United States would not be considered a reading disability case, even though he did have an instructional problem. He may need to start learning to read elementary English, but he cannot be called a disabled reader. He should have material different from that for the six-year-old beginner, and he will need special methods of instruction. But he is not a disabled reader. He is a child who cannot read English because he did not have the opportunity to learn.

The role of lack of opportunity to learn is even more complicated than is indicated in the case of the child who has not yet entered school or is from another country. Some children will be disabled in reading in comparison to their other intellectual achievements, because they did not start to learn to read as early as they started other verbal learnings. A gifted child, for example, who is just entering the third grade may have the verbal facility of the usual sixth-grade child. He could not be expected to read as well as a typical sixth-grade child, because he has received reading instruction for only two years while his general language has developed over a period of eight years.

Verbal Competency

The aural verbal ability of a child frequently is used to indicate the level at which we could expect him to read. If the child has a superior listening vocabulary, he may be expected to read at a higher level than can other children of his age. If the child is able to understand paragraphs of more than usual difficulty read aloud to him, he should be able to read better than those children who have less aural verbal ability. The child's verbal ability, as measured by a test such as the Durrell-Sullivan Reading Capacity Test* gives a good indication of the level at which he should be reading. A marked discrepancy between his aural verbal capacity and his reading ability is an indication that he may be a disabled reader.

There are two considerations the diagnostician must recognize in using the child's general aural verbal stature as an indicator of the reading level at which he can be expected to attain. The first is that it may not be safe to assume that a child who is low in both reading and verbal ability does not have a reading disability. The poor performance on the aural tests may indicate that the child has had one avenue of developing verbal ability closed to him. A child, for example, who has been a poor reader from the first grade to the sixth will not have had an opportunity to develop language equal to that of his natively equal counterpart who always has been a good reader. The poor reader will not have had as much experience with words because he has not read as widely. Nor will he have had as much experience in understanding paragraphs. Bond and Fay (24), among others, have shown that poor readers are considerably lower in the vocabulary items in the Stanford-Binet Intelligence Tests than are good readers of equal intelligence. Similarly, Farr (71), Strang (198) and Huelsman (110) have found that the disabled readers score lower on the verbal scale of the Wechsler Intelligence Scales than they do on the Performance Scale. These findings could indicate either that these children have native limitations in verbal ability compared to their general intelligence and are therefore poor readers, or that they are limited in developing language because they are poor readers and therefore lack verbal experience. The authors, through experience with hundreds of reading cases, take the latter point of view, while they recognize that a few children fit the first explanation. An able child who is a poor reader cannot be expected to develop as extensive a vocabulary nor to be as experienced in interpreting paragraphs as the good reader can. The use of aural verbal ability alone as a criterion for classifying children as reading disability cases might classify certain children as verbally

* See Appendix V for list of reading tests.

inept although, in truth, they are reading disability cases who would profit much from remedial instruction.

The second problem in using a discrepancy between aural verbal ability and reading as a means of classifying a child as a disabled reader is that it does not take into account the opportunity of the child to learn. Two children, for example, may have the same measured verbal ability. One, however, is only a second-grade child while the other is a sixth-grade child. The second-grader has had only one year of reading instruction while the other has had five. The younger child cannot be expected to read as well as the older child, who has had five times as much reading instruction, even though they measure the same on an oral vocabulary test or a test of ability to understand paragraphs read aloud.

Verbal competency should be one consideration in classifying a child as a disabled reader, but it will often mislead the teacher or diagnostician if used as the only one. The length of time in school and the opportunity to learn to read also must be considered. The accuracy of the estimate of verbal aptitude also must be taken into account if all the children who are in need of specific help in reading are to be located and if a child is not to be misjudged.

Success in Nonreading Fields

In identifying the child who is a disabled reader, teachers often compare his reading achievement with his degree of success in subjects requiring a minimum of reading. Arithmetical computation is used frequently as one subject in which success is less influenced by reading ability. If the child is doing well in arithmetic and poorly in reading, he is likely to be a disabled-reader. Such information adds considerably to the accuracy of locating children who are disabled readers rather than poor readers who are doing almost as well as can be expected.

In cases in which the child appears to be emotionally disturbed, for example, the comparison between reading ability and success in arithmetic computation gives some evidence of the relationship between the personality problem and reading ability. If the disturbed child is intellectually capable and still is poor in both reading and arithmetic, it is likely that his lack of achievement is the result of a more deep-rooted personality problem. If, however, a child's reading achievement is considerably below his arithmetic, it is likely that his personality difficulty centers around his lack of success in reading. This judgment cannot always be accepted because in a few cases, the disturbed child may have achieved a feeling of success in arithmetic and therefore applied himself with unusual vigor to that field. The child's lack of success in reading may have aggravated an existing insecurity, so that reading was rejected in favor of the field in which he found more immediate success.

Success in nonreading fields does indicate in most cases how well the child is able to apply himself to learning situations other than reading. If he has a general personality problem, he is likely to show ineffective learning of these fields as well as of reading. If he has limited general capability he will do as poorly in nonreading fields as in reading. But when a child is successful in nonreading fields, yet has difficulty in reading, he is likely to be an intelligent, well-adjusted child who is a disabled reader because of some faulty learning. This child usually can be helped a great deal by remedial instruction in reading. While success in nonreading fields is insufficient evidence in itself to classify a child as a disabled reader, it often is used as one fact to be considered in making such a classification.

Monroe (141), for example, uses arithmetic achievement as one of the criteria for selecting children who will profit from remedial instruction in reading. She uses a reading index (R.I.) to find those children who are more retarded in reading than is to be expected. The index is determined by using the child's average reading age (R.A.), chronological age (C.A.), arithmetic age (A.A.), and mental age (M.A.). The reading index (R.I.) can be calculated by using the following formula:

$$\text{R.I.} = \frac{\text{R.A.}}{(\text{C.A.} + \text{M.A.} + \text{A.A.}) \div 3}$$

Experience shows that a child with a reading index of 0.80 or below is practically always a reading disability. Those with indices between 0.80 and 0.90 tend to be borderline. Some of the latter will need remedial instruction, others will not. All of those who are borderline should be tested further to see if irregularities in their reading profiles indicate serious problems.

Mental Ability

Mental ability is related to reading achievement. The mere fact that the child has high intellectual ability itself does not guarantee that he will be successful in reading, especially in the early years. Nor does the fact that a child has trouble in reading indicate that he is mentally limited. There is ample evidence to show that the relationship between intelligence and reading success becomes closer when populations are sampled at successively higher grade levels. The correlation between mental age, as measured by individual Stanford-Binet tests, and reading comprehension at the end of the first grade is approximately .35; at the end of the fifth grade, it is approximately .60; during the high school years, it approaches .80. These correlations indicate that factors in addition to mental age influence a child's success in reading. Some children, who begin relatively slowly in the primary grades, later increase their rate of learning and surpass some of their contemporaries. Thus, early success does not necessarily indicate ultimate reading capability.

These comparative relationships seem reasonable. In the early stages of their reading development, children are concerned with the mechanical aspects of reading. For instance, word-recognition skills lean heavily upon visual and auditory discrimination. In the higher grades, the complexities of reading and study demand fine verbal discrimination, logical reasoning, abstract analysis, and other comprehension skills which require a high level of mental ability. It is not surprising that mental age and reading capability become more and more closely related, as the reader progresses into more and more mature materials and reads for more and more mature purposes.

The mental ability of the child is used most often as the basic criterion with which to compare his reading capacity in order to judge the existence of a reading disability. The customary method of making this comparison is to use the mental age or grade of the child as the key to reading expectancy. When the child's average reading is felt to be significantly lower than his mental age, he is thought to be a disabled reader. While undoubtedly the true mental ability of the child should be used as a basic consideration in classifying a child as a disabled reader, caution is necessary for two reasons. First, the determination of mental capacity of a poor reader is difficult. Second, the problem is complicated by the fact that although mental age is calculated from birth, the child is not introduced to systematic instruction in reading until he is six or more years old.

ASSESSING MENTAL AGE. There are many types of tests which may be used to assess mental age. Four general types of measurement are commonly used. They are verbal group mental tests, nonverbal group mental tests, individual mental tests, and individual performance mental tests. Each of these tests has its advantages and limitations. In classifying a child as a disabled reader, the particular measure of mental ability used must be considered carefully.

VERBAL GROUP MENTAL TESTS. These are of little use in selecting children who will profit from remedial work in reading. These tests are to a great extent, reading tests and therefore the poor reader cannot demonstrate his true mental ability. Clymer (38) has shown that at the fifth-grade level, certain group intelligence tests give no valid measure of the mental ability of the children who are reading in the lowest forty percent of the class. To show the extent of misinterpretation possible by the uncritical use of such tests for disabled readers, Mary's case can be cited. Mary was brought to the University of Minnesota Clinic for study. Her cumulative record was assembled. At the end of kindergarten, she was given a Stanford-Binet mental test which indicated that she had an I.Q. of 115. In grade four, she was given a verbal group test and was appraised to have an I.Q. of 80. Inasmuch as her reading ability and general school performance was consistent with the 80 I.Q., no mismeasurement was suspected. She went into junior high school and in the ninth grade was given another, and this time a more verbal group test, one that was almost a power of comprehension reading test—at least it was for one who read as poorly as Mary. She received an I.Q. of 56. This measurement, while somewhat consistent with her scholastic performance, seemed unreasonable to the counselor, so a complete study of Mary was made. When an individual Stanford-Binet mental test was given, the results indicated that she had an I.Q. of 104. Mary, in reality, was a marked reading disability case. Her reading score indicated only third-grade ability. It was found that she seemed to be attempting to learn all the 800,000 words in the language by memorizing the spelling of each. She could comprehend but little and therefore could not show her true mental ability on a test that required reading. Such tests all too frequently are used in making comparisons between reading growth and mental growth. The one advantage to such tests is that they can be given to large groups. The results are useful in making most comparisons for the usual student. But they are worse than worthless in the case of poor readers, because the results often are considered accurate.

NONVERBAL GROUP TESTS. These tests often are used as a criterion for determining reading expectancy. They can be given to large groups and therefore save a great deal of testing time. They are useful in selecting children who have a notable discrepancy between their mental age and their reading age. These tests, although paper and pencil tests, do not require reading matter as a means of presenting the items. Therefore the disabled reader can take these tests unhampered by his poor reading ability. The major difficulties with these tests are two: first, they are not as accurate in measurement as desirable for individual diagnosis; second, they do not appear to measure the type of mental ability needed for success in reading. They are, to some degree, performance tests rather than tests of reasoning ability. Nonetheless, they have merit as screening tests and can be administered by the classroom teacher, thus saving testing time. When reading disability is suspected, however, the results should be checked by more accurate, individual tests.

INDIVIDUAL MENTAL TESTS. These are the most suitable measures of mental growth to be used with reading cases. The Stanford-Binet and the Wechsler Intelligence Scale for Children* are the most popular and useful

* See Appendix III for representative intelligence tests (also see Buros [35] for a critical evaluation of these tests).

tests of this type. They give an accurate measure of mental ability for able readers and are affected only slightly by the lack of reading ability of disabled readers. Bond and Fay (24) have shown, however, that the disabled readers do have appreciable difficulty with the items in the Binet directly related to reading growth, such as vocabulary, reading and memory, minkus completion, abstract words, and dissected sentences. This handicap may be as much as from 5 to 20 I.Q. points underestimation for poor readers of fifth-grade age. In the case of Mary, cited above, the difference between the 115 I.Q. at kindergarten age and the 104 I.Q. when she was in the ninth grade could be accounted for by the tendency of the test to underestimate the mental ability of the disabled reader. If the clinician is alert to this possibility, individual mental test are accurate. Of course, the worker can say only that Mary's I.Q. in ninth grade was at least 104, while in all likelihood it was somewhat higher. Individual mental tests are the most desirable measures to use in estimating reading expectancy. They are limited, however, by the fact that they are time-consuming and require trained examiners.

INDIVIDUAL PERFORMANCE TESTS. These are useful additions to other tests for supplying information to be used to diagnose certain types of reading problems. They aid in measuring the mental ability of children who are hearing-impaired, those who have marked oral-expressive problems, or those who have other handicaps. These tests have the same limitations as other individual tests, since they are time-consuming and require trained examiners. Another limitation is that they do not emphasize the verbal aspects of intellectual growth.

Relating Mental Growth to Reading Expectancy

The problem of relating a child's mental growth to his reading growth in order to estimate the level at which he should be able to read is a complicated one. The usual way in which this judgment is made is to consider that the child should have reached a reading age or grade roughly comparable to his mental age or grade. Then, if a given child's reading grade is significantly lower than his mental grade, he is classified as a disabled reader. The amount of discrepancy between reading grade and mental grade considered significant, increases as the child grows older. In the primary grades, from one-half to three-fourths of a grade difference is taken to be enough to classify the child as a disabled reader. In the intermediate grades, a difference of one to one and three-fourths grades is used. A second-grade child whose mental grade is 2.8 and whose reading is 2.2

would be thought a disabled reader. Likewise, in the second grade, a very able child whose mental grade is 4.0 and whose reading grade is 3.4 would be considered disabled. There is serious question as to whether this latter conclusion is justified.

For example, the child with 150 I.Q., who enters the first grade at the age of 6.5, cannot be expected to read at a 4.3 grade level even though that would be about his mental grade. As a matter of fact, this child would be able to read little, if anything, because he has not yet been taught. He has had no real opportunity to learn to read.

There are many possible ways of using the general intelligence of the child as a yardstick against which to judge his reading growth. The results of mental tests in classifying a child as a disabled reader have been used with the mental age or grade as the level at which the child is expected to read. Most studies of over- and underachievement have used the mental age criterion to estimate who were the good and who were the poor achievers. These studies have found universally that bright children underachieve and dull children overachieve in comparison to their mental age.

The assumption that a child should be achieving up to his mental age needs careful inspection. Although it is true that learning such as listening or speaking vocabulary can be so judged, other learning cannot be expected to be related in the same way. The child of 150 I.Q. who is ten years old has a mental age of fifteen. For example, this means that he should, on the basis of his mental grade, be doing mathematics equal to that of about a tenth-grader instead of a fifth-grade child. But it is doubtful if such a child would know algebra and geometry, because he has not yet met them. Reading achievement acts in much the same way.

Systematic instruction in reading usually is not begun before the first grade. The typical child, regardless of his I.Q., has little if any measurable reading ability when he starts the first grade. At this time, he would be said to read at the 1.0 grade level. If we assume that the I.Q. is, in one respect, an index of rate of learning, we can estimate the reading potential of each child by means of the *reading expectancy* formula:

$$\left(\frac{I.Q.}{100} \times \text{years of reading instruction}\right) + 1.0 = \frac{\text{Reading}}{\text{Expectancy}}$$

The 1.0 is added because the child who just starts to learn to read is given a 1.0 grade score, and after one year of instruction the typical child will be classified as a 2.0 reader.

By this formula, the typical child with an I.Q. of 70 could be expected to read at the level of 1.7 at the end of one year of instruction, and at the end of two years of reading instruction, he should read at 2.4 grade level. Still using the same formula, the child with 100 I.Q. would be expected to read at 3.0 after two years of reading instruction, and the able child with 150 I.Q. would be expected to read at 4.0. At the end of three and one half years, a child with a 130 I.Q. could be expected to read at a 5.55 grade level. Placing the numbers in the formula, $(\frac{130}{100} \times 3.5) + 1.0 = 5.55$, which is the reading expectancy for that child. To the extent that all other elements that influence reading success are favorable, he would learn somewhat faster than the typical child with 130 I.Q., thus exceeding his reading expectancy. If, on the other hand, these other conditions were unfavorable, he would not read up to his expectancy level and might even be so retarded that he would be a disabled reader.

Experience and research have shown this formula to be surprisingly accurate in estimating the potential reading ability of the typical child. As can be seen, the formula is easy to calculate, but the following considerations should be kept in mind:

1. The time of reading instruction is the years and months in school from the time systematic reading instruction was started. This typically begins with first grade. (Some slow-learning children may have a delay of a year or so in starting to learn to read.)

2. Readiness training in kindergarten is not counted even though such programs do much to diminish the chances of disabilities from occurring once reading instruction has started.

3. If an I.Q. obtained from a Binet or Wechsler Intelligence test is not available, it is suggested that a Slosson Intelligence Test given by the teacher or a group performance intelligence test score be substituted temporarily.

We now must consider the extent of discrepancy between the child's reading expectancy grade level and his actual average reading grade which would indicate that he is a disabled reader. Table 1 shows that this discrepancy increases grade by grade. In the first grade, for example, one-half year is a sufficiently large difference between reading expectancy and reading achievement to indicate a serious problem. Even children who are three-tenths of a year lower in reading achievement than we would expect them to be, are considered seriously enough retarded to be studied further as having a possible disability. At grade seven or above, the difference must be two or more years to be classified as a disability, and have a 1.3- to 2-year lag to indicate a possible disability, if supported by other evidence.

A child with superior intellect who is classified as a possible reading disability case may appear to be progressing reasonably well in reading in comparison with the other children in his grade. He may appear, for example, to be an efficient reader of third-grade material even though he is only just finishing the second grade. His achievement in reading in comparison with his reading expectancy would place him in the region of

Table 1

*Discrepancies Between Reading Expectancy and Achievement Which Indicate
Disability at Each Grade Level*

| | GRADE IN SCHOOL | | | | | | |
grade score discrepancy	1	2	3	4	5	6	7 and above
Indicating Disability	0.5 or more	.66 or more	.75 or more	1.0 or more	1.5 or more	1.75 or more	2.0 or more
Indicating Possible Disability	.3–.5	.4–.66	.5–.75	.7–1.0	.9–1.5	1.1–1.75	1.3–2.0

doubt (a possible disability), but not significantly low enough to classify him as disabled. A study of his reading profile on a group reading diagnostic test might show irregularities in his skill development, indicating that he was using faulty skills which, if allowed to persist, would limit him at more advanced levels.

Many reading cases which could have been discovered early may not show up until unfortunate techniques have become so entrenched that they interfere with good reading at a more mature level. The tasks involved in reading change as the materials become more difficult in structure and place greater demands on the reader. Skills that may suffice at grades one or two, when used by an intellectually superior child, may enable him to understand the content of primary books, but cause him trouble later on. For example, a child might use a letter-by-letter spelling attack for word recognition. This child, with high learning ability, might read reasonably well materials with the limited vocabularies introduced in the primary grades, but would be handicapped severely with the greatly expanded vocabularies encountered in the intermediate grades. His dependence upon the superior use of a spelling attack on words would preclude the development of more diversified work-recognition skills. As a result, the child would become a disabled reader whose educational career would be seriously impaired. His problem might have been solved easily if his potential disability had been identified and corrected early.

The disabled reader is, in general, one who has had an opportunity to learn to read, but who is not reading as well as could be expected by his aural verbal ability, his mental capacity, and his success in nonreading learnings. He is, in reality, the child who is at the lower end of the reading distribution when compared with other children of his age and general capability. He is at the lower end for reasons which will be discussed in the chapters that follow. It should be noted, however, that there are other children of his general capability who are as far advanced in the reading distribution as the disabled reader is retarded. These advanced readers have been fortunate indeed and probably have been endowed with all the other factors which influence effective reading growth.

CATEGORIES OF READING DISABILITIES

The children who have been classified as disabled readers can be grouped into descriptive categories which help to explain the general nature of reading disability. There are, among the children who are disabled readers, the following groups:

1. Simple retardation cases

2. Specific retardation cases

3. Limiting disability cases

4. Complex disability cases

Simple retardation cases is the way we label those disabled readers who lack general maturity in reading. They are significantly retarded in reading when compared with other children of their general reading expectancy, but there is no unusual or limiting characteristic about their reading pattern. Though they are immature in reading, there is nothing especially wrong with the reading they do. John, a fifth-grade boy of average intelligence, shown in figure 2, has not been as interested in reading and has read only about half as much as the typical child reads at a level only halfway through the third grade. He is a good reader of third-grade material and his entire profile on a diagnostic battery of tests looks like any normal third-grade pattern. This case is one of simple retardation. The problem can be solved by giving John more experience in reading and systematic instruction at his level of reading ability. Such cases are frequent among disabled readers. These children do not constitute a reeducation problem, but they do need adjustment in material and instruction. If they are forced to read books too difficult for them or if they are not given systematic instruction in reading development at their level, they very likely will become more complex reading disability cases. There are many reasons, other than lack of interest, which result in the prevalence of such reading cases.

Specific retardation cases are those children who have specific limitations in their reading profiles. In general, these children are competent readers and may or may not be classified as disabled. They are classified as disabled if they are weak in enough areas of reading to lower their average performance sufficiently. Mary, shown in figure 2, is a reader who is able to read and understand the general significance of paragraphs difficult enough to challenge the reading capacity of children of her age and intelligence. She, however, cannot read to follow directions or to organize longer interrelated selections. She has acquired the general basic reading skills and abilities, but she has not learned to adapt them to all her reading purposes. She may be inexperienced in noting relationships and in organizing what she has read. She needs training in the areas in which she is weak rather than reeducation in the basic skills and abilities. She is fundamentally an able reader, but she is retarded in ways that do not limit her general growth in reading.

Limiting disability cases are those disabled readers who have serious deficiencies in their basic skills and abilities, which limit their entire reading growth. Children who have a word-recognition deficiency, limiting mechanical habits or inability to sense thought units, and so on, would fall into this category. The principal fact about the children in this group is that they need reeducation. They need to unlearn some of the things they have learned or to learn some new basic approaches to reading. They have failed in some learning essential to reading growth, have acquired an unfortunate attack on reading, or have overemphasized one needed skill so much that they lack balance in their reading attack. These children require the help of well-planned remedial programs to correct their faulty reading patterns and to develop such skills as they need.

George, represented in figure 2, has a limiting disability. He is a capable fifth-grade boy who is quite low in all types of reading. His high intelligence enables him to grasp the significant ideas in a passage he is reading relatively well, even though he reads less well for specific detail. His ability to recognize words is even more immature. The profile shows that he is low in recognizing words in isolation, though he is getting some aid from context clues. His basic problem appears to be an inability to locate visually the usable parts of words, even though his knowledge of the same word elements, when isolated for him, is somewhat advanced. He also experiences difficulty in recombining the word elements he recognizes into word entities. These two limitations (visual analysis and word synthesis) are basic to effective word identification. These limitations are not only the probable cause of George's reading disability, but they also threaten to impede any future growth unless corrected by careful remedial work. The types of training necessary for such cases will be described in chapter 10.

Complex disability cases are really a subgroup of limiting disability cases, children who have deficiencies in their reading patterns which limit further growth in reading. Their reading is complicated by unfortunate attitudes toward reading and by undesirable adjustments to their failure to progress. Reeducating these children may be complicated further by sen-

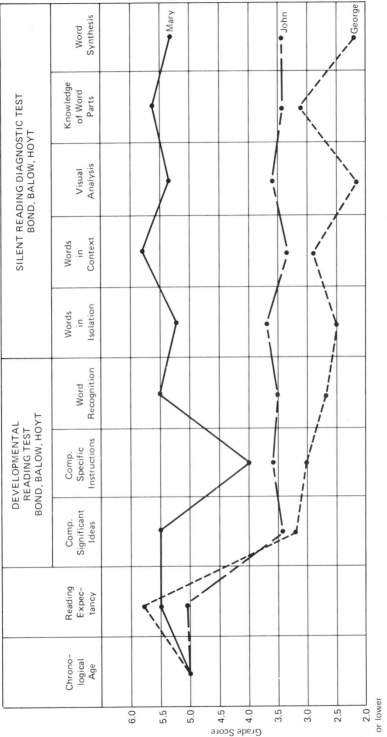

Fig. 2 *TYPES OF DISABLED READERS.*

sory, physical, or other handicaps. Each of the children classified as a complex disability case needs a remedial program carefully devised to meet the particular complexities of his problem.

A more extensive diagnosis will be needed to determine whether George, shown in figure 2, has only a limiting disability or is in fact a complex disability case. At this point in the study, it has become clear that George has an inconsistent profile which shows a marked limiting condition in need of correction. Personality and attitude appraisals are needed, and also measures of his sensory, physical, and emotional characteristics. The various constitutional and environmental factors to be discussed in the next two chapters will have to be explored in order to clarify the category into which this child should be placed and to design a remedial program which will correct his difficulty. The modifications needed in the remedial treatment of complex disability cases are discussed in chapter 12.

SUMMARY

The disabled reader is more than just a child who cannot read well. He can be found among children at almost any level of general intellectual capability. He is a child who is not reading as well as could be expected for one of his intellectual or verbal maturity. No two disabled readers are the same, and it is likely that no two disabilities were caused by the same set of circumstances. Many disabled readers become discouraged and frequently develop emotional tensions when in reading situations.

The classification of a child as a disabled reader rather than as just a poor reader must be based upon his opportunity to learn, his verbal ability, his demonstrated ability to apply himself in learning situations other than reading, and his general mental ability. The mental ability of the child is used most often in assessing his reading expectancy. Care must be taken in measuring the mental ability of the disabled reader, because most tests require reading ability. For this reason, individual mental tests are the most suitable instruments.

The problem of using mental growth as a means of assessing reading expectancy is a complicated one. The use of mental age or grade as the sole criterion of expected attainment in reading is of questionable validity. A more sensible and useful approach would be to depend on calculations based on years of reading instruction and the child's I.Q.

Disabled readers can be grouped into descriptive categories according to the seriousness of the problem and the nature of the adjustment needed. Simple retardation cases are those children whose reading ability is generally immature but otherwise well balanced. Children with specific retardation are low in one or more types of reading but are competent in basic reading skills and abilities. Children with limiting disability are deficient in basic reading abilities that preclude further growth in reading. Children with complex disability in reading are those who cannot grow further in reading because of deficiencies in basic reading abilities. Their problems are complicated by conditions such as their rejection of reading, accompanying personality problems, sensory or physical limitations, and other learning handicaps.

SELECTED READINGS

BURMEISTER, L. E., *Reading Strategies for Secondary School Teachers,* chap. 1. Reading, Mass.: Addison-Wesley, 1974.

HARRIS, A. J., and E. R. SIPAY, *How to Increase Reading Ability* (6th ed.), chap. 1. New York: David McKay, 1975.

KENNEDY, E. C., *Classroom Approaches to Remedial Reading* (2nd ed.), chap. 3. Itasca, Ill.: F. E. Peacock Publishers, 1977.

OTTO, W., R. A. MCMENEMY, and R. J. SMITH, *Corrective and Remedial Teaching,* chap. 6. Boston: Houghton Mifflin Co., 1973.

TINKER, M. A., and Constance M. MCCULLOUGH, *Teaching Elementary Reading,* chap. 25. Englewood Cliffs, N.J.: Prentice-Hall, 1975.

VERNON, M. D., *Backwardness in Reading.* New York: Cambridge University Press, 1960.

WILSON, ROBERT M., *Diagnostic and Remedial Reading for Classroom and Clinic* (3rd ed.), chap. 3. Columbus, Ohio: Charles E. Merrill Publishing Co., 1977.

Causes
of
Reading
Disability:
Physical Factors

four

Causes of reading disability are numerous. Rarely will a teacher or clinician find that a single factor has caused a child to be disabled in reading. It is almost always true that a reading disability is the result of several factors working together to impede successful reading progress. Reading is a complex process. Proficient reading depends upon the acquisition and versatile application of many intricately coordinated skills. These skills are acquired only through long, motivated practice under good guidance. Because the reading process is so complex, there are many opportunities for unfortunate complications to retard its growth. Various factors, operating singly or more often together, may block further progress in reading until they are discovered and eliminated, or until corrective instructional procedures can be devised to adjust to, or to circumvent, their effects.

Labels, such as dyslexia, sound serious, but do not provide so much as a hint of how to help a child, do not even have an accepted meaning, and certainly do more harm than good. Labeling usually does not provide useful remedial information. Finding out as precisely as possible what is needed to teach a child to read and then providing that help is more beneficial. A further complication in some cases is that it is difficult or impossible to distinguish cause from effect. It is easy, for example, to mistake emotional stress or behavioral problems as the cause of reading failure, when they often are the effect of a child's awareness of his failures in reading.

This chapter will discuss and evaluate the roles of various physical deficiencies or conditions as contributing causes of reading disability. Visual, auditory, speech, and intellectual deficiencies, and conditions of general health and neurological status all will be considered.

VISUAL DEFICIENCIES

Rutherford (168) cites an extreme case of visual disability. Janice seemed to be a well-adjusted child before entering first grade but then had great difficulty learning to read. Professional examination revealed severe visual impairment. On the way home, after receiving her corrective lenses, she asked her mother about the signboards along the street, the rear lights of cars, and even the leaves on trees. Of course Janice had seen them before, but not in the form and dimension in which they now appeared to her, which made them look so different that she could not identify them. It is no wonder that Janice was not able to learn to read before getting glasses.

It seems axiomatic that ocular comfort and visual efficiency are prerequisite to easy reading. When a child shows signs of becoming a disability case, the tendency of both teachers and parents is to think of visual deficiencies. It is true that a child's eyesight may be so poor that it is practically impossible to read. There are a number of less severe eye defects which handicap children in the reading situation. When they attempt to read, they become uncomfortable, squirmy, fatigued, and so distraught that they can continue for only a short time. They may refuse to read at all. Although certain mild defects may not interfere with learning to read, they may make reading for a lengthy period fatiguing. It is not surprising, therefore, that many studies have concentrated upon visual deficiencies as causes of reading disability.

Considerable historical research relating visual deficiency to reading difficulty has resulted in somewhat conflicting findings. An extensive bibliography of current research compiled by Weintraub (224) indicates that this disagreement and controversy still persists. However, some fairly consistent trends have emerged:

1. There is a slightly greater percentage of visual defects among children with reading disability than among children without reading disability.

2. Children with visual defects, as a group, tend to read more poorly than children without visual defects.

3. On the other hand, many children with visual defects learn to read as well as or better than children without visual defects.

4. No matter what kind or type of visual deficiency is studied, some children can be found who have that specific kind or type of visual deficiency and who are making good progress in reading.

Most types of visual defects appear to increase the possibility of reading disability, but none of these appear to be sufficient in itself to preclude reading success. Perhaps the answer is that some children with visual defects fail to learn to read because of the extra effort required of them to master reading, whereas other children with the same visual defects do learn to read successfully because they, for one reason or another, try so hard that they overcome their handicap. In any event, children with visual deficiencies who do read well, probably have learned under conditions of visual stress and fatigue. The wise teacher is alert to signs of fatigue among visually impaired children when they are required to complete demanding visual tasks and makes appropriate adjustments. The appropriate educational adjustments for these visual problems will be discussed in chapter 12.

Types of Visual Deficiency

Faulty focus of light rays that enter the eyes, *refractive errors,* may be associated with reading disability. However, research by Eames (66), Farris (72), Taylor (202), and Young (234) suggests that certain types of refractive errors are more closely associated with reading disability than others. The farsighted, *hyperopic,* child who can bring far targets into clear focus easily, but finds it difficult to focus clearly on near targets, is more likely to be reading-disabled than is the child with normal vision. On the other hand, the nearsighted, *myopic,* child who easily can bring near targets into clear focus but finds far targets difficult, is less likely to be reading-disabled than is the child with normal vision. This seems reasonable when one considers the nature of the reading task which involves prolonged periods of close visual inspection of near targets. However, if the teaching method relies heavily on the use of experience charts and much chalkboard work, the nearsighted child may have difficulty.

Problems in focusing the two eyes precisely and simultaneously on a target, *binocular difficulties,* are more common among disabled readers than among successful readers. Lack of binocular coordination because of muscular imbalance of one or both eyes, *strabismus,* causes images to be blurred, or in more severe cases, causes two images of a single object to be seen. The result is confusion, fatigue, or suppression of one eye when the child attempts to read. It has been demonstrated that one-eyed students progress better in reading than those with muscle imbalance.

Another binocular characteristic connected with success in reading is precision of focus so that images may be fused into a single, clear picture. Eames (66), Taylor (202), Spache and Tillman (188), and Witty and Kopel (230) report research suggesting that fusion difficulties are associated with reading difficulties. Not only accuracy of fusion, but also speed of fusion seem to be related to reading success. Ocular images of a fixated target that are unequal either in size or shape in the two eyes, *aniseikonia,* also has been found to be related to reading difficulties. Dearborn and Anderson (55) conclude, on the basis of their research, that aniseikonia is one of the many factors which may contribute to the causation and persistence of disability in reading.

Although many children with visual defects are quite successful in reading, visual defects often may contribute to reading failure. Children with visual defects are more likely to get into difficulty in reading and are more difficult to teach. Correction of visual defects is essential for all children with visual deficiencies, whether they are experiencing reading difficulties or not. Correction of visual defects enables children to learn to read more easily, but rarely, if ever, is such correction sufficient to relieve reading disability. Once correction has been made, however, most students will be able to progress more easily when given appropriate remedial instruction.

Identification of Visual Defects

Accurate identification of all visual defects depends on the cooperation and coordinated efforts of home, school, and eye-care professions. For an overview of vision screening, including screening of preschool children, see Lin-Fu (132); for a simple pamphlet for parents, Eberly (67) is recommended; and for excellent practical suggestions for organizing visual screening programs in the schools, see Jobe (115).

Extensive research by Knox (124) and Kozlowski (126) strongly suggests that observation by the teacher, combined with visual screening tests given by the school, provide more accurate identification of children in need of visual care than either teacher observation or school-administered visual screening tests alone.

However, as Jobe cautions, visual screening tests must be given only for the purpose of identification. Pupils who already have, or may develop problems requiring the care of a specialist must be referred to a vision-care specialist. Screening tests are not diagnostic, and neither teachers nor school nurses should ever attempt to diagnose or treat visual problems.

Visual Screening Devices

Some of the more widely accepted school-administered visual screening devices are:

Keystone Visual Survey Tests, Keystone View Company, 2212 E. Twelfth Street, Davenport, Iowa 52803.

Massachusetts Vision Test, Welch-Allyn, Auburn, New York or American Optical Corporation, Southbridge, Massachusetts 01550.

School Vision Tester, Bausch and Lomb, Rochester, New York 14602.

Sight Screener, American Optical Corporation, Southbridge, Massachusetts 01550.

Titmus School Vision Tester, Titmus Optical Vision Testers, 1312 W. Seventh Street, Piscataway, New Jersey 08854.

Teacher Observation

Knox (124) believes, based on extensive research on the identification of children with visual problems through observation with subsequent validation by an eye specialist, that the following behavioral symptoms are most useful:

1. Facial contortions.
2. Book held close to face.
3. Tense during visual work.
4. Tilting head.
5. Head thrust forward.
6. Body tense while looking at distant objects.
7. Assuming a poor sitting position.
8. Moving head excessively while reading.
9. Rubbing eyes frequently.
10. Tendency toward avoidance of close visual work.
11. Tendency to lose place in reading.

When two to four of these symptoms are noticeable and persistent, it is the teacher's responsibility to work with the parents, the school, and the eye-care professional to ensure that the child receives a proper vision examination. If a vision defect is diagnosed by a vision-care specialist, cooperative efforts must be made to provide proper vision care for the child and to make appropriate educational adaptations within the school. Suggestions will be found in chapter 12.

Visual Processing Defects

Research on the relationship between visual perception, visual memory, visual sequencing, and reading disability has been contradictory and confusing. Vernon (219) concluded from a review of research relating deficient visual perception to severe reading difficulties, that deficient visual perception is one of the characteristics of severely disabled readers, but that deficient visual perception is so often associated with a general maturational lag that it may be but one symptom of a general immaturity which also includes language development and personality development.

Robinson (163) found that students with deficiencies in visual perceptual abilities also had lower IQs than children who did not. Bryan and Bryan (33) found from a review of recent research on visual processing—specifically visual memory and visual sequencing—that the relationship between these abilities and reading disability was not clear. Two major reasons for the ambiguity were cited. The first was a validity problem, specifically that researchers could not convincingly measure visual processing abilities. The second was that among the children studied, visual processing abilities were so intermingled with other factors usually considered detrimental to reading success, that determining the cause of reading difficulty was not possible. Vernon and Robinson also expressed concern for the contamination of results of research on children with visual processing problems. In the clinic, however, children who do appear to have visual processing problems, as well as extreme reading disability, often benefit greatly from the Kinesthetic-Auditory-Visual methods of reading instruction described in chapter 11.

AUDITORY DEFICIENCIES

Under certain circumstances, auditory deficiencies may be a primary cause of reading difficulty. Research shows a direct, though low, correlation between certain auditory characteristics and reading success. See Weintraub (222) for a comprehensive bibliography. In addition, clinicians such as Durrell and Murphy (63), report numerous cases in which auditory deficiencies were associated with reading failure.

The importance of auditory abilities can be appreciated when one considers that each child learns to read utilizing the language that he understands and uses, which is influenced by the language he has heard. Further, it should be remembered, that most beginning reading instruction involves much oral teacher direction. Therefore, the child who does not hear well or who does not listen well, learns at a disadvantage compared to other children who have good hearing and good listening habits. Both research and clinical experience provide evidence that some children overcome auditory disadvantage whereas others do not. The severity and type of auditory impairment, the length of time it remains undetected, the quality of the educational program, the coordination of the efforts of parents, specialists, and others, the desire of the child to read, and other causal factors all work together to affect the eventual outcome.

Types of Auditory Deficiency

Weintraub (222) identifies three major areas of concern:

1. Auditory acuity (hearing)
2. Audition (listening)
3. Auditory processing (working with sounds)

Much of the confusion in research, clinical work, and teaching results from the difficulty in separating the effects of hearing loss, listening skills, and auditory processing. Often a student may have difficulty with all three aspects of hearing, but sometimes the difficulty may be specific. For example, some children with no measurable hearing loss have difficulty hearing sounds in words but no difficulty understanding the meaning of spoken sentences. Other children with hearing loss have difficulty with all the auditory aspects of language, speech, and reading. Still other children have specific difficulty blending sounds into whole words and recognizing the meaning of the words. There are many kinds and types of auditory deficiency and what is best for one child with an auditory impairment may not be best for another child with a different auditory impairment.

Although research studies disagree, apparently because of dissimilar techniques of measurement and lack of uniform standards for differentiating hearing-impaired from nonhearing-impaired children, it is safe to say that a large number of school children—about five percent—have serious hearing losses. Apparently, many more children have slight hearing losses which may later become more serious unless proper medical treatment is given.

The relationship between hearing loss, especially a high-frequency hearing loss, and reading difficulty is well documented by Bond (22), Henry (103), Kennedy (120), Johnson (116), Poling (155), Reynolds (161), Robinson (164), and Witty and Kopel (230) among others. Although children with severe and extreme hearing losses always have great difficulty learning how to read, those with lesser impairments often do reasonably well if the hearing loss is identified early and appropriate medical and educational measures are taken. From the teacher's or the reading clinician's point of view, proper management of phonics instruction is crucial. For appropriate educational adjustments see chapter 12.

The relationship between audition and auditory processing, and reading disability is quite controversial. Bryan and Bryan (33), Groff (97), and Hammill and Larsen (99) offer critical reviews of the research. Clinical experience stresses that for some children, improving listening skills and auditory processing abilities is essential to successful remediation.

Identification of Auditory Defects

As with vision, successful identification of all auditory defects depends upon the cooperation and coordinated efforts of home, school, and auditory specialists. Early screening of very young children has been very beneficial in many cases. Auditory screening programs in the schools are very important.

Auditory Screening Devices

Hearing loss is determined most accurately by means of an audiometer such as:

Ambco Audiometers, Ambco Electronics Inc., 1222 W. Washington Boulevard, Los Angeles, California 90007.

Beltone Audiometers, Beltone Electronics Corporation, 4201 W. Victoria Street, Chicago, Illinois 60646.

Grason-Stadler Audiometers, Gen Rad, Environmedics Division, Route 117, Bolton, Massachusetts 01740.

Maico Audiometers, Maico Electronics, Inc., 7573 Bush Lake Road, Minneapolis, Minnesota 55435.

All companies have models especially adapted to school use.

Teacher Observation

An alert teacher will note signs of hearing difficulty from careful observations of children's behavior. Hearing impairment may be suspected if a child shows behavior such as:

1. Inattention during listening activities.

2. Frequent misunderstanding of oral directions or numerous requests for repetition of statements.

3. Turning one ear toward the speaker or thrusting head forward when listening.

4. Intent gaze at the speaker's face or strained posture while listening.

5. Monotone speech, poor pronunciation, or indistinct articulation.

6. Complaints of earache or hearing difficulty.

7. Insistence on closeness to sound sources.

8. Frequent colds, discharging ears, or difficult breathing.

For informal screening, a whisper or low-voice test can be used. Four or five children are lined up in a row in a quiet room about five feet from the examiner and with their backs to him. The examiner stays in one place and gives directions to the children, speaking in a distinct, low tone. Directions are like the following: "Take five steps forward; raise your right arm; take two steps forward; hold up three fingers"; and so forth. By watching the children, the examiner can see those who hesitate, turn to see what other children do, look back at the examiner, or fail to follow directions. The children who get to a position approximately twenty feet from the examiner without signs of seeking help have normal hearing. Hard-of-hearing children can be detected readily. Whisper tests may be given by softly saying single words with the child standing about twenty feet away with one ear turned toward the examiner, i.e., a distance at which most children can hear in the particular room used. The child tries to repeat each word as he hears it. If necessary, the examiner moves closer until responses are correct. Each ear is tested separately.

Although whisper or low-voice screening tests are valuable when they can identify a child with a hearing loss, these methods sometimes miss children with less severe hearing losses. For this reason, routine audiometric screening of all children before entering school, and from time to time during the school years, is preferable to total reliance on any informal method.

As with vision, the purpose of identification of hearing loss is to refer the child to a hearing specialist for proper treatment. In addition, educational services and instructional adaptations, as discussed in chapter 12, must be provided.

SPEECH DEFECTS

Defective speech is associated with reading difficulty, according to research by Bond (22), Lyle (135), Monroe (141), and Robinson (164). Usually, inaccurate formation of speech sounds, *articulation disorders,* are found to be more closely associated with reading disability than are the faulty rate of production or repetition of speech sounds, *fluency difficulties*. Generally it is agreed that in many cases, both inaccurate articulation and reading difficulties are associated with other factors such as slow intellectual development, neurological involvement, or inability to discriminate sounds in words. Nevertheless, clinical experience suggests that for some children defective speech itself is a causal factor.

Monroe (141) notes that faulty articulation may directly affect reading by causing confusion between the sounds the child hears others make and the sounds the child hears himself make when he is asked to associate print symbols with sounds in reading. Clinical experience and research by Bond (22) show that reading methods which require individual letter-by-letter sounding and blending can cause extreme difficulty to a student with faulty articulation. If the student has auditory limitations as well, the difficulty is augmented. Methods stressing visual-mental word analysis enable such a student to progress in reading much more successfully.

Confusion also may arise when a student hears words spoken one way when *he* reads orally, but another way as he sees the words in his book while *others* read them aloud. This confusion not only affects sound-symbol associations but also may interfere with the student's understanding of what is read. The child thus may become increasingly confused about not only how words are pronounced but also about what they mean.

Some children with speech defects become obviously upset when they are asked to read aloud. This is usually because the student is sensitive about his articulation errors and dislikes displaying them in an oral reading situation. Clinical experience reveals that many children with speech defects, even very minor, barely noticeable problems, insist that they do not want to read aloud but are willing to read silently. In fact, clinical experience shows that insistence upon oral reading has been known to turn some children with speech defects against all reading.

Research by Bond (22) and Monroe (141) suggests that speech defects are not associated with silent reading achievement but are associated with oral reading disability. Some evidence suggests that the strongest association of all may be between speech defects and poor oral reading when it occurs together with adequate silent reading.

The child with speech defects usually needs the assistance of a speech specialist to remedy his speech problem plus an appropriate reading program. Emphasis on visual-mental word analysis and silent reading usually is best. Planning a suitable reading program for a child with speech defects becomes more complicated when other factors, such as slow intellectual development, neurological impairment, or auditory discrimination difficulties also are present.

Suggestions for educational adjustments are made in chapter 12.

GENERAL HEALTH PROBLEMS

Learning to read is a difficult, even arduous task. To succeed, the learner must be an attentive, active participant in the learning process. Any physical condition which lowers a child's vitality makes it difficult for him to sustain active attention to learning.

Chronic Illness and Malnutrition

Chronically ill or malnourished children often are unable to sustain attention to demanding learning tasks. These children are likely to miss much instruction due to frequent absences, which make learning even more difficult. When learning to read becomes a matter of having to catch up on a week's missed work, while feeling insecure about how to proceed, tired, unwell, and perhaps hungry, it is little wonder that some children begin to dislike and avoid reading.

What is the teacher's responsibility in regard to poor general health, malnutrition, and frequent absence?

1. When a general health problem is suspected, the teacher, school nurse, parents, and others should discuss the matter and decide what to do. Often the appropriate action will be to refer the child for a medical diagnosis. In this case, it is important to alert the doctor or diagnostic team to the nature of the behavior in the home and in the school, which prompted the referral.

2. Although malnutrition is still an important problem for many children, the schools have taken an increasingly important role in combating it through various lunch, milk, and breakfast programs. Some teachers, especially those who use behavior modification techniques, also provide some students with tiny amounts of nutritious food as part of their teaching procedures.

3. In the case of absenteeism, it is the teacher's responsibility to provide special assistance to ensure that children have not missed essential skill development, and that they do not feel confused or insecure about proceeding with their work. Depending upon the circumstances, the teacher may provide this assistance directly, use other resource personnel within the school, or enlist the parents' aid.

General Fatigue

In a reading clinic, it often is discouraging to hear a chronically fatigued and disabled reader give a detailed rendition of last evening's late, late television movie. It is especially so when follow-up questioning reveals that the student watches a great deal of television, usually far into the night. In this case, the child's television viewing habits must be discussed with his parents and the child himself. Often, viewing habits will be changed; sometimes they will not. It is tempting to believe that extensive television viewing or other factors which seem to be interfering with proper rest are causing a student's reading difficulty and in some cases, this is true. In other cases, overuse of television or other activities may be a child's way of escaping from the frustrations he feels, including the frustration of reading failure.

GLANDULAR DISTURBANCES

Glandular disturbances, especially thyroid dysfunctions, have long been known to be associated with reading disability. A thyroid deficiency, *hypothyroidism,* often results in marked obesity and "mental" sluggishness; a thyroid excess, *hyperthyroidism,* often results in weight loss, overactivity, fatigue, and irritability. Neither condition is conducive to effective learning. Both have been found to be factors in specific cases according to Harris and Sipay (100), Olson (149), Robinson (164), and Witty and Schacter (233).

Recently, a more subtly related condition has been suspected. Park and Schneider (152) compared blood samples from a group of fifty-three disabled readers with blood samples from a similar age group of successful readers. Although the disabled readers revealed no detectable illness when examined by physicians and showed no behavioral evidence of hyperthyroidism, the thyroxine content of their blood was found to be elevated compared to that of the nondisabled readers. Compared to normal standards of thyroxine content, all the successful readers were within normal limits as were ten of the unsuccessful readers. However, forty-three of the unsuccessful readers had thyroxine contents elevated beyond normal limits, suggesting an association between reading disability and systemic metabolic irregularity. Further research is needed to confirm this single finding. Assuming metabolic differences are commonly associated with reading difficulty, it will be important to know whether these differences cause reading difficulty, or are a stress reaction to reading difficulty. It also will be important to know if there are any medical and educational implications.

In cases of true hypothyroidism, Witty and Schacter (233) and Austin, Bush, and Huebner (2) report that when proper medical treatment was given, children made dramatic gains in reading. Any child suspected of thyroid dysfunction or any other glandular disturbance should be referred to a physician.

NEUROLOGICAL LIMITATIONS

Among children who have not yet acquired the ability to read, there are a very few who have sustained known brain damage before, during, or after birth. Some of these children suffer severe handicaps, such as aphasia, cerebral palsy, marked mental retardation, or debilitating motor problems. They obviously require highly specialized medical assistance and educational programming. Other children with known brain damage are much less handicapped. They, too, require medical assistance and educational programming. However, for reading instruction, appropriate educational programming may or may not be much different from good reading instruction for the typical learner, depending on the needs of the individual child. Recent case studies from the Geneva-Medico-Educational Service (90) suggest that known brain lesions, unless very severe, often do not retard learning, and that many children with verifiable brain damage do make good progress in reading. Educational adjustments for such children are discussed in chapter 12.

Besides the concern for the child with known brain damage, there has been a great deal of recent concern, research, speculation, opinion, and clinical data reported regarding *suspected* brain damage and reading difficulties. Such terms as developmental dyslexia, primary reading retardation, minimal brain damage, maturational lag, and others have been used to refer to suspected brain damage in the absence of medically verifiable brain pathology. Bender (8), Critchley (46), and Rabinovitch (160), among many others, have argued persuasively in favor of some type of neurological impairment, other than known brain pathology, as a probable cause of reading difficulty. A careful and perceptive review of relevant research by Balow, Rubin, and Rosen (5) suggests that subtle, often undetected, neurological impairment associated with complications of pregnancy and birth is a cause of later reading disability among some children. Rourke (166) also presents compelling evidence for the view that neurological dysfunction, in the absence of known brain damage, is a common associate of reading disability.

On the other hand, Spache (184) provides a highly critical review of the overwhelming abundance of current literature relating suspected neurological impairment to reading disability. He warns that some specialists

appear to be attributing almost all reading difficulties to suspected neurological impairment, not only in the absence of known brain damage, but
even in the absence of *any* signs of abnormal neurological functioning. Isom
(112) cautions that the assessment of a child's neurological development
and its relationship to reading is extraordinarily complex. His thoughtful
review of neurological research relevant to reading indicates that among
children who show signs suggestive of neurological impairment, some have
no reading difficulty, some have moderate reading difficulty, and some
have serious reading disability. He emphasizes the critical need for competent research comparing the frequency of occurrence of presumably abnormal neurological signs found in reading-disabled children with the
frequency of occurrence of the same signs among their nonreading-disabled
peers. In a somewhat related study, Larsen, Tillman, Ross, Satz, Cassin,
and Wolkin (130) found that among a group of one hundred children referred to a center for learning disabilities, signs of neurologic impairment
were no more common among those who were reading-disabled than
among those who were making normal progress in reading.

In a study comparing reading-disabled children with and without
clinical signs of neurological dysfunction, Black (16) found no real differences among the groups in severity of reading problems, overall cognitive
functioning, or behavior. He concluded, from his research, that suspected
neurological dysfunction was *not* an important factor in planning proper
remediation of reading disability. Black (14) also compared children who
were suspected of neurological dysfunction with children with known brain
damage. Once again, patterns of behavior, cognitive abilities, and academic difficulties noted for these groups were similar enough to suggest
that specialized remedial programs differentiating between children with
documented brain damage and suspected brain dysfunction are probably
unwarranted. Black concluded that remedial programs should be based *not*
on probable neurological causation, but rather on the instructional needs
of each child.

In the authors' opinion, a medical referral for neurological assessment
should be made when:

1. There is an extreme discrepancy between a child's reading expectancy and
   reading achievement in spite of appropriate educational experiences.

Or when:

2. Despite a wide discrepancy between expectancy and achievement, a
   child's progress in a carefully planned and well-taught reading program is
   persistently and unexplainably slow.

Practically speaking, what should the reading teacher or reading clinician do about suspected neurological involvement among poor readers?
The best initial referral for neurological assessment is usually to a coopera-

tive pediatrician who has had extensive experience with both normal and neurologically impaired children. Often no real evidence of neurological impairment will be found, sometimes an unexpected physical deficiency of a different sort will be uncovered, and sometimes evidence of neurological impairment will be revealed. If any type of physical condition which requires medical assistance is found, appropriate measures, of course, should be taken. Any suggestions a physician offers which might serve to enhance a child's learning should be followed. However, reading instruction for the disabled reader who shows medical signs of neurological impairment, as for any other disabled reader, should proceed according to a careful plan based on a diagnosis of the child's particular reading deficiencies and instructional needs. Methods of proper diagnosis and treatment of reading difficulties are included in chapters 6 through 16.

When progress is slow, much slower than the child's reading expectancy would suggest, special effort must be made to ensure that the child knows that he *is* making progress and feels that he is succeeding. Clinical experience suggests that neurologically impaired children with low average, average, or above average intelligence almost always learn to read, often—in time—to read well. But for many of them, the experience is a very unpleasant, personally destructive one. Teaching such children to read is difficult but possible. Making this process a constructive experience in the child's life is much more difficult and much more important.

LATERAL DOMINANCE

The role of lateral dominance in reading disability is a controversial issue. The literature on the subject is extensive and equivocal. It is possible to indicate here only the trends of the evidence and to evaluate it.

Lateral dominance is the consistent preference for using and for using more skillfully the muscles on one side of the body. Lateral dominance is illustrated by "handedness" which involves preferred use of either right or left hand for skilled manipulations, and by "eyedness" which involves preferred use of right or left eye for such tasks as aiming or examining things through a monocular microscope. Crossed dominance, which is less common, occurs when the preferred eye and hand are on the opposite sides. A few people are neither dominantly right- nor left-sided, i.e., are ambidextrous, as skillful with one hand as with the other.

Orton (150), a neurologist, has proposed a much discussed cerebral dominance theory of laterality in relation to reading disability. It has been established that the right cerebral hemisphere controls movements on the left side of the body and that the left hemisphere controls the right side. He suggests that memory images or records of letters and words exist in the brain on both the right and left, one in each hemisphere like mirror images. Orton claims that learning to read involves selecting the memory images in the dominant hemisphere. When there is marked cerebral dominance, usually manifested by either dominant right- or left-handedness, the child ordinarily has no difficulty in learning to read. However, if the child has not developed either right or left dominance by the time he begins to learn to read, difficulties will arise; the two sides of the brain will conflict. Either the right or left orientation of letter sequences may be stimulated by looking at a word, according to which hemisphere happens to take the lead. The result is a tendency to make reversals in reading. Although Orton's theory has found favor with some, it is by no means universally accepted. As pointed out by Jastak (113), Orton fixed his attention on a group of symptoms and then worked out an *ad hoc* neurological theory to explain them. For a well-documented and research-based criticism of the cerebral dominance theories of reading disability, see Spache (184).

In using reversals as a symptom of reading difficulties, it is wise to remember that many beginning readers, including even the most successful, will show some reversal tendencies. Such tendencies are most apparent when the beginning reader feels tense or uncertain. However, with a little concern and attention from the teacher, his confusion usually is soon overcome. But it is important to be aware that excessive and persistent reversal difficulties sometimes are associated with extreme reading disability. Further discussion of reversal tendencies among severely disabled readers is provided in chapter 11.

Clinical evidence of a relationship between laterality and reading disability is given by Dearborn (51, 52, 53, 54). Among his clinical cases, he found a greater incidence of left dominance, crossed dominance, and lack of dominance among poor than among good readers. He notes that reading difficulties are most likely to appear among children who have been changed over in handedness or whose lateral dominance has never been well established. Additional supporting clinical evidence is reported by Eames (65), Crosland (47), Witty and Kopel (232), Teegarden (203) and Monroe (141).

When Cohen and Glass (41) tested first- and fourth-grade pupils, they found no significant relationship between dominance or directional knowledge and reading achievement among fourth-grade pupils. Among first-grade pupils, poor readers were more likely to lack hand dominance and to be confused about left and right than were good readers. In other investigations, no evidence was found supporting a relationship between lateral dominance and reading achievement, including studies of beginning readers. Noteworthy are the studies of Douglas and others (60), Bennett (9), Haefner (98), Tinker (208), Gates and Bond (86), Witty and Kopel (232), Muehl (144), Balow and Balow (4), Belmont and Birch (7), Coleman and Deutsch (43), Hillerich (108), Koos (125), and Goodglass and Barton (93).

The studies disagree probably because research on groups of good and poor readers in the classroom tends not to show a statistically significant association between laterality and reading difficulty, while at the same time, studies of individual severely disabled readers often do find laterality closely related to a certain child's disability. Weintraub (223) concludes from his review of laterality research that evidence collected from *nonclinical* subjects shows little if any relationship between laterality and reading achievement. Thomson (206) points out that relationships between laterality and reading vary considerably as do the various methods and populations used in the specific studies.

When the incidence of dominance anomalies in groups of poor readers is compared with the incidence in groups of successful readers, left-handedness, mixed dominance, or lack of dominance is found in both groups. Therefore, it seems reasonable to assume that dominance anomalies alone do not necessarily cause reading disability and that good readers overcome them. However, dominance anomalies in combination with other handicaps may be important factors in the reading difficulties of poor readers. Clinically, dominance anomalies can be very important for certain children.

Certain secondary conditions arising from laterality also should not be neglected. The naturally left-handed child who has been forced to change to his right hand may be attempting to learn to read under considerable stress, caused by the constant tension of attempting to use his "wrong" hand throughout the day. Even without a change-over, the left-handed child may develop considerable tension in adapting to many school and other activities which are structured to be done with the right hand. Handwriting difficulties are just one example. Teachers can help by being sensitive to the left-hander's plight and by making appropriate educational adaptations. Forcing a naturally left-handed child to behave as if he were right-handed is a mistake, and is the most costly to the child when he is forced to write with his right hand. Children who are not obviously right- or left-handed, those who do not have clearly developed hand dominance, have somewhat different needs. A careful judgment must be made as to which hand is favored and then the child should be encouraged and guided to use that hand. Clinically, among severely disabled readers, left-handedness and lack of hand preference do appear to be associated with directional confusion in reading.

Measurement of Lateral Dominance

Accurate determination of hand and eye dominance can be accomplished by the following, uncomplicated procedures:

To test handedness, note which hand is used to perform several tasks, such as throwing a ball, cutting paper, picking up a small object, hammering a nail, erasing the chalkboard, threading a needle, and the like. Do not test use of eating utensils or writing implements, as the child may have been made to do these tasks with his right hand. Be sure that the child has equal opportunity to use either hand. This means that both hands must be free and that it is equally convenient for the child to use either hand. Several trials should be given and the results tabulated. Examination of the records will reveal definite handedness, or a tendency to use both hands almost equally often.

Sighting tests usually are used to determine eye preference. To do this, a teacher may request a child to aim a pencil held upright at arm's length at the teacher's nose or to look at the teacher through a hole punched in a sheet of paper or through a cardboard tube. The teacher then can easily and accurately determine whether the child's left or right eye is in direct alignment with the pencil, punched hole, or cardboard tube.

Commercial devices such as the Harris Test of Lateral Dominance (Psychological Corporation, New York City) also may be used to assess hand and eye dominance.

INTELLECTUAL LIMITATIONS

Although reading achievement is related to intelligence, according to Beldin (6), Bond and Wagner (26), Kirk and Elkins (123), Sewill and Severson (173), Strang (197), Traxler (213), and Wheeler and Wheeler (226), intellectual development alone does not determine how well a given child will or should read. See also Black (15), and Durrell (61). The precise assessment of reading achievement and of intelligence is complex and difficult. Both are influenced by other factors, and both are difficult to measure fairly and accurately. Nevertheless, for proper diagnosis of reading disability, the relationship between intelligence and reading achievement is very important. This is especially true for children with below-average intelligence.

As Durrell (61) cautions, the relationship between intelligence and reading achievement never must be used to set any limit on how much or what a child can learn. The relationship between intelligence and reading achievement should be used to identify the child who is failing to progress in reading commensurate with what is most reasonable to expect of him. Discrepancies between reading expectancy and achievement which indicate disability by grade level can be found in chapter 3.

The implication for the intellectually limited child is that if educational adaptations are made which are suited to his needs, he can and will make continuous, appropriate progress in reading. Clinical experience shows that children and youth of quite limited intelligence can and do learn to read if the proper educational adaptations are made. Although their achievement remains very low in comparison to others of their age, they are able to master reading skills useful to them throughout their lives.

But as Kirk (122) points out, low intelligence can be a cause of reading disability when appropriate educational adaptations are not made. For example, if a child with low intelligence is expected to read before he has been taught appropriate prereading skills, or if he is expected to progress through sequential reading instruction without adequate opportunity to securely learn essential reading skills, then he is likely to fail to make reasonable progress in reading. This child is reading-disabled not because his reading achievement is low, but because it is unreasonably low. Methods of adapting reading instruction for the intellectually limited child will be described in chapter 12.

When a child progresses in reading much more slowly than his peers, it is natural for his teachers to think that he may have low intelligence, especially when there are no other obvious reasons for his slow progress. However, it is not correct to assume that the child's intelligence is low, rather, it is imperative to refer the child to a specialist, such as a school psychologist, for further assessment. Either the *Wechsler Intelligence Scale for Children (Revised)* or the *Revised Stanford-Binet Intelligence Test* should be used for most children for this assessment. Results from group intelligence tests requiring the child to read as a part of the intelligence testing procedure must not be used, because the child who cannot read well cannot do well on these tests, no matter how well he might have performed if proper testing procedures had been used.

SUMMARY

This survey suggests that any one of a number of physical conditions may be involved as a contributing factor in reading disability. Much of the evidence is equivocal. It is obvious that any single factor seldom if ever causes reading disability. As emphasized throughout this chapter, reading disability tends to be caused by many factors. Several hindering factors combine as a pattern in producing the disability.

A more detailed summary together with selected readings will be found at the end of the next chapter.

Causes of Reading Disability: Emotional, Environmental and Educational Factors

five

In the preceding chapter, a number of physical conditions possibly affecting reading disability were surveyed. In this chapter, various emotional, environmental, and educational factors and how they may contribute to reading disability will be examined.

PERSONAL AND SOCIAL ADJUSTMENT

When the behavior of disabled readers is compared to that of pupils making normal progress, it becomes obvious that there are differences in personal and social adjustment. Children who are failing to learn to read well are more likely to show signs of emotional and social maladjustment than are their more successful peers. Most children with reading difficulties manifest some sort of maladjustment ranging in degree from very mild to quite severe. Symptoms of maladjustment vary, and it has not yet proved possible to discern any clear pattern of traits which characterize poor readers. It also is difficult to determine the relationship of emotional problems to reading problems. Although it is common for a reading disability to cause an emotional reaction, which in turn causes increased difficulty in reading, it also is common for previous personal and social problems to impede reading progress from the beginning.

When working with reading-disabled children in a clinic, it soon becomes apparent that they are laboring to learn under stress. In the classroom, children with reading problems also manifest symptoms of stress in one way or another. Some reading-disabled children appear shy or listless; some seem unable to concentrate; others show nervous mannerisms such as nail biting. Often reading-disabled children lack self-confidence. They become discouraged easily and tend to give up when work becomes difficult. Often the child with reading problems is easily irritated. Because of frustration or other reasons, reading-disabled children sometimes become aggressive in the classroom thereby gaining the attention, but rarely the approval, of others; on occasion they even manage to disrupt the entire class.

It is the teacher's responsibility to aid and assist these children in proper classroom behavior for the benefit of both the child and the rest of the class. It is crucial, as Gates (83) noted many years ago, not to assume that a child's instability is permanent or inalterable. It is necessary, if emotional or adjustment problems appear severe enough, to seek the aid of professionals such as school psychologists or social workers. It is important to remember that many children with serious emotional or adjustment problems learn to read and to read well.

Research Studies

When groups of poor readers are compared to good readers, the results usually show a somewhat larger percentage of pupils with signs of personality maladjustment among the poor readers. In most instances, the differences are not great (Bennett [9] and Ladd [128]). According to Sornson (182), children who become reading-disabled in the primary grades develop feelings of insecurity and show less satisfactory forms of personal and social adjustment than do their more successful peers. Studying children at the upper elementary level, Zimmerman and Allebrand (235) found that in contrast to good readers, poor readers willingly admitted feelings of discouragement, inadequacy, and nervousness. Gann (80) reported that the behavior of poor readers had more unfavorable signs than did normal readers. Stevens (193) found that fourth-grade students, identified as remedial readers, were less accepted than others in their classrooms, and that they had poor self-concepts. Using various measures of self-concept, Herbert (105) and Prendergast and Binder (156) report that ninth-grade students with low reading achievement also tend to have a poor self-concept.

In these group comparisons, poor readers felt less adequate than did good readers and also demonstrated more behavior problems. It should be remembered that many of the good readers also showed some signs of personality maladjustment; some reported that they felt inadequate, and some demonstrated adjustment difficulties.

There is some evidence that certain types of disabled readers exhibit more unfavorable traits than others. Karlsen (119) found that word-by-word readers rated low in attention, motivation, and social confidence, while context readers rated high on these characteristics.

Some studies have been concerned with the possible effect of adjustment difficulties on progress in reading. Feldhusen, Thurston, and Benning (74) identified a group of aggressive-disruptive children for comparison to a group of children who behaved more appropriately. When the school achievement of the two groups was compared five years later, the school grades of the maladjusted group were found to be significantly lower than those of the normally adjusted children. Wattenberg and Clifford (221) studied the relationship of self-concept of kindergarten children to beginning reading achievement. They found that the children's attitudes about themselves were more closely related to success in beginning reading than was intelligence. The researchers suggested that self-concept is causally related to reading achievement. Black (17) confirmed that children with reading difficulties tend to have a negative view of themselves. He also noted that older children with reading problems felt more negatively toward themselves than did younger children.

Reports of clinical studies such as those of Robinson (164), Gates (82), Bird (13), Blanchard (19), Witty and Kopel (231), and Martyn (140), indicate that the incidence of emotional problems among clinical cases of reading disability is high. The listed personality handicaps which interfere with learning include introversion or preoccupation with one's own thoughts, shyness, lack of self-confidence, fear of the reading task, antagonism toward reading, overdependence on approval, nervous tensions, obnoxious compensatory behavior, withdrawal from ordinary associations, truancy, and giving up easily. In only a few instances was there evidence of constructive compensatory behavior, such as intensive devotion to drawing or dramatics or some other activity.

Although case studies of children often find an intimate relation between a child's emotional problems and his reading difficulties, most research studies comparing the personality characteristics of retarded readers to those of good readers have failed to show any consistent group differences. Harris and Sipay (100) suggest that "this is probably due to the mistaken attempt to find a common personality type or problem in the reading disability cases" (p. 301).

Successful reading requires application and sustained concentration. Whatever emotional problems prevent a pupil from paying attention and concentrating also interfere with his learning to read. Harris and Sipay outline several types of emotional problems that may contribute to reading disability: conscious refusal to learn, overt hostility, negative conditioning to reading, displacement of hostility, resistance to pressure, clinging to dependency, quick discouragement, extreme distraction or restlessness, and absorption in a private world (daydreaming). Although in some cases, the underlying emotional difficulties may be similar, the symptoms or forms of expression may differ so widely that attempts to place them in useful categories would be futile. Blanchard (19) has shown that reading cases do not fall into neatly separated types. It also should be kept in mind that reading problems tend to have several causes rather than just one. The more inhibiting factors that are present, the greater is the possibility that a reading disability will occur.

Effects of Lack of Success

The inability to learn to read satisfactorily usually means severe frustration for the child. When his unsuccessful attempts to read make him conspicuous in a socially unfavorable way, the child is hurt and ashamed. His continued lack of success with attendant frustration and feelings of insecurity bring on emotional maladjustment (Sornson, 182). Some of these children easily become convinced that they are stupid. This feeling is frequently enhanced by the attitudes of their classmates, their parents, and even the teacher, if she fails to understand the real problem. The reading-disabled child comes to dislike reading and seeks opportunities to avoid it. Sometimes failure leads children to become timid, withdrawn, and they frequently daydream. In other cases, the children show their insecurity through nervous habits such as nail-biting, or through hysterically motivated illnesses such as headaches. Still others may compensate for their feelings of inferiority by developing various forms of antisocial behavior.

Most children who enter school with well-integrated personalities are eager to learn to read. Such children thrive on success and approval. For some of them, though, learning to read will mean only the failure and frustration of reading difficulties. When success is denied and approval withheld, as failure and frustration increase, an emotional reaction is a natural consequence. From this, personal and social maladjustment often follow. Reading disability has led to personal maladjustment.

Emotional Maladjustment as a Cause

Occasionally a child has become emotionally unstable before he even begins school. The basis of this maladjustment may be constitutional or environmental or may be due to a series of unfortunate incidents during the preschool years. Whatever the basis, some children exhibit impulsive responses, negative attitudes, irritability, attention difficulties, and lack of energy. These children are unable to achieve the cooperation and sustained effort required in learning to read. Until their emotional adjustment is improved, there will be little progress in learning to read. Psychiatric aid is indicated.

The personality patterns of backward readers in two special classes were explored by Frost (78). He found that forty percent of the children were rated as maladjusted and another forty percent were unsettled or likely to become maladjusted. The outstanding characteristic of these children was depression.

When we examine the conclusions of those who have investigated emotional maladjustment as a cause of reading difficulty, we find they differ greatly. In the many studies cited by Vernon (218), various and sometimes unclear results are reported. In particular, some investigations do not differentiate between moderate and severe reading disability. As Vernon puts it, "One difficulty in reaching any conclusive answer is that, as we have noted so frequently, mild cases of retardation which often show little sign of maladjustment have often not been differentiated from severe cases of real failure to learn to read. Even among the latter, however, it has not always been possible to detect any obvious signs of emotional maladjustment. . . . Undoubtedly many of these cases have not been investigated very thoroughly, and it is possible that more deeply seated types of disorder have passed unnoticed" (pp. 147-148).

Emotional Maladjustment: Cause and Effect

When reading disability is accompanied by emotional involvement, the question arises as to whether the personality maladjustment is primary or secondary. There is no consensus among writers and investigators on this point. Gann (80) is at one extreme: she believes that every personality tension unfavorable to learning to read occurred before entering school. She does not believe that personality maladjustment may be due to reading disability. Fernald (75) is at the other extreme: her analysis of the school histories of seventy-eight children with extreme reading disability treated in her clinic revealed only four who had given evidence of emotional instability before entering school. The other seventy-four were happy, well balanced, and eager to learn when they entered school. With them, the emotional upset occurred only when they were frustrated in their attempts to learn to read. As they did learn to read, their personality maladjustments diminished and then disappeared. Similarly, Wilkins (227) reviewed thirty studies and discovered only one case reported in which the reading disability was caused by previous emotional maladjustment.

Gates (83) is in an intermediate position, feeling that about seventy-five percent of the children with severe reading disability also will show personality maladjustment. He believes that, for about twenty-five percent of those reading cases showing personality maladjustment, the emotional difficulty was a contributing cause of the reading failure. That is, emotional difficulty contributed to reading failure in about twenty percent of the children with serious reading difficulties. Harris and Sipay (100) consider emotional difficulty to be a more frequent cause of reading failure as does Robinson (164). Robinson also considers emotional difficulty to be both a cause of reading disability and an effect of the failure to learn to read.

It is not surprising that emotional maladjustment associated with reading disability can be both cause and effect. Examination of reported evidence and the views of writers and clinical workers suggests that in only a few cases does a previous personality maladjustment prevent a child from learning to read. In a larger number of cases, emotional difficulties appear to be due to failure in reading. There are no data available which can assign exact percentages to the proportion of instances in which emotional difficulties are causes rather than effects. Examination of all the evidence does make it fairly clear that emotional maladjustment is much more frequently the effect than the cause of reading disability. This view is supported by the fact that in most instances, emotional difficulties clear up when reading disability is alleviated by remedial instruction.

When emotional and personality maladjustment involves both cause and effect of reading disability, as noted above, the interaction tends to become circular. In many cases, it is probable that there is a reciprocal relationship. Lack of success during early attempts to learn to read causes tension, stress, and frustration usually accompanied by feelings if inadequacy and often by negative behavior. Resulting personal and social adjustment difficulties then handicap further progress in learning to read. Thus a vicious circle is formed. The reading disability and the emotional and behavioral reactions to the reading disability interact, each making the other more intense. Robinson (164), Bennett (9), and Monroe (141), among others, concur in this view. For an in-depth view of self-concept and reading, with practical suggestions on how to build positive self-concepts among all readers, see Quant (159). Suggestions on how to help poor readers attend to and complete reading tasks are given in chapter 12.

ENVIRONMENTAL CAUSES

Achievement in reading depends on the child's personal strengths and the demands of the reading program. Children with a background of family tension may approach reading as unhappy and insecure learners. Children from a culture different from that of the teacher and different from that portrayed in the materials they read may experience unusual difficulty in learning. Children who feel comfortable listening to and speaking a language or dialect different from the teacher's and different from that in their books may find learning to read unusually demanding.

Some of the children who are from unstable homes, or who must make cultural or language adjustments, do learn to read. Many teachers are sensitive to the students' needs and adapt instruction accordingly. Many students can adjust to the school's demands, even though they must try harder than the typical child.

Home Environment

Some children come from a home environment which provides love, understanding, an opportunity to develop individuality, and a feeling of security. Others do not. Quarreling parents, broken homes, child neglect, child abuse, overprotection, parental domination, anxiety, or hostility, or destructive rivalry among siblings are likely to produce nervous tension and feelings of insecurity. There is more evidence of family conflict in the homes of poor readers than in those of children with no reading difficulties, according to Seigler and Gynther (172). Disturbed parent-child relations, marked sibling jealousy, and unfavorable attitudes toward school were characteristic of the poor readers studied by Crane (45). Thayer (204) counseled disabled readers and their parents, and then compared the reading progress of these pupils to that of those who had had no counseling. The former had made large gains while the latter had made none. These results suggest that improvement of home conditions facilitates improvement in reading. Gates (85) discussed the possibility of personality maladjustment occurring when a child becomes the center of a parental conflict. A child's unsuccessful attempts to maintain loyalty to both parents may produce emotional reactions with feelings of insecurity unfavorable to learning. The conflict due to divided loyalty in a broken home may produce a similar effect.

Neglect or lack of sympathetic understanding may cause a child to feel that he is not loved or not wanted. Apparent indifference on the part of a parent or overconcern for a child's difficulties in learning may cause anxiety, lack of confidence, and perhaps attention-seeking behavior.

Overprotection or domination of a child by his parents can lead to adjustment difficulties. Too much parental control can prevent a child from developing initiative and cause him to become so dependent on others that he is unable to learn independently. If a parent attempts to dominate all a child's activities, including learning to read, the child may rebel against such domination and against reading as well. A parent's solicitude for every phase of a child's reading activities may produce anxiety to the point at which the child may reject reading entirely.

When a child's reading achievement is compared unfavorably to that of a brother or sister, it may have a bad effect. A child who cannot compete successfully may attempt to escape from competition and may refuse to continue to learn to read.

Any conflict between parent and teacher over a child's reading is likely to have negative consequences. For instance, if a child who is failing to progress satisfactorily in reading makes a disparaging remark about his teacher, and a parent agrees with the child and also makes negative remarks about the teacher, the child will have an excuse for failing to learn. The child's attitude toward his teacher even may interfere with future reading progress.

A child under unusual stress from conditions at home may become an anxious, insecure learner or give up much too easily when reading becomes demanding. Some children react to home stress by disrupting the classroom. In certain other instances, the result is quite different. Some children find reading alleviates personal anxiety and insecurity, and use it and school success as an escape from environmental pressures. But usually home tension and pressures hinder rather than help reading progress.

Austin, Bush, and Huebner (2) point out that, although certain home factors have been shown to be partly responsible for a child's reading difficulties, these can almost never be cited as the single causal factor.

Attitudes

It is important that the child develop a good attitude toward school, his teachers, his classmates, and toward reading. While favorable attitudes foster progress in learning to read, unfavorable attitudes may result in reading disability. Personal and social adjustment, home conditions, peer relationships, teacher-pupil relations, and the instructional program all influence attitudes toward reading.

Although most children begin school eager to learn to read, some do not. Occasionally there will be a beginner who, for one reason or another, is antagonistic toward learning in general or toward reading in particular. It requires tact, patience, and sympathetic understanding and guidance from the teacher if these children are to form positive attitudes toward reading.

In most instances, unfavorable attitudes toward reading comes after, rather than before, the child is exposed to reading instruction. A consensus of investigators, including Ladd (128) and Sandin (170), report that successful achievers form positive attitudes toward reading and school, while slow-progress pupils and reading-disabled children have negative attitudes. Sound reading instruction emphasizing each child's successes does much to ensure that he will maintain and acquire positive attitudes toward reading and other school activities—in short, that he will like school.

Implications of Evidence

Reading disability generally is accompanied by emotional involvement which adversely influences the personal and social adjustment of the child. This personality maladjustment may be due to constitutional factors, to one or more of a variety of pressures in the child's environment, or to failure in reading. The degree to which reading disability is a cause or an effect of personality or emotional maladjustment often is not clear. Examination of the available data suggests the following:

1. A relatively small proportion of children are emotionally upset and maladjusted when they enter school. Many of them will find learning to read difficult.

2. A relatively large proportion of children who experience reading disability began school well-adjusted and reasonably secure. The frustration of failing to learn to read causes some sort of emotional reaction. Here, reading disability has caused the emotional reaction.

3. Emotional maladjustment often may be both an effect and a cause of reading disability. The emotional reaction to reading failure then may become a handicap to further learning. A vicious circle is formed; there is a reciprocal relationship between the emotional conditioning and the reading disability.

4. If the personal and social maladjustment is due to reading disability, it usually disappears when the child becomes a successful reader.

5. A few children need to be referred to a specialist for psychological assistance. These include two types of poor readers. First, there are those who are so emotionally upset that they do not respond to the best efforts of the remedial teacher. Second, with a very few children, the emotional maladjustment associated with past reading failure is so ingrained that it remains even after they learn to read well. They need special help to overcome their unrealistic anxiety and insecurity toward school achievement.

6. Adverse attitudes toward reading, the teacher, classmates, and school itself are due frequently to failure in reading. The best remedial techniques are directed not only toward helping students learn to read better, but also toward helping them develop more positive attitudes.

Cultural and Language Differences

There is little doubt that the child who approaches reading from a cultural or language background different from that of his teacher and different from that of the material he is expected to read is at a disadvantage.

When cultural and language differences also are accompanied by poverty, poor food, poor sanitation, poor housing, and poor medical care, the disadvantage is compounded. (Birch and Gussow [11]). When home conditions prompt the teacher to expect little from the student, the pathway to failure has been prepared (Rist [162].) Although, as Cohen and Cooper (40) argue, it is not the role of education to eradicate all social ills, a major contribution can be made by teaching poor children adequate reading skills. The best way to do this, according to Cohen (39), is to provide intensive, quality instruction, based not on race or social condition, but on the learning needs of each child.

There are many kinds and types of cultural differences. They can affect the teachers' perceptions of their students, and the childrens' perceptions of their teachers, their behavior in school, and the nature and importance of reading. For example, there are cultural differences in how a child should behave when an adult is speaking, the desirability or undesirability of answering when unsure, the amount of competition or cooperation he displays to his peers, the amount of physical aggression he should use, and the amount of control he asserts over his own destiny. A child may be misunderstood by a teacher with a cultural heritage different from the child's, unless the teacher is aware of the differences and of the implications of such cultural differences.

If reading materials deal with events, activities, ideas, and ideals quite different from those in the child's own experiences, reading itself may seem to be for someone else, and may be rejected or considered unimportant for that reason. If a child's books negatively portray people from his culture, he may reject reading, or may learn to read, but develop adverse feelings about himself or his family. Spache (183) provides a list of realistic, yet positive books from which appropriate selections could be made for children from various minority groups. But, as Vick (220) points out, there are many excellent materials available which have content suitable for all children.

Language differences pose an additional problem in instruction. Some children speak a dialect variation of the standard English used in the classroom. Other children speak a foreign language, such as Spanish. These language differences increase the difficulty of learning and of teaching reading.

Simons (176), commenting on the mismatch between dialect and standard English, states that this causes reading interference. He criticizes both the unsystematic attempts to teach standard English along with reading and also readers in which the stories are written in dialect. He feels that teaching standard English as a part of the reading lesson interferes with learning to read. Dialect readers are unpopular, because not all children who speak a dialect speak the same one. Simons and others, including

Venezky and Chapman (217) and Rystrom (169), believe that the teacher's knowledge of dialect differences and her attitude toward children who do not speak standard English are more important than dialect or materials.

Although dialect differences interfere with learning to read standard English, language differences create even more serious problems. There is a great need for bilingual teachers who understand the positive qualities and are sensitive to the real needs of the non-English–speaking child. In an extensive review of the literature, Engle (69) was unable to determine whether minority children in a bilingual culture should be taught to read in their native language or the dominant language. She pointed out that any method which undermines a child's pride in his native language or culture, or places a child in a situation in which he cannot understand the teacher's instruction, will be unsuccessful. Thonis (207) is a valuable resource for those teaching Spanish-speaking children.

In summary, most authors agree that teachers of children with cultural or language differences must understand these differences in order to be effective in teaching reading. A good attitude also is necessary, as is the ability to communicate to each child a sense of his dignity and worth.

The educational problems in improving the reading growth of children with cultural and language differences belong to the developmental reading program rather than to the remedial program. The educational program of these children should be adjusted to meet their individual needs.

Children from homes in which a language other than English is spoken may know little or no English. They may be unable to understand or to speak English well enough to participate in ordinary classroom activities. These children may appear to be of low mental ability, because it is difficult to obtain a fair estimate of a child's intelligence when he can neither understand nor speak English, no matter which type of test is used.

The reading difficulties of children who are learning English as a second language tend to be due to their inability to understand or speak English. The procedures ordinarily used in teaching beginning reading in our schools assume that each child already has learned to understand and speak the language. Language-handicapped children first need a program to improve their English. A preparatory instructional period ordinarily should have three simultaneous activities: first, building up a basic vocabulary for understanding and speaking; second, improvement of facility in oral communication; and third, providing a background of meaningful experiences. Words and concepts associated with experiences must be in English. Thus the child learns to speak and understand a vocabulary before he encounters it in reading. It is probable that much of the training in the understanding and use of spoken English should be carried out in sessions not concerned with reading. In general, lessons in reading should not be complicated by simultaneous training in pronunciation. All this does not mean that no reading is done while the child is being taught English. Although the two can be done concurrently, they should be in separate class periods.

These children do not become reading disability cases if an appropriate teaching program is organized early in their school lives. Nevertheless, the development of an adequate background in English will be gradual. Until this is achieved, these children will be at a disadvantage in all school activities. The program may need to be continued throughout the elementary school years.

Children from culturally different environments and speaking a dialect other than standard English have a somewhat different problem. Preschool-level programming is especially beneficial to culturally different children. As Lloyd (133) points out, language patterns are established firmly by the time a child is six years old. Therefore, it is desirable to encourage early language development and build essential concepts in young preschool children. Such development of language and of necessary concepts is especially important for the culturally different child. This is part of the role of the various programs for preschool children such as Operation Head Start. When James B. Conant said that the more disadvantaged a neighborhood is, the more important it is to have kindergarten and prekindergarten schools, he was referring to those needs now fulfilled partly by Operation Head Start.

These preschool programs are important in helping disadvantaged children prepare for reading and other learning. Special teaching also is needed to help the disadvantaged child progress through the elementary grades.

A continued emphasis upon real experiences, field trips, audio-visual presentations, story telling, puppetry, and role playing should be maintained throughout the school years. The language used in these experiences is beneficial to disadvantaged children and is an important part of beginning reading instruction. In this approach, immediately tied to a real experience, the children tell a story which the teacher writes down verbatim. The children then review the story and work on certain activities associated with the story, such as reading sentences, matching words, or drawing pictures to illustrate the story. For a child with experiential differences, language differences, or dialect differences, this approach is useful in that it deals with experiences he has had, and uses words and language structures with which he is familiar and comfortable.

Some of the children with dialect differences or those for whom English is a second language will have reading difficulties that can be corrected by specific remedial training. They should receive immediate help. These children should be treated like others disabled in reading; their reading patterns should be diagnosed, their basic reading problems isolated, and individual remedial plans formulated.

The fact that a given child, for example, has a dialect difference itself should be taken into account in the remedial plan, and the techniques used should include the language experience approach. Silent reading exercises always should use interesting meaningful material. Any oral reading errors related to the child's dialect should be ignored.

It should be remembered that children with dialect differences understand radio and television well. Although when they discuss what they have heard or seen, they tend to use their own dialect, rather than the standard English used in the radio or television programs. This should not be criticized or belittled.

We suggest that these children do much independent reading of material written in standard English. The material should be very easy for each child to read, and the child should be allowed to discuss it as he likes. We also suggest that the child, for example, might select parts of a story most liked, most exciting, most humerous, or well written. He then might choose a part of the story to read aloud to others. He should read this material as it is written. It might be even more helpful if he pretended to be a television personality and read as he would on a real television program.

EDUCATIONAL CAUSES

Among all the factors that are considered possible causes of reading disability, the group of conditions classed as educational stand out as tremendously important. Careful consideration of various learner characteristics which predispose children to experience difficulty in learning to read does not diminish the importance of the educational program as the major cause of reading difficulty. Rather, it shows how necessary it is for each child's instruction in reading to meet his individual learning needs. In the vast majority of reading disability cases, careful diagnosis reveals that there is faulty learning or a lack of educational adjustment in the student's instructional program.

Reading, as discussed earlier, is a complex process made up of many interrelated skills and abilities. As a child progresses through the reading program there is constant danger that he may fail to acquire these essential learnings or that he may get into difficulty because he may over- or underemphasize any one of them. Under the broad category of educational causes, several educational practices must be considered. Although this book discusses them separately, it should not be supposed that they operate in isolation, but rather are related and interacting.

School Administrative Policies

Success in teaching children to read depends on the teacher. Thus we must examine the role that certain administrative policies play in determining how effectively a teacher can organize and carry out her reading program. Some of the policies which hinder even the best of teachers will be considered briefly.

READING VERSUS PUPIL DEVELOPMENT. Whether reading or child development should be the chief concern of the school during the early grades is controversial (Dolch, 59). Some educators believe that the emphasis should be almost entirely on developing reading skills. Others object to this and feel that the school's chief concern should be the happy, balanced development of each child's personality. Many teachers are not only aware of the issue between these two but also may be under pressure to stress one approach at the expense of the other. The argument of those opposing effective reading in the primary grades is that putting pressure on the children to read sometimes produces personality maladjustments. They claim that emphasis upon reading destroys interest in learning since, as they claim, reading is an activity foreign to the real interests of children in these grades. Actually, there need be no serious conflict between well-balanced child development and all-around development which includes reading, if the reading is taught properly. With individualized instruction, including reading readiness, development of reading can become an integral part of the program to develop a balanced personality. This program means that only those who are ready begin to read early in grade one. Other children start later, when they are capable of succeeding. When frustrations arise, it is likely to be because of the method of instruction. Reading instruction will suffer when administrative pressure overemphasizes or underemphasizes reading in the primary grades.

PROMOTION POLICY AND CURRICULUM RIGIDITY. In 1938, Cole (42) stated that the reason for the prevalence of remedial reading classes was the failure of schools to adjust the curriculum to the current promotion policy. To some degree, this indictment is still valid. She was referring to promoting children mainly by age rather than by achievement with no accompanying change in curriculum requirements. This produces a wider and wider range in reading ability in successively higher grades. At the same time, the curriculum requirements have remained fairly rigid. When pupils are promoted by age, not achievement, and there are no instructional adjustments made, then much of the material assigned to pupils in the higher grades will be too advanced for the poorer readers' level of reading competence. The poorer readers also will not receive needed instruction in certain reading skills, because these skills are not usually emphasized in the higher grades. For some pupils, the result is reading disability. Yet it is not the yearly promotions per se which have caused the reading difficulty, but rather the failure to adjust instruction to the individual needs of certain students. If alternative materials are assigned and if essential skills are taught, then reading disability need not result from promotion by age.

Lack of Readiness for Beginning Reading Instruction

Success in beginning reading largely depends on the child's overall level of maturity. The pattern of growth entails many types of abilities, acquired behaviors, and specific knowledges. Although some aspects of reading readiness come with inner maturation, many of the most important ingredients are learned and therefore can be taught. This means that when a child approaches beginning reading lacking certain essential skills and knowledges, these can and should be taught before or during beginning reading instruction. Research by Spache and others (189) has demonstrated the effectiveness of appropriate training in visual and auditory perceptual skills for children who needed such skill development to succeed in beginning reading. The evidence suggests that the training was effective in developing visual and auditory perceptual skills before beginning reading instruction, and that in addition, such prereading skill development facilitated initial reading success. Other beginning reading achievements, such as knowledge of word meanings, attention to oral directions, ability to work independently and to work cooperatively in groups, and even the desire to read, can be taught.

Many first-grade children are not ready to learn to read in the typical program and therefore instructional modifications must be made if they are to experience initial success in learning to read. Reading disability frequently is caused by starting a child in a standard reading program before he is ready. Because of his lack of experience, verbal facility, visual or auditory perceptual development, overall immaturity, or a combination of these, he is unable to achieve what is expected of him daily and therefore he does not succeed.* Instead of learning to read, the most he can do is acquire only bits of, reading skills which he is unable to use. Thus he falls farther and farther behind. The outcome will not be reading well, but frustration and failure perhaps leading to feelings of inadequacy, inferiority, insecurity, and even rebellion. Such a child even may come to hate reading and all persons and activities connected with it.

The many failures in reading during the primary grades are due in part

* See Appendix IV for representative reading readiness tests (also see Buros [34] for a critical evaluation of these tests).

to the lack of instructional adaptation to differences in readiness for beginning reading instruction. Any educational program or administrative policy which provides exactly the same formal reading instruction for all pupils at the beginning of grade one causes reading failure for many pupils.

Lack of Adjustment to Individual Differences

Beginning in grade one and in every grade thereafter, reading instruction can be effective for all pupils only when there is satisfactory adjustment to individual differences. Without such adjustment, reading difficulties arise. This topic has been considered in detail in an earlier chapter.

Methods of Teaching

Most reading cases are caused by the child's failure to acquire necessary learnings, or by faulty learnings, as he goes through the reading program. The complexity of the reading process offers many opportunities for the child to get into difficulties. Sometimes coupled with this is *ineffective teaching*. For one reason or another, there may be a lack of educational adjustment to the needs of certain pupils, so that they do not acquire essential learnings.

A number of factors may lead to ineffective teaching. Curriculum requirements may take so much of the teacher's time that she is unable to individualize the program satisfactorily. At the same time, the methods or materials used may be too difficult for certain youngsters. Under these conditions, it is probable that certain pupils are pushed through the program too rapidly to learn what the program is designed to teach.

Using materials and methods that seem dull and unimportant *to the pupil* is another part of ineffective teaching. In beginning reading, for instance, it is important that the child develop the attitude of insisting on understanding what is read. To do this, the reading material either should tell him a story (have a plot) or should give him some information. This cannot be done by excessive use of badly constructed and insipid experience charts, nor by reading dull and anemic materials made up of almost meaningless sentences, or isolated drill on word parts. One youngster, on being exposed to such material, said to his teacher, "That sounds silly." It is not surprising that some children react strongly to such reading, and acquire unfortunate attitudes which become obstacles to learning to read.

Similarly, procedures which do not tie class activities to the reading program may lead to reading disability. When reading is taught separately, as something of little consequence, it is no wonder that the child sees no reason for learning to read. In contrast, if there is a relationship between reading and class activities, so that reading itself is a tool for those activities, the child becomes motivated to learn to read. It is desirable that reading activities affect some of the important things the child is doing in the class, and that many of the class activities grow out of the reading program. Then the child can see a reason for reading, and interest and motivation are maintained at a high level.

It should be emphasized here that interest is not synonymous with entertainment. Real interest backed by strong motivation is not found by flitting from one amusing incident or story to another. Much better is a program in which reading is tied carefully to activities in the classroom.

This program would imply coordination among the language arts, speaking, writing, listening, spelling, and reading. Difficulties arise, for instance, when a youngster is expected to spell a word and use it in his writing when he has not learned to recognize it in his reading.

Excessive emphasis on isolated drill kills interest. As we shall see later, some drill is desirable and necessary. Sometimes, however, drills are so far from the act of reading that the child cannot bridge the gap. Not only is he unable to transfer what is learned in the drill to actual reading, but he also cannot see the reason for the drill. Methods concentrating on isolated drill with phonics elements, or excessive devotion to reading and recitation of isolated facts rather than sharing stories and experiences, lead to loss of interest and inhibit the desire to learn to read.

Inappropriate emphasis on the basic reading skills may prevent effective reading. The basic skills include a sight vocabulary, word-recognition techniques, word meanings, reading by thought units or phrasing, comprehension, and study skills. Either underemphasis or overemphasis may lead to difficulties. Probably more children have difficulties due to underemphasis than to overemphasis. The basic skills underlie efficiency in reading. Stories and other reading matter in books are simply materials enabling the teacher to teach the child how to read. To do this, the skills and abilities should be properly stressed and systematically ordered.

Many youngsters are in trouble because progressive tendencies in teaching are not well thought out. It should not be forgotten that progressive tendencies which ignore systematic, orderly development of the essential skills and abilities are not beneficial to the pupils. It is difficult to imagine proper emphasis on these skills and abilities without an orderly, sequential, basic reading program. It is impossible to keep the sequence in mind and have reading a by-product of something other than an important reading program. Some of the cases referred to the Minnesota Reading Clinic appear to result from teaching reading as a by-product of social studies and other subjects. McKee (136) concurs in this view. He points out that the perfunctory, unorganized, and meaningless teaching of the content subjects as carried out in many schools is partially responsible for the retardation in reading ability found among pupils. Teaching of the content subjects can contribute to effective reading if training in the basic skills and abilities is an integral part of that instructional program. The introduction to reading content materials should be made in a well-organized basic program which shows the child how to read by teaching him the essential skills and abilities.

When the emphasis upon mechanics of reading leads to neglect of meanings, the child is in difficulty. Undue stress on word recognition, perfection of enunciation, and speed may lead to verbalism, the pronunciation of words without understanding their meanings. A girl in one of our remedial reading groups could read aloud fourth-grade materials without error, but she could comprehend practically nothing of what she "read." To pronounce words without understanding their meaning is not reading. It is merely word-calling. This girl was a reading disability case.

Overemphasis on phonic analysis as a word-recognition technique frequently causes disability. The child is so intent upon sounding out most of the words he encounters that he cannot attend to meanings. Or he laboriously separates a new word into its component sounds and then is unable to blend the separate sounds into a recognizable pronunciation of the word. Such cases usually have an insufficient sight vocabulary and are unable to make adequate use of context clues for word recognition.

To progress satisfactorily in learning to read there must be a proper balance among many skills and abilities. A sight vocabulary, various techniques for word recognition, concepts and word meanings, reading in thought units, comprehension and study skills, and many other abilities must not be taught separately. They are all part of an integrated sequential program. There is a balanced relationship between them that must be striven for. The pupil who gets into difficulty is quite frequently the child for whom a balance among them has not been maintained.

We grant that it is difficult to imagine a teacher who is able to handle a class of twenty to thirty children and at the same time keep account of all the essential balances while carrying out her sequential program in a systematic and orderly fashion. But the teacher should never forget the importance of the balanced program and do what is possible to achieve it. The smaller the class, the greater is the possibility of maintaining the balance.

Role of the Teacher

The role of the teacher herself is important. She can have a positive or negative influence upon progress in learning to read. Pupils are fortunate indeed if their teacher is so able, well trained, and sympathetic that she maintains good pupil-teacher telationships and is able to achieve a proper balance in developing skills and abilities in the reading program. When teachers deviate from this, reading instruction is apt to suffer. The teacher who is inept because of either poor training, lack of experience, or a slavish devotion to inflexible routine, will be unable to adjust reading instruction to the varied needs of her pupils.

Gates (83) and Witty and Kopel (231) have stressed the effects of unsatisfactory teacher-pupil relationships. A teacher's personality, especially when she has a negative attitude toward a particular pupil, may cause or intensify the emotional stress associated with his failure in reading. Apparent indifference, hostility, or any obvious anxiety in the teacher when a pupil has difficulty in reading, intensifies the child's emotional reactions and feelings of insecurity. We have to face it—in many cases, the teacher is not without blame when a child becomes a reading disability case.

Role of the Library or Media Center

The school library or media center also plays an important part in the total reading program. While the teacher develops the child's reading skills by means of the formal program of instruction in the classroom, it is through the school library or media center that the child's interests in reading are pursued and expanded. The librarian can provide teachers with materials for developmental reading programs as well as for individual and remedial programs. Within the library or media center, there can be attractive book displays, book talks, and story-telling hours to make reading exciting to the pupils. The library's varied book collections offer students opportunities for reference reading, research, and additional reading at each grade level.

Secondary schools lead in library services for their pupils; many elementary schools have been much less fortunate in their library facilities. In fact, some elementary schools have no books at all other than textbooks. Other schools have small classroom collections, while still others fortunately, have a library room or media center with a trained librarian or media expert.

The value of a library or media center to the elementary pupil's advancement in reading cannot be overemphasized. Gaver (89) evaluated six school libraries and their services, as well as quantity and quality of reading done by the pupils. She found that higher educational gains were made when there was a school library, and students read more and better books when there was a library.

SUMMARY

The possible causes of reading disability are numerous. A single factor seldom causes reading disability. In all but the mildest cases, the difficulty is due to a composite of related conditions. The contributing factors interact in a pattern. The view taken in this book, therefore, is that reading disability is due to multiple causation.

Although the evidence concerning the relation between specific eye defects and reading disability is ambiguous, there are certain relevant trends. (*a*) Eye defects appear frequently among both good and poor readers and can be a handicap to either group. Comfortable and efficient vision should be provided for all children whenever possible. (*b*) There is evidence that farsightedness, binocular incoordination, fusion difficulties, and aniseikonia may contribute to reading disability. When there is a visual defect, there are usually other associated contributing causes. (*c*) Visual examinations are essential to diagnosing reading disabilities.

Hearing impairment can be a handicap in learning to read. This is particularly true when the hearing loss is severe enough to intefere with normal auditory discrimination. There is evidence that hearing impairment may be associated with reading disability as a contributing cause when (*a*) the hearing loss is severe, (*b*) the child has high tone deafness, and (*c*) pupils with hearing loss are taught reading by predominantly auditory methods. All pupils who become reading cases should have a hearing test.

Although motor incoordination is sometimes associated with reading disability, a causal relationship has not been established. Both the motor incoordination and reading disability may be due to a condition such as minor birth injuries. Defects in articulation which complicate word discrimination and recognition may contribute to reading disability. Any severe emotional involvement created by speech defects tends to inhibit progress in learning to read. In certain cases, glandular dysfunction, particularly hypothyroidism, may contribute to reading disability .

Various conditions associated with poor health can be detrimental to normal progress in reading. Brain damage is seldom a cause of reading disability, but when present, a very difficult instructional problem exists.

Reading disability usually is accompanied by emotional involvement adversely affecting the child's personal and social adjustment. This personality maladjustment may be due to constitutional factors, to pressures in the child's environment, or to failure in reading. In a relatively small number of cases, the child is emotionally upset when he arrives at school. Such a child is apt to have difficulty in reading. For many, the frustration arises from failure to learn to read. In these cases, the reading difficulty causes the emotional upset. It seems that emotional maladjustment may be both effect and cause. When emotional disturbance arises from reading disability, it then may become a handicap to further learning. There is, in such cases, a reciprocal relationship between emotional conditioning and the reading disability. When personality maladjustment is due to reading failure, it tends to disappear when the child learns to read satisfactorily. When the emotional maladjustment is deep-seated, psychiatric help will be needed.

Lower than normal intelligence need not be a cause of reading disability. But when instructional procedures are not adjusted to a child's slow learning ability, an accumulation of partial learnings will make it impossible for him to profit from regular classroom instruction.

Frequently, reading disability is due largely to educational factors. Any administrative policy which prevents sufficient individualization of instruction, including emphasis upon reading readiness, will prevent effective progress in reading. Failure to acquire the necessary learnings or the acquisition of faulty learnings is most frequently due to ineffective teaching. One or more of the following factors may be involved in the ineffective teaching which brings about reading disability; too rapid progress in the instructional schedule, isolation of reading instruction from other school activities, inappropriate emphasis on some technique or skill, or treating reading as a by-product of content studies. Frequently, the difficulty occurs because the instructional program has failed to maintain a balance in the growth of the large number of skills and abilities involved in learning to read.

For children who are learning English as a second language, ordinary reading instruction usually will not be productive until they have been taught to understand English quite well. However, as soon as the teacher considers it feasible, they can be taught reading concurrently while improving their English.

Disadvantaged children benefit greatly from preschool programming. Good health, sound nutrition, a positive self-concept, and language development all are helpful. In the preschool and the school years, opportunities to participate in real experiences and to utilize audio-visual presentations are especially beneficial to many disadvantaged children. The language experience approach can be an important part of beginning reading instruction for many children with experiential, language, or dialect differences.

If one conclusion were to be made, it is that there is no one cause for all disability cases. Each case is unique. Only when there is a valid diagnosis, will there be a sound basis for planning an individual remedial program to alleviate the disability.

SELECTED READINGS

HARRIS, A. J., and E. R. SIPAY, *How to Increase Reading Ability* (6th ed.), Chaps. 10, 11, 12. New York: David McKay, 1975.

JOHNSON, D. J., and H. R. MYKLEBUST, *Learning Disabilities: Educational Principles and Practices,* Chap. 5. New York: Grune and Stratton, 1967.

QUANT, I. J., *Teaching Reading: A Human Process,* Chap. 15. Chicago: Rand McNally, 1977.

STRANG, R., *Diagnostic Teaching of Reading* (2nd ed.), Chap. 9. New York: McGraw-Hill, 1969.

SPACHE, G. D., *Investigating the Issues of Reading Disabilities,* Chaps. 1–9. Boston: Allyn and Bacon, 1976.

ROSWELL, F., and G. NATCHEZ, *Reading Disability: Diagnosis and Treatment* (2nd ed.), Chap. 1. New York: Basic Books, 1971.

VERNON, M. D., *Reading and its Difficulties,* Chap 1. Cambridge, England: Cambridge University Press, 1971.

WILSON, R. M., *Diagnostic and Remedial Reading,* Chap 3. Columbus, Ohio: Charles E. Merrill, 1977.

Basic Considerations in Diagnosing Reading Difficulties

six

Remedial work not based on a thorough diagnosis is likely to waste time and effort for both the student and the remedial teacher. Moreover, remedial work done without adequate diagnosis is likely to fail. A student who has had difficulty with reading already may be insecure. Continued failure in the remedial program would be unfortunate. The person responsible for the remedial program should be aware of the possible results of failure, and should make every effort to ensure that each child will be successful and recognize that success.

GENERAL PRINCIPLES OF DIAGNOSIS

An adequate diagnosis determines in no small measure the success of the remedial program. Since reading is a complex process, there is no one single or simple cure for reading disability. Remedial training that is effective in one case might be detrimental or wasteful in another. It is only through understanding the underlying factors of disability of any given case that an adequate remedial program can be formulated. For example, two students have difficulty with reading. The appraisals show that both are low in reading comprehension. Further analysis of the difficulty indicates that one student is low in comprehension because of inadequate recognition vocabulary. The other student is low because he is a word-by-word reader who is so conscious of words that he is unable to group them into thought units. The first student needs remedial work to build up his awareness of words and ability to inspect them in detail. Obviously, this procedure would be detrimental to the second student's need for overcoming his overemphasis on isolated words.

The problem of helping the disabled reader is complicated further by the many characteristics of the child and his learning environment that affect his reading growth. It is necessary to adjust to some of the variations within the physical, emotional, educational, intellectual, and environmental factors if reading growth is to progress smoothly or at all. Sometimes these same factors need to be corrected before remedial programs can be effective.

It is little wonder, then, that the classroom teacher, attempting to correct disabilities in this intricate learning for a wide variety of children in trouble, finds that no two cases have the same instructional needs. Any attempt to give a child remedial instruction must be based on a thorough diagnosis of his unique reading needs and personal characteristics. This diagnosis is the very core of successful correction programs, whether they are for the less complex problems met in the classroom or for the more complicated problems of the clinic.

The classroom teacher may need special help in diagnosing or correcting some of the more complex disabled readers, or when limitations in reading are so subtle that a diagnosis, more detailed and more penetrating than the teacher has time or training to give, is required. Frequently it is necessary to study the reading pattern of a disabled reader by means of individual appraisals that take several hours to administer. It is expedient to have the more detailed diagnoses conducted by someone who can work individually with the children over a long period of time. At times, the diagnosis requires special equipment available only in a reading clinic. In many cases of disability in reading, it is necessary to obtain evaluations and corrective help from other specialists, such as social workers, psychologists, physicians, or psychiatrists.

Of course, the teacher should diagnose and correct as many of the reading difficulties as she can. The early detection and correction of these problems will prevent many from becoming more complex reading cases. There are many diagnostic procedures that the classroom teacher can use in studying the moderately disabled reader. In the more subtle cases, an outside diagnosis may be needed to help the teacher formulate the kinds of remedial treatment she can provide in the classroom. In some instances, both the detailed diagnosis and the therapeutic treatment should be given in special reading centers or clinics. But in every reading disability case, whether simple or complex, a diagnosis is necessary.

A DIAGNOSIS IS ALWAYS DIRECTED TOWARD FORMULATING METHODS OF IMPROVEMENT. In studying a disabled reader, whether in the classroom or clinic, the diagnosis should collect information necessary for planning a corrective program. There are two types of diagnosis—etiological and therapeutic. Etiological diagnosis finds out what originally caused a child to get into difficulty. This often is impossible and frequently useless for formulating a remedial program. It is of little use, for example, to search the records and find that a child is in difficulty in reading in the fourth grade because he was absent from school with the measles when he was in the first grade. Nothing can be done now to give him the help that should have been available when he returned to school after a month's absence during the first grade. This information, collected and summarized for research purposes, would be useful to prevent reading difficulties, but it is not useful for the immediate job of correcting a reading disability that began several years earlier.

Therapeutic diagnosis is concerned with the conditions now present in the child in order to plan a program of reeducation. The therapeutic diagnostician searches for the reading strengths and limitations of a child and for any characteristics within this child's present environment or makeup that need to be corrected before remedial instruction can be successful, or for conditions that need to be adjusted to before he can be expected to make progress. The diagnostician would be more concerned about a current hearing loss, for example, than he would be about finding out that the child was in difficulty because he had had a temporary hearing loss several years ago.

DIAGNOSIS IS MORE THAN APPRAISAL OF READING SKILLS AND ABILITIES. The complex nature of reading disability and the many factors related to achievement in reading make it necessary to explore the child's many traits and reading skills and abilities for an adequate diagnosis. Besides discovering the deficiencies in reading that are at the root of the disability, it is frequently necessary for the diagnostician to appraise the physical, sensory, emotional, and environmental factors that could impede progress. In some cases, the diagnosis will require other expert help. The diagnostician should be alert to the possible effect of conditions within the child or his environment that require specialized help such as the services of a social case worker, psychologist, physician, otologist, ophthalmologist, psychiatrist, or neurologist. All appraisals made in more complex cases should be extensive enough to pinpoint the existence of such limitations. The measurements used in a reading diagnosis will be discussed in the following chapters. It is enough to say here that the diagnosis should supply all the information pertinent to correct the disability.

THE DIAGNOSIS MUST BE EFFICIENT. The diagnosis of some disabled readers is often lengthy and intricate. In other cases, the child's instructional needs can be isolated relatively easily and quickly. A diagnosis should proceed as far, and only as far as is necessary to formulate a remedial program for each specific case. The diagnosis should proceed from group measurements to the more detailed individual measurements needed for the case under study. The diagnosis should be reached by measuring first the relatively common types of problems and then the more unusual ones.

It would be expected, for example, that one would give routinely to all suspected reading disability cases measurements of general reading capability and of general mental ability. It would be only in an unusual case that a complete neurological examination would be required. The procedures in diagnosis are much like successive screenings in which only the more complex and subtle cases are retained for further measurement and study. There are, then, various levels of diagnosis: (*a*) appraisals which are made routinely for all children in the schools or for all children referred for special study, (*b*) appraisals more detailed in character and made only in those instances when more analytical study is warranted, and (*c*) appraisals which are individual in nature made only in more subtle cases.

In reading diagnosis, as in all educational diagnosis, there are three levels of study. The level reached in any one case depends on the characteristics of that particular case. The three levels through which some cases must be carried are: general diagnosis, analytical diagnosis, and case-study diagnosis.

General diagnosis has three purposes. First, it gives information necessary to adjust instruction to meet the needs of groups of children in general. For example, a fifth-grade class as a whole may be found to be relatively weak in reading ability. If so, the conclusion may be that more attention should be given to reading instruction than had been given in the past. Second, the general diagnosis can give the information necessary for adjusting instruction to individual differences in reading found within the class. It can, for example, indicate the range of general reading capability with which the instruction must cope and also indicate the individuals that would profit from modifications usually made within a class to adjust to individual differences. Third, a general diagnosis can help to find the children in need of a more detailed analysis of their reading disability.

Analytical diagnosis makes two important contributions to the correction of reading disability. First, it locates those areas of limited ability that need to be explored more fully. Second, it often can indicate by itself the instructional adjustments required. Many cases, however, will need a more detailed study of their reading problems and limiting characteristics than can be made at the analytical level.

Case-Study diagnosis is necessary for many disabled readers. This level of diagnosis involves a more detailed, thorough, and time-consuming study than is warranted for children with less complex reading problems. Many children's learning problems may require only a general study of their educational achievement and intellectual capacity. Other children's difficulties may require differential or analytical study to locate the specific areas of limitation. Some of these children's problems may be so subtle or complex that a detailed case study is required before a remedial program can be designed.

USE INFORMATION FOUND IN CUMULATIVE RECORDS. The yearly records of the school will give the diagnostician information about the progress the student has made throughout his school life. They also will indicate the subjects that have been difficult for him. They will tell, too, about any periods of prolonged absence or changes of school. These records also help to establish the grade level at which the trouble with reading may have started. The examiner should make a careful study of the school history of the student and should record upon the diagnostic record inventory those circumstances that are related to reading. Such a study often eliminates duplicate testing and gives information not available from other sources.

ONLY PERTINENT INFORMATION SHOULD BE COLLECTED. There is a tendency for clinicians and teachers to add tests to their routine diagnostic programs on an experimental basis. This is as it should be, but when such tests are found to have little diagnostic value, they should be discontinued. The time, energy, and expense involved in getting the necessary information is so great that everyone making diagnoses should appraise the measuring instruments being used to make sure they are efficient and that they add to the understanding of the children's instructional needs. There should be grave concern if there is unnecessary overlap in testing. The more reliable and valid measures should be used.

The child should be given every consideration when administering tests in a diagnosis. Indiscriminate testing may set a child against the whole procedure or even may cause him to doubt his capability to learn. The clinician should investigate thoroughly the reading profile of each reading case, obtain a valid estimate of the child's learning capability, and satisfy himself that the child's sensory equipment is normal or has been corrected as far as possible. He should explore the child's personal makeup and any special psychological and neurological characteristics only when there is an indication that these data are pertinent to the optimal adjustment of the child being studied. It is advisable to intersperse reading measures with others of a different kind since many children in serious trouble become resistant in reading situations. They easily become discouraged or even uncooperative if they are subjected to a long, uninterrupted series of reading tests.

A test for group measurement should be used whenever the results justify it. Although it is true that anything worth measuring at all should be measured well, it is equally true that the diagnosis should avoid wasteful and nonessential methods. This does not mean that cutting down on the information needed to diagnose correctly should be condoned. It does mean that undiscriminating and inefficient measurement must be avoided.

WHENEVER POSSIBLE, STANDARDIZED TEST PROCEDURES SHOULD BE USED. In diagnosing the learning difficulty of a disabled reader, his reading, his physical and sensory characteristics, and various personality and environmental factors must be analyzed. The authors of this book wish to make it clear that they fully appreciate the interrelationships which exist among the child's development, his other achievements, his personal qualities, his environment both in and out of school, and his reading capabilities. However, after a child has had reading disability identified as his major problem, it becomes necessary to investigate thoroughly his reading pattern to establish the root of his difficulty. This is always one of the major concerns of the diagnostician when studying a reading disability case, because without locating the particular reading anomalies, little if anything can be done to correct the reading disability.

It may be, for example, that a disabled reader is found to be farsighted, and correction is made with glasses. He is now comfortable visually. He stands a more reasonable chance of learning to read, but he is still a disabled reader. His reading should be analyzed to locate the faulty learnings, which may have been caused in part by his visual difficulty, in order to plan instruction to correct his reading disability. No matter what physical, environmental, or personality problem caused the reading difficulty, it is necessary to study and correct the reading disability. The other factors associated with the reading difficulty also need to be studied so that the correction in reading can be made most efficiently and so that the other conditions may be improved.

There are two general types of appraisals used in diagnosing reading disability. First is the application of precise units and numerically expressed norms, such as age or grade norms, percentile norms, or standard score norms requiring measurement by standard procedures. Second are qualitative appraisals for which norms expressed in numerical terms either are not available or are inappropriate. This second type of appraisal often is called an evaluation. This kind of appraisal is limited in one sense in that the procedures are not systematic and in that the varying degrees of the diagnostician's personal bias may enter into the appraisal. These appraisals gain their merit from the fact that they allow the diagnostician to obtain information about things for which no standardized measures are available.

Standardized tests are valuable instruments for analyzing the child's reading strengths and weaknesses. They also are needed for collecting many of the related facts entering into the formulation of a remedial program. Methods of appraisal involving accurate measurement should be used whenever possible. When using standardized tests it is necessary for the diagnostician to follow precisely the procedures for giving and scoring the instruments as specified in the accompanying manuals. Any variation from standard procedures may affect the use of the norms supplied.

The results of normative data obtained from standardized tests, both survey and diagnostic, must be interpreted carefully. The norms supplied for such tests indicate the performance of typical pupils in a sample of typical learnings within the field being measured. Therein the standardized tests have their strength and also their weakness. Disabled readers are far from being typical learners. They are designated disabled readers because they are atypical. Standardized tests allow the diagnostician to compare a disabled reader with his more fortunate typical counterpart. This is how strengths and weaknesses can be located with a minimum of clinical bias.

Much caution and considerable insight must be used to interpret the results of the measurements. A child of sixth-grade age, for example, with a reading expectancy of 6.0 may measure 3.0 in reading. An uninitiated examiner might assume that this child needs the reading materials and methods suitable for the typical third-grade child. This usually is not the case. This sixth-grade child is not a typical third-grade reader. He is a sixth-grade child with sixth-grade interests, drives, motives, and friends. He is not even a third-grade reader, for further study very likely would indicate that his basic reading skills and abilities, and therefore his instructional needs, are closer to those of a second-grade child. His degree of mental maturity enables him to use his limited basic reading skills better than does the typical child with 2.0 reading ability. He has 6.0 potential to which to apply his 2.0 reading skills. He is able to measure somewhat higher, namely, 3.0, because of his greater mental maturity than the second-grade child with 2.0 reading ability, 2.0 potential, and 2.0 chronological age and experience. This is but one illustration of the care with which the diagnostician of reading cases must work. The standardized test usually is, however, his most reliable instrument of measurement. They give him normative data with which he can judge what is best for the atypical learning he is trying to remedy. A reading diagnosis is likely to be accurate to the extent of the numerical data upon which he bases his judgments. Diagnostic methods will be described in the chapters that follow.

INFORMAL PROCEDURES SHOULD BE USED. Even though the greater part of a diagnosis is based on standardized data, the need often arises to study areas for which standardized tests have not been developed. The diagnostician should feel free to explore further, by informal means, any leads to the nature of a particular reading disability discovered during the standardized procedures. Often informal explorations supply more insight for planning a remedial program than does the standardized diagnostic program. Most diagnosticians combine formal testing with informal inventories of reading skills, abilities, interests, attitudes, and the like, for optimal understanding of a child's difficulty.

Informal appraisals also are valuable in that they often are the only or the best method of gaining information. There are no standardized tests, for example, to measure the child's attitude toward reading. Probably the diagnostician has to ask the child what he thinks of reading or watch informally the child's reactions to reading. This information may be significant in formulating a remedial program and should be collected, even though sometimes it may be of questionable validity. The good diagnostician probably will be aware of the confidence to be placed in such information. Specific informal diagnostic techniques are discussed in chapter 7.

DECISIONS IN DIAGNOSIS MUST BE BASED ON PATTERNS OF SCORES. When the information about a disabled reader has been collected, it must be arranged so that the various numerical scores can be compared with one another. An adequate diagnosis is made from these comparisons. High as well as low scores must be considered in estimating the instructional needs of the disabled reader. Often, disability is the result of an unfortunate overemphasis in the reading program. One child's sight vocabulary may be low because he has always been so good at using word-attack techniques, that he has found little need to remember words at sight. Another child may have such a compulsive need to be accurate in reading that he cannot become a fluent reader. He is always one-hundred percent accurate, and even if more detail about a passage was required, he would know that, too. No minutiae escape him, but this takes up too much reading time. These lacks of balance can be detected only by making comparisons among standardized norms.

If the diagnostician fails to compare the child's performance in the separate skills with his general reading ability, there will be many mistakes in planning remedial work. For example, when a fifth-grade child has only third-grade ability in syllabication, the diagnostician may think his lack of ability to break words into syllables is at the root of the difficulty. But when it is noted that the child's general reading ability is only that of the typical second-grade child, his ability to syllabify becomes a strength rather than a weakness.

Most standardized diagnostic tests in reading are arranged so that such comparisons are made easily. Even the range of tolerance frequently is indicated so that the diagnostician will not place too much emphasis upon some low or high score which is not significantly out of range as compared with the overall reading capability of the child.

After the numerical data are compared and judgments are made, decisions should be modified in accordance with the qualitative data gathered from evaluative techniques and other informal approaches. The diagnostician should be careful not to let isolated observations or bits of information alter drastically the judgments he has made from reliable and valid measurements.

DIAGNOSIS SHOULD BE CONTINUOUS. Occasionally, a child fails to respond to remedial instruction based upon the original diagnosis. In this case, after two or three weeks of instruction, the diagnosis should be reevaluated, perhaps with additional measurements and other appraisals. Some vital factor in the case may have been overlooked in the original diagnosis.

When the remedial program is successful, reading disability is dynamic rather than static. The original diagnosis indicated the instructional needs of the disabled reader at the time remedial instruction was undertaken. The remedial program based on it was designed to alter the child's reading profile in ways that would encourage better overall growth in reading. As remedial work progresses, study of the child should be continued. If the remedial instruction has been effective, the needs of the child will have changed and the remedial program may require modification. Diagnosis must therefore be continuous.

At the start of remedial instruction, a child may have been insecure in reading situations. The diagnostician may have recommended that a chart be kept to show him his progress. After a time, as the child gains security, the chart can be discontinued. Another child may have been relatively poor at using context clues as aids to word recognition and was depending solely upon analytical approaches. The remedial instruction may have been directed toward encouraging the use of context. After a time, it may be noted that the child was neglecting careful inspection of the words and making seemingly random guesses. The guesses made sense but not the correct sense. By continuous diagnosis, the remedial worker could detect when the problem changed and thus maintain a better balance between the word-recognition techniques. In these two examples, the remedial work had to be altered because the instructional needs of the child had changed.

ANALYZING READING DIFFICULTIES

The amount of diagnostic effort to formulate remedial programs for disabled readers varies widely. Some children, suspected of being disabled readers, later are found not to fit this classification but have other problems. This chapter will not go into the diagnosis necessary to solve the many types of problems sometimes confused with reading disability. Our present concern is limited to the diagnostic procedures needed to locate and analyze reading disability cases of various kinds.

Sometimes, the diagnosis of reading disability will point out other areas to be studied because, if not tended to, they will interfere with the correction of the reading problem. Under such circumstances, the appropriate course of action will be indicated, but in certain instances the diagnoses in related fields will be left to discussions in references dealing with those problems. For example, a child's reading disability may be difficult to correct because of a deep emotional disturbance. It is not the province of this book to describe how the emotional problem should be diagnosed or treated. Nevertheless, the reading diagnostician has to be alert to such problems and should include in his case study observations that will identify related problems needing further study by other specialists. In formulating a remedial program, the diagnostician must always take into account the presence of conditions that need treatment elsewhere.

The screening approach, in related problem areas, should be one that if any error is made it should be in referring false positives rather than in neglecting a case requiring specialized diagnosis. For example, the reading diagnostician does not diagnose visual defects, but he does screen for the possibility of visual handicaps. It is better for him to refer, for expert attention, two possible cases which do not need visual correction than it is to miss one which does.

A reading diagnostician needs to find the answers to some specific questions about the disabled reader before an effective remedial program can be formulated. Our discussion of the analysis of reading difficulties will be in terms of these questions:

1. Is the child correctly classified as a disabled reader?

2. What is the nature of the training needed?

3. Who can give the remedial work most effectively?

4. How can improvement be made most effectively?

5. Does the child have any limiting conditions that must be considered?

6. Are there any environmental conditions that might interfere with progress in reading?

Is THE CHILD CORRECTLY CLASSIFIED AS A DISABLED READER? Poor reading ability is so interrelated with other characteristics of child growth and development that it often is extremely difficult to determine whether the reading disability or some other condition is the basic problem. Not all children who are poor readers are reading disability cases. There are many children low in reading ability who can in no way be considered reading disability cases. A few children who are disabled readers have a more important problem that should be remedied before correcting the reading. First, the teacher or diagnostician must identify the true general nature of the child's problem and decide whether the child will profit from remedial instruction in reading or whether some other adjustment is required.

The child who is considered disabled because he is not as good in reading as other children of his age may be reading better than could be expected of him. The most obvious example of this erroneous classification is the child with low verbal intelligence. This child cannot be expected to grow as rapidly as can other children in reading. His problem will not be solved by a remedial reading program, but it can be eased by curricular changes and by methods better suited to his limited learning ability. He cannot be classified as a disabled reader but rather should be considered a slow learner. For this reason, no child should be considered disabled in reading, unless there is a discrepancy between his learning capacity or general verbal intelligence and his reading performance.

Physical anomalies may cause a child to be classified as a disabled reader when whom he needs to see is a doctor, not a remedial teacher. Among the more common physical conditions erroneously classified are glandular conditions limiting a child's energy. The child with a glandular limitation, even though he is bright, may not be able to sustain the high level of concentration needed to read intently during a testing period or long enough to finish an assignment. This child would measure low in reading performance even though he might have well-developed skills and abilities in reading. Even if he has not been able to develop reading competency, his underlying problem still is medical. Reading instruction, properly adjusted, should be continued while the physical limitation is being treated, but a concentrated program in remedial reading for many of these cases would not be advantageous. To instill a sense of inadequacy in the child would limit seriously his future reading growth.

Children with spastic conditions, epilepsy, chorea, or other neurological problems cannot be expected to develop reading capabilities as rapidly as can their equally intelligent but neurolgically sound contemporaries. Spastic children, for example, can learn to read, but because of difficulties in coordination, they may be expected to learn more slowly than normal children. As long as he maintains a relatively even reading profile, a spastic child cannot be considered a disabled reader even when there is a discrepancy between his mental maturity or level of learning ability and his reading grade.

Some neurological problems are more difficult for the educational diagnostician to detect and are suspected only after considerable remedial instruction has been given with unsatisfactory results. The diagnostician should be alert to the possibility of neurological limitations, especially in those children high in intelligence and low in other organized learnings such as arithmetical computation. The reading diagnostician and remedial worker must be aware that not all human deficiencies can be corrected by education.

When children have neurological impairments, the reading teacher often must be satisfied with less than usual results. In many of these cases, both the neurological limitation and the reading problem can be remedied simultaneously. The remedial reading program in such cases is designed to give the child the individualized help he needs. His problem usually is not unfortunate reading growth patterns, but rather a restricted, overall reading development produced by the neurological limitation. A more detailed treatment of the visual and perceptual problems encountered by the neurologically impaired child will be given in chapter 12.

The relationship between reading disability and emotional maladjustment often makes it difficult to classify a child's major problem as a reading disability. The dual relationship between reading disability and emotional insecurity already has been discussed. Sometimes the poor reader is an emotionally disturbed child and reading ability suffers along with other school learnings. More often, the emotional disturbance is brought about by the failure to make normal progress in reading. Here, immediate attention to the reading problem will correct both the reading and the emotional problems. Sometimes, the child may be so confused that the help of a specialist in emotional problems may be needed. The specialist may decide that the emotional problem must be treated before further reading instruction is given. Even in those cases in which deep-seated emotional tensions are suspected of making the child an inefficient learner, emotional therapy and remedial instruction in reading can be given concurrently, to the mutual benefit of both.

The reading diagnostician should study the emotional reactions of a child who is reading below expectancy in terms of his learning ability. The child who is inefficient in learning in general and who is emotionally disturbed, is more likely to have an emotional problem than is the child who is low in reading and reading-related subjects alone. The emotionally tense child who is better in nonreading subjects than he is in reading, and who is considerably better in silent reading than in oral reading may have a reading-centered emotional problem. Unless a qualified expert in emotional problems has recommended a delay of the reading instruction, it is the opinion of the writers that the child, whether the emotional disturbance is the cause or the result of the reading disability, should be considered a reading disability case and treated as suggested in chapter 12 as a specially handicapped child.

Determining the child's basic problem frequently is difficult and requires an alert diagnostician. A careful study of his achievement scores and mental ratings, parental interview blanks, physiological records, and personality inventories often is necessary to decide correctly whether the child should be classified as a disabled reader. This problem alone may have been what has led some psychologists with a flair for sweeping statements to claim that to understand reading disability in all of its ramifications is to know all there is to know about psychology and reading instruction.

WHAT IS THE NATURE OF THE TRAINING NEEDED? The training needed by a disabled reader is indicated by his reading strengths and weaknesses. Establishing the reading limitation is the most important phase of a diagnosis for formulating a program of correction. The diagnostician's main problem is that of finding just what, in the reading pattern of the disabled reader, is retarding his reading growth. The diagnostic study of what is really wrong with the child's reading, what faulty techniques he is using, what abilities he is overemphasizing, what abilities he lacks, is essential to formulating a remedial program.

There are some limitations in the child's reading profile which have little effect on his reading growth in general. A child may be unable to read science materials or he may be weak in one of the study skills. Under such circumstances, the limitation can be found readily and work begun to overcome the specific limitation. Many children have these minor and easily corrected reading limitations. A general and analytical diagnosis can and should discover such problems. Once found, the training needed becomes clear: the child should have training in the weak area pointed out by the diagnosis. This type of limitation is specific and has no repercussions on other aspects of the child's reading growth. The diagnosis and planning of remedial instruction is relatively simple in these cases.

There are other limitations in disabled readers' reading patterns that have more far-reaching and devastating effects. Failure to establish certain skills and abilities, overemphasis of others, failure to learn essential knowledges, or adoption of faulty approaches may interfere with the child's entire reading development. The lack of flexibility and adaptability may limit seriously the child's ability to adjust his reading skills to the needs of particular reading material or to certain purposes for reading.

WHO CAN GIVE THE REMEDIAL WORK MOST EFFECTIVELY? There are three places in which remedial work can be given, the classroom, the school reading center, and the clinic. The regular classroom teacher can and should give remedial instruction to most children moderately disabled in reading. The size of the class, other responsibilities, and her training limit the teacher to the solution of only the less complicated reading problems. She always must decide just how much attention can be given to one child at the expense of many. If adequate programs of measurement, efficient class management, and materials designed to aid the teacher in adjusting to individual differences are used, many reading difficulties can be detected early and corrected by the classroom teacher. Even under these circumstances, the teacher frequently may need the help of an expert diagnostician to aid her in the formulation of a classroom remedial program.

The second place in which remedial work in reading is given is at a reading center or resource room within the school. This center is usually a room well stocked with materials for reading and for special practice exercises. Here a remedial teacher works with individual children or groups of children needing more specialized and individual attention than can be given by the classroom teacher.

In general, the smaller the group, the greater are the returns for each child. There seems to be little advantage, however, in having groups of less than six children for instruction to moderately disabled readers. The remedial teachers working in school reading centers need special training to handle the problems they meet. These remedial teachers should be able to diagnose the less complex reading cases and offer remedial suggestions for those children who are to be treated by the classroom teachers. The teachers in charge of remedial rooms or centers within a school should be successful classroom teachers who have had additional training in reading and in diagnosing and treating reading disability. Reading disability is no simple thing to be solved by a novice or merely by a set of exercises purporting to be suitable for all cases.

The third place in which remedial work is given is at an educational or reading clinic. These clinics frequently are found in the major universities or teachers' colleges. Many enlightened school systems have child study clinics which include sections devoted to educational disability and reading difficulty. This is indeed fortunate, because there will be many children with learning difficulties as long as we try to teach all children to read. The more complex problems are best diagnosed and treated in these clinics. However, the demand for the services of these educational clinics so far exceeds the available personnel and facilities, that only those children who cannot be helped in the other two places should come to the clinic for remedial work. In a complex case, the child should be excused from part of his regular class work and given careful individual, clinical attention. The teacher and parents must be informed of the child's problem so that his entire reading environment may be attuned to his needs.

The clinic's greatest contribution to a public school system is in making more thorough diagnoses than can be obtained elsewhere. Only the more subtle and complex reading cases need clinical remedial training. To sum up, many disabled readers should be corrected in the classroom; some of them, however, will be given remedial instruction in a school reading center or resource room; and others will be referred to a clinic for treatment. However treated, every case must be diagnosed accurately.

To decide where the child with a reading difficulty can most effectively be treated, the diagnostician first needs to decide into which of the general descriptive categories the child fits. These are described in chapter 3.

RECOMMENDATIONS FOR SIMPLE READING RETARDATION. Children who are significantly retarded in reading but show no unusual or limiting characteristics in their reading patterns and no personal rejection of reading and no disturbance from it can be treated effectively in the regular classroom. They are cases of *simple retardation,* immature in reading but needing no marked reeducation. They do need instruction for their level of advancement, a rigorously motivated reading program, and an opportunity to read a lot.

Some children in this category will be treated better in the school reading center. The amount of a child's retardation and his grade level will determine which place is better. If the child is so low in reading ability that he cannot profit from most of the instruction given in the lowest reading group in the class, he would be taught more productively by the remedial teacher in the school reading center. Most reading cases of secondary school age might be assigned to a remedial teacher. It is difficult for the secondary teacher, who works with about 150 pupils a day, to know any one child well enough to overcome an extreme case of simple retardation.

The impersonal nature of the secondary school makes the classroom teacher's problem of helping the disabled reader more difficult than it is in the elementary school in which the teacher works the entire day with a single class. No case of simple retardation in the elementary school needs to be referred to the reading clinic for individual treatment.

The child with simple retardation in reading usually can be discovered by general diagnosis, using achievement tests and nonverbal group mental tests. He may not be isolated until the analytical level of diagnosis is reached. The child with simple retardation in reading is one who has a low but relatively uniform reading profile and who has no adverse reactions to his poor reading. He is disabled only because he is not reading as well as he could be expected to read. A study of his reading scores shows that he has normal reading patterns for the typical child of equal reading attainment. There is no interfering habit nor faulty attitude present to impede future growth.

RECOMMENDATIONS FOR SPECIFIC READING RETARDATION. Children best described as cases of *specific retardation* are those who are limited severely in one or more areas of reading but who demonstrate that they have developed the general basic skills and abilities well enough to be able readers in other areas. Practically all of these cases can be given the remedial work they need by the classroom teacher. The skills or abilities in which the child needs further training and experience have been found. Then, as the child participates in the regular developmental reading program, the teacher increases emphasis on specific areas in which the child is weak. If there are two or three children needing the same emphasis, from time to time, the teacher can give them remedial training as a small group. In some instances, children with specific limitations from several classes of about the same grade level can be sent to the school remedial center for group instruction, but for the most part, they should be given training by the classroom teacher. The prognosis for overcoming specific retardation is exceedingly good even though the degree of retardation is sometimes great.

A child with specific retardation in reading is discovered through reading tests that are more analytical than are those customarily used in general diagnosis. Tests that give scores in various important areas of reading are needed to diagnose the child with specific retardation. Indications of attainment in the more common types of comprehension and study skills are needed to pinpoint the area of specific limitation. If a child scores high in some of the comprehension tests but low in other tests, he is correctly described as a case of specific retardation and no further diagnosis is needed. The child's high scores indicate that there is no basic limitation in his reading. His low scores isolate the areas needing attention.

RECOMMENDATIONS FOR LIMITING DISABILITY. The child who has serious deficiencies in basic reading skills and abilities which impede his entire reading growth is best described as having a *limiting disability*. Such a child is low in all types of reading, because he has acquired interfering habits or has failed to learn one or more essential skills. His reading profile does not indicate the healthy reading growth of the simple retardation case but rather an unfortunate reading pattern.

Most children with limiting disability should be given remedial work in a school reading center. A few could be corrected by the classroom teacher, but usually reeducation takes more time and careful planning than she is able to devote to it. Some of the more difficult cases of this type should be referred to the reading clinic for remedial work. Any decision must rest on a thorough case-study diagnosis, usually conducted at a child study center or psychoeducational clinic. The results of the complete diagnosis and the recommended remedial program should be discusssed with the remedial teacher in a case conference. In practice, the clinics are frequently so overcrowded that case reports are sent to the remedial teacher who, in turn, discusses the problem with the concerned school personnel.

RECOMMENDATIONS FOR COMPLEX DISABILITY. Children who are best described as *complex disability* cases include the disabled readers whose problems are more subtle and complicated. These children are always severely retarded in reading. They are frequently bright, capable youngsters who demonstrate antagonism toward reading and who feel embarrassed about their inability to read. They sometimes make a good adjustment to their reading difficulty by doing outstanding work in fields such as art or arithmetic computation which do not require reading ability. More often, they merely take on unfortunate modes of adjustment to their lack of success in reading which spread to general ineffectiveness in other school work. In many cases, they lack persistence and tend to retreat from school in general and from reading situations in particular. They are absent from school frequently and sometimes they become delinquent.

Complex reading disability cases include not only those who have made a faulty adjustment to their unfortunate reading growth, but also those who have other handicaps of one sort or another. The remedial programs are further complicated for children who are poor readers and also need their remedial programs modified to adjust to physiological, emotional, intellectual, environmental, or other atypical conditions.

Many children with complex reading disability become blocked and so tense that they are ineffective learners. They get into a downward spiral that increases tensions and causes ever greater inefficiency in learning. A child with a complex disability in reading often is found to have anxiety and worry about reading and fear of reading. He tends to be insecure and defeated. Children who are classified in this category need careful, individual, clinical attention. A complex reading disability case needs clinical diagnosis of his problem, and often the reading diagnostician must enlist the services of other specialists in order to appraise the child's needs accurately and thoroughly.

Often the remedial work for such children should be done in the clinic. In some cases, of course, it can be done at the school reading center when there is time to give the child the necessary individual help that he requires.

How can improvement be made most effectively? The answer to this question is extremely important because the corrective program must be efficient in order to develop reading capability at an accelerated rate. Extensive diagnosis of the nature of the reading problem will have pointed out the type of instruction that is necessary. The purpose of the remedial program is to overcome unfortunate approaches to reading that have already limited or are likely to impede the child's reading growth. The information gained from the study of the child must enable the diagnostician to make several decisions which will increase the efficiency of the remedial instruction. First, the decision must be made as to the proper level of difficulty of the material; second, the material must deal with topics that are interesting to the child, or at least, as compatible as possible with interests of children of his age and general capability; third, the diagnostician must suggest the methods by which the child will be informed of his progress; fourth, the diagnostician must estimate the length of the instructional period; and fifth, he must give the necessary information for planning the types of independent work that the child needs.

DETERMINING THE PROPER LEVEL OF DIFFICULTY OF MATERIAL. The diagnostician must make a careful estimate of the level of difficulty of the material that is to be used at the start of remedial instruction. Usually the child who is in difficulty with his reading has been having trouble for some time. It thus becomes vital to select material for him at the appropriate level of difficulty. This material should be that in which the child can feel competent. The problem of selecting material of the right difficulty is complicated by the fact that the disabled reader cannot read as well as would be expected of a child of his age and mental maturity. Some diagnosticians think that the correct approach for estimating the difficulty of material is to study the results of standardized tests and thus ascertain the child's general reading level. They think that if a child measures, for example, 2.5, he should start his remedial instruction in material suitable for the typical child halfway through the second grade. But research and experience have shown that for most disabled readers this would be an overestimation of the level at which their instruction should start.

Let us suppose that a child who measures 2.5 on a standardized reading test is one with a reading expectancy of 5.0. The child really is not a typical 2.5 reader. He often is a reader with considerably less skill development than a typical 2.5 child. This child is able to bring to the reading scene a much broader background of experience, a keener evaluation of the concepts, a higher level of reasoning ability than can the typical child who is halfway through the second grade. He may measure as much as a year higher in general comprehension than he would in basic reading abilities such as the ability to recognize words or to phrase them effectively for comprehension.

In judging the level of difficulty for initial remedial instruction, the diagnostician must consider, in addition to standardized tests, other evidence of the child's level of skill development. Such evidence as his ability to read material aloud should be investigated. In oral reading situations, does he make more than one error in every twenty running words? What is his skill in phrasing? What word-recognition techniques does he use? What about his ability to answer various types of comprehension questions about the material read? The level at which the child can read comfortably and effectively can be estimated by trying the child out in a series of basic readers and finding the level most suitable for him. He may be started, for example, in a book at second-grade level of difficulty. If this book proves to be too difficult, a first-grade book can be tried. If this is still too difficult, a primer could be used. The diagnostician may find that the first book he chooses is too easy, that the child can read the second-grade book with great fluency. Then he would try a third-grade reader. The diagnostician would sample books in the series until the level was found at which the child could read with reasonable ease. This informal approach gives a rough estimate of the level of difficulty suitable for a given child.

It is possible to estimate this in another way. Some of the results of standardized diagnostic tests will indicate the level at which remedial instruction should be started. If it is found, for example, that in the skill areas the child measures around 2.0, even though his general reading level on the basis of comprehension tests is 2.5, the appropriate level at which to start the child's remedial instruction is likely to be toward the end of a first-grade reader, or approaching the 2.0 level. These evaluations will give the diagnostician a general estimate of the level of material suitable for beginning instruction, but it must be modified in accordance with the type of remediation the child needs.

A second consideration in selecting material is the nature of the disability. The diagnostician must consider the instructional outcomes to be gained from its use. For example, if the child's major problem is developing greater speed, the material selected should be considerably easier than that normally appropriate to the child's general level of attainment. If the child can read comfortably material of fourth-grade level, then material that is from a half-year to a year easier should be selected for increasing speed of reading. The material should contain no more than one word that would cause the child difficulty, in every hundred running words. If the child's problem is developing knowledge of visual, structural, and phonetic elements, he should be given material that is rather difficult, material in which he is likely to meet one word that he needs to analyze in every twenty running words. He may be given exercises that require the phonetic analysis of a high percentage of the words. Such exercises would be too difficult for general reading purposes but would be suitable to this specific problem. It should be noted that in these exercises, the child must have a reasonable chance for success. The selection of materials at the appropriate level of difficulty for a specific case is probably one of the most important decisions the diagnostician makes.

ESTIMATING WHAT MATERIAL IS SUITABLE IN INTEREST AND FORMAT. An important consideration in selecting material to be used for remedial treatment is that it should be suitable to the child in both interest and format. Securing this material is another major problem for the remedial teacher. The diagnostician must estimate the type of material the child will be interested in and the best format. The problem resolves itself into finding material that will be relatively mature in content and format but which requires only the reading ability of the disabled reader. Workbooks accompanying the basic readers may contain the material with which it will be necessary to start the remedial instruction. Or, the teacher may have to prepare her own materials. More frequently, the problem can be handled successfully by using material of appropriate difficulty and by enabling the child to use the results of his reading in ways important to him. For example, a boy of high school age may be willing to read in a fourth-grade science book an account of the way to connect a battery to a bell in order to make it ring, if he actually is allowed to do it.

The task of the diagnostician is that of estimating the level at which the child should be expected to read from the point of view of difficulty, the areas of interest that seem to be most acceptable to him, and the degree to which he will be adaptable to somewhat immature format. Estimates of all these conditions are made on the basis of reading tests, interest inventories, informal appraisals, and work samples with various types of materials. See appendixes I and II for sources of graded book lists and materials.

SELECTING MEANS OF SHOWING PROGRESS. The diagnostician should suggest appropriate means of demonstrating to the child that he is making progress in reading. He also should estimate the amount of attention that should be given to demonstrating to the child that now he is learning to read. The method of demonstrating this growth will be determined by the remedial training to be given. If, for example, the child's problem is one of oral reading, the diagnostician may suggest that a tape recording of the child's oral reading be made at intervals throughout the remedial instruction. Then, from time to time, the child should be allowed to listen to his recordings and note the growth that is taking place.

The amount of time that should be devoted to making his growth in reading apparent to the child depends upon the child himself. If he is insecure in the reading situation, or if he has demonstrated personality problems which are coupled with his lack of success in reading, more time should be devoted to this phase than would be necessary with a child who is not so insecure.

These judgments will be based upon an inspection of the child's reading profile and also upon evaluations of the child's attitude toward reading or his emotional adjustment.

ESTIMATING DESIRABLE LENGTH AND FREQUENCY OF REMEDIAL LESSONS. The diagnostician must estimate the length of time for each training period and also the frequency with which training should be given. These estimates are made from three types of appraisals. *First,* the results expected from remedial instruction must be considered. If the child needs to increase his speed of reading, the actual lesson should be relatively short and highly motivated. Between lessons the child may continue to emphasize speed of reading, independently.

The second consideration used in judging the length of the remedial sessions is the physical stamina of the child. If he tires easily, or if he is emotionally upset, the length of the training periods should be short. If he is physically strong and emotionally relaxed, the training periods can be longer.

Third, any condition, such as poor vision, that limits the child's ability to pay close attention to reading instruction over a period of time, will shorten the length of remedial sessions. It is often better to have two short sessions a day than to have one longer one.

A careful inspection of all information available about the youngsters is necessary to make a reasonable estimate of the length of time for each training period and the frequency of the remedial lessons.

PLANNING FOR INDEPENDENT WORK. The final consideration in determining how improvement can be made most efficiently is planning independent work for the student. The child's reading disability will not be corrected in the remedial periods alone. He must extend his remedial reading experiences into his independent work. The level of difficulty of material used for independent work should be considerably easier than that studied during the remedial lessons. The independent work will be somewhat different from work done in remedial lessons. In planning independent work, the diagnostician must judge how best to motivate it and what type of exercises might be most profitable for the child to engage in independently. We may ask, for example, if the child is trying to build a larger sight vocabulary, would it be best for him to have a pack of word cards on which he drills himself, or stories containing words in contextual settings, or would workbook-type exercises be best? These decisions are made by the diagnostician on the basis of the nature of instruction needed, the characteristics of the child, and the characteristics of his general environment.

DOES THE CHILD HAVE ANY LIMITING CONDITIONS THAT MUST BE CONSIDERED? In formulating a remedial program, all causes of reading disability considered in Chapters 4 and 5 must be appraised by the diagnostician and he must decide what expert help is needed. For the reeducation program to be effective, any limitations within the child which might influence his reading growth detrimentally must be located. If the child has poor vision, an examination by a competent expert is required. Whenever possible, the visual defect should be corrected. Whether corrected or not, modifications in the remedial program will be necessary. Such modifications are described in a later chapter dealing with the specially handicapped child.

If poor hearing is suspected, an otologist should be consulted. Again, the mere correction of the auditory limitation will not improve the reading disability. It will, however, make the child more trainable. The child with poor auditory capacity will need modifications in his instructional program. See chapter 12 on the specially handicapped child.

All of the factors that cause reading disability in the first place may also become conditions within the child which need correction or to which the program must adjust. Whenever possible, such limitations should be corrected before the start of remedial training. When no correction is possible, the program must be altered to allow for the known limitation. It should be recognized that the correction of a limiting condition does not alter the reading needs of the child. If the child, for example, has third-grade reading ability before a visual correction, he still will have third-grade skills and abilities in reading after the visual correction. The correction of an unfortunate characteristic will not alter the need for remedial reading instruction. However, it will, improve his chances for learning to read efficiently and effectively.

ARE THERE ANY ENVIRONMENTAL CONDITIONS THAT MIGHT INTERFERE WITH PROGRESS IN READING? The diagnostician must study the child's entire environment, for it may have limitations that could influence the success of the remedial program. Sometimes, in their zeal to help their children, parents create emotional tensions that do not help the reading and disturb a child greatly. Or, parents may try to help their child in ways that are detrimental to his reading growth. Parents can contribute much to the success of a remedial program by remembering that they should:

1. Take an interest in the independent reading work that the child brings home.

2. Give the child a good place in which to work without interruption.

3. On the advice of the remedial teacher, secure materials that will be the child's own.

4. Hide their anxieties about the child's reading problem.

5. Tell the child a word if he has difficulty doing his independent reading at home.

6. Read the independent material and discuss it with him.

7. Avoid ridicule or making comparisons among siblings.

8. Let the child know that they appreciate his many accomplishments and that they have confidence in him.

9. Recognize that the child's "don't care" attitude toward reading is often a "do care very much" one and that it is wise to let him adopt this apparent attitude as a "safety valve."

Not only the home conditions and child-parent relationships, but also the school situation should be studied. All too frequently, improvement of reading is left to the remedial program alone. Often the school environment is not conducive to effective reading development for the disabled reader. The child's entire reading environment should be coordinated if he is to progress. Sometimes a teacher does not recognize fully the seriousness of having a child try to read material that is so difficult that it can be nothing but frustrating to him. At other times, the teacher is not aware that a child's lack of attention may be the result of a hearing loss. The authors of this book have yet to see the parent or teacher who would not do everything in his power to cooperate in helping a disabled reader if the child's problems were explained.

The diagnostician must try to find any irritant in the child's environment which will impede his progress in learning to read.

ILLUSTRATION OF AN ANALYSIS OF READING DIFFICULTIES

The following illustration of reading diagnosis shows how the study of a fifth-grade class progresses from general diagnosis to analytical diagnosis to case-study diagnosis. It also indicates how the answers to various questions are secured.

General Diagnosis in Reading

The first level of diagnosis can be called general diagnosis and is concerned with information about children's levels of performance in the more common aspects of reading growth. To adjust instruction to individual differences, school systems frequently give periodic achievement tests. When no such tests are given, the diagnostician should give these as the first step in his diagnosis. A general diagnosis also should include an estimate of the child's intellectual level.

The diagnostician can compare the child's mental status, reading grade status, and level of performance in other fields. He then can judge whether a child is a disabled reader. If the child's reading grade is about the same as his reading expectancy and as his success in other fields of learning, we judge him to be progressing as well in reading as can be expected. This is true even if his reading ability is somewhat poorer than the reading of other members of his class. Such a child will need no further diagnosis in reading even though he may need certain adjustments for the slow learner, to be described in a later chapter. The classroom teacher constantly should watch each child she teaches in the developmental reading program. In regular class work, the teacher systematically studies every child's performance in an analytical, diagnostic manner.

If a child is considerably lower in reading ability than his reading expectancy indicates that he should be and than he is in the subject-matter fields that are independent of reading success, further diagnosis is needed. The general diagnosis helps the diagnostician to discover those who are educationally handicapped by ineffective reading and those who need curricular adjustments. Standardized survey tests, achievement tests, mental tests, informal objective tests, and general observations are used in making these judgments.

An examination of a typical fifth-grade class of thirty-five pupils helps to show the result of a general diagnosis. Table 2 gives the results of a survey of reading capabilities, mental ability, and arithmetical computation obtained at the beginning of the school year. The *Gates Reading Survey* for measuring reading ability and the *Stanford-Binet* for measuring intelligence were used. The scores in arithmetic are obtained from the norms given in the *Modern School Achievement Test*. The reading grade scores are obtained from the table of norms given in the test booklet. The mental and chronological ages of the children were converted into grade scores, enabling comparisons among reading grade, mental grade, arithmetic grade, and chronological grade to be made.

A study of table 2 gives much useful information. The class is somewhat better than average. The average mental grade is 5.5 which is advanced for a typical beginning fifth-grade class. The class grade score in arithmetical computation is 5.5, which is average for a class of this general capability. The average reading grade of 5.4 is about the same as the men-

Table 2
Test Information About a Beginning Fifth-Grade Class

grade score	CHRONO- LOGICAL GRADE	MENTAL GRADE	GATES READING SURVEY				ARITH- METICAL COMPU- TATION
			power of compre- hension	*vocabu- lary*	*speed*	*average reading grade*	
Above 9.0					1		
8.5-8.9		1		1	0	1	1
8.0-8.4		2	1	2	1	1	2
7.5-7.9		2	3	1	2	2	3
7.0-7.4		3	2	2	2	1	2
6.5-6.9		2	3	2	3	3	3
6.0-6.4	1	4	2	3	2	4	3
5.5-5.9	10	4	4	5	4	3	4
5.0-5.4	18	5	5	5	5	6	6
4.5-4.9	6	3	4	4	4	4	4
4.0-4.4		4	5	4	5	5	3
3.5-3.9		3	3	2	3	3	2
3.0-3.4		1	1	3	1	1	1
Below 3.0		1	2	1	2	1	1
Median Scores*	5.3	5.5	5.3	5.5	5.4	5.4	5.5

Calculated from ungrouped data.

tal grade, indicating that this class is doing fairly well in reading. A further inspection shows that the class is rather uniform in its average reading attainments. The average power of comprehension is 5.3, average vocabulary 5.5, and average speed of reading 5.4. It seems from the above average performances of this class that there is no real reading problem here.

A further study of the class, however, reveals that there is a rather large problem of adjusting materials and methods to individual differences. There are thirteen children who are instructionally suited to a fifth-grade basic reader. There are ten children who are below 4.5 in reading ability and need to be taught with simpler material. There are twelve children who are reading at 6.0 or higher and need an expanded reading program.

Figure 3 shows the profiles of three members of this fifth-grade class. The general diagnosis shows that two of them should be considered disabled readers while one of them should not. The figure shows that Alice is a child of less than average mental ability. Her chronological grade of 6.2

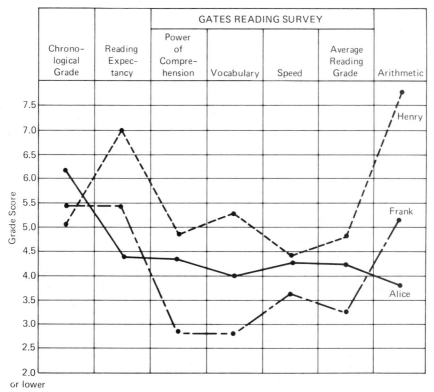

Fig. 3 *PROFILES OF THREE CHILDREN BEGINNING FIFTH GRADE*

shows that she is the oldest child in her class. She has been retarded one year in school. Her reading expectancy grade is one of the lowest in the class and her I.Q., which is 70, is the lowest. Yet Alice is doing a creditable job in learning to read. She is reading about a half-year lower than would be expected of a child with her mental ability who had been in school five years. Alice needs the type of instruction, described in chapter 12, suitable to a slow-learning child.

Frank is a disabled reader. He is more than two years behind in his reading development, compared to his reading expectancy. He is of average intelligence, so should be reading about 5.3, but is reading 3.0. He needs to be studied further in order to plan a remedial program to improve his reading ability; his relatively successful performance in arithmetic shows that he is able to achieve in areas other than reading.

Henry is a reading disability case, although he is reading only two months below his grade placement. He is one of the youngest members of the class, but he is the most capable intellectually. His reading expectancy grade, estimated from his 150 I.Q., indicates that he should be reading at seventh-grade level instead of 4.8, his average reading grade. His arithmetic grade is high (7.5) and more in keeping with his mental ability. Henry has a reading disability. A further diagnosis of Henry's reading disability is needed in order to plan his remedial program.

Analytical Diagnosis in Reading

The analytical diagnosis separates the reading act into some of its more specific skills and abilities. It enables the diagnostician to detect the areas of a child's difficulty. It will show whether the child's difficulty is in a specific type of comprehension, in word-recognition techniques, in reading efficiency, oral reading, or basic study skills. An analytical diagnosis also might indicate how well the child is able to adapt his reading abilities to meet the demands of the specific content fields. There are many tests which give the type of information needed for analytical diagnosis. Some of the more useful ones are listed in chapter 7.

Figure 4 shows the results of an analytical diagnosis of three members of the fifth-grade class. The general diagnosis, it will be remembered, revealed that Frank and Henry were disabled readers needing further diagnosis. Barbara has not shown such an overall deficiency, but an inspection of her relative scores on the analytical diagnosis in figure 4 on page 145 shows that she has a specific retardation. Barbara is, in general, a competent reader. Her profile shows that she is low in one type of reading—reading to follow directions—in which she is more than a year and a half lower than would be expected of a girl with her mental capability and general reading ability. This is not a serious matter, but it is probable that a short

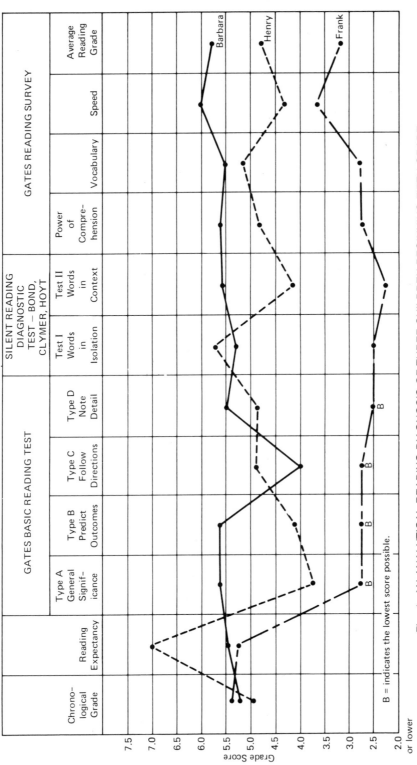

Fig. 4 AN ANALYTICAL READING DIAGNOSIS OF THREE CHILDREN BEGINNING FIFTH GRADE

period of emphasis on this type of reading would make Barbara as proficient in reading to follow directions as she is in other comprehension abilities. She needs no further diagnosis.

Figure 4 shows that Henry has a very uneven profile. Henry's analytical diagnosis shows that he is low in the more general types of reading comprehension. It also shows that he is considerably better at recognizing words in isolation than he is at recognizing words in context. He is a very slow reader. It is reasonable to suspect that Henry is an overanalytical reader, and that he fails to use the more rapid word-recognition techniques. The precise nature of instruction he needs will have to be determined by further study in a diagnostic case study.

Frank is seen to be low in all types of reading in figure 4 and must be studied further. This analytical diagnosis shows him to be a reading disability case and that only the speed of reading score (though still low) even approaches what could be expected of him. An inspection of his performance on the speed test shows a high degree of inaccuracy. Even the speed test cannot be considered good performance because to obtain speed without accuracy is a questionable asset. It is apparent, on the basis of the analytical diagnosis, that Frank has something basically wrong with his reading. The difficulty appears to be in the word-recognition area, but even this suspicion awaits case-study diagnosis before it will be verified.

Case-Study Diagnosis in Reading

Standardized tests for general and analytical diagnosis, individual standardized tests, detailed silent reading diagnostic tests, and informal study of a child's approaches to the various aspects of reading are used in a thorough case-study diagnosis. This diagnosis also includes an analysis of the child's strengths and limitations as an individual—his sensory capacities, emotional reactions, and attitudes toward reading. A case-study diagnosis also should study the child's general school environment, the methods of instruction used in his school, and home conditions that might be specifically related to reading and that might influence his reading growth. The last kind of appraisal should find out how the parents feel about their child's reading problem, and how much they will cooperate in overcoming the difficulty. A case-study diagnosis must give answers to the specific questions concerning the disabled reader that have been discussed in this chapter.

The first question, *whether the child is correctly classified as a disabled reader,* is answered frequently by the general diagnosis. In some cases, the case-study approach will indicate that a child's major problem is not disability in reading. The detailed case studies of Henry and Frank did not reveal any condition which would lead to a classification other than reading disability. The general diagnosis showed, on the other hand, that Alice's problem was one of low mentality and that she could not be classified as a disabled reader.

The second question, dealing with the problem of *who can give the remedial instruction most effectively,* sometimes can be answered in the general diagnosis and other times in the analytical, but frequently must await the completed case study. The general diagnosis showed that Alice's problem could be remedied more adequately by an adjusted program and realistic expectations. Certainly her basic problem was not reading disability nor could it be expected that she would be helped by remedial training in reading.

The analytical diagnosis showed that Barbara was weak in just one type of reading. She had a specific retardation in reading which could be handled adequately by the typical classroom teacher.

As a result of a thorough case study, it was judged that Henry would profit from remedial reading in a group at the school reading center; while Frank's problem was so complex and charged with emotional rejection of reading that it was felt that he would need to get his remedial work at a reading clinic.

The third question, dealing with *the nature of the training needed,* was answered, for Alice, in the general diagnosis. She needed training in reading suitable to a slow-learning child. The training needed for Barbara was decided by the analytical diagnosis, which showed that Barbara needed training in following exact directions. The case-study diagnosis showed that Henry was, indeed, an overanalytical reader. He had a high score in knowledge of phonetic elements, and he attempted to use this means of word recognition even with words that he could recognize at sight when they were flashed before him with a speed that allowed him only a glance at the word. He also demonstrated a tendency to pay marked attention to word endings and to neglect somewhat the beginning elements of words. In addition, he was very poor at making adequate use of context clues. Henry has a marked limiting disability in word recognition. The remedial work that Henry needs will be described in a later chapter dealing with word identification and recognition.

The training needed by Frank also was indicated by the case-study diagnosis. Frank's problem is complex. He has failed to develop a systematic attack on words. He is a marked reversal case and had emotionally rejected reading. In addition, there was evidence that Frank had a visual handicap which should be corrected before remedial work was undertaken. The necessary remedial work is one of the types discussed in chapter 11, dealing with left-to-right orientation in reading and word perception, and in chapter 12 on the especially handicapped child. He also needed more work on word recognition as described in chapters 9 and 10.

The fourth question that must be answered by the diagnosis deals with *how improvement can be brought about most effectively.* This question could have been answered for Alice in the general diagnosis and for Barbara in the analytical diagnosis. Alice should be given material at approximately the middle of the third-grade level. She needs encouragement, success, and many opportunities to use the results of her reading in constructive activities, such as building models or helping make displays and things of that sort. She needs concrete illustrations of what she is reading. Alice should read for only one, well-defined purpose at a time because she has low intelligence and finds it difficult to attend to several purposes at the same time.

For general purposes, Barbara should read material at 5.5 level of difficulty. But in the exercises designed to increase her ability to follow exact directions, her remedial instruction should be started with material somewhat less difficult. The purposes for which Barbara reads this material should be to emphasize reading to organize, to get the sense of a sequence of ideas, and to follow exact directions. Special exercises such as the *Gates-Peardon Practice Exercises, Type C* might be good material with which to start Barbara's corrective instruction. It would be desirable to keep a chart indicating her speed and accuracy in doing these exercises. As she increases in accuracy, she can be encouraged to read somewhat more rapidly and the difficulty of the material can be increased. Barbara can be expected to develop readily the ability to organize and to follow exact directions.

Complete case-study diagnoses were necessary to find out how improvement could be brought about most efficiently in the cases of Henry and Frank. Henry should have a time chart indicating the speed at which he reads during exercises designed to increase his speed. He should be given remedial instruction in material about half-way through the fourth grade in difficulty. Henry should have a lot of recreational reading. He should be given exercises designed to encourage the use of context clues, exercises approximately fourth-grade in level of difficulty.

Frank's problem is much more difficult. He will need to read material at approximately the second-grade level of difficulty. It would be desirable to use material that is as mature in format as possible—workbook material might be used. The remedial teacher must be optimistic and demonstrate to Frank that he actually is growing in his reading capability. He should make a picture dictionary in which he can see that the number of words he recognizes is increasing. He could dictate some stories of his own and if his tendency to reverse words persists, it may be necessary to use sound tracing methods, described in a later chapter.

The fifth question is concerned with *limiting conditions within a child* that must be considered in formulating his remedial program. From a thorough case-study diagnosis, it became clear that Henry had no limiting characteristics to which the program needed to adjust or for which there had to be a correction made before remedial instruction. Frank was found to have two limiting conditions. The first was his emotional rejection of reading. This must be taken into consideration in formulating his remedial program, but it was not felt serious enough to warrant treatment by a specialist. The fact that Frank's arithmetic score was nearly equal to his reading expectancy indicated that in situations not involving reading Frank was able to apply himself reasonably well. Frank's second limitation was his eyesight. There was some indication that Frank was farsighted, and that he found it difficult to focus on the printed page at reading distance. A thorough visual examination was recommended before Frank was to undertake remedial instruction.

The sixth question deals with *environmental conditions that might interfere* with the progress of remedial work. It was found that for three of the children, Henry, Frank, and Alice, the school would have to make some adjustments to their needs. For Alice, the adjustments would be those expected in general adjustment to individual differences in any class. It was found, for example, that in science and social studies, the same textbooks were used by all the children in the class. Alice could not be expected to use this material. A thorough study of Alice's placement will need to be made, but from the information available, a further diagnosis of her reading is not indicated.

Henry, who had been in the middle reading group, should be kept there. But it was found that he could not read profitably some of the material of the content fields. Somewhat less mature reference material should be made available for him.

The school adjustments necessary for Frank are more complicated. Frank should not attempt to read the materials in the content fields, but should use this reading time to read materials at his level of advancement. He may listen to the discussions in the classroom and participate in the creative activities.

There were no indications of unfortunate circumstances in any of the homes of these children, with the possible exception of Frank. Frank's parents were very concerned about his poor reading ability. They had attempted to teach him to read using a strictly phonetic approach, recommended in a series of articles in their local newspaper. After about a month of instruction, they wisely judged that Frank not only was getting worse in reading, but that he was becoming highly disturbed by their instruction and by his own seemingly inadequate response. Frank's parents were eager to cooperate with the school and the reading clinic. They agreed to set aside a place for Frank to keep his reading materials, and they welcomed the suggestion to discuss with Frank the stories he read and to help him by pronouncing words he found difficult.

Each of the cases from this fifth-grade class was different. Some of the children needed no further study beyond the general and analytical diagnoses. Two of the boys needed detailed case-study diagnoses, which were made at a reading clinic. It was necessry for the diagnostician to have consultations with both the classroom teacher and the parents of the two boys.

In making the case-study diagnoses of the reading disability cases, both standardized and informal procedures were used, and in one case, the services of an outside expert were needed. The reading diagnostic tests most useful in case-study diagnosis will be described in detail in the next chapter.

SUMMARY

The correction of reading disability is complicated by the intricate nature of the reading process and by the many differences in children and their environments influencing reading growth. It is little wonder that no two cases of reading disability confront the teacher or diagnostician with exactly the same problem. It is apparent that any remedial instruction must be based on an adequate diagnosis. The more complex and the more subtle cases of reading disability often require more detailed and more penetrating study than the classroom teacher has the time or training to give. Sometimes the services of a clinical diagnostician may be required. In such instances, it is sometimes necessary to enlist the services of other specialists as well, such as social case workers, psychologists, physicians, or psychiatrists.

The diagnosis of a disabled reader must be directed toward improvement of instruction. Therefore, the therapeutic type of diagnosis is better than the etiological, i.e., the one that seeks causes only. The diagnosis is more than an appraisal of reading skills and abilities. It also must assess the mental, physical, sensory, emotional, and environmental factors that could impede progress.

The diagnosis must be efficient and should proceed only as far as necessary to formulate a remedial program. Some children's instructional needs can be found through general diagnosis, others will need a more thorough study by analytical means, and still others may need a complete clinical case study of their reading disability. Since diagnosis of reading disability is detailed and time-consuming, only pertinent information should be collected and by the most efficient means available.

Standardized measurements are essential to reliable diagnosis of reading disability. Even the results of standardized tests must be interpreted with care, because the disabled reader has an atypical and subtle problem. It often is necessary to resort to informal procedures for information not obtainable from standardized measurements.

The remedial program is planned by first taking into account the numerical data and then modifying it in accordance with whatever other information is obtained. The diagnostician should treat the data objectively so that the case can be judged accurately. After a reasonable period, if the remedial work proves unsuccessful, a reevaluation should be made to find the correct diagnosis. Even in successful cases, diagnosis should be continuous because reading disability is one aspect of a dynamic process which alters during remedial instruction, and the remedial program must be changed to meet the new needs of the disabled reader.

A diagnostician must make recommendations in six areas.

1. He must find out whether the child is correctly classified as a disabled reader or if some other problem of child growth and development is the basic difficulty.

2. He must recommend where the remedial work can be given most effectively. Should the child be reeducated in the classroom, school reading center, or clinic? The answer to this question lies in the nature of the case. Most simple retardation and specific retardation cases should be given remedial training in the classroom or school reading center. Children with limiting disability should be corrected at the school reading center or clinic, while complex disability, for the most part, should be corrected at a clinic.

3. The nature of the training needed must be discovered. Identification of the particular character of the reading limitation is the most important part of the reading diagnosis. The reading pattern of the child must be studied to pinpoint the specific faulty learning impeding his reading progress. This requires a thorough appraisal of the skills and abilities involved in reading.

4. The most efficient methods for improving the child's reading should be recommended. These include levels and types of material to be used, ways of demonstrating progress in reading to the child, and plans for extending the reading instruction with exercises or assignments that can be done independently.

5. The diagnostician must locate any condition within the child that might be detrimental to reading growth. He should utilize other expert help whenever it is needed for diagnosis and correction. He should recommend needed modifications in the remedial program to adjust to any limitations.

6. He must evaluate the child's entire learning environment in order to find any conditions that might interfere with progress in reading. He should recommend how the parents and the school can contribute to the solution of the child's reading problem.

SELECTED READINGS

DURRELL, DONALD D., *Improving Reading Instruction,* chaps. 5, 16. New York: Harcourt, Brace and Jovanovich, 1956.

HARRIS, ALBERT J. AND E. R. SIPAY, *How to Increase Reading Ability* (6th ed.), chaps. 8, 9. New York: David McKay, 1975.

MYKLEBUST, HELMER R., ed., *Progress in Learning Disabilities.* Vol. 1. New York: Grune and Stratton, 1968.

OTTO, W., R. A. McMENEMY, AND R. J. SMITH, *Corrective and Remedial Teaching Principles and practices* (2nd ed.) chaps. 3–5. Boston: Houghton Mifflin, 1973.

Specific Approaches to Diagnosis

seven

The preceding chapter discussed six questions that should be answered in any diagnosis of reading disability. In addition, an illustrative analysis was given to show how the sequence of general, analytical, and case-study levels of diagnosis helped to answer each question. The question that is the major responsibility of the reading specialist is the one concerned with the nature of the specific types of training needed to correct reading disabilities. The following classification of the more prevalent reading difficulties includes the types of defects that must be found if a diagnosis is to indicate clearly the precise kinds of instruction needed:

CLASSIFICATION OF READING DIFFICULTIES

A. Faulty word identification and recognition.
1. Failure to use context and other meaning clues.
2. Ineffective visual analysis of words.
3. Limited knowledge of visual, structural, and phonic elements.
4. Lack of ability in auditory blending or visual synthesis.
5. Overanalytical.
   a. Analyzing known words.
   b. Breaking words into too many parts.
   c. Using a letter-by-letter or spelling attack.
6. Insufficient sight vocabulary.

       7. Excessive locational errors.
         a. Initial errors.
         b. Middle errors.
         c. Ending errors.

B.   Inappropriate directional habits.
     1. Orientational confusions with words.
     2. Transpositions among words.
     3. Faulty eye movements.

C.   Deficiencies in basic comprehension abilities.
     1. Limited meaning vocabulary.
     2. Inability to read by thought units.
     3. Insufficient sentence sense.
     4. Lack of paragraph organization sense.
     5. Failure to appreciate author's organization.

D.   Limited in special comprehension abilities.
     1. Inability to isolate and retain factual information.
     2. Poor reading to organize.
     3. Ineffective reading to evaluate.
     4. Insufficient ability in reading to interpret.
     5. Limited proficiency in reading to appreciate.

E.   Deficiencies in basic study skills.
     1. Inability to use aids in locating materials to be read.
     2. Lack of efficiency in using basic reference material.
     3. Inadequacies in using maps, graphs, tables, and other visual materials.
     4. Limitations in techniques of organizing material read.

F.   Deficient in ability to adapt to reading needs of content fields.
     1. Inappropriate application of comprehension abilities.
     2. Limited knowledge of specialized vocabulary.
     3. Insufficient concept development.
     4. Poor knowledge of symbols and abbreviations.
     5. Insufficient ability in using pictorial and tabular material.
     6. Difficulties with organization.
     7. Inability to adjust rate to suit purposes and difficulty of material.

    G. Deficiencies in rate of comprehension.
1. Inability to adjust rate.
2. Insufficient sight vocabulary.
3. Insufficient vocabulary knowledge and comprehension.
4. Ineffectiveness in word recognition.
5. Overanalytical reading.
6. Insufficient use of context clues.
7. Lack of phrasing.
8. Using crutches.
9. Unnecessary vocalization.
10. Inappropriate purposes.

    H. Poor oral reading.
1. Inappropriate eye-voice span.
2. Lack of phrasing ability.
3. Unfortunate rate and timing.
4. Emotionally tense oral reader.

These defects in reading patterns that must be appraised in a thorough diagnosis show that reading disability is not a simple condition that can be corrected by a single approach. Information on a child's strengths and weaknesses in these areas is obtained from a variety of evaluative techniques. A competent diagnostician uses both standardized and informal procedures in studying the nature of reading deficiencies so that appropriate remedial programs can be designed. Detailed procedures for overcoming each of these specific deficiencies will be discussed further, beginning with chapter 8.

The whole field of testing and evaluation procedures is used by the reading specialist in appraising the needs of the disabled reader. The diagnosis usually starts with giving achievement tests, a reading survey test, and an individual mental test. It may continue until the diagnostician has measured such details as how many independent letters are unknown to the child or which of the important digraphs he does not know. A study of the possible limitations should go as far as necessary to formulate the nature of reading instruction needed.

In this chapter the specific approaches to diagnosis will emphasize the case-study level of diagnosis as conducted by the reading specialist. Preceding chapters have indicated the role of the general and analytical levels of diagnosis as used by the classroom teacher. The tests used at these two levels are group tests that can be administered by the teacher. The results of such testing also are necessary for and important to the diagnostician as well. The reading specialist must collect and study all pertinent information obtainable in order to arrive at a valid diagnosis of a disabled reader's total reading problem.

TESTS USED IN GENERAL DIAGNOSIS

A general diagnosis must include a *general achievement test* which measures the relative strengths and weaknesses of pupils in the various areas of the curriculum. They usually are given periodically throughout the school. A second type of test used for general diagnosis is a *reading survey test.* These tests are used to obtain a valid estimate of the pupils' *average reading grade* and to determine their relative strengths and weaknesses in such attributes as power of comprehension, word recognition, and rate and accuracy of reading. The teacher can use these results to aid her in adjusting to individual differences within her classroom, and to help find the areas of reading that need corrective treatment.

General Achievment Tests

A profile of the disabled reader's relative proficiencies in the curriculum's major fields, as measured by general achievement tests, enables the reading specialist to isolate the content areas in which a student may have trouble adapting his reading to the specific content fields. When this trouble is found, the diagnostician then uses evaluation techniques to pinpoint the exact nature of the problem. She also would inspect the profile to see if the disabled reader were significantly higher in nonreading subjects than in the reading section of the tests. If so, it could be assumed that reading might be a basic problem. A marked variation in the profile might suggest that the student was deficient in a certain specific comprehension ability or in the basic study skills. All of these irregularities would indicate that a further extension of reading diagnosis is needed. A few typical examples of *General Achievement Tests* useful in general diagnosis are listed below. The list is not complete. For examples and evaluations, see Buros (35).

California Achievement Tests: 1.5–2.5, 2.5–4.5, 4–6, 6–9, 9–12: Reading (vocabulary, comprehension, total); Mathematics (computation, concepts and problems, total); Language (mechanics, usage and structure, total); Spelling; Total.

Iowa Tests of Basic Skills: 3–9: Vocabulary, Reading Comprehension, Language (spelling, capitalization, punctuation, usage, total); Word-Study Skills (map reading, reading graphs and tables, knowledge and use of reference materials, total); Mathematics Skills (mathematics concepts, mathematics problem solving, total); Total.

Metropolitan Achievement Tests: 5.0–6.9, 7.0–9.5: Reading (word knowledge, reading, total); Language; Spelling; Mathematics (computation, concepts, problem solving, total); Science; Social Studies.

Stanford Achievement Test: 3.5–4.4, 4.5–5.4: Reading Comprehension, Word-Study Skills, Total; Mathematics (concepts, computation, applications, total); Spelling, Language, Social Science, Auditory (vocabulary, listening comprehension, total); Total.

Reading Survey Tests

One measure basic to any reading diagnosis is the *average reading grade score.* This score is obtained by averaging the grade scores of the subtests of a reading survey test. The subtests usually include *power of comprehension, word recognition,* and *speed of reading.* This average grade score is used to determine whether a poor reader is actually a disabled reader. It is compared with the *reading expectancy score,* discussed in chapter 3.

The average reading grade score has an even more important role to play in the entire study of specific patterns of scores of reading skills and abilities of disabled readers. The average reading grade score is used as the basis for judging the significance of each reading item of diagnostic information. For example, if the grade score on a test of sight vocabulary is significantly lower than the average reading grade score, it indicates that remediation should focus upon enlarging the child's sight vocabulary. If sight vocabulary is found to be significantly higher than the average reading score, it indicates that the child depends too much on sight vocabulary at the expense of other word-recognition skills, such as meaning clues or phonics skills.

The reading survey test has a third role in reading diagnosis. Such tests themselves are analytical to some extent. This is because the complex nature of reading growth and development requires that no single type of test be used as the sole criterion of a child's reading stature. Each subtest of a survey test is in itself a measure of an important reading outcome. The score of each subtest can be compared with the average reading score to see if a child is weak in power of comprehension, word recognition, speed, or accuracy. If a given score were significantly lower than the average reading score, the area of reading needing further study would be isolated.

The tests listed below are samples suitable as reading survey tests for general diagnosis. They also have some analytical value.* For more examples and evaluations of them, see Buros (34).

* See Appendix V for representative reading and study skill tests.

American School Achievement Tests: Part 1, Reading: 2-3, 4-6, 7-9: sentence and word meaning, paragraph meaning, and total.

Davis Reading Test: 8-11, 11-13: level of comprehension and speed of comprehension.

Gates-MacGinitie Reading Tests, Survey: 4-6, 7-9, 10-12: speed and accuracy, vocabulary, and comprehension.

The Nelson Reading Test, Revised Edition: 3-9: vocabulary, paragraph comprehension, and total.

TESTS USED IN ANALYTICAL DIAGNOSIS

Analytical diagnosis explores systematically specific areas of reading weakness. This level of diagnosis identifies such problem areas as those listed as major headings under *Classification of Reading Difficulties* presented at the beginning of this chapter. Analytical diagnosis, for example, will indicate that a disabled reader's problem is a deficiency in the area of basic comprehension abilities, but it will not isolate the exact limitations involved and in need of remediation. An analytical diagnosis may indicate the instruction needed for the first two types of reading cases, i.e., simple retardation and specific retardation. The tests used in analytical diagnosis do not go into enough detail to plan remedial instruction for those cases classified as a limiting disability or a complex disability.

Many standardized group tests are available that can make a systematic analysis of the various areas of reading growth. Some reading problems can be identified clearly enough to enable the diagnostician or the classroom teacher to develop an individual remedial plan to overcome the specific retardation. Other problems indicated by the analytical diagnosis will need further study using case-study techniques, before a suitable remedial plan can be formulated.

If the diagnosis requires a case-study approach, the diagnostician will need to include all of the information acquired in the general and analytical levels of diagnosis, and any other data she requires to complete the case study. The reading specialist making the case study especially will need the average reading grade score for comparison with the grade scores of the various subheads listed in the classification of reading difficulties. She also will need the chronological grade of the disabled reader and his mental grade. These latter grade scores are necessary to compare with the individual characteristics that are related to physical growth and those that are related to mental growth.

A few examples of group tests for analytical diagnosis are listed below. The list is not complete.* for more examples and critical evaluations, see Buros (34).

Gates Basic Reading Tests, 3–8: appreciate general significance; predict outcomes; understand directions; note detail.

Iowa Test B—Basic Study Skills—Elementary Battery, 3–5: reading maps; use of references; use of index; use of dictionary; alphabetizing.

Iowa Test B—Basic Study Skills—Advanced Battery, 5–9; reading maps; use of references; use of index; use of dictionary; reading graphs, charts, tables.

New Developmental Reading Tests: Primary Reading: vocabulary; general comprehension; specific comprehension.

New Developmental Reading Tests: Intermediate Grades, 4, 5, 6: basic reading vocabulary; reading for information; reading for relationships; reading for appreciation; literal comprehension; creative comprehension; general comprehension.

†*Silent-Reading Diagnostic Tests:* For disabled readers of any age with average reading grades from 2.0–7.5: words in isolation; words in context; visual-structural analysis; syllabication; word synthesis; beginning sounds; ending sounds; vowel and consonant sounds; words omitted; errors; initial errors; middle errors; ending errors; orientation errors.

†*Stanford Diagnostic Reading Tests:*
Red level, 1, 2: phonics skills; auditory vocabulary; word recognition; sentence comprehension; paragraph comprehension.
Green level, 3, 4: auditory discrimination; phonetic and structural analysis; auditory vocabulary; literal and inferential comprehension.
Brown level, 5–8: phonetic and structural analysis; auditory vocabulary; literal and inferential comprehension; reading rate.
Blue level, 9–12, and Community College: phonetic and structural analysis; reading vocabulary; literal and inferential comprehension; reading rate; scanning and skimming.

REPRESENTATIVE INDIVIDUAL CASE-STUDY TESTS

The group tests used in the general and analytical levels of diagnosis form the basis of the case study. For some disabled readers, these tests give the diagnostician sufficient information to develop an *appropriate individual plan*

---

* See Appendix V for representative reading and study skill tests.
† These tests are group tests frequently used in case studies of elementary and high school students with limiting and complex disabilities.

of remediation, and a case study is not needed. For the disabled readers who have not yet been diagnosed adequately, a study of their test results usually will indicate the areas of reading limitation that should be explored further during the case study. The techniques used in a case study are confined mostly to individual testing procedures that require special training and some supervised clinical experience for valid results.

The techniques of individual diagnosis described here are representative but by no means inclusive of all the programs described in the literature.* The reader should bear in mind that each of these techniques (and others not described) has had successful use in the field. Some of the strong points of each will be noted.

The descriptions in this chapter are designed to give the reader merely a general impression of the main characteristics of the diagnostic tests together with examining procedures and uses. Actual use of any diagnostic test will be based upon the detailed directions accompanying the test.

A. DURRELL ANALYSIS OF READING DIFFICULTY

The Durrell procedure for discovering cases of disability and the diagnosis upon which remedial programs are to be based is outlined in three steps:

1. Discrepancies between mental ability and reading achievement are determined. The *Revised Stanford-Binet Scale* and an appropriate reading test may be used for this. For children in grades three to six, Durrell suggests the *Durrell-Sullivan Reading Capacity Test* and the *Durrell-Sullivan Reading Achievement Test,* which are standardized on the same population. The *Reading Capacity Test* is entirely nonverbal in the sense that no reading is required. This is actually a listening comprehension test. It measures the child's understanding of spoken language both for word meanings and paragraph comprehension. The scores are combined to give grade or age level for hearing comprehension. This is compared with level of achievement on the *Reading Achievement Test* to discover discrepancies indicating reading disability.

2. The next step is a thorough physical examination of those children with a serious discrepancy between their mental ability and their reading achievement. In this examination, special attention is given to hearing and sight as well as to any physical condition which may result in chronic fatigue.

---

* See Appendix V for representative reading and study skill tests (also see Buros [34] for a critical evaluation of these tests).

3. The third step consists of a detailed analysis of reading difficulties by means of the *Durrell Analysis of Reading Difficulty,* revised edition. This consists of a series of individual tests in oral and silent reading, word perception, visual memory of word forms, auditory analysis of word elements, plus systematic observing and recording of certain responses and forms of behavior which will be described below.

Tests and Procedures (Durrell)

Oral Reading is the first test in the Analysis series. Eight paragraphs of reading material are printed on cardboard and assembled in a booklet. The child is started with a paragraph on which it is quite certain he will make no error—a "basal paragraph." The reading continues in succeeding paragraphs until seven or more errors are made on a single paragraph, or until the time required for reading any parapraph is more than two minutes (upper level). A detailed record is made of all errors such as omitted words, words inserted, mispronunciation, words not known, and so on. All behavior symptomatic of reading difficulties is noted on the check-list in the record blank. A list of comprehension questions is asked at the end of each paragraph. Grade norms, based on the time required for reading, are provided. High, middle, and low positions within each grade are given. If two or more comprehension questions are failed, the child is rated low on that paragraph.

Silent Reading is the second test. A different set of paragraphs are used. They are graded in difficulty and printed on cards in a booklet, as in Test 1. The child reads paragraphs of the same difficulty as he did in the first test. As each paragraph is completed, the child is asked to tell everything he can remember in the story. The material in the examiner's copy is arranged to facilitate recording the ideas recalled. Any relevant reading difficulties are checked on the list accompanying this test. Grade norms based upon time and memory scores are provided.

Listening Comprehension comprises Test 3. Paragraphs of the same levels of difficulty as those in preceding tests are used. Each paragraph is read aloud by the examiner and a set of questions is asked the child. The listening comprehension is ascertained from the level where not more than one question is missed.

The *Word Recognition and Word Analysis Test* comes next. For this test, lists of words are printed on strips of cardboard for presenting in a cardboard tachistoscope (short exposure) device. Separate lists of words are employed for grade one and for grades two to six. One of these lists of words suitable to the child's reading ability, is presented in the tachistoscope so that the words appear one at a time for one-half second each. Both correct and incorrect pronunciation are checked appropriately. When a child fails to grasp a word in this flash test, the shutter of the tachistoscope is opened so that the child can study and try to work out the pronunciation of the word. This provides a test of word-analysis skills. Correct and incorrect responses during this analysis are recorded. Difficulties in word analysis and word recognition are noted on the accompanying check-list. Successively more difficult lists of words are presented until the child fails on seven successive words of a single list or the hardest list in the series is completed. There are grade norms both for word recognition (flash presentation) and for word analysis.

The next series of tests is comprised of *Naming Letters, Identifying Letters Named, Matching Letters,* and *Writing Letters.* These tests are designed for the severely retarded reader or for any child when it is suspected that he does not know the names of the letters.

The test for *Visual Memory of Words—Primary* is to be used with children whose reading grade is three or below. *Visual Memory of Words—Intermediate* is for children with reading grades four to six. The child is shown a letter or word in the tachistoscope for two to three seconds. When this is covered, he turns to the record booklet and marks from memory the item shown.

A series of tests deals with the auditory analysis of word elements: *Hearing Sounds in Words—Primary* tests ability to identify beginning sounds, ending sounds, and both beginning and ending sounds in words. A child who fails the preceding test should be given the test on *Learning to Hear Sounds in Words.* This will provide information on the severity of his difficulty in perceiving sounds in words. To discover which letter sounds and blends are not known, the test for *Sounds of Letters* is given to children with less than second-grade reading ability.

The *Learning Rate* test is given to severely retarded readers to discover the degree of difficulty a child has in remembering words taught.

Additional tests are *Phonic Spelling of Words,* a *Spelling Test,* and a *Handwriting Test.*

A form is provided for a detailed analysis of faulty pronunciation or spelling. This will provide information on vowel errors, consonant errors, reversals, addition of sounds, omission of sounds, and substitution of words.

Standardized tests are not available for gathering information on certain reading habits and skills, for this can be done just as well informally. Durrell suggests informal tests for the following: (*a*) reading interest and effort, (*b*) suitability of the level of reading materials used in the classroom, (*c*) speed of reading, (*d*) word skills, and (*e*) speed and accuracy in locating information.

Advantages of the Durrell Program

The *Durrell Analysis of Reading Difficulty* has certain distinct advantages: (*a*) Directions for administering the tests are complete and clear. (*b*) The type of case for which each test is needed is indicated. (*c*) The series of tests requires a reasonable amount of time to administer. (*d*) As emphasized by Durrell in the Manual of Directions, "The check-lists of errors are more important than the norms." This check-list is probably the most detailed and complete of its kind. Appropriate use of these check-lists, which accompany the diagnostic tests, will provide sufficient information for diagnosing reading difficulties in a majority of cases.

B. THE GATES-McKILLOP READING DIAGNOSTIC TESTS

The Gates-McKillop program for analysis of reading difficulties is described in the 1962 revision of *Gates-McKillop Reading Diagnostic Tests*. This program of diagnosis, in its third edition, is based largely upon about forty years' experience of Gates at Teachers College, Columbia University.

In the Gates-McKillop procedure, the formal identification of reading disability requires that we measure mental age and silent reading ability, and know the child's actual grade placement. Mental age as determined by the Stanford-Binet test is considered to provide the best criterion of a child's verbal ability with which to compare his reading, although some other good, individual test, such as the *Wechsler Intelligence Scale for Children —Revised,* may be used. Then, one or more standardized silent reading tests appropriate to the child's reading level are given. The mental age and silent reading scores are converted to grade scores. Finally, to determine whether or not a child should be able to keep up with his class, his average silent reading grade is compared with his grade location.

Ordinarily the more important comparison is between average silent-reading grade and mental grade. This comparison will reveal the degree of reading retardation in relation to the child's intelligence level or learning ability. Comparison of reading grade either with actual grade placement or with mental grade is made by reference to a table which indicates ratings that are respectively average (or at grade), low, or very low. The degree of retardation that is given a rating of low or very low varies with grade level. For example, at grade 3.0 a child reading between grades 1.7 and 2.2 is rated low; and at 1.6 (or below), very low. But at grade six, a reading grade of between 3.9 and 4.5 is rated low; and of 3.8, very low. A child whose average silent reading is either low or very low in comparison with his mental grade is considered a reading disability case. To discover the specific kinds of difficulties involved in a case of reading disability, we resort to the detailed diagnostic tests. It will not be necessary, however, to give all the diagnostic tests to all reading cases. The skilled examiner will be able to select those tests essential to secure the diagnostic information he needs as a basis for determining the proper remedial instruction for a particular child.

Tests and Procedures (Gates and McKillop)

The diagnostic tests will be described briefly in the order in which they are listed in the test materials. Note will be made of only one form since the two forms are equivalent.

ORAL READING TEST. This test is composed of seven paragraphs of increasing difficulty. The child begins with the first paragraph and continues until he makes eleven or more errors in each of two consecutive paragraphs. The child's errors are recorded for each paragraph. Grade scores range from 1.6 to 7.5. Also, information on the child's behavior while the reading is going on should be recorded using the check-list or notes. These data supplement the error analysis in an important way. An outline form is given for the scoring summary and another for analysis of errors. Analysis of the errors plus reference to the appropriate tables will indicate whether the child is making excessive errors in each of the following categories: words omitted, words added, repetitions, mispronouciations, full reversals, reversals of parts, total of all reversals, wrong beginnings, wrong middles, wrong endings, wrong several parts. Observation of performance during the reading yields such information as degree of skill in the use of various word-recognition techniques and clues, signs of nervous tension, ability to phrase, and enunciation habits.

WORDS—FLASH PRESENTATION. The test consists of four columns of ten words each. The first twenty words (two columns) progress from short, easy words to longer, more difficult ones; for example, from *so* to *superstition.* The second twenty words are arranged similarly. All forty words are used. Starting with the easy words, the examiner exposes each word through a rectangular window in a card (tachistoscope) for one-half second. The first two columns of words are used and then the other two columns. This flash presentation test is employed to determine how well a child can recognize at a single glance words increasing in difficulty. The number of correct responses is converted to a grade score for comparison with other results, such as mental grade and average reading grade.

Words—untimed presentation. The material of the test consists of four columns of words, each column arranged from easy to difficult. The test may be shortened by using either two or three columns. The words are read horizontally, i.e., the first word of each column, the second word of each column, and so on. This test determines the child's ability to unlock each isolated word, one after another. Plenty of time is allowed for each word. The child is encouraged to employ whatever techniques of analysis he possesses, but he is not to be helped in his analysis. The test is continued until ten consecutive words have been missed. Every mispronunciation is written in the blank. From observation of the child's behavior and from analysis of his errors, the accompanying check-list of difficulties is filled in. The total score for the test is converted into a grade score for comparison with other results. For instance, a comparison with silent or oral reading grade will provide an estimate of how well the child uses context clues in reading. These clues are, of course, present in silent and oral reading but not in the perception of isolated words. An appreciably higher score either in silent or oral reading than in either the timed or untimed word perception would suggest that the child makes very good use of context clues when they are available. The principal contribution this test makes is to provide an opportunity to observe the techniques a child uses to work out the recognition and pronunciation of words.

Phrases—flash presentation. The materials consist of twenty-six phrases of two to four words each. Starting with short phrases, the examiner exposes each through the window in his tachistoscope card for one-half second. All phrases in the first column are presented before those in the second column. The recording is the same as for flash presentation of words. The total score, converted into a grade score, may be compared with silent reading scores or other test scores available.

Recognizing and blending common word parts. This and the following three tests deal with knowledge of word parts and word attack. The tests consists of twenty-three "words" such as "spack" listed in the left column. The child reads down the column, pronouncing each "word." If he fails a word, columns 2, 3, 4 are uncovered so that the line appears:

spack / sp / ack / spack

The child then tries to sound the initial consonant blend, the rest of the "word," and then to blend the parts to read the "word" in column 4. The pupil's performance on this test will determine whether the next three tests should be given. It is suggested his performance be compared with what he does on certain other tests.

NAMING CAPITAL LETTERS AND NAMING LOWERCASE LETTERS. Results are compared with those on certain other tests.

The next four tests require recognizing the visual forms of sounds.

NONSENSE WORDS. In this test the material consists of twenty lines of four words each. The child listens while the examiner says one of the words in each line. The pupil circles the word pronounced. A second trial is given to allow the pupil to check his response. This test supplies valuable information concerning the child's ability to associate sounds he hears with letter combinations he sees.

INITIAL LETTERS. The examiner pronounces a series of nineteen words while the child listens carefully to the sound at the beginning of the word and then circles the letter in the booklet that represents the sound. A second trial is given for each word to allow the child to check his response.

FINAL LETTERS. The pupil listens for the sound at the end of each of fourteen words spoken by the examiner. For each word, the child circles in a row of five letters the letter that comes at the end of the pronounced word. A second trial is given for the child to check his response.

VOWELS. The five vowels are named for the child as they are pointed out in the test material. Then the examiner pronounces the ten words of the list while the child tries to identify the vowel in the middle of each word and points to it in the list of vowels. A check trial is given.

AUDITORY BLENDING. The examiner pronounces by parts (i.e., he sounds) each of fifteen words. There is a brief pause of about one quarter of a second between the parts of a word. The child then tells what the whole word is.

SPELLING. The material consists of two columns of twenty words each. In each column, the words increase in length and difficulty, e.g., from *is* to *philosopher.* The examiner pronounces each word for the child and asks him to spell it aloud. A check-list is given to facilitate recordings of kinds of errors and methods of spelling.

ORAL VOCABULARY. This test of thirty multiple-choice items ranging from easy to difficult may be used when a pupil's score on the vocabulary test in the Stanford-Binet test is not available. It is especially designed for pupils in grade four and above. This test is not very reliable when applied to pupils of average and lower ability in the first three grades.

SYLLABICATION. The material consists of twenty "words," each of two or more syllables. These sound somewhat like real words although they are not, e.g., "foter" and "bashola." It is a test of ability to combine syllables into words, not just to identify the syllables.

AUDITORY DISCRIMINATION. The material consists of fourteen pairs of words. In some pairs the two words are the same; in others they are different. The examiner pronounces the two words of a pair while the child, sitting with his back to the examiner, listens. The child decides whether the two words spoken are the same or different. Each pair of words is pronounced once only.

GENERAL STATEMENT. Gates and McKillop state which tests may be omitted if previous responses have been adequate. Along with the directions for scoring, suggestions for interpreting results and hints as to what remedial methods to use are given. All the tests were standardized on the same population.

Advantages of the Gates-McKillop Program

The Gates-McKillop program for analysis of reading difficulties possesses the following favorable features: (*a*) It is perhaps the most complete program of diagnosis available. (*b*) The program is adapted readily to a case of reading disability of any degree of severity by a judicious selection of tests. (*c*) The provision for converting raw scores into grade scores is especially helpful in identifying and evaluating difficulties. (*d*) All tests in the series are carefully standardized. (*e*) The suggestions for remedial work are helpful. (*f*) In addition to directions for evaluation, the examiner is told what to look for throughout the testing.

C.   THE SPACHE DIAGNOSTIC READING SCALES

The *Spache Diagnostic Reading Scales* consist of a series of integrated tests developed over a period of eight years to provide standardized evaluations of oral and silent reading skills and of auditory comprehension. The tests were planned to determine the proficiency of normal and retarded readers at elementary school levels and of retarded readers of junior and senior high school age.

Tests and Procedures (Spache)

In the test battery are three word-recognition lists, twenty-two reading passages of graduated difficulty from grades 1.6 to 8.5, and six supplementary phonics tests. The testing materials consist of a reusable booklet for the pupil, a record booklet for the examiner's use, and the examiner's manual. The first part of the manual contains a description of the scales with data on their reliability and validity. Part 2 describes uses of the scales, with interpretation of results. Part 3 gives directions for administering and scoring the tests.

In general, the reliability and validity coefficients of the tests are relatively high. The first word list ranges in difficulty from grades 1.3 to 2.3; the second list from grades 2.3 to 5.5; and the third list from grades 3.8 to 6.5. The reading passages are arranged in eleven steps in grade placement, ranging from grades 1.6 to 8.5. Comprehension questions with answers accompany each selection. The six supplementary phonics tests are tests of consonant sounds, vowel sounds, consonant blends, common syllables, blending, and letter sounds. The last three pages of the record booklet provide a thorough check-list of reading difficulties, a summary record blank, and space for a summary of the case including background data and recommended remedial procedures.

Use of the Scales

Administration of the word-recognition lists serves three purposes: (*a*) To estimate the level at which to start the oral reading passages. (*b*) To reveal the pupil's methods of word attack and analysis. The kinds of errors the pupil makes in reading the words reveal the kinds of difficulty he has in analyzing words. These errors are classified by use of the word analysis checklist provided. If further study of procedures in word analysis seems warranted, the supplementary phonics tests are given. (*c*) To evaluate the pupil's sight vocabulary.

In oral reading, the pupil's errors and his comprehension scores will enable the examiner to determine which is for him the most suitable level of instructional reading materials. The proper instructional level, determined by noting the number of oral reading errors, is that at which teaching oral reading occurs. Its materials must not present undue difficulties for the pupil. The independent reading level is the grade level for recreational and supplementary reading at which the child can read silently with satis-factory comprehension. Although he will encounter some word-recognition difficulties at this level, these will not be great enough to block comprehension or prevent his taking pleasure in his reading.

The potential reading level is the maximum level to which it is estimated a pupil's reading may be raised by remedial or classroom training. Knowledge of the potential reading level reveals whether the child is reading below, or up to his capacity.

The six phonics tests are designed to provide a detailed analysis of the child's ability to relate symbols and sounds. Their use helps the clinician or teacher to identify the needs of a pupil in the recognition and use of letter sounds, use of consonant blends, identifying common syllables, and blending.

Advantages of the Spache Program

The Spache program for analysis of reading difficulties has the following favorable features: (*a*) Tests may be used to determine the proficiency of normal readers in the elementary school as well as of retarded readers in both elementary and high school. (*b*) There is ample provision for summing up the results of testing and listing medical checks, home conditions, and the like, plus tentative remedial recommendations. (*c*) Directions for administering tests and interpretation of results are clearly stated with adequate precautions. (*d*) The suggestions to de-emphasize adhering to rigid standards are useful both to clinician and classroom teacher. (*e*) The Diagnostic Reading Scales are useful for dealing with cases of mild, moderately severe, and severe difficulties. (*f*) The tests may be administered either by an able and alert classroom teacher or by a clinician.

REPRESENTATIVE GROUP CASE-STUDY TESTS

Traditionally, any system of case-study diagnosis of reading difficulties has required individual testing. These tests usually have used samples of oral reading to locate the specific reading skills and abilities needing remedial attention. The next two tests explore reading skill patterns by means of group silent-reading samples. In this way, they measure silent-reading skills and abilities, thus emphasizing the kind of reading done most frequently. They may be given to groups or to individuals, as desired.

A.   SILENT READING DIAGNOSTIC TESTS
(BOND-BALOW-HOYT)

The Silent Reading Diagnostic Tests, published in 1970, are based upon twenty years of research and use in regular classrooms and clinics. Five experimental editions preceded the revised 1970 edition. The tests are designed to be used with pupils of any age whose average reading scores are second-through sixth-grade levels. The reading skills tested are those usually taught in the elementary school, those skills generally found necessary for functional reading ability. The tests also are useful in formulating remedial reading programs in the junior and senior high schools for pupils with relatively severe reading retardation.

Tests and Procedures
(Bond-Balow-Hoyt)

The *Silent Reading Diagnostic Tests* have eight subtests that serve to evaluate the most important areas of word recognition.

Test 1: *Words in Isolation,* composed of fifty-four items in which the pupil selects a word that describes a picture. This test gives a measure of the child's recognition vocabulary plus his errors, which are classified according to the location of an error within a word (wrong beginning, wrong middle, and wrong ending), and on the basis of reversals.

Test 2: *Words in Context,* composed of thirty items in which the pupil selects a word that logically completes a sentence, thus indicating his ability to use context clues in word recognition. Errors are classified as in Test 1. The errors in Test 1 and Test 2 then are added to determine the pupil's error tendencies.

Test 3: *Visual-Structural Analysis* utilizes thirty words containing the most common prefixes, suffixes, and variant endings. When the pupil can separate the stimulus word from variant endings, prefixes, and suffixes, he will know the root word. Although introductory work is provided in the primary grades, visual-structural analysis is taught more intensively in the intermediate grades. This test measures as low as second grade and extends well into the seventh.

Test 4: *Syllabication* measures ability to separate words into syllables. This test also measures knowledge of the six rules of syllabication having greatest applicability. The test ranges from second to mid-seventh grade.

Test 5: *Word Synthesis* measures ability to blend words together visually. The series of paragraphs used has many lines ending in hyphenated words. The hyphen separates a common blend, syllable, or affix from the remainder of the word. The test works well in grades 2 through 7.5.

Test 6: *Beginning Sounds.* Thirty items are used containing common initial blends and digraphs. The pupil selects the letter combinations that have the same sound as the beginnings of the words read by the examiner. This test functions from grades 2 through 7.5.

Test 7: *Ending Sounds.* Auditory and visual discrimination are involved. The child selects the letters that represent the same sound he hears at the end of the stimulus word read by the examiner. Most of the thirty items represent the most common endings. The test measures responses from grade 2 through 7.5.

Test 8: *Vowel and Consonant Sounds.* The pupil selects the letter that represents the initial sound in the word pronounced by the examiner. It tests knowledge of phoneme-grapheme association, with its thirty items measuring up to the seventh grade.

The raw scores for each of the tests and types of errors are plotted on a *Graphic Profile.* This profile indicates the grade level and the amount of deviation of each from the case's *average reading score.* The profile also enables the diagnostician to locate those areas of reading in which the disabled reader has limited ability, and also the areas of overemphasis. A study of the profile gives the diagnostician an indication of the types of errors the child makes in recognizing words. It shows the efficiency with which he uses context clues; it indicates the relationship between word recognition and comprehension; it shows the ability to analyze words visually into usable parts; it measures the child's knowledge of phonics and locates areas of weakness; it gives an indication of the over-analytical as well as the under-analytical cases; and it measures the ability of the disabled reader to synthesize word parts visually. This battery of tests are valuable to classroom teachers in diagnosing the needs of pupils with reading difficulties, as well as to the clinician studying severe reading disabilities.

Advantages of the Bond-Balow-Hoyt Program

Diagnosis of reading difficulties by means of these *Silent Reading Diagnostic Tests* has certain advantages: (*a*) The test can be administered and the results interpreted and used by any competent classroom teacher. (*b*) Directions for scoring and interpretations are clear, direct, and relatively uncomplicated. (*c*) The tests are economical in time; they can be given to a whole class at once. (*d*) Identification of reading difficulties is easily and quickly achieved by means of the profile. Use of the profile avoids the laborious task of referring to tables of norms. (*e*) The technique provides an important practical aid for planning individual remedial instruction. (*f*) Emphasis is upon diagnosing *silent* reading abilities and skills in contrast to most other detailed diagnostic tests. (*g*) The tests provide a complete diagnosis of the essential skills. (*h*) The tests are useful for diagnosing severely disabled junior and senior high school pupils.

B.   STANFORD DIAGNOSTIC READING TEST
(KARLSEN—MADDEN—GARDNER)

The *Stanford Diagnostic Reading Test* contains a series of measures designed to identify needed areas of instruction in the fundamental skills of reading. It is intended for use in the early part of some instructional sequence, such as at the beginning of the school year. The assumption is that, in order to improve pupil competence in a certain area, it first is necessary to find out what learning problems a pupil has and then to eliminate them as completely as possible.

These tests are for group administration and are to be given by the classroom teacher. Although the use of the test results is centered around classroom instruction, the findings also are valuable in a clinic setting.

Tests and Procedures
(Karlsen—Madden—Gardner)

These tests have been prepared on four levels (red, green, brown, and blue) with two forms at each level. The *red level* is for grades 1 and 2 and for reading cases in succeeding grades. The tests include measures of basic phonics skills, auditory vocabulary, word recognition, and sentence and paragraph comprehension. The *green level* is for grades 3 and 4 and for reading cases in grade 5 and beyond. It includes measures of auditory discrimination, phonetic and structural analysis, auditory vocabulary, and literal and inferential comprehension. The *brown level* is for grades 5 through 8 and reading cases of high school grades. The tests include measures of phonetic and structural analysis, auditory vocabulary, literal and inferential comprehension, and reading rate. The *blue level* for grades 9 through 12 and for community college includes measures of phonetic and structural analysis, reading vocabulary, literal and inferential comprehension, reading rate, and scanning and skimming.

After the tests have been scored, a maximum amount of information on pupil achievement is obtained by (1) converting the raw scores for each student into norms such as percentile ranks or stanines (tables are employed to do this); (2) summarizing the test performance of individual pupils; and (3) summarizing test performance for the class as a whole.

The norms, or converted scores, allow the teacher to make judgments about the level of performance of a pupil or a group of pupils. The authors of the test recommend that stanine scores be used but provide a table of percentile scores for use if desired. A stanine is a value on a simple nine-point scale of standard scores. Scores are expressed along a scale ranging from 1 (low) to 9 (high), with the value 5 always representing average performance for pupils in the norm group. This nine-point scale presents as fine a classification as the teacher or counselor needs for adapting instruction or for appraising strengths and weaknesses of a pupil.

Advantages of the Stanford Diagnostic Reading Test

This battery of tests has certain advantages: (*a*) It may be used effectively by teachers with pupils needing individualized help or by a reading specialist. (*b*) Directions in the manual are clear and complete. (*c*) Suggestions for remedial instruction are included in the manual. (*d*) Because it is a group test, it is economical in terms of time. (*e*) It emphasizes silent reading abilities. (*f*) It is effective in diagnosing reading disability cases from grade 3 through the college level.

INFORMAL DIAGNOSIS

The diagnosis of reading ability and deficiencies is best achieved through using standardized tests and procedures. It is possible and almost always desirable to extend the diagnosis by less formal procedures. The classroom teacher constantly makes informal diagnostic appraisals during the various steps involved in teaching reading selections in the developmental program. She notes each child's successes and errors in word recognition, his ability to anticipate the words he will meet by using meaning clues, and his tendency to regress when he needs to reestablish understanding of what he reads in order to correct a faulty word recognition. She appraises any tendency to omit or add words which change the meaning of what he is reading. She notes each child's growth in developing the skills necessary to decode graphic clues, such as phonic and structural aids to word recognition. Perceptual habits of the child in recognizing words are noted. All of these observations are important to evaluating reading instruction.

Knowing all this, the classroom teacher can make instructional adjustments for each child. When she discovers that a child is in serious difficulty, she or a reading specialist may resort to more systematic informal diagnostic appraisals.

There are two reasons for such a systematic informal diagnosis. The first is to estimate the child's three reading levels—the child's independent reading level, his instructional level, and the reading level at which he becomes frustrated. The second is to make a qualitative evaluation of the child's word-recognition and comprehension strengths and weaknesses.

Estimating Reading Levels

The reading levels of a child can be estimated by using a carefully graded series of basic readers. The series should be one which the child has not used before. Selections of 100 to 150 words are chosen from each successive book in the series. For any grade level, e.g., grade 3.0, material is selected at about twenty pages from the beginning of the first book at that grade. Similarly, for halfway through a grade (grade 3.5, etc.) material is selected near the beginning of the second book for that grade. A few questions involving both some ideas and some facts are constructed for each selection. After the pupil, starting at a relatively easy level, has read each selection aloud to the teacher, or to the examiner in an individual testing situation, he then answers the comprehension questions based upon its content. If the material in the book he starts with is not handled easily, he is moved back to a still easier level. The child then reads the successively more difficult selections until his reading levels are determined. Betts (10) has outlined reading levels as follows:

1. The child's *independent reading level* is ascertained from the book in which he can read with no more than one error in word recognition (pronunciation) in each one hundred words and has a comprehension score of at least ninety percent. At this level the child must read aloud in a natural conversational tone. The reading should be rhythmical and well phrased. At the same time he is free from tension and has good reading posture. His silent reading will be faster than his oral reading and free from vocalizations. This is the level at which the child should do extensive supplementary reading for enjoyment or for information in line with his interests. At this *independent reading level,* the child has complete control of experience (concepts), vocabulary, construction, and organization. He has, therefore, maximum opportunity for doing the thinking that is required for a full understanding of what he is reading.

2. The *instructional reading level* is determined from the level of the book in which the child can read with no more than one word-recognition error in each twenty words and has a comprehension score of at least seventy-five percent. At this level the child reads orally, *after silent study,* without tension, in a conversational tone, and with rhythm and proper phrasing. Silent reading is faster than oral, except at the beginning levels. The child is able to use properly word-recognition clues and techniques.

This is the level at which a pupil is able to make successful progress in reading under a *teacher's guidance*. When using challenging materials at this level, and with purposeful reading directed by the teacher, the result should be maximum progress in acquiring reading abilities.

3. The *frustration reading level* is marked by the book in which the child "bogs down" when he tries to read. He reads orally without rhythm and in an unnatural voice. Errors and refusals are numerous. Tensions are obvious. The child comprehends less than half of what he is trying to read. The test should be stopped as soon as it is clear that the child is at his frustration level.

No child should be asked to go on reading at the frustration level when he is being taught or in any other situation. The teacher, however, should recognize that such a level exists. Too frequently children are found to be working at their frustration levels in classes in which instruction is not satisfactorily adjusted to individual differences.

Informal Diagnosis of Word-Recognition Difficulties

Word-recognition difficulties are diagnosed effectively by evaluating oral reading behavior. Most of the standardized individual diagnostic tests, described previously in this chapter, have used quantitative measures of oral reading performance to find the strengths and weaknesses of the disabled reader. Often additional insights into the disabled reader's problems can be obtained by informal qualitative appraisals of his oral reading habits and errors.

After the child's reading levels have been determined, as described above, the diagnostician selects a story from a basic reader more advanced than one at the child's instructional level, so as to get a good sample of reading errors but still to be below the level of frustration, so that meaningful reading is possible. The child should be told to read the selection aloud without any help. He also should be told to guess any of the words he does not know, and also told that he will be asked to retell the story when he finishes it. Every error should be recorded so that it can be classified according to the phase of word recognition in question. A tape recording of the oral reading sample might be helpful in order to make a careful study of the errors.

We have found that three types of classification are necessary in order to obtain a complete understanding of disabled readers' word-recognition problems. First, we classify the errors to indicate the child's phonic and structural decoding strengths and weaknesses. The error classifications we use are similar to those developed by Monroe (141). Her error classifications include:

Faulty vowels. In his mispronunciation the child may have altered one or more vowel sounds, as *dig* read *dug.*

Faulty consonants. Here, one or more consonant sounds are altered, as *send* read *sent.*

Reversals. A mispronunciation reveals a reversal in the orientation of letters (*dig* read *big*), or in a sequence of letters (*was* read *saw*), or in a sequence of words (*he said* read *said he*).

Addition of sounds. The child wrongly inserts one or more sounds in a word, as *tack* read *track.*

Omission of sounds. The mispronunciation involves omission of one or more sounds in the test word, as *blind* read *bind.*

Substitution of words. The child substitutes a word unrelated in form or sound, as *lived* read *was.*

Repetition of words. Each test word repeated, whether read correctly or incorrectly, is counted as a repetition as, *"a boy a boy had a dog"* (two repetitions).

Addition of words. The child inserts a word into the text, when *once there was* is read *once upon a time there was* (three word additions).

Omission of words. The child omits a word from the text, as *a little pig* read *a pig.*

Refusals and words aided. The child refuses to attempt a word or a word has to be supplied by the examiner after a delay of fifteen seconds.

The remedial suggestions for such decoding problems are discussed in chapters 10 and 11.

Next, we study possible faulty perceptual habits, such as those classified in the oral reading section of the Gates-McKillop Reading Diagnostic Tests, discussed earlier in this chapter. The perceptual errors include the following types of mispronunciations: (1) full reversals; (2) reversal of parts; (3) wrong beginnings; (4) wrong middles; (5) wrong endings; (6) wrong in several parts. The remedial suggestions for eliminating such perceptual errors are discussed in chapters 10 and 11.

The third type of diagnosis of oral reading behavior deals with limitations in the use of meaning clues to word recognition. We have found helpful a somewhat modified use of the linguistic classification of oral reading miscues, suggested by Goodman and Burke (95). We are interested especially in word miscues that indicate: 1) ineffective use of expectancy clues gained from the reader's background (for example, a child might quickly recognize a word, such as *rhinocerous,* if he were reading about a trip to the zoo); 2) miscues that indicate little use of syntactic aids derived from knowledge of language structure (for example, *"They all were happy,"* read as *"They all where happy"*); 3) miscues that indicate a lack of use of semantic aids gained from an ongoing understanding of the content presented (for example, *"The boy was riding a horse,"* read as *"The boy was riding a house"*).

We assess the reader's limitations in the use of meaning clues in anticipating the next word, or words, to be read. Skill in using meaning clues facilitates any necessary decoding or even makes possible instant recognition by effective use of perceptual skills. We also diagnose the disabled reader's difficulties in using meaning clues to check the accuracy of decoded, unknown words. These last two limitations are identified by the number of repetitions made, the compatability of the errors made with the ongoing content, and the omissions or additions of words that alter the meaning of the passage being read. If a more systematic diagnosis of meaning-clue deficiencies seems desirable, the clinician should refer to the *Reading Miscue Inventory-Manual* developed by Goodman and Burke (96).

Having the child pronounce words from the word lists at the end of basic readers provides additional information about word-recognition skills. The words should be selected from the list at the child's instructional level. Errors are recorded and analyzed. Next, we have the child again try to pronounce the missed or refused words to discover his identification patterns. After this, the words missed are presented orally to the child for him to use in oral sentences to ascertain whether they are part of his meaning vocabulary.

All of the remedial exercises throughout this book emphasize the use of meaning clues, because all the skills are taught in meaningful reading situations rather than in isolated drills. The remedial methods suggested in chapter 9 are specifically designed to correct deficiencies in meaning clues to word recognition.

Suggestions for the Diagnostician

Many clinicians find it convenient to make an informal, diagnostic booklet. This booklet can be made easily by using selected passages at various grade levels of a basic reading series. The oral reading passages should be affixed to the left-hand page of the booklet, and a comparable selection for silent reading is affixed to the right-hand page. On the next page, a list of comprehension questions for each passage should be listed in the following order: first, a summary question should be used, then two factual questions, one inference, and one vocabulary if possible. On the fourth page, a list of words selected from the back of the basic reader used, at approximately the same level from which the oral and silent reading passages were taken, should be typed on the page for use as a vocabulary test, as described above. The same four-page procedure is repeated, using selections, at half-yearly intervals, from the same series of basal readers. Grade-level tabs should be attached to the selections at the edge of the booklet for quick selection.

A diagnostician collecting information from sources of evaluation rather than measurement, should follow certain procedures which will enable the data he gets to be as accurate as possible. These suggestions may be helpful for collecting evaluative data:

1. ISOLATE SPECIFIC OUTCOMES OR CHARACTERISTICS TO BE EVALUATED. If, for example, information is needed on the method of attack a child uses on words in isolation when working orally, the observer should be alert to all of the approaches that might be used by the child.

2. THE DIAGNOSTICIAN SHOULD DEFINE THE OBSERVABLE RESULTS OR CHARACTERISTICS IN EXACT TERMS. The diagnostician should have before him, for example, a check-list of possible methods that the child might use when he is orally solving a word-recognition problem.

3. THE INFORMAL SITUATION IN WHICH THE CHARACTERISTIC IS TO BE OBSERVED SHOULD BE WELL PLANNED AND SUITABLE TO THE RESULTS TO BE OBSERVED. The child whose methods of word study are to be observed should be given a list of words of increasing difficulty and he should be requested to work out the unknown words aloud so that the diagnostician may note which word-recognition approaches the child is using.

4. INFORMATION SHOULD BE CLASSIFIED IN UNIFORM AND USEFUL WAYS. The diagnostician studying word recognition may wish to classify the errors made by a child as to both location within the word (beginning, middle, ending, or reversal errors) and phonetic types (vowels, consonant blend, digraph, addition of sounds, omission of sounds, or transposition of sounds). He should classify the analytical attack under categories such as: spelling, letter-by-letter sounding, phonic, structural, syllabic, or a combination of these forms of attacks on words. He also should notice if the child tries to recognize each word as a sight word without any otherwise discernible form of attack.

5. A RECORD SHOULD BE MADE OF WHAT HE FINDS WITH ILLUSTRATIVE SAMPLES OF THE PERFORMANCE ON WHICH THE JUDGMENTS WERE MADE. Using the methods of word study just described, the child might be found to be attempting a phonic approach to the problem, but his knowledge of word elements may be weak. Sample words should be listed to show: (*a*) vis-

ual separation of the words; (*b*) the elements miscalled; (*c*) any difficulty in synthesis that results; and (*d*) the final pronunciation of the word. In addition, a summary of the diagnostician's opinion, at that time, should be recorded.

6. THE SIGNIFICANCE OF OBSERVED BEHAVIOR OR CHARACTERISTIC SHOULD BE EVALUATED. The diagnostician, in the example cited above, should indicate the importance of the information to the understanding of the instructional needs of the child he is studying.

The usefulness of information from informal procedures depends on the experience of the observer, the number of observations, the degree to which the observations are unbiased, and the relevance of the information to the understanding of the case. Many elements in reading diagnosis must be determined by informal procedures.

The information acquired by informal approaches should be gathered as systematically as possible, and it must be interpreted and used with caution. Many misjudgments are made if the personal biases of the diagnostician are allowed to influence his judgments, even on normative data. Misjudgments are even more prevalent when the data are collected informally. For example, a diagnostician may have a special interest in reversals. When a child makes a few, as most children do, they may be overemphasized by the diagnostician. As a result, the child may be classified as a reversal case while his true difficulty is something quite different.

Informal procedures have merit because they allow the diagnostician to explore further some characteristic suspected from more standardized measurements. Many times, when giving a standardized diagnostic reading test, the examiner notices in the child a reading tendency which he wishes to study further. He may complete the test as designed so that he can use the norms, but then he may explore, informally, the items he wishes to check because of his "hunch." For example, the diagnostician may be giving a standardized list of isolated words to find out how well a child can work out the pronunciations in an untimed situation. He gives this child the list of words according to directions and determines the child's score. He may have noted, however, that the child seemed to have trouble in visually separating the words into usable elements. The diagnostician may wish to go back to some of the words missed and, by covering up parts of the words, show the child the correct way to analyze them. He might then see whether the child could have recognized the words, had his visual analysis been correct. This information would be recorded but would not enter into the application of the normative data.

The following *Informal Diagnostic Inventory* has been organized to facilitate recording data obtained during informal diagnosis.

INFORMAL DIAGNOSTIC INVENTORY

Name _____ School _____ Grade _____ Age _____ C.G. _____

Mental Test _____ I.Q. _____ M.A. _____ M.G. _____ Date _____

Standardized Group Reading Tests: *Reading Expectancy Grade* _____

1. _____ R.G. _____   2. _____ R.G. _____

3. _____ R.G. _____   4. _____ R.G. _____

Reading Levels   *Average Reading Grade* _____

1. Independent _____ 2. Instructional _____ 3. Frustration _____

Oral Reading from Basic Reader at Grade Level _____ *Basic Series* _____

1. Oral Reading Skill
   - (a) Slow Rate _____
   - (c) Over-fast Rate _____
   - (e) Faulty Enunciation _____
   - (g) Unusual Posture _____
   - (i) Signs of Tension _____
   - (b) Poor Comprehension _____
   - (d) Inappropriate Phrasing _____
   - (f) Faulty Expression _____
   - (h) Pointing _____
   - (j) Word-by-word _____

2. Word Recognition Difficulties
   - (a) Omissions _____
   - (c) Repetitions _____
   - (e) Wrong Beginnings _____
   - (g) Wrong Endings _____
   - (i) Refusals _____
   - (k) Semantic Miscues _____
   - (m) Limited Expectancy Clues
   - (b) Additions _____
   - (d) Reversals _____
   - (f) Wrong Middles _____
   - (h) Wrong in Several Parts _____
   - (j) Limited Self-Correction _____
   - (l) Syntactic Miscues _____
   - (n) Others _____

Silent Reading: continue in same book as above

1. Rate: Words per Minute _____   2. Comprehension: % Correct _____
3. Lip Movements _____   4. Audible Speech _____
5. Finger Pointing _____   6. Head Movements _____
7. Signs of Tension _____   8. Distractibility _____

Word Pronunciation: from Word List *in same basic reader*

1. Technique Used
   - (a) Whole Word _____
   - (c) Syllabic _____
   - (e) Letter-by-letter _____
   - (b) Structural _____
   - (d) Phonics _____
   - (f) Spelling _____

2. Errors
   - (a) Faulty vowels _____
   - (c) Reversals _____
   - (e) Omission of Sounds _____
   - (g) Faulty Visual Analysis _____
   - (i) Words Refused _____
   - (b) Faulty Consonants _____
   - (d) Addition of Sounds _____
   - (f) Substitution of Words _____
   - (h) Faulty Blending _____
   - (j) Others _____

Other Relevant Data

1. Hearing _____   2. Vision _____
3. Handedness _____   4. Eyedness _____
5. Speech _____   6. Any Physical Difficulties _____
7. Language Usage _____   8. Fluency _____
9. Ability to concentrate _____ 10. Persistence _____
11. Emotional reactions (confident, shy, over-aggressive, negative, cheerful, etc. _____
12. Attitudes toward (school, teacher, reading _____

13. Home environment _____
14. Other observations _____

Tentative diagnosis of case: 1. _____
2. etc. _____

Suggested appropriate remedial plan: 1. _____
2. etc. _____

(Permission for duplication and use of the *Informal Diagnostic Inventory* is hereby granted.)

Informal observation of the child's oral reading when confronted with selections of increasing difficulty provides many clues to his problems. The diagnostician should be especially alert to any sign of word-by-word reading, failure to use context clues, inability to group words into thought units or language patterns, limited sentence sense, or any other indication of a basic comprehension problem. Many of these basic abilities are most easily detected by the way in which a child reads aloud a passage that is rather difficult for him.

USE OF STANDARDIZED READING DIAGNOSTIC TESTS IN COMBINATION WITH INFORMAL PROCEDURES

In clinical diagnosis at the case-study level, a combination of standardized diagnostic tests and brief informal check tests can be used. In this way, the diagnostician has the advantages of the impartial standardized procedures and the freedom to design his own reading and learning tasks using whatever materials seem most appropriate.

For example, after considering referral information, intelligence testing results, and results of standardized group reading tests, a clinician might choose to administer the word list and paragraph sections of either the *Spache Reading Diagnostic Scales* or the *Durrell Reading Analysis*. From such limited use of a standardized reading diagnostic test, the clinician would have adequate information to judge the student's relative strengths in reading comprehension, rate of comprehension, and general word recognition.

If word recognition and reading comprehension appeared to be strengths, but the rate of comprehension noticeably slow, the clinician could proceed directly to refinement and verification of the diagnosis. Using materials at the reading level indicated by the diagnostic test just administered, the clinician could set specific purposes for rapid reading to appraise whether the slow rate indicated inefficient word recognition, overconcern with detailed comprehension, or was simply a habitual response to all reading tasks.

Similarly, in the area of comprehension, a case-study level, diagnostic finding could be sharpened. For example, a student who was not accurate in factual detail recall, could be given a suitable selection and asked several questions requiring recall of factual detail. The clinician then could ask the student to explain how he arrived at his answers. In this way, misunderstandings of word meanings in context reading or insufficient attention to syntactic clues to precise understanding often are uncovered. The diagnostician should review *all* answers and should not indicate whether she considers any answer to be good or bad. It is diagnostically important to know how the child arrived at his answers and the exact nature of his understandings and misunderstandings. The child also should be directed to find where in the passage the relevant information is. It is important to determine how efficiently this is accomplished and whether, in the review process, the student is able to clear up spontaneously any of his own confusions.

Similar diagnostic procedures can be used in most areas of comprehension difficulty. It is important to assess how the child approaches comprehension tasks, the nature of his misunderstandings, and his ability to correct his own errors when his attention is specifically focused on a single aspect of reading comprehension.

When the diagnostic concern is centered on word recognition difficulties, the diagnostician must make, refine, and verify judgments about its various aspects. Using referral information and a child's performance on the word list and paragraph sections of the standardized diagnostic test, a clinician might decide his weakness included lack of instant recognition of common words the child should know by sight at his level of reading development. This judgment could be verified and refined by additional testing, using word lists from the child's own reading series or from remedial instructional materials. A trial lesson might be taught by the clinician to determine whether any special methodologies, such as a word-tracing method, would enhance learning.

When word recognition difficulties appear to result from inadequate analytic techniques, diagnostic information obtained from word lists and paragraph sections of standardized diagnostic tests often are found to give insufficient information to enable the clinician to turn directly to informal diagnostic methods. For a complete, unified, standardized picture of word recognition techniques as used in silent reading, a diagnostic instrument such as the *Silent Reading Diagnostic Tests* should be used. From a comparison of results obtained from this instrument along with diagnostic insights from referral information, and word lists and paragraph reading, the clinician will be able to evaluate the relative strengths and weaknesses within the broader general area of word recognition. Informal procedures then can be used to refine and verify the diagnosis. For example, if a student appeared to be ineffective in using meaning clues as an aid to word recognition, the clinician could have the student complete some simple cloze passages and discuss how he decided upon his answers (see Bormuth, 27). Similarly, if the student demonstrated difficulty with word beginnings and with beginning sounds, the diagnostician might want to check more thoroughly the exact nature of the student's confusion by having him read aloud a list of common words beginning with the essential beginning blends and digraphs. A few sample exercises and activities also might be tried in order to help the clinician decide how the child might be helped most effectively to gain a functional knowledge of common word beginnings.

When the major diagnostic concern involves word-recognition techniques used in oral reading, the clinician first should obtain a complete, unified, standardized picture of oral word recognition by means of an oral reading diagnostic instrument such as the *Gates-McKillop Reading Diagnostic Test*. When using this instrument, subtests 1 through 5 should be administered as well as any additional subtests the clinician considers useful to a more complete understanding of a child's word-recognition difficulties. Appropriate comparisons of results obtained from these subtests together with referral information and other standardized and informal diagnostic assessment will suggest weaknesses which can and should be understood even more completely through informal testing procedures.

In the classroom, reading center, resource room, or clinic, standardized tests serve best in putting in perspective major areas of reading competence or concern. Informal methods are best, once an area of concern has been established, to clarify what exactly should be taught and how learning can be enhanced.

SUMMARY

A classification of reading difficulties shows that both standardized and informal procedures must be available to diagnose the needs of disabled readers. The diagnosis is a series of screenings going as far as needed from general diagnosis to analytical diagnosis, to case-study diagnosis, until all the information necessary to develop an appropriate individual plan of remediation is gathered.

Several representative detailed techniques have been described. The Durrell program is most appropriate for use with the less severe cases of disability. It is uncomplicated and takes only a moderate amount of time to administer. Basically, the program consists of a standardized method for observing, recording, and interpreting errors and faulty habits during reading and word perception.

The Gates-McKillop program is perhaps the most comprehensive, in that it is applicable to any degree of retardation in reading. Only part of the tests need be used with the less severe cases. Two equivalent forms are available. The examiner must be a trained clinician, as the procedures themselves, the scoring methods, and the final interpretations are complicated. The basic analyses are derived from tests of oral reading and word and phrase recognition, and with more severe cases, visual and auditory skills are examined.

The Spache program is well adapted to diagnosing the reading proficiency of normal readers in the elementary school and of both the moderate and severe disability cases in both elementary and high school. Either an able teacher or a trained clinician can administer the tests.

The *Bond-Balow-Hoyt Silent Reading Diagnostic Tests* identify reading difficulties through group testing of silent reading. The analysis is based upon responses to eight diagnostic tests. The tests may be given and interpreted by the classroom teacher. The program is particularly useful for diagnosing reading problems of students from second grade into high school whose general reading grade level is from 2.0 to 7.0.

The *Karlsen-Madden-Gardner Stanford Diagnostic Tests* are an excellent series of silent reading group tests for diagnosing reading instructional needs of students from grade 2 through the community college level. A systematic, informal diagnosis is presented in detail, and includes a sample *Informal Diagnostic Inventory*.

Whenever detailed diagnosis of reading difficulty is called for, the examiner should choose the most appropriate evaluative techniques including both standardized and informal procedures. Skill in choosing the proper technique, in testing and in interpreting results, comes from experience; but therein lies much of the skill in diagnosis.

SELECTED READINGS

HARRIS, A. J., and E. R. SIPAY, *How to Increase Reading Ability* (6th ed.), chaps. 8, 9. New York: David McKay, 1975.

KENNEDY, E. C., *Classroom Approaches to Remedial Reading* (2nd ed.), chaps. 4, 5. Itaska, Ill.: F. E. Peacock, 1977.

OTTO, W., C. W. PETERS, and N. PETERS, *Reading Problems: a Multidisciplinary Perspective,* chap. 9. Reading, Mass.: Addison-Wesley, 1977.

ROSWELL, F., and G. NATCHEZ, *Reading Disability* (2nd ed.), chap. 2. New York: Basic Books, 1971.

SPACHE, G. D., *Diagnosing and Correcting Reading Disabilities,* chap. 7. Boston: Allyn and Bacon, 1976.

STRANG, R., *Diagnostic Teaching of Reading* (2nd ed.), chap. 10. New York: McGraw-Hill, 1969.

WILSON, R. M., *Diagnostic and Remedial Reading* (3rd ed.), chap. 4. Columbus, Ohio: Charles E. Merrill, 1977.

Planning
Appropriate
Remediation

The clinician or reading teacher studies the diagnostic findings and then arranges learning conditions in which the disabled reader can grow in reading at an accelerated rate. In making an *appropriate educational plan of remediation,* it is necessary to identify the specific limitations in the disabled reader's reading profile that are impeding reading growth. Methods, motivation, and materials are considered in formulating the education plan that will be most suited to the disabled reader's remedial program.

The remedial program must be based on more than an understanding of the child's reading needs. It also must be based on the child's characteristics. The child who is hard of hearing needs an approach to reading different from that for his counterpart with normal hearing. The one with poor vision needs adjustment in methods and, if his limitation is severe enough, in materials also. The child who is a slow learner needs modified methods and so does the one who is emotionally disturbed. The modifications of instruction for such children will be discussed in a later chapter.

As each case is different, there can be no "bag of tricks." Nor can there be a universal approach which will solve disabled readers' problems. Many times, remedial training suited to one child would be detrimental to another. If, for example, a remedial program has been planned to develop more adequate phrasing, the child might be required to do considerable prepared oral reading in order to help him to read in thought units. This same recommendation would do serious harm to the disabled reader who already is overvocalizing in his silent reading. It would exaggerate the faulty habit he had acquired and increase his disability. To sum up, every remedial program must be planned on the basis of a thorough appraisal of the child's instructional needs, his strengths and weaknesses, and the environment in which correction is to take place.

The appropriate remedial plans should be in written form indicating in some detail what is to be recommended for each case. This must be done because it is too difficult to remember each child, his needs, the level of his attainments, and his limitations with the exactness that is necessary for an effective corrective program. The written case report should indicate the nature of the disability and the type of exercises recommended to correct it. It should identify the level of material to be used. The written plan should state any physical or sensory characteristics that need to be corrected or for which the program needs to be modified. Any indication of faulty personal adjustment or unfortunate environmental conditions should be included. Interests, hobbies, and attitudes should become part of the written record. Most important, it should include a description of the remedial program recommended and the types of material and exercises to be used.

The original individual plan of remedial work is not to be considered permanent. It will need to be modified from time to time as the child progresses in reading. Often a disabled reader changes rapidly in his instructional needs. The better the diagnosis and the more successful the remedial plan, the more rapidly his needs will change. One disabled reader, for example, may have failed to build analytical word-recognition techniques but depends on sight vocabulary and context clues to recognize new words. He would be given remedial work designed to teach him the analytical techniques. After a time, he may develop considerable skill in word study, but he may not make a corresponding gain in rate of reading. His problem would no longer be one of developing word analysis. In fact, emphasis on this phase of the program might become detrimental to his future reading growth. The use of larger word elements and other more rapid word-recognition techniques and further building of sight vocabulary would be advisable. As the problem changes, so must the plan of remediation in order to meet new reading needs.

Because the child's instructional needs change rapidly, it is unwise to put him into a remedial program that resembles a factory production line. Such a program assumes that once a given child's level of reading performance is identified, all that is needed is to put him through a set of exercises uniform for all children. The disabled reader whose needs change rapidly as his limitations are corrected is in dire need of a program that readily adjusts to every change in his reading pattern. To achieve success, a remedial program must be based on a continuous diagnosis, and the basic plan must be modified somewhat as the instructional needs change.

In some instances, the original plan of remediation does not result in improvement. When this occurs, a reevaluation of the diagnosis and perhaps additional appraisals should be made. A somewhat altered approach to instruction may be necessary for success.

Inasmuch as an *appropriate individual educational plan of remediation* is necessary for correcting each disabled reader's problem, the following elements should be considered:

1. Remedial plans must be individualized.
2. The remedial plan must encourage the disabled reader.
3. Materials and exercises must be appropriate.
4. The remedial plan must use effective teaching procedures.
5. The plan must enlist cooperative efforts.

REMEDIAL PLANS MUST BE INDIVIDUALIZED

The disabled reader is one who has failed to respond to reading programs designed to meet the instructional needs and characteristics of the majority of children. The onset of reading disability usually is gradual. The child who becomes a disabled reader gets into a moderate amount of difficulty, misses some instruction, or in some way falls behind or gets confused. The reading curriculum and the class itself go on, while the child is left behind. Soon he finds himself hopelessly out of things. He can no longer read well enough to keep up with his group. He may develop an aversion to reading and is quite likely to develop unfortunate reading habits. All of these things accumulate until it is apparent to the teacher that the child has become a disabled reader. He has not learned the skills and abilities essential to effective reading. Faulty habits and unfortunate modes of reading have become established. He is developing or has already developed a disliking for and antagonism toward reading and his sense of defeat mounts higher and higher.

This child's difficulty has been produced gradually through his failure to progress in the usual fashion. The teacher, concerned with all the other children, at first failed to see the child's need or did not take the time to adjust the instruction to his requirements. The child thus developed an unfortunate variation in his reading skills and abilities.

A plan designed to treat reading disability is based on the assumption that children learn differently and need programs that meet their individual requirements. Such programs must be based on a recognition of a particular child's physical and mental characteristics and must be designed individually to be efficient in overcoming his difficulties.

The Remedial Plan Should Be
in Keeping with the Child's Characteristics

The expected results of instruction and the methods used will need to conform to the child's characteristics. If the child is lacking in general intelligence, he cannot be expected to reach the goals in reading for children of greater mental capability nor can he be expected to progress as rapidly. The remedial teacher would be wise to modify the goals of the program. The prognosis for rate of gain is usually directly proportional to the general intelligence of the child and the seriousness of his problem. In addition to lowering the results she expects, the remedial teacher would be wise to modify the methods of instruction also to meet the slow-learning child's needs. All these children need more concrete experiences, more carefully given directions, and more repetition and drill than do children of higher intelligence.

If a child has poor vision or poor hearing, modifications in methods will need to be made. Such limitations make learning to read more difficult but in no way preclude the child from achieving. Even deaf children have been taught to read effectively (Thompson, 205). Children with visual defects have learned to read well, but they are more likely to get into difficulty. The disabled reader with lesser sensory handicaps can be taught more efficiently if his limitations are known and modifications in methods of instruction are made. The adjustments in methods that have proved helpful will be discussed fully later in this book.

Remedial Instruction Should Be Specific, Not General

The remedial teacher should focus instruction upon the child's specific reading needs. The diagnosis usually has indicated that there is something specifically wrong with the pattern of his reading performance. One child, for example, may have learned to read with speed but falls short of the accuracy required in certain situations. This child should read material with factual content, and should read for purposes that demand the exact recall of those facts. Another disabled reader may be so over-concerned with detail that he reads extremely slowly, looking for more facts than the author wrote. He becomes so concerned with the detail that he cannot understand the author's overall intent. The teacher would endeavor to make him less compulsive so that the rate of reading and its results can be compatible with the purposes of this particular reading.

The principle that remedial instruction should be specific and not general means that the remedial teacher should emphasize those phases of reading development that will correct the reading limitation. It does not mean that just one type of exercise should be used, nor does it mean that a specific skill or ability should be isolated and receive drill. For a disabled reader with an insufficient knowledge of the larger visual and structural elements used in word recognition, the teacher would be in error if she used a method that gave isolated drill on word elements. A better procedure would be to have the child read a basic reader at the proper level of difficulty. He would read for the purposes suggested in the manual, but when he encountered a word-recognition problem, the teacher would help him by emphasizing the larger elements in the word. When the exercises given in the manual for developing basic skills and abilities were studied, the remedial teacher would have him do those that gave him experience in using the larger visual and structural parts of words. The teacher could find or construct additional exercises that would provide experiences with the larger elements in words he already knew so that he could learn to use these larger word elements in recognizing new words. The teacher also could construct exercises similar to those suggested in manuals of other basic reading series using vocabulary known to the child.

The workbook exercises accompanying basic readers also should be used. The disabled reader may need to do only certain pages selected for him. This is because he has an uneven profile, and he may have emphasized one phase of reading instruction to the detriment of another. The child who needs a greater knowledge of large visual and structural elements may have failed to develop them because he had overemphasized letter-by-letter sounding in word recognition. Such a child should avoid exercises that teach the knowledge of letter sounds.

Use a Variety of Remedial Techniques

There is an unfortunate tendency, once remedial instruction has been prescribed, to stick to one specific type of exercise to overcome a known deficiency. Basing a remedial program on a diagnosis does not imply that a given exercise can be used until the child's reading disability is corrected. There are many ways to develop each of the skills and abilities in reading. An effective remedial plan will include a variety of teaching techniques and instructional procedures.

Many sources describing teaching techniques are available to the remedial teacher. Professional books on remedial instruction in reading give suggestions for correcting specific types of reading difficulties. Russell and Karp (167) have compiled a group of remedial techniques. Manuals and workbooks accompanying basal reading programs are the most fruitful source of teaching techniques. The exercises suggested for teaching the skills and abilities when first introduced in such manuals and workbooks are the sorts of things that prove beneficial to remedial programs. If, for example, a fifth-grade child has difficulty with finding root words in affixed words, the teacher can find many and varied exercises in second- and third-grade manuals and workbooks to teach this skill. As she examines the teaching techniques suggested in these materials, the remedial teacher can accumulate a variety of exercises for each of the important types of disabilities listed in chapter 7. She can keep the program dynamic and interesting to the child by using a variety of teaching techniques and at the same time be sure that the instruction emphasizes the skill development indicated in the *individual educational plan of remediation.*

In using a variety of teaching methods and techniques, care must be taken that the teaching approaches do not confuse the child. The directions should be simple and the teaching techniques should not be changed too often. The exercises should be as nearly like reading as possible. Artificial or isolated drills should be avoided. The child should not have to spend time learning complicated procedures or directions. Enough variety should be introduced, however, to keep the program stimulating.

The Remedial Plan Should Assure Energetic Learning

Growth in reading presupposes an energetic learner. Of course, the child must learn to read by reading. He must attack the printed page vigorously and often if he is to succeed. A fatigued child cannot be expected to make gains during the remedial period. Therefore, the length of the period for remedial instruction should be such that concentrated work is possible. The disabled reader frequently finds it difficult to read for any considerable length of time. His lack of attention may be due to a variety of causes. It may be lack of physical stamina, it may be that he is not getting enough sleep at night, or it may be that his emotional reactions to reading sap his vitality. His inattention or lack of vigor may be due to habits of escaping from an unsuccessful and uncomfortable situation. Whatever the cause, most children, if properly motivated, can apply themselves to reading at least for a short period of time. Obviously, if the lack of attention and vigor result from a condition that can be corrected, the correction should be made. In any case, the length of the remedial reading period should be adjusted so that an energetic attack can be maintained.

Frequently it is necessary to divide the remedial sessions into short periods. The child may work with the remedial teacher for a period of forty-five minutes. At the start of the remedial training, it may be necessary to have him read from a basic reader for only ten minutes for specific purposes and then have him use the results of his reading in some creative activity, such as drawing, constructing, modeling, discussing, or the like. Then he might work on some skill development exercises which emphasize the training he needs. These exercises might entail rereading the material he read at the first part of the session or they may be word-recognition drill on new words introduced in the basic reader. Finally, the child might be asked to tell about the book he has been reading independently. As he gains in reading growth, the length of concentrated reading time should be increased. Soon the child who has no physical limitation will be reading longer without interruption. When this is so, creative activities can be used less frequently. Then he can read for several days during the remedial periods before he utilizes the results of reading. He still will need to discuss what he has read and do the related exercises.

THE REMEDIAL PLAN MUST ENCOURAGE THE DISABLED READER

Most disabled readers are discouraged about their failure to learn to read. They frequently think that they cannot learn. This lack of confidence in their ability to learn is detrimental to possible reading growth. The effective learner is a confident and purposeful learner, one who has a desire to learn and finds pleasure in working toward this goal. In order that a disabled reader may go ahead rapidly in learning to read, it is necessary for him to know that he can learn and to see that he is progressing satisfactorily.

Frequently the disabled reader is emotionally tense or insecure. He has had no real opportunity to gain confidence in himself because most of the school day is spent reading. For some time he has been much less effective in school work than his intellectual level would indicate that he should be. This child may become submissive or demanding, aggressive or withdrawing, or show his basic insecurity in a variety of ways. He may develop attitudes of indifference, dislike, or rejection. He may resist help, display few interests, or be antagonistic toward reading instruction. Remedial reading programs must overcome these attitudes and compensatory modes of behavior.

One of the first responsibilities of the remedial teacher is to develop in the child a need for learning to read. The second is to gain his confidence to such a degree that he will know that she has taken a personal interest and that she will solve his reading problem. A direct attack on the reading problem by a businesslike, considerate adult will do much to overcome tensions and faulty attitudes. When a child recognizes that an interest is taken in him and his problem, it will give him the much-needed sense of personal worth and the confidence in himself that he hitherto has lacked.

The Plan Should Emphasize Success

In order that the remedial program may be encouraging to the child, his successes rather than his mistakes should be emphasized. Teachers have a tendency to point out errors to children rather than to make them feel that for the most part they are doing particularly well. A disabled reader who is reminded continually of his errors may become overwhelmed by a sense of defeat. A wise teacher will start him in a remedial program that is somewhat easy for him so that his successful performance will be immediately apparent. As he gains confidence, the difficulty of the reading materials may be increased. The teacher should always be quick to recognize when the child has put forth a real effort and has done something well. Many times, particularly at the start, recognition will have to be given for activities related to the reading rather than the reading itself. Gradually the teacher will find more opportunities to give praise for the actual reading that is well done. At all times it should be remembered that the effectiveness of remedial instruction depends in no small measure upon the child's gain in confidence. This gain in confidence is brought about through successful experiences with reading which in the past had caused him so much difficulty.

The emphasis upon success does not mean that errors are to be overlooked. A child's faulty reading, of course, must be brought to his attention. Errors in word recognition must be pointed out. Faulty habits in reading which limit his speed must be recognized by him before they can be corrected. Sometimes it is necessary to demand greater exactness in reading. While it is true that the teacher must point out his mistakes, she must at all times indicate that he is improving and that for the most part he really is doing well. If, for example, a child should call the word *house, horse* in the sentence "The dog ran up to the house," the teacher should point out to him that he had the sentence nearly correct, but that in order to be exactly right he should have looked at the center part of the last word a little more carefully. As a matter of fact, the child did recognize most of the words in the sentence. He made an error that indicated that he was using the context well and that his error was a very slight one indeed. The words *house* and *horse* do look much alike.

In a comprehension lesson, the child may give the wrong answer to a question. Instead of saying that the answer is wrong, it would be far better for the teacher to say, "Let's see what the book says about this" and then find out why the child made his error. It frequently will be found that he did not understand the meaning of a word or that he failed to notice a key word such as *not,* or that he had not grouped the words into proper thought units. Whatever the cause, it should be found and the child should be shown the correct way to read the passage. The attitude of the teacher should be not one of pointing out errors but one of helping the child learn to read.

An effective remedial program must be one that is satisfying to the child, makes him feel that he is getting along well, and keeps at a minimum any anxiety which he feels about his reading progress. The teacher's responsibility in encouraging the child to read energetically is great. She should neither hurry him unduly nor allow him to dawdle; she should be sure he is working hard and yet avoid putting pressure on him. Practically all children can be expected to work intently in developing reading ability. This is especially true if the reading materials are at the right level, if the child is properly motivated, and if he is reading for purposes that are real to him. There should always be a friendly atmosphere, but one that keeps uppermost the point of view that the child is there to learn to read.

Growth in Reading Should Be Demonstrated

The disabled reader needs to have his reading growth demonstrated to him. There are many ways to do this. The diagnostician has isolated the child's needs and indicated the amount of emphasis that should be given. The method for demonstrating progress to him depends upon the nature of the reading problem. If, for example, the child is trying to develop a sight vocabulary, he could make a picture dictionary of the words he was trying to learn. As the dictionary became larger, he would recognize that he had increased his sight vocabulary. The child who is working on accuracy of comprehension could develop a bar chart (figure 5) in which he would indicate his percent of accuracy from week to week. If he failed to gain over the period of a week, the teacher could simplify the material or ask more general questions so that accuracy would increase. Then as the child gained confidence, the difficulty of the material again could be increased gradually. It is good for the child to go back, from time to time, and reread something that he has read previously. He will discover that material that was difficult for him a short while ago is now relatively easy for him to read. This will be especially true if the teacher takes time to prepare him to read it.

Whatever the nature of the difficulty, it is important for the remedial program to be organized to demonstrate to the child that he is progressing toward his goal of better reading. The disabled reader who has been in

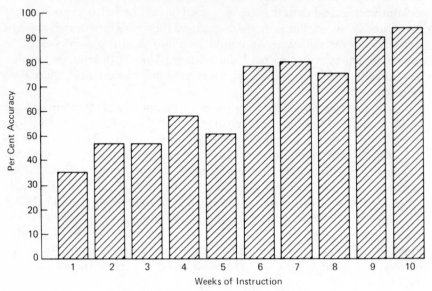

Fig. 5. *AN ACCURACY BAR CHART.*

difficulty for a long time needs whatever encouragement can be given him. He needs not only to be in a comfortable learning situation but also to see that he is making effective advancement in reading.

Remedial Programs Should Not Be
Substituted for Enjoyable Activities

The remedial teacher must organize the periods of instruction so that children are not required to come for training at a time that competes with other activities of great importance to them. For example, it is a frequent practice to have them come to a clinic after school. This is a bad time for a boy who enjoys outdoor sports with his friends, and who finds this the only time that outdoor games are played in his neighborhood. In scheduling summer reading programs, it is wise to delay their start until a week or so after school is out, and the children have found that they have time that they do not know what to do with. Even then, the better scheduling time for classes is probably in the morning because the majority of things that the child likes to do, such as going swimming or playing baseball, are done in the afternoon.

The busy classroom teacher often finds it difficult to give a child the attention he needs when the class is in session. She may select recess time or the time in which other children have their hobby clubs, or are in the auditorium viewing a movie, for helping a child with his reading. Such a practice is understandable but is not good for the correction of a reading disability. A better time would be to work with the children needing reeducation while the rest of the class is busily engaged in studying or reading independently. Whatever time is used for giving remedial help, it is important that it does not conflict with activities which are important to the child.

MATERIALS AND EXERCISES MUST BE APPROPRIATE

The selection of appropriate material for remedial work in reading is one of the main problems the remedial teacher has to solve. Some teachers feel that the most important element is that the material deal with a subject in which the child is interested. Others feel that the level of difficulty is of even greater importance. Still others believe that having material compatible with the nature of the remedial instruction is of paramount importance. There can be no doubt that all three of these elements enter into the selection. Without trying to decide between them, we may conclude that the more important considerations in selecting material are:

1. The materials must be suitable in level of difficulty.
2. The materials must be suitable in type.
3. The materials must be at the appropriate level of interest and format.
4. The materials must be abundant.

The Materials Must Be Suitable in Level of Difficulty

The child grows in reading by reading; therefore the material that is used for remedial instruction should be of a difficulty level that enables him to read comfortably and with enjoyment. The diagnosis will have disclosed the level at which the disabled reader could be expected to read. The remedial teacher must pick out materials at that level to suit the child. The difficulty of material can be judged in many ways. Readability formulas, such as the Lorge formula (134), the formula of Dale-Chall (49), and that of Spache (185) are useful in estimating reading level. Sources of graded book lists are given in the Appendixes I and II. Most basic readers are graded carefully and indicate the level of reading maturity necessary for their use. In general, basic readers of second-grade level are suitable to the child whose skills are of second-grade maturity. Third-grade books are suitable for the child whose skill development is approximately that of a third-grade child. Ungraded materials can be estimated by formula or by using a basic reading series as a difficulty-rating scale. The difficulty of an ungraded library book, for example, may be judged by comparing it with the various grade levels of a basic reader. The book can be compared with a third-grade reader, and if it is judged to be harder, it then may be compared with a fourth-grade reader, and so forth, until the approximate level of difficulty can be estimated. In making the judgment, the teacher should look at the number of unusual words it contains, the length of its sentences, the number of prepositional phrases, the number of unusual word orders, and the complexity of the ideas it includes. In judging level of difficulty, it is important that the remedial teacher remember that the results of standardized survey tests tend to overestimate the skill development of a reading disability case. Therefore, it is usually wise to start remedial instruction with material that is somewhat lower than the child's general reading score indicated by standardized tests.

The difficulty of the material appropriate for remedial instruction will vary somewhat with the nature of the disability. The teacher should modify the level of difficulty according to the goals of instruction to be achieved by the use of that material. For example, if the child's major problem is one of developing sight vocabulary, the material should be relatively easy with few new words being introduced. Those that are introduced should be used often in the material. For this child, a relatively easy level in a basic reading program would be desirable. For the child who needs training in analyzing words effectively, a higher concentration of new vocabulary would be desirable. The child could meet one new word in approximately every twenty running words. This would give him an opportunity to use the techniques of word analysis that he needs to develop, and at the same time it would enable him to maintain the thought of the passage so that meaning clues could be used as a means of checking the accuracy of his word recognition.

A child who is trying to increase his speed of comprehension should use material that is easy for him. This would have few if any word-recognition problems for him. But the child who is trying to increase his power of comprehension should use material which challenges him; but he must have a reasonable chance of successfully comprehending the material.

The Materials Must Be Suitable in Type

It often is said that any kind of material suitable for teaching reading in the first place is suitable for remedial instruction. While this is true, it is important to recognize that the material must be nicely selected to meet the disabled reader's instructional needs. The type of material that is suitable for one kind of disability is not necessarily appropriate for another. If the major problem is that of increasing speed of reading, the best material would be short stories with fast-moving plots. The material should be easy not only in reading difficulty, but the content should be such that the child can read it to gain a general impression or the general significance. If the problem is one in the word recognition area, a basic reader along with the exercises found in the manuals and workbooks related to the word-recognition problem would be the best reading material to use. If the problem is in the comprehension area and increased accuracy in reading is sought, science or social studies material with a lot of facts should be used. In every instance, the material should be at the appropriate level of difficulty, but also it should be conducive to the goals of reading expected.

The Materials Must Be at the Appropriate Level of Interest and Format

A relatively mature and intelligent twelve-year-old usually will not find first- and second-grade material interesting, nor will he find the format very attractive. A child with second-grade reading ability nevertheless must use material that he can read. The problem facing the remedial teacher in this respect is very great. Second-grade books are designed for children seven or eight years of age. The pictures are of small children and the print looks large and juvenile. The topics are for the seven- or eight-year-old and not for a twelve-year-old. Many books that might be used for remedial reading instruction lose some of their value because they lack interest and have the wrong format. Nonetheless, there can be no compromise with using material that is at the appropriate level of difficulty. The problem is how to find material at a suitable level and as appealing as possible to a child of more mature age.

An increasingly large number of books for remedial work are being developed. There are books designed primarily for the less capable reader. They include *The Cowboy Sam Series* (44), *The Deep-Sea Adventure Series* (56), *Everyreader Series* (70), *The Morgan Bay Mysteries* (143), *Interesting Reading Series* (111), and *Xerox Pal Series* (151).

Happily, there is more material designed to aid in developing the skills of disabled readers who are diagnosed as having specific instructional needs. *The Macmillan Reading Spectrum* (138), *The S.R.A. Reading Laboratories* (191), and *Barnell-Loft Specific Skills Series* (190) all are helpful in correcting some deficiencies in disabled readers' skills.

Phonetically regular materials and certain word-recognition skill books are useful for reading disability cases who are weak in the phonic aspects of word recognition. Such series as *McGraw-Hill Story Books* (200), *Phonetic Reader Series* (153), *Breaking the Sound Barrier* (177), *Eye and Ear Fun* (194), and *The New Phonics We Use* (146) will prove helpful when used judiciously.

A new type of material that appears to have promise for disabled readers is programmed-learning material. An example of this is *Programmed Reading* (201). Other organized learning programs are forthcoming.

The workbooks that accompany basic readers also are excellent. The workbooks look considerably more mature than the basic readers they accompany. The drill exercises give no indication of the maturity level of the children who are expected to read them. There are many lists of books that can be used in remedial work. Many of these lists indicate the level of reading maturity required to read the books and also indicate the maximum age of a child who will enjoy reading the material. Sources of graded book lists are given in Appendixes I and II.

The Materials Must Be Abundant

In selecting material for remedial work, the first consideration is that it must be at the correct level of difficulty. The second is that it should be appropriate in type. The third is that it should have the proper format and meet the interest level of the child. Another consideration in reading is that the materials be abundant. There should be a wide variety of material meeting many interests and at various levels of difficulty. For any one child, there should be ample material for him to read. There should be material for his remedial instruction and also for his independent reading. The independent reading for a remedial reading case should be considerably easier than that used in remedial instruction. The material for independent reading needs to be on many topics because the children will have a wide variety of interests. The material that the disabled reader is to read independently should fulfill an existing interest which he already has, while the material that is used for instructional purposes must be such that he can be motivated to take an interest in reading it.

THE REMEDIAL PLAN MUST EMPLOY EFFECTIVE TEACHING PROCEDURES

During the discussion of planning for the treatment of reading difficulties, it was implied that remedial instruction is the application of sound teaching procedures directed toward the specific needs of the child. Instruction in remedial reading is not unusual in character nor does it need expensive

and artificial equipment. Skills and abilities should be emphasized in actual reading situations free from isolated drill. Sound teaching procedures
such as those used for introducing the reading skills and abilities in the first
place should be used. The materials best for remedial instruction are those
that are best for the developmental program.

The difference between remedial instruction and the developmental
program is in the extent of individualization and in the study of the disabled reader rather than in the uniqueness of its methods or materials. The
diagnosis will have indicated the type and level of material to be used. The
authors consider the reading of selections to be at the core of a remedial
plan. The remedial plan for every disabled reader should include the reading of selections, taught in much the same way that they are in a developmental reading program. In teaching a selection, there are a series of steps
necessary to foster reading growth wherever taught—in the classroom,
reading center, or clinic. These steps are essential to good teaching of reading at any level from first grade through college. They form the lesson plan
for teaching a selection step by step, as follows:

1. Building readiness.
2. Introducing new or difficult words.
3. Setting purposes for reading.
4. Guiding silent reading.
5. Discussing content read.
6. Rereading if desirable.
7. Developing specific skills and abilities.
8. Extending to related supplementary material.
9. Utilizing the results of reading.

Some of these steps in reading instruction, unfortunately, sometimes
are neglected in remedial work. Readiness should be built carefully for
every topic and every selection to be read by the disabled reader. This includes the creation of interest in, the development of background for, and
the introduction of new words for each selection the disabled reader reads.
The child who has difficulty in reading, just as the other children who do
not, should understand the purposes for reading before the reading is done.
Another step of teaching a selection that never should be neglected is developing specific skills and abilities. For remedial instruction, this step is of
paramount importance. Having disabled readers merely read and discuss a
selection will not itself develop the skills and abilities necessary for orderly
growth in reading capability. The most important phases of instruction
take place in the preparatory activities, during which new vocabulary is

introduced and purposes are set, and in follow-up skill and ability exercises. A teacher demonstrates her teaching skill when she shows the disabled reader how to read and when she provides him with the experiences and the drills necessary for establishing the specific skills and abilities that make for mature reading.

Many types of reading disability cases need reinforcing exercises beyond those for students with normal reading growth. In the following chapters on remedial instruction for specific reading problems, sample types of supplementary reinforcing exercises are suggested.

The disabled reader also should use the results of his reading in a creative enterprise. If, for example, he has read a selection about flood control to find what techniques are used, it would be as important for him to make a diagram of a river bed illustrating what he had learned, as it would be for children in the developmental reading program. Using the results of their reading is a good procedure for all children. It is essential practice, though often neglected to those who are disabled readers. How the results of reading may be used may be a discussion, a picture drawn, a chart made, a map planned, or any one of such enterprises. There should be relatively little time given to these things, but above all, the creative work should be the child's own.

The remedial teacher will find it helpful to keep a cumulative account of the child's progress. The record should include the books read, the type of exercises used and the success of each, any charts used to show the child his progress, and the results of periodic tests. Any indications of interests and anecdotal accounts of the child's reactions to the remedial program should be included. By studying this record, the teacher can compare periods of rapid growth with the type of exercises used and books read. A study of past records will recall those approaches that were successful with other similar cases. The teacher can assemble a file of such folders, arranged according to the specific problem involved.

The Reading Processes Must Be
Made Meaningful to the Learner

One reason why the disabled reader is in difficulty is because he does not understand the process involved in being a good reader. The remedial teacher has the responsibility not only for maintaining orderly sequences of skill development but also for making these steps understood by the child. The teacher not only should teach him to use context clues in word recognition but also should let him see how helpful it is in word recognition. The teacher also should show him how to organize the material he reads for effective retention. She should show him why it is effective. The child should understand the importance of reading certain material carefully with attention to detail, while other material can be read rapidly to understand its general ideas.

If the remedial teacher expects the child to retain a knowledge of word elements, it is important for her to show him how much they will aid him in recognizing new words. For too long, many remedial teachers have felt that if the child is stimulated to read material at the correct level of difficulty he automatically will develop the needed skills. This point of view can be questioned. A more reasonable assumption is that the child should be shown how to read and how much he can use each added reading accomplishment. Suppose a child, for example, has learned by rote to pronounce a list of isolated prefixes—how much better it would have been to point out to him the prefixes in words and show him how they change the meaning of the root words.

The remedial teacher will find that explaining the processes of reading to the learner helps to solve his reading confusions. Drill on isolated parts of words is not as effective as is a meaningful approach to reading. Modern developmental reading programs are planned to enable the child to develop the needed skills and abilities and to understand the usefulness of each. The remedial program should be concerned even more with explaining reading processes to the child. The day has long since passed when it was assumed that if we but interested the child in reading, he would go ahead on his own to develop skills of which he was unaware.

Remedial Procedures Should Be as Nearly Like the Reading Act as Possible

Although there are available many devices and mechanical aids for remedial instruction, most reading growth will come from training allied with reading itself. Most expensive equipment is unnecessary and often wastes time that could be used for more productive reading activities. In establishing a reading center or clinic, priority should be given to obtaining varied reading materials. These include books, pamphlets, and skill-development books of a wide range of reading difficulty. A typewriter, with primer-size type, is another desirable item to have available. A typewriter is useful to the teacher in constructing materials to meet specific needs and vocabularies.

The exercises should not only be designed to develop specific skills but also should utilize these skills in meaningful reading content. For example, even in a simple exercise for developing rapid sight recognition of words, it is better to have the child read the word flashed before him, and at the same time tell whether it names an animal, or is an action verb, rather than just to identify the words without giving any thought to their meaning. In reading, the child must not only identify a word but also must associate meaning with it. Exercises that place the skill development in context rather than in isolation are superior to those that do not. The remedial suggestions made in the following chapters illustrate this principle of remedial instruction.

The more that exercises used in building skills and abilities approximate real reading, the more likely they will be transferred to reading. For example, enlarging the knowledge of phonics in recognizing words needed by a child for understanding content more likely will lead him to use them in identifying new words by himself than he would if the same elements had been taught by use of isolated drill exercises. Not only will he be more likely to transfer what he has learned in new situations, but also he will establish the habit of noting the phonetic patterns within troublesome words and discover many more useful aids to word recognition.

The Teacher Must Be Optimistic

A teacher helping a child overcome a reading disability should be a buoyant, energetic person. She must make the disabled reader sense her confidence in him. The problems in correcting a complex reading disability may seem to be almost insurmountable. Nevertheless, the teacher must show each disabled reader that she knows he will learn to read. This attitude comes from a thorough understanding of the child's instructional needs, a sound diagnosis, and a remedial program planned well enough in advance so that it is clearly in mind. The teacher gains immediate confidence through knowing exactly what is going to be done during each remedial lesson. A well-prepared teacher who knows exactly where each session is going will instill confidence in the child. With preparation, there usually will be progress in reading.

The teacher may be optimistic because most reading disability cases do show immediate gains from remedial instruction. If the child's reading problem and his characteristics have been evaluated carefully and if the program has been based upon an appropriate individual remedial plan, success is practically assured. Of course, the teacher's confidence sometimes may be shaken. There are periods during the corrective treatment of practically every remedial case when there is little evidence of new growth. But all the same, confidence in the child's ultimate success must remain even when things do not appear to be going well. Under some circumstances, the remedial plan should be restudied and the diagnosis reviewed, but all this need not diminish confidence in the child's ultimate success.

The Child Needs Group as Well as Individual Work

The disabled reader needs to share experiences with other children just as much as, or even more than, the child whose growth in reading is normal. Not only should his classroom work be organized so that he can participate in some of the important activities of the class, but also he should see that there are other children with similar difficulties. It is recommended that disabled readers work in groups whenever possible. Much can be gained by the disabled reader seeing other children right around him with similar difficulties who are making progress in overcoming them. It often is assumed that remedial reading instruction is a formal procedure in which the child is separated from other children and drilled until his disability is corrected. Such instruction is most unwise. It is a boost to the child to know that there are other children who are learning to read and who are able to use their newly gained proficiencies in reading.

The summer program at the University of Minnesota Psycho-Educational Clinic is a good illustration of how a child can be given both individual and group remedial work. Of course, the school reading center or the typical reading clinic would have to make slight modifications. The children who come to the summer reading clinic at the University of Minnesota mostly are extremely disabled readers. The great majority would be described as complex or limiting disability cases. The most successful approach that we have been able to devise for these children has been to separate them into groups or classes of about fifteen to twenty. They work with a classroom teacher for an entire morning. In the classroom, there is a regular unit of instruction, using topics found in readers and selected for the reading level at which the greatest number in the class can read comfortably. These topics are supplemented by a variety of reference books in the room. For some of the children, picture books or pictures in books which supply information are used. Besides the unit the children are reading, there is group instruction using basal material at the appropriate level for each group within the class. Then, for a half hour to an hour every day, each child is withdrawn from the class, either in small groups of four or five or for individual instruction, whichever is deemed best. The children are given remedial instruction designed for their specific remedial problems. Children in the same major classification of disability form the small groups. Children who do not fit into any group are handled individually. In a typical school reading center, the remedial reading teacher would not have additional personnel to handle small groups. Therefore, the modification recommended for the school reading center would be to have those children who were less seriously disabled or who constituted a similar type of disability, such as the slow readers, brought together for instruction in relatively large groups. Those children with more complex disabilities could be handled in smaller sections. These group sessions could be conducted during the morning. Then the remedial teacher would be free in the afternoon to handle smaller groups or individuals.

THE PLAN MUST ENLIST COOPERATIVE EFFORTS

Although implementation of the remedial plan may be the direct responsibility of the remedial reading teacher, many other people should be involved in formulating and helping to implement an *individual plan of remediation* including outside consultants, classroom teachers, parents, and the remedial reader himself.

The Remedial Plan Should Involve Outside Consultants

It would be rather unusual for such professionals as the school principal, the school psychologist, the school social worker, a physician, a media expert, a speech pathologist, or the school nurse to be in any way involved in the direct remediation of a disabled reader. Nevertheless, the insights of one or more of these professionals may prove invaluable to the formulation of the appropriate individual remedial plans. Knowledge of a student's reading difficulties and a remedial plan help other professionals coordinate their efforts. Some children receive not only remedial reading services but also the services of other professionals such as a social worker or a speech pathologist. It is important for the remedial reading teacher and such other professionals to share information, insights, and concerns on a regular basis.

The Remedial Plan Should Involve Classroom Teachers

In most people's minds, including those of most reading-disabled children and their parents, success or failure in reading is measured not in the school reading center or resource room, but in the regular classroom. That is where the child spends the greater part of his day and that is where he must establish social relationships with his peers. If a child is to really find success in school, he must find it in the classroom. For this reason, it is imperative for classroom teachers to be cooperatively and closely involved in initial planning and to maintain involvement in order to coordinate their efforts with those of the reading specialist. Direct observation of a student's classroom behavior by the remedial reading teacher, and consultation with the classroom teacher enable the remedial reading teacher to plan activities which benefit the child directly in the classroom. For example, if students in the classroom have been told that they may make an optional, brief, oral report on a book that they think others in the class might enjoy, the remedial reading teacher could encourage an insecure reading-disabled child to do so. The remedial reading teacher could aid the child in the selection of a book which he could read successfully, but which also would appeal to his classmates, and she could give him an opportunity to practice his presentation privately in order to gain the confidence he needs to speak effectively to the class. In consultation with the remedial reading teacher, the classroom teacher can adapt and adjust classroom expectations to ensure that when the reading-disabled child exerts honest effort, he will be successful. Although a student may be making real and rapid progress in reading in the reading center or resource room, he will be denied a true sense of accomplishment if the rest of his day is filled with reading demands which are far beyond him. He will lose the opportunity to practice his newly acquired reading skills in the regular classroom; he will lose the opportunity to view himself and have his classmates view him as a reader; he will lose the positive attitudes he may have acquired about reading; and he will lose that sense of confidence necessary to learning.

The Remedial Plan Should Involve the Parents

Parental cooperation is beneficial to successful remediation, for two reasons. First, parents can make a unique contribution to a teacher's understanding of their child. Parents are concerned with their children's behavior in nonschool settings and for this reason often are aware of certain attributes which teachers are less likely to see. For example, it is often the parent who serves to alert the remedial reading teacher to signs of tension or frustration which in school a child has hidden. It is the parent who is the first to sense that positive change of attitude which characterizes a child's response to successful remediation. The second reason parental cooperation is so beneficial is because parents are very important people in a child's life. When his parents understand the remedial plan and support it, a child receives a form of encouragement which helps him overcome his reading difficulty.

Furthermore, parents are concerned about their children's difficulties, sometimes extremely concerned. Complete understanding of the remedial plan and information about the program's outcome helps to relieve the extreme anxiety some parents feel when their children have reading problems. Some parents of disabled readers become interested in directly aiding their children in reading. Parents can do much to help their children with reading, but their efforts will be most beneficial when they receive guidance from the remedial reading teacher and serve to enhance and support the remedial plan.

The Remedial Plan Should Involve the Child

The true focus of every successful remedial plan is the disabled reader himself. It is the child, after all, who has to learn. If the child is not enthusiastic about the plan or does not believe in it, the efforts of consultants, teachers and parents will have little effect. The child should aid as much as possible in formulating the plan; older students often have valuable insights into the nature of their reading problems. At the secondary level, many wise remedial reading teachers have found that enlisting students' cooperation in planning activities, choosing materials, and setting goals was a necessary first step in provoking interest in improving reading. Discussing with a child his feelings and attitudes about reading and about plans for reading improvement is an essential beginning to helping him develop more positive feelings and attitudes about reading, about learning, and even about himself. It is important for everyone concerned, most of all the child, to understand the remedial program, to support it, and to cooperate with it.

SUMMARY

In making an *appropriate educational plan of remediation,* it is necessary to identify the specific limitations hindering reading growth. Although the remedial work for each disabled reader must be different in certain respects, there are some common elements among the corrective programs. The remedial program must be designed to emphasize the child's instructional needs as shown by the diagnosis, and therefore there can be no universal approach to all cases. The remedial program for each reading case must be planned carefully and written down. It will be necessary to modify the program from time to time to keep abreast of the child's changing instructional needs. Even though the program is planned to emphasize overcoming a specific disability, a variety of remedial techniques should be used. The remedial teacher will find manuals and workbooks in basal reading programs a good source of teaching techniques.

Remedial reading programs must be individualized and must be designed in keeping with the child's instructional needs and characteristics. It is necessary to modify the approaches to reading in order to adjust limitations such as poor hearing or poor vision. Remedial instruction should not drill on one specific skill or ability in isolation, but should provide new experience in whatever skills are needed in connection with purposeful reading. The length of remedial sessions should be planned so that the child will not become fatigued or inattentive.

Reading instruction for the disabled reader must be well organized so that skills and abilities may be developed smoothly with no undue burden on the child, with little chance for overemphasis, and with no omission of essential learnings. The teacher should not only maintain an orderly sequence of skill development but also should make the steps understood by the child.

The remedial reading program must encourage the child since much of his trouble was because he had lost confidence in his ability to learn. The teacher should be optimistic, the child's successes should be emphasized, and his progress should be demonstrated to him. Materials must be geared to the child's reading abilities and instructional needs; they should be at his level of difficulty and type of content; they should be as near as possible to his interests; and they should look "mature" to the child. The materials used for remedial instruction must be of such difficulty that the child can read them and of such maturity that he will be motivated to read them. There can be no compromise with the difficulty level of the material, because the child will not be interested in reading material he cannot read, no matter how attractive the subject matter. In all remedial work, sound teaching procedures should be used and artificial devices and isolated drill should be avoided.

Needed resource experts—the classroom teacher, the parents, and most of all, the disabled reader himself—should have an active part in formulating the *individual plan of remediation.*

SELECTED READINGS

DURRELL, DONALD D., *Improving Reading Instruction,* chap. 14. New York: Harcourt Brace Jovanovich, 1956.

HARRIS, ALBERT J., and E. R. SIPAY, *How to Increase Reading Ability* (6th ed.), chap. 13. New York: David McKay, 1975.

KENNEDY, E. C., *Classroom Approaches to Remedial Reading* (2nd ed.), Itaska, Ill.: F. E. Peacock, 1977.

OTTO, W., and R. A. MCMENEMY, *Corrective and Remedial Teaching: Principles and Practices* (2nd ed.), chap. 3. Boston: Houghton Mifflin, 1973.

SPACHE, G. D., *Diagnosing and Correcting Reading Disabilities,* chap. 10. Boston: Allyn and Bacon, 1976.

TINKER, M. A., and C. M. McCULLOUGH, *Teaching Elementary Reading* (4th ed.), chap. 25. New York: Appleton-Century-Crofts, 1975.

ZINTZ, M. V., *Corrective Reading* (2nd ed.), Chaps. 3, 4. Dubuque, Iowa: Brown, 1972.

Correcting Deficiencies in Meaning Clues to Word Recognition

nine

Skill in word recognition is a fundamental part of the equipment of a capable reader at any level. As the child matures in reading, the materials and methods used in teaching him gradually demand more and more independent word recognition. The child who has failed to establish effective means of identifying and recognizing words for his level of advancement will be handicapped in all other aspects of reading.

Modern approaches to teaching word recognition must be based upon integration of the unique nature of reading growth, as analyzed by reading research workers, and oral communication, as described by linguistic research workers. The first-grade reading studies sponsored by the United States Office of Education gave some new insights into the development of word-recognition skills. The major conclusions reached by Bond and Dykstra (23) resulting from their analyses of the combined data compiled from the twenty-seven individual studies offer some definitive evidence of the importance of word-study skills to reading success. They found that regardless of the approach to reading instruction used in the first grade, word-recognition skills must be emphasized. A second year follow-up study (64) indicated that this was true for the second grade as well.

The combined analyses also showed that much of the variation in success in reading during the first two years of reading instruction could be accounted for by attributes the children brought to the learning situation. Capabilities such as auditory and visual discrimination, and pre-first-grade familiarity with print are related substantially to success in learning to read, whatever approach to initial instruction is used. These attributes are considered by some authorities to have a direct relationship to the child's preschool interest in words and their printed symbols. These capabilities are readiness factors for the development of word-recognition skills.

The combined data from these extensive studies further show that combinations of methods including such components as basal readers, phonics and linguistic training, and language experiences, are superior to any of these approaches used alone. Those programs which were especially effective in developing word-recognition skills were not as productive in the comprehension areas. Conversely, those programs which emphasized meaning, such as the language experience and basic reader approaches, needed to be augmented by a more intensive word-recognition program.

These studies further indicated that initial reading programs should strive for a better balance between phonetically regular words, as emphasized by some linguists, and high-utility words, emphasized in many basal readers. The use of vocabularies selected largely on the basis of their frequency of use or utility can generate word-recognition problems. It also was evident that the sole use of words spelled in a phonetically regular way makes meaningful reading difficult to acquire.

The analyses also showed that encouraging children to write the words as they learned to read them and to associate words with sounds and meanings was helpful in developing word-recognition skills.

How to correct difficulties in the *word-perceptual* skills, necessary in recognizing the printed symbols of word meanings, will be the concern of the next two chapters. These skills must be taught so as to encourage a child to attempt *rapid recognition* of known or partially familiar words, so that he will be able to group them into thought units. At the same time, training in *word identification* must be given so that the learner can develop skill in decoding the printed forms of words that these symbols represent when he first sees them in their written forms. These skills are not easily developed, and it is little wonder that some children run into difficulties before they acquire them. In fact, most severely disabled readers have weaknesses in the word-recognition area.

Word study involves two types of goals. The first is expanding meaning vocabulary and teaching the word-recognition techniques so that meanings accompany the identification of the symbols. The child must learn to associate meaning with printed symbols. His meanings must be clear and precise if he is to comprehend the material he is reading. He also must be able to select, among all the meanings of a word, the one that is correct for the particular context in which the word is used. The word *run*, which is used in most pre-primers, has fifty-six different definitions even in a dictionary used in the elementary grades. The child must learn to use context as he recognizes the printed symbols to help him select the correct meaning. For example, the meaning of *run* can be derived from the content in the statements "He was tired after the long run," and "All will turn out well in the long run." Often the sentence alone will not give the meaning of a word; only the gist of the passage will. For example, the precise meaning of *run* cannot be derived from the sentence "He was out of breath after he made the run." In order to understand the word *run*, the reader must know not only that the boy was playing baseball, but also that he scored rather than chased a fly ball. The development of word meaning will be discussed in detail in chapter 13; but it is important to teach the word-recognition techniques in such a way that words will be rapidly recognized and the proper meanings associated with them.

The second goal of instruction in word study is the development of a set of flexible skills and knowledges that will enable the child to recognize words he already knows and identify new words with speed and understanding. *Word identification* and *word recognition* are closely related features of word perception. First contact with a new word form calls for identification of the printed symbol in terms of its sound and meaning. Subsequent contacts develop recognition. In this text, the development of word recognition implies identification as the first step in the process. Until a printed symbol is grasped at a glance, until it has become what we term a *sight word*, recognition requires some degree of identification. Instruction in word recognition is designed to enable the child to do three interrelated tasks. *First,* he must be able to recognize known words rapidly with a minimum of analysis. For example, if he knows the word *think* as a sight word, he should not analyze it into *th-ink,* pronouncing each part and then blending it into the word *think.* Indeed, to do so again and again would be most detrimental to his reading ability. There are children who are in difficulty in reading for just this reason. *Second,* he should be skilled in recognizing partially known words with little analysis. If the child knows the word *think,* he should be adept at identifying it in all of its variant forms. Applying syntactic skills, he should need but a glance at the word to enable him to recognize and know the meaning of *think, thinks, thinking,* and as he gains maturity, *unthinkable.* In such words, the child should learn to identify the root word, recognize the modified form rapidly, and understand the changed meaning. *Third,* the child must develop a flexible set of skills that will enable him to identify new words by himself. As he matures in reading, he must be able not only to pronounce the new words, but also to be so skilled that he can recognize them silently without interrupting the thought of the passage.

Instruction in word identification is complex indeed. It is understandable why reading instruction has progressed through a series of methods from the spelling approach of the *Blue-Back Speller* days, to the whole-word approach of the *Quincy Method,* to the phonetic emphasis of the *Beacon* and *Gordon* systems, to sentence or context emphasis, to the modern composite methods using context, whole-word, phonics, and structural analysis as aids to word identification. The major problem in the modern approach is teaching the flexible set of skills needed so that none will be omitted or over- or underemphasized and so that the more analytical and time-consuming aids to recognition will be used only when needed. To teach the child the word-recognition techniques necessary for him to recognize known words and to identify new ones visually or phonetically, at least five sorts of "balance" must be maintained.

First, a balance between the establishment of *word-recognition techniques* and the development of *meaning vocabulary* is desirable for reading growth. If there is too much isolated drill on word parts, the child may become a capable word-caller, but he may not understand what he is reading. The child may be able to make a fairly accurate attempt at pronouncing new words, but unless what he pronounces has meaning accompanying it, the results may be erroneous. Even though the early lessons in reading use very common words, the teacher who neglects to introduce the words in context may encourage an overemphasis on analytical techniques at the expense of word meaning. Conversely, the teacher who neglects to teach identification skills, may cause the child to make random attempts to say any word that comes to mind or it may make the child too dependent on her. Word-recognition skills should be taught in context and in words rather than in isolation. They must be taught and learned as part of the coordinated program.

Second, a balance between the acquisition of *sight vocabulary*—words the child knows at a glance—and the establishment of *word-recognition skills* is essential. The child must learn to recognize at sight an ever-increasing number of words, because it is on these that his fluency as a reader depends. These words also provide much of his ability to derive meaning from printed matter. If the child is led to place too much emphasis on either one of these learnings at the expense of the other, the results will be serious. The teacher may place so much emphasis upon building sight vocabulary that the child fails to establish the needed word-recognition techniques. This child may seem to progress well at the start, but he soon will become a disabled reader. He will lack independence, since he has no way of identifying new words by himself. A reading program that stresses word-recognition skills and neglects to build sight vocabulary is encouraging the child to become a slow, laborious, and overanalytical reader. The child needs to build both an ever-increasing sight vocabulary and a more diversified set of word-recognition techniques. The child who excludes one in favor of the other will have serious trouble reading. This is one of the most difficult balances to achieve. As a result, there are many children who go to work using analysis on words that they really know at sight, and other children are at a loss to work out the pronunciation of new words independently because they are weak in the identifying skills.

Third, there must be a balance between the *meaning clues* and the *analytical aids* to word recognition. The child who depends too much on meaning clues to recognition will make many errors that have little relationship to the appearance of the word he miscalls. These errors are in substituting words that make sense though they are not the words of the author nor do they evoke his meaning. For example, this child might read the sentence "The ship sailed over the equator," as "The ship sailed over the seas." Such a reader is often inaccurate and misses out in comprehension. The child, on the other hand, who depends too much upon analytical and blending aids to the exclusion of meaning also may be inaccurate. The errors might reflect reasonable letter-sound associations, but they make no real sense. For example, the sentence "The Scotch girl's dress was plaid," might be read "The Scotch girl's dress was played." In either this case or the former, little or no understanding results. The child must develop both abilities and when he has done so, he can use them to reinforce one another. The child who lacks the analytical techniques is handicapped because exact recognition often is impossible from context alone. The child who depends too much upon word analysis is unable to use context to speed recognition and to check the accuracy of his recognition through the sense it makes.

Fourth, a balance between *phonic* and *structural* techniques must be maintained. If the teacher places too much emphasis on phonetic training, the child may fail to develop the ability to use larger structural elements in the recognition of words. The result may be an element-by-element, sound-blending approach which is unfortunate as a major means of word recognition. This emphasis may teach the child to separate words to such an extent that synthesis or blending of sounds into one word becomes impossible. But if the emphasis on larger structural and visual elements is too great, the child may not have skill in using smaller elements or letter sounds sufficiently developed for him to recognize certain words, such as unusual names that require sounding. Many children with reading disability have failed to establish this balance and hence have become either overanalytical or lack sufficient knowledge of phonics.

Fifth, there must be a balance between the emphasis placed on *knowledge of word parts* and the *orderly inspection of words* along the line of print from the left to right and from the beginning of the word to the end. If too much stress is placed, for example, on word families such as the *at* family in *cat, sat, fat, hat,* the child may neglect the beginning elements of words and thus make an unreasonable number of errors in them. Another child using this emphasis may become a difficult reversal case, because he has the habit of looking at the end of words to pick up his clues to recognition. When a child makes an excessive number of errors in any specific location within words, it usually indicates that knowledge of word parts has been emphasized at the expense of orderly inspection from the beginning to end of each word he studies. In this respect, another balance is required in the orderly inspection of words, which is that the child must develop flexibility in his visual analysis of the word he is trying to recognize. For example, suppose the word is *frighten;* the child selects *fri* as the first element he recognizes.

Unless he quickly rejects this result of his visual analysis, he will be unable to work out the rest of the word, because *ght* will not be very helpful to him. He may try to sound each letter, *g—h—t,* and then get into marked confusion. A child who was more flexible in the visual analysis of words would reject the first separation of the word and break it into more suitable parts, such as *fr—ight—en.* Then, applying his knowledge of the elements, he would be able to pronounce the word with little difficulty.

Word recognition is much more complex than is assumed in programs emphasizing a single set of skills or in instruction placing the child in a stimulating reading environment and expecting him to discover all the needed skills and to maintain the balances among them. Word recognition entails too many interrelated learnings to allow the program to be narrow or incidental.

The major source of word-recognition difficulty is in the child's failure to establish one or more of these basic learnings or overdependence on any of them. Word-recognition problems often are found to be at the root of the difficulty of those disabled readers who fall into the categories of *limiting* disability and *complex* disability. The more prevalent meaning-clue disabilities are listed below. Each will be discussed along with the methods of correction that have been found helpful.

1. Failure to associate meaning with printed symbols.

2. Insufficient sight vocabulary.

3. Failure to use meaning clues.

FAILURE TO ASSOCIATE MEANING WITH PRINTED SYMBOLS

The real goal of all word recognition is to enable the child to identify words and to associate the correct meanings with them. Often programs of word recognition emphasize oral word study and pronunciation so strongly that the child fails to establish the habit or to sense the importance of understanding the meaning of printed symbols. The child may give fairly close approximations to the pronunciation of the words he studies, but he may not have identified the word as one he knows in his listening or speaking vocabulary. Sometimes the teacher can detect mispronunciation that indicates that the word was almost, but not quite, recognized. At other times, it will be necessary to ask the child what the word means in order to detect whether he is having this basic difficulty. Of course, a relatively low level of performance by a child on oral vocabulary or meaning vocabulary tests, when compared to his skill in word-recognition techniques, such as knowledge of word elements and visual analysis of words, indicates this type of difficulty.

Remedial work for such cases should emphasize the basic comprehension abilities and reading for meaning that will be described in chapter 13. In all word-recognition exercises, the meanings of the words should be kept in the forefront. Drill on isolated word elements should be rejected for this type of case, as indeed it should be for most children, lest the development of this type of disability be encouraged. The word-identification exercises should be whenever possible in contextual settings so that there is the need to recognize not only the word but also its meaning to complete successfully the tasks.

There are methods related to real reading which will help the child develop the habit and ability of associating meanings with the word symbols. For example, the child may be requested to draw illustrations for a story he is reading. To do so, it is necessary for him to attend to the meaning of descriptive words. If the child is expected to retell a story in his own words rather than to repeat the words in the book, he soon will learn to interpret the meaning of the word symbols. Any comprehension exercise which does not allow verbalism, by which we mean merely repeating the words of the book, will encourage the association of meaning with the words read.

Besides emphasizing word meanings in all reading comprehension, the child always must develop his word-recognition techniques in relevant settings, if he is to be encouraged to associate precise ideas with the printed symbols. The child who is limited in this ability may profit from exercises such as the following:

1. Exercises to develop clear sensory impressions.

    a. What did you hear:

    when a stone hit the water?
    splash   cr-ack
    when the branch broke?
    bang   cr-ack
    when the gun went off?
    splash   bang

    b. An animal with stripes on it is a:

    elephant   horse   zebra

    c. Match the words with the phrase that tells the same thing.

    Put the number of the word before the phrase.

    1. lagged   _____flowed with force
    2. gushed   _____moved slowly
    3. gurgled   _____made a noise as it flowed
    4. rushed   _____moved rapidly along

    d. Put *J* before each word that would tell about a jolly person.

        ———merry   ———laughing   ———joyful
        ———sober   ———gay   ———droopy
        ———beaming   ———bitter   ———dreary

2. Exercises to develop precise meanings.

    a. In each line, find the two words that have opposite meanings.

many	some	no	few
tall	slim	short	little
good	tired	sad	bad
right	bad	wrong	trouble
wet	dry	damp	moist

    b. Find the words that have a similar meaning.

glow	bright	shine	spark
rushed	walked	ran	hurried
replied	said	answered	wrote
center	middle	around	point

    c. Complete the sentences with the best word from those listed below it.

        1. When the boy saw the people far away he ——— to them.
          said   shouted   whispered   muttered
        2. The cruel boy rode the horse ———.
          roughly   glaringly   harshly   sharply

3. Exercises to develop extensiveness of meaning.

    a. Tell the difference in meaning of *pound* in these sentences.

        1. We ate a *pound* of candy.
        2. See him *pound* the nail.

    b. Tell the difference in the meaning of *roll* in the following sentences:

        (1) We ate a *roll* for lunch.
        (2) We watched the big waves *roll* along the beach.
        (3) Get a *roll* of paper.
        (4) Please *roll* the ball to Jim.
        (5) The dog could *roll* over.
        (6) The teacher called the *roll.*
        (7) We could see the *roll* of the hills.
        (8) We could hear the *roll* of the drums.

    c. Put the number of the right definition in front of each sentence.

      trunk   (1) The main stem   ———He picked up
                 of a tree   peanut with his
                                   trunk.
             (2) A box used to   ———The trunk of the
                 carry clothes.   oak was rough.

(3) Part of an   _____He put the trunk
     elephant   on the train.

bark   (1) Cry of a dog   _____He peeled some
                                   bark to make a
                                   rope.

     (2) Part of a tree   _____He heard a loud
                                     bark across the
                                   bay.

     (3) A sailing boat   _____He saw the bark
                                     on the sea.

Exercises such as those given above and the suggestions made in chapter 13 will aid in building the habit of attending to word meanings and also will develop skill in associating meaning with word symbols. Many times a child makes a close approximation to a word by the use of phonics and other word-recognition techniques, but unless he keeps the context in mind, the word will remain unidentified. In addition to exercises, extensive reading coupled with the habit of noticing expressive use of words will aid in encouraging the child to associate meaning with printed symbols. Since the goal of all reading is to derive meaning from the printed page and since this goal must be achieved by recognizing printed symbols and their meanings, all word-recognition exercises should demand not only the identification of words, but also an understanding of their meanings.

INSUFFICIENT SIGHT VOCABULARY

The importance of forming the habit of rapidly recognizing known words, rather than studying each word encountered as though it never had been seen before, cannot be emphasized too strongly. The child who fails to build a large sight vocabulary and who does not have the habit of recognizing these words at a glance cannot hope to become an able reader. He will be limited not only in his ability to group words into thought units, necessary for comprehension and fluency, but he also will be seriously handicapped in identifying new words. This latter limitation comes about in two ways. First, the child will be unable to use context clues effectively, because the vocabulary load of unknown words will be too great. Second, he will be inefficient in the more mature methods of word study. Affixed words, for example, will be difficult to recognize because the child does not know the root word, since for him it is not a sight word. Compound words also will present him with a tough problem, since he has not developed the habit of sight recognition of the two smaller words from which the compound is made. The child who does not have a substantial sight vocabulary, and who does not have the habit of recognizing those words as known units, will find learning to read a most confusing enterprise. For these reasons, modern instruction in reading emphasizes the building of a sight vocabulary from the start.

There are children who have too early an introduction to analytical techniques or who are drilled so thoroughly on isolated word parts that all words fall to pieces before their eyes. Such children may become so adept at working out words that they fail to have an immediate need for building a sight vocabulary. In the early grades, the teacher may find it difficult to detect that these children are not building a sight vocabulary. If they are allowed to persist in this practice, the results will be disastrous to their reading growth. Either they will have to reject this detailed study of each word and build a sight vocabulary, or they will become severe disability cases.

In other children, a limited sight vocabulary is easily detected. They may be word-by-word readers, making phonetic errors with words they should know at sight or they may fail to phrase well in oral reading. Another indication is the tendency for the child to make about an equal number of errors regardless of the difficulty of the material he is reading. If a child, for example, makes about the same percentage of errors in reading a second-grade reader as he makes in a fourth-grade reader, he is likely to be limited in his development of a sight vocabulary. If he tends to make more mistakes on small common words than he does on polysyllabic words, he probably is limited in sight vocabulary.

The teacher easily can measure sight vocabulary by rapid-exposure techniques. She can flash words printed on cards for quick exposures. The child who cannot readily identify common words at a glance has failed to develop a sight vocabulary. When using flash cards, if the child makes a considerably greater number of errors than he does when looking at the same words for an unlimited time, he can be assumed to have an insufficient sight vocabulary. These indications of limited ability in recognizing words at a glance would mandate remedial work in building a larger sight vocabulary.

Remedial training for increasing the sight vocabulary of a disabled reader is done best by using a basic reader at a level of difficulty that is somewhat easy for the child. The exercises that require rapid reading to locate a specific statement or to understand the general significance of the passage should be emphasized for a child who is trying to increase his sight vocabulary. He should be given all the exercises suggested in the manual which require the new vocabulary to be read as whole words, and all those which require the analysis of words should be avoided. Workbook pages that emphasize rapid word recognition rather than analysis should be used. Extensive reading of material related to the topic in the basic reader then being used is desirable. Such material should be at a level of difficulty that is easy for the child so that rapid recognition of the words is encouraged.

The following illustrative types of exercises, using the basic vocabulary that is being developed, have proven effective as additional reinforcement of the habit of reading words at a glance.

1. Exercises in which the word is so much expected that the recognition be rapid.

    a. A cowboy rides a ————.
        tree   horse   farm

    b. In winter there is ————.
        snow   house   well

2. Exercises in which a child finds the correct word in a list on the chalkboard as the teacher gives the clue.

    a. Find the word in this list that tells us where we:

Clue	*Words*
buy food	farm
go swimming	table
find cows	store
eat dinner	beach

    b. Find the word that tells us what animal:

gives us a ride	dog
gives us milk	horse
barks loud	duck
swims under water	cow
says, "Quack"	fish

3. Exercises that require meaningful scanning of a list.

    a. See how fast you can draw a line around all the things that can run.

horse	house	girl	pig
tree	dog	road	man
cat	boy	store	window

    b. See how fast you can draw a line around all the things that are good to eat.

candy	pie	trees	cake
mud	meat	nuts	pencils
soup	boards	fruit	dessert

4. Various word games that call for immediate responses and require sight recognition of words and their meanings.

    a. Cards with names of animals printed on them can be used. Two children can play together. One child can flash the cards and the other can respond. Words like the following can be used:

chicken	elephant	bird	goose
dog	duck	pony	donkey
horse	goat	wren	fish

One child may tell which name an animal with four feet as the cards are flashed. Then the other may tell which can fly.

b. Another set of cards could be made of verbs and the child could tell which words on the cards tell movement. The types of words that might be used are:

afraid	listen	march	walk
jump	roll	sleep	feel
think	skip	ride	guess
flew .	know	slide	was

c. A fish-pond game is played in which words are attached to paper clips and the child uses a pole with a magnet on the end of the line. If the child can read the word that he fishes out of the pond, at a glance, it is caught. If he has to study the word, that fish gets away, but he may be able to catch it at another time. Any words that caused the child trouble in the basal reader could be used in this game as well as other words that he knows well.

d. A game similar to "authors" can be played with words. The words are grouped in sets of four similar things, such as clothes, animals, trees, time, food, toys, people, and colors. Four children may play together. Each child gets eight cards and the remaining cards are placed in a pile in the center. The children take turns drawing one card from the center pile and then discarding one. The child who first gets two complete sets of four similar words wins the game. The set of word cards for this game might be these:

Clothes	*Animals*	*Trees*	*Time*
coat	lion	oak .	afternoon
hat	elephant	maple	spring
shoe	donkey	fir	tomorrow
dress	horse	willow	morning

Food	*Toys*	*People*	*Colors*
bread	doll	aunt	yellow
pudding	wagon	father	green
peanuts	football	uncle	blue
strawberries	balloon	mother	brown

Furniture	*Flowers*	*Fruit*	*Meals*
chair	rose	peaches	breakfast
table	tulip	bananas	dinner
bed	daisy	apples	lunch
desk	poppy	pears	supper

e. Many other games such as Wordo (like Bingo), Old Maid, Spin the Wheel, Climb the Ladder, Dominoes with words, and Grab Bag can be played.

All of the above exercises and activities can be developed using phrases too.

5. One of the best exercises involves the rapid recognition of groups of high-utility words. These words are typed on flash cards and are presented rapidly.

  a. Giving directions. The child demonstrates understanding through action.

jump up	point to me
sit down	open the book
come here	look at the door
raise your hand	go to the window

  b. Classifying. The child demonstrates recognition by indicating whether the words tell about something one would find in a home or at a zoo.

table and chairs	barking seal
lion and tiger	iron cage
set of dishes	baby elephant
pretty picture	pots and pans
big red rug	little brown monkey

The exercises used in building sight vocabulary should encourage the child to inspect the words rapidly rather than to resort to detailed study of them. The words should be presented in contexts that require understanding of the word meanings.

The child should be reading material that introduces new words gradually and repeats them at well-spaced intervals. Basic readers are the best material for expanding sight vocabulary. If the child is motivated to read the selection, if the new words are introduced before the selection is read, and if the purposes require rapid reading, the child should increase his sight vocabulary. When this instruction is reinforced with exercises like those described above, using the words being emphasized, the gains should be even greater. In all reading and drill, recognizing the meaning of the words should be required and pronunciation held to a minimum. Permitting pronunciation of the words encourages a slower type of recognition than is desired. What the child with an insufficient sight vocabulary needs is experience in recognizing the word and its meaning at a glance.

FAILURE TO USE MEANING CLUES

Meaning clues are among the most important aids to word recognition. The effective adult reader uses these clues in all word identification and recognition. Meaning clues enable the reader to anticipate new or unfamiliar words before he actually sees them. No matter what other aids to recognition are used, the proficient reader always uses some form of *meaning clue*, such as: anticipating words he might expect within a given topic (*expectancy clue*), a knowledge of the meaning of a passage (*semantic clue*), or a knowledge of the structure of a sentence (*syntactic clue*) to aid him.

The authors of this book agree with Goodman (94) that word recognition is, in a sense, "a psycholinguistic guessing game." In word recognition, the child does three things: He anticipates the word through expectancy clues, semantic clues, and syntactic clues. Then he applies word-recognition skills, such as perceptual skills, for instant recognition, or decoding skills for more intensive identification, if necessary. Simultaneously, he checks the correctness of his "guess" by the sense it makes in relation to the preceding content. He sometimes resorts to rereading if he doubts accuracy or if the "guess" does not satisfy the content immediately following.

Many disabled readers have failed to acquire this ability and they are ineffective in word recognition. The failure to use meaning clues precludes the acquisition of such mature reading skills as grouping words in thought units. It also limits the development of accuracy in using the other word-recognition techniques. The ineffective use of meaning clues forces the child to analyze carefully many words that should be identified with a minimum of inspection.

Meaning clues can be divided into two types. The first are *expectancy clues* which enable the mature reader to anticipate the sorts of words and concepts that he is likely to encounter when reading about a given topic. If, for example, a mature reader is reading about soil conservation, he might expect to meet such words as *erosion, soil, depletion, levee, irrigation, rotation, drainage,* and many others. This anticipation would make the recognition or identification of the words more rapid than if they unexpectedly appeared in prose on some other subject. The second type of meaning clue is the *context clue*, which is even more helpful. The use of context clues is a sort of rapid recognition technique in which a word or phrase is so completely anticipated from the meaning of the sentence or paragraph that the merest flick of a glance is all that is needed to confirm that it is that expected word or phrase. Even if the word symbol is unfamiliar, the context plus a minimum of inspection is all that is needed for its identification.

Weakness in Use of Expectancy Clues

The child who does not anticipate words that he is likely to meet when reading about a specific topic or within a specific field is to some degree handicapped in word recognition. There are many children and even some adult readers who fail to use their knowledge of a subject as an aid to word identification and recognition. There are many adult readers, for example, who skip the graphic presentation of the facts discussed in the running comment. A brief study of the table, chart, or graph would enable them to anticipate the context and the words within the passage. The reader who uses the pictorial aids effectively becomes a more fluent and understanding reader of a passage, partly because he is prepared for those words. He can identify them with ease and devote himself to the meaning of what is read rather than to the mere recognition of words. For the younger reader, picture clues operate in much the same way. A well-illustrated book builds expectancy clues. However, the child must be taught to use such pictures effectively. Modern basic reading programs use pictures as a means of building the habit of anticipating words and concepts. There is a possibility of danger in the overuse of pictures. If the picture tells too much of the story or if all the concepts are illustrated, they lose their value because they leave so little for the child to discover by reading. The readiness activities preceding reading on a topic, which include the planning, development of background, and introduction to new words, are a form of building expectancy clues for the youngsters. Programs that neglect such essentials of reading instruction predispose the child to be weak in using expectancy clues.

The ineffective use of expectancy clues in word recognition can be detected by noting unusual difficulty in recognizing the words specifically related to a topic. It also can be suspected of the child who is always weak in telling words he might expect to find in a passage about some given topic. If, for example, a child is asked to tell what words might be used in a story about a rabbit and if he could not mention some such words as *jump, carrot, run, hop, long ears, cotton tail,* and *burrow,* he is probably weak in using expectancy clues.

The remedial work for this child would be, for the most part, to place greater emphasis on the readiness development which precedes the reading of a topic and on each selection within the topic. The child who is weak in using expectancy clues needs more attention given to the introductions of units and selections, more picture study before reading, more opportunity for vocabulary development on a particular topic or selection to be read, and more careful planning of the results expected. Thoughtful reading rather than just recall should be emphasized. Suggestions for the introduction and building of readiness can be found in most of the manuals that accompany basal readers. Basic readers which have such suggestions in their manuals would be good material from which to develop the habit of anticipating words and concepts. The instruction need not be limited to this material, even though the methods should be the same.

There are certain exercises which also help develop effective use of expectancy clues. The following illustrate some of the types that are useful:

1. Exercises using pictures to build expectancy clues.

   a. Look at the picture above. In it you will see some animals. They are doing funny things. Then look at the sentences below. Draw a line around the name of the animal that the sentence is about.

      He is opening his mouth for a peanut.
      elephant   hippopotamus   monkey
      He is walking back and forth.
      giraffe   elephant   kangaroo
      He is in the water.
      elephant   hippopotamus   kangaroo

   b. Studying the picture illustrating a selection before reading it.

      The unit to be read may deal with various types of animals in the zoo. A study of the picture would enable the children to anticipate the names of the animals. Then, before each selection is read, a review of the names of the animals in the selection can be made. The picture clues become a great aid to recognition of such difficult words as *baboon, kangaroo, hippopotamus, elephant, orangutan, zebra, panther,* and *crocodile.*

2. Exercises using knowledge of the topic to build expectancy clues.

   a. Mark the words you would expect to read about in a farm story, *F.* Mark those in a city story, *C.*

stores	cattle	tractor	streets
chickens	bus	escalator	traffic
crowds	hay stack	silo	meadow

   b. Which of the following phrases would you expect an old seafaring man to use? Put *S* before them.

      _____ a square-rigged ship
      _____ pretty autumn leaves
      _____ over the bulwarks
      _____ the larboard boats
      _____ the well-filled silo
      _____ port the helm
      _____ a ship of the desert

Failure to Use Context Clues

The child who has failed to develop ability in using context clues as an aid to word recognition is indeed in difficulty. This ability is one of the most important, if not the most important, means of word recognition. It is a rapid technique which enables the reader to identify a word immediately. For example, in the sentence "The man put his hat on his_____," it is not difficult for the child to know from the context that the missing word is *head.* At least the meaning of the sentence enables the child to anticipate the few words it could possibly be, rather than one of the 800,000 it might be if it were just any word, without regard to context. In addition, the use of context clues makes the selection of the correct meaning of the word possible. In the sentence used in the example above, the word *head* could have been a part of only the man, it could not have been the *head of a stream* nor a *head of steam.*

The reader who uses contextual aids is more likely to recognize a new word correctly than if he were using no such aid. He often can make an approximation of the pronunciation of a word from his analytical techniques. The context clues enable him to identify the word even though he picked up only an approximation of the actual word from his analysis. Context clues usually work in combination with other word-recognition techniques. These meaning clues make the application of analytical techniques much more rapid and accurate.

An equally, if not more, important use of context clues is that they act as a check on the application of all the other recognition techniques. Just as in subtraction, it pays to add afterwards so as to check the answer, so in reading it pays to check the meaning of the sentence to see if the problem in word recognition has been solved correctly. When the child has figured out a word, he must be aware whether it makes sense in the context in which it is found. If it does, he probably has found the correct solution. If it does not, he should reinspect the word because he undoubtedly has made a mistake. Without at least a fair degree of skill in the use of context clues, the child will be slow and inaccurate in word recognition. With this skill, he can be a good reader if he also has other word-recognition techniques well developed. A child who depends on contextual clues alone also will be inaccurate and become a disabled reader. It is important to know that many children who are thought to be in difficulty in reading because of limited skill in analytical techniques or because they have insufficient knowledge of phonetic, structural, or visual elements, are really in difficulty because they are not using context clues well.

The child who is limited in the use of context clues is spotted easily. If he makes as many errors when reading words in context as he does when he is reading a list of words, then he is not making sufficient use of the meaning of sentences or paragraphs as an aid to recognition. If the child's errors do not fit the meaning of the sentences and tend to be far afield, he is not using context clues. If, for example, the child reads the word *cat* as *sat* in the sentence "The dog ran after the cat," he is not using context because *sat* makes no sense at all. If, however, he read *cat* as *car,* he is probably using context because *car* would make sense. Another way of detecting this limitation is by comparing standardized test results. If, for example, the child makes a relatively high score on Test I, "Reading Words in Isolation" as compared with Test II, "Reading Words in Context" on the Bond-Balow-Hoyt *Silent Reading Diagnostic Tests,* he would be using context clues ineffectively. Ordinarily this difficulty is corrected readily.

Remedial training in the use of context clues should have the child read materials at a level of difficulty in which he encounters about one new word in every forty running words. He should be reading for purposes that demand thorough understanding of the content. In the more severe cases of this type, a separate and immediate purpose for each paragraph or sentence should be stated. This will emphasize reading for meaning and will enable the child to recognize known words at a glance and use context clues as an aid to other techniques in the identification of unfamiliar words. The teacher may need to ask the child from time to time what he thinks the word might be, or have the child use the context plus the initial sound to help him solve his word-recognition problems.

In addition to the above suggestions, the following more formal exercises will encourage the child to use context clues:

1. Exercises in which the meaning of the sentence indicates the word to be recognized.

   a. The boys rode over the snow on it. What was it?
   boat   store   sled

   b. Mother put a candle on the cake for Bob's _____.
   football   birthday   bedroom

2. Exercises in which the child reads a paragraph, filling in the missing words, using the initial elements given. He does not need to write them but reads the sentences to himself. Comprehension questions can be asked.

   Billy caught the ball.
   Then he th_____ the ball to his father.
   Father c_____ the ball, too.
   Billy and his father were pl_____ catch.
   A dog came to play.
   He j_____ up and got the ball.
   Then he ran a_____ with it.

3. Exercises in which context plus initial elements are used as aid to word recognition.

   a. We will get some apples at the st_____.
   store   steep   farm

   b. The car went down the str_____.
   strong   road   street

4. Riddles in which the context gives the answer.

   It lives in a zoo.
   It hops about.
   It carries its baby in its pouch.
   It is a _____.
   elephant   crocodile   kangaroo

5. Closure-type exercises using syntax clues and initial-element clues.

   a. They went sw_____ at the beach.

   b. Tom l_____ candy.

   c. Mary likes h_____ new doll.

   d. The boys w_____ to play, but they d_____ not have a ball.

6. Pure Cloze exercises in which the student must fill in the blank from sentence and paragraph meaning.

   > Mary and John went to the _____ to buy some candy.
   > On their way home they met their _____ Tom.
   > Tom was riding his _____ bicycle.

   In this type of exercise it is imperative that the reading be at an easy level for the student. For this use of the Cloze technique, any word which fits the meaning and the structure of the sentence will do.

7. Deletions of nonsense additions. Exercises in which the child reads a paragraph and deletes the words which do not belong because they do not make sense.

   > Mary and John went dog to the store to barn buy some candy. On their zoo way home they met their friend Tom. Tom was kangaroo riding his new bicycle.

SUMMARY

Meaning clues are helpful to word recognition in three ways. *First,* they enable the reader to anticipate the words he is to read. This makes the recognition of known words rapid and accurate, and allows the reader to work out the identification of unfamiliar words with a minimum of study. *Second,* the use of these clues is essential as a check on the accuracy of his recognition. If the word recognized does not make sense, it should be his habit to study further the word missed. *Third,* the application of other word-recognition techniques frequently gives the child only an approximation of the word; then the meaning clues enable him to recognize the word correctly.

A more detailed summary together with selected readings will be found at the end of the next chapter.

Correcting Faulty Perceptual and Decoding Skills in Word Recognition

Proficiency in both the use of meaning clues and the application of analytical word-recognition techniques is required if the reader is to associate the correct concept with the printed symbol. Meaning clues alone are not enough for good reading at any level. They must be accompanied by the use of a flexible set of word-recognition skills. It is through the interaction of all the word-study skills that a competent reader builds his reading structure.

The set of skills needed to reinforce the meaning clues to word recognition can be grouped under three types of interrelated learnings: (a) flexible visual perceptual habits; (b) knowledge of phonics and structural word elements; (c) fluent oral and visual synthesis of word parts. Weakness in any one, or any combination, of these types of achievements, will preclude adequate growth in reading. Disabled readers, deficient in word-recognition skills, would be classified as having a limiting or complex disability. This chapter will discuss the basic problems of faulty word-study skills, under the following headings:

1. General suggestions for correcting word-recognition difficulties
2. Ineffective visual perceptual habits
3. Limited knowledge of word elements
4. Lack of fluent oral and visual synthesis

GENERAL SUGGESTIONS FOR CORRECTING
WORD-RECOGNITION DIFFICULTIES

To correct limitations in word-study skills, the instructional procedures must be planned carefully according to the findings of a thorough diagnosis. There are certain general suggestions that will aid in making the remedial teaching effective. These suggestions, suitable to any type of word-skill deficiencies, are:

1. TEACH WORD RECOGNITION IN MATERIAL THAT IS AT THE DISABLED READER'S INSTRUCTIONAL LEVEL. Any material that is used for reading is helpful in teaching word recognition. There are certain precautions that must be observed, however. The material should not have too many new words. Obviously, if the disabled reader is to use the meaning of the printed page and context clues to aid him in word recognition, he must know a sufficient number of sight words, so that the meaning will not become lost. In the initial lessons, it is especially important that new words should not be too numerous.

2. TEACH WORD RECOGNITION WHEN IT IS IMPORTANT TO THE DISABLED READER TO RECOGNIZE THE WORD. If the purpose for reading is real to the disabled reader and if he has accepted it, he will make a more vigorous attack on difficult words that prevent him from reaching his goal. This will make him persist in recognizing the words even though it entails careful analysis.

3. ALWAYS TEACH WORD RECOGNITION IN MEANINGFUL MATERIAL. Because the objective of all word-recognition techniques is to recognize words, it is better to develop the techniques in the content in which they are going to be used, meaningful content. This allows the disabled reader to use not only the analytical techniques, but also the various meaning clues. It teaches him to interpret a word in the context in which he finds it. Word recognition is not word calling, but is the recognition of the correct meaning of a word in a given situation. Teaching word recognition in context encourages a balance between the development of meaning vocabulary and the word-recognition techniques.

4. UNDERTAKE THE MORE ANALYTICAL TYPES OF WORD RECOGNITION TECHNIQUES ONLY AFTER THE DISABLED READER IS AWARE OF THE MEANINGFUL NATURE OF READING, HAS ESTABLISHED THE HABIT OF RECOGNIZING WORDS AS WHOLE WORDS, AND HAS BUILT A SUPPORTIVE SIGHT VO-

CABULARY. This enables the disabled reader to use meaning clues, and it also encourages him to use more rapid recognition techniques.

5. BE SURE THAT THE DISABLED READER KNOWS THE MEANING OF THE WORDS HE IS TRYING TO IDENTIFY OR HAS THE BACKGROUND NECESSARY TO DERIVE THEIR MEANING. It is obvious that the disabled reader should have, or be able to secure, the meaning of the word he is attempting to recognize. It is difficult enough for him to use identification clues when meaning is present. But if meaning is absent, he may not know whether he has studied the word adequately.

6. TEACH THE DISABLED READER TO ANALYZE THE WORD VISUALLY BEFORE HE ATTEMPTS TO SOUND IT OUT. Visual analysis always must precede sounding, because it is through visual analysis that the reader isolates usable word elements to be sounded. A large proportion of the ability to decode words effectively is the ability to locate usable elements. Frequently, through isolated drill, certain word elements are taught to children who find this learning of little use, because they cannot find elements within large word patterns fast enough. How much better it would be to proceed from location of the elements within a word through rapid visual study, to sounding, and then to recognition, rather than attempting faulty and unwarranted sounding and blending because the proper elements have not been isolated through such a visual inspection. Flexible study of words is essential, because a faulty start will have to be rejected quickly if words are to be recognized by analytical means.

7. DEVELOP THE HABIT OF NOTICING SIMILARITIES AND DIFFERENCES AMONG WORDS. Through many comparisons, most of which he himself will make, the disabled reader can establish this habit—one that encourages careful and rapid inspection of words and helps to develop many of the word-recognition techniques. The disabled reader can use this procedure, for instance, to build his own families of words and to notice similarities in meaning and configurations of words with the same roots. This habit encourages building large sight-recognition vocabularies and discourages overanalysis.

8. TEACH THE ABILITY TO LOCATE A NEW WORD-RECOGNITION ELEMENT IN KNOWN WORDS BEFORE APPLYING THAT ELEMENT TO IDENTIFY NEW WORDS. The disabled reader is led to *discover,* for example, the initial-letter sound in the known words: *run, ride,* and *rat,* before he uses this knowledge in identifying the new word, *rabbit.*

9. BUILD THE HABIT OF INSPECTING WORDS RAPIDLY, THOROUGHLY, AND SYSTEMATICALLY FROM LEFT TO RIGHT. Many of the difficulties in

word recognition result from failure to study the whole word systematically, starting at the left and looking completely through the word from left to right. Reading seems to be the only task in which recognition must be systematically carried on in one direction. The disabled reader who fails to make this left-to-right inspection may recognize a word like *stop,* as *pots* at one time, and *tops* at another. Although the parts are recognized adequately, the order of those parts is confused, and he is therefore in difficulty. Many reversal cases are caused by failure to establish a systematic left-to-right inspection of words. The neglect of any part of the word in that inspection also may cause difficulty.

10. ADJUST INSTRUCTION IN WORD-RECOGNITION TECHNIQUES TO THE INDIVIDUAL. In developing word-recognition techniques, it should be kept in mind that there are some disabled readers who do not profit from certain types of instruction. For example, for a disabled reader with auditory deficiency, it is unfortunate to emphasize phonic approaches. Sometimes phonic approaches may have to be omitted entirely. In developing independence in word recognition for a disabled reader with faulty vision, more dependence should be placed on large word elements, such as syllables, than would be necessary for the child with more normal vision.

11. AVOID DRILL ON ISOLATED WORD ELEMENTS OR USE OF ARTIFICIAL TEACHING DEVICES. Whenever possible, the disabled reader should recognize and remember words as sight words. Drill on isolated elements tends to cause the disabled reader to analyze words that he otherwise might have recognized quite easily at sight. Isolated drill on word elements, such as *tion* and *tr,* is a relatively easy teaching technique and therefore is frequently overused. Such drill, however, hinders rapid word recognition. If it is transfered into actual reading, it may slow it up and interfere with understanding the meaning. For this reason, it generally is unwise to use isolated drills on discrete word endings and on discrete phonic and visual elements.

12. DISCUSS WITH THE DISABLED READER EXACTLY WHAT HIS PROBLEM IS AND LET HIM AID IN FORMULATING HIS INDIVIDUAL REMEDIAL PLAN. The disabled reader will be more motivated in the necessary drill-type work if he is working toward known goals. He also can offer useful suggestions and will feel a sense of accomplishment when he achieves his own reading goals.

INEFFECTIVE VISUAL-PERCEPTUAL HABITS

The ability to read depends upon a group of visual-perceptual skills and habits essential to decoding the printed symbols. These skills must be highly coordinated and flexible, if a reader is to read in thought units at speeds that far exceed the rate at which he can listen. The thought units are made up of words that are so quickly perceived that they can be grouped together and recognized at a single glance. The disabled reader is often in major difficulty because his reading perceptual habits preclude such rapid recognition of words. His problem may be in any one, or in any combination, of the following interrelated perceptual defects:

1. Faulty visual analysis of words

2. Excessive word-perceptual errors

3. Overanalytical habits

Faulty Visual Analysis of Words

Visual analysis of an unfamiliar word always must precede the application of knowledge of word parts. Both of these come before the final synthesis of the parts into recognition of a word. For example, a child unfamiliar with the word *something* might visually separate the word into *so—met—hing*. He then would apply his knowledge of the parts, pronouncing each in turn. Then he would try to blend the parts and find that he had failed in his attempt because his original visual separation of the word was wrong. He would have to reject his first visual analysis and make another one. This time he might see the first of the two small words from which the word *something* is made and separate the word into *some—th—ing*. Then applying his knowledge of the parts and synthesizing them, he would be able to recognize the word. Of course, this approach to recognizing the word *something* would have been rather immature. A more advanced reader would have visually analyzed the word into the largest known elements, *some* and *thing*. He would visually recognize these parts and then synthesize them. Aided by context clues, the separate parts would not have to be spoken and blended, but the whole word, *something,* would have been recognized at a glance. Nonetheless, the word would have been visually analyzed, knowledges applied and then synthesized, all with great rapidity. The visual analysis of words must be flexible and diversified if the child is to become an able reader.

To do so, the child must develop great skill in the visual analysis of words. He must, at a glance, be able to separate the word into elements useful in recognizing it. An element useful in one word may not be so in another. For example, the element *on* in the word *upon* is useful, but separating *on* out of the word *portion* would be detrimental to recognizing the whole word. The child must be flexible so that when one method does not work, he can quickly reexamine the word and reanalyze it visually. He must analyze a word only when he does not know it as a sight word, and even then, he should select the largest usable elements in the word rather than resort to piecemeal analysis.

The child who is disabled in the visual analysis of words can be identified by the classroom teacher in two ways. *First,* when pronouncing words verbally he will select inappropriate elements to sound out and often he will try again and again to use the same analysis even if it does not work. *Second,* when the examiner shows him how to analyze the word by covering up parts of it, if the child is able to recognize it, then at least one of his problems in word recognition is faulty visual analysis.

The remedial training for a child with this kind of disability must focus on two results. *First,* it should give the child help in finding the most useful structural, visual, and phonic elements in words. *Second,* it must develop flexibility in the visual attack on words, teaching the child to use the larger elements first, but to change quickly from an analysis that does not work to one that does.

The most effective remedial measures are similar to those used by the teacher when first developing this ability. In introducing unfamiliar words during the preparatory phase of teaching a selection, the teacher should work carefully in showing such a disabled reader how to analyze visually the new words. In the follow-up phases of teaching a selection, the visual analysis skill should be emphasized. Such training as finding similarities in known words like *fight* and *sight* or *three* and *throw* gives the child experience in visual analysis. The material for such training should be at the instructional level of difficulty so that the child will be forced to analyze words visually. Help in finding parts of compound words or in isolating root words in affixed words is excellent experience in visual analysis. Syllabifying words also is useful. Reinforcing exercises like the following, first using known words and then having the child find similar elements in unknown words, should be used liberally with a child seriously deficient in visual analysis of words:

1. Exercises in finding the root word in words with variant ending forms.

    a. Find the root words from which these words are made.

(1) looks	looking	looked
(2) worker	worked	working
(3) washes	washing	washed

    b. Find the root words in words having variant endings, such as: *want* in *wanting; wait* in *waited; swim* in *swimming.*

2. Exercises having the child use syntax clues in choosing between variant forms, such as:

               wanting
a. The bear   the honey.
               wanted

                  talk
b. The man was talking to them.
                  talked

            make
c. Mother is   a cake.
            making

3. Exercises that require finding similar blends.

    a. You see the picture of the clown, say clown. Look at the words here and put C on the ones that begin like clown and that tell something we can do.

clap	clean	clocks
come	clothes	play
climb	cook	clam

4. Exercises that emphasize seeing similar word parts.

    a. Put C on the right word.

        (1) <u>She</u> wanted to _____ for joy.
            sing   shout   shoe

        <u>Str</u>ing is not as _____ as rope.
            street   big   strong

    b. Draw a line under the right word.

        (1) The sun cannot be seen at _____.
            fight   night   right   sight

        (2) The train runs on a _____.
            sack   black   track   tack

        (3) Baseball is a _____.
            game   same   came   tame

5. Exercises that teach syllabication.

    a. Say the words below and decide how many parts you hear. These parts are syllables. Write the number of syllables after each word.

about_____	surprise_____	something_____
rabbit_____	together_____	thermometer_____
cat_____	wonderful_____	banana_____

    b. Show the syllables in these words, as: dif/fer/ent.

ahead	forgotten	furniture
yellow	interested	tomorrow
after	moment	electricity

6. Exercises that emphasize seeing both parts of compound words.

   a. Find the two small words in each compound word and tell how they help us know what it means.

fireplace	baseball	sailboat	policeman
fireside	football	rowboat	fireman
firefly	basketball	ferryboat	fisherman

   b. Take one of the little words from each compound word below the sentence and make a new compound word to fill in the blank.

   (1) We were seated by the _____ to get warm.
   firehouse   inside

   (2) The wind makes the _____ go fast.
   sailfish   steamboat

7. Exercises that develop skill in analyzing affixed words.

   a. Draw a line around the part of the word that means *again*.

relive	remake	retell
rework	replay	relearn

   b. Draw a line around the prefix and tell how it changes the meaning of the root word.

unhappy	retake	unknown
mistrust	displease	repay
unkind	dislike	mislead

   c. Draw a line around the suffix in these words. Put the right number after the words to show what the suffix means. The first one is done for you.

(1) without	(2) in that way	(3) full of
bravely__2__	thoughtless____	thoughtful____
careless____	wonderful____	sadly____
careful____	strangely____	thankful____

   d. Draw a line around the root word, the word from which the larger word is made. Tell how the prefix and suffix change the meaning of the root word.

unfriendly	unthankful	distrustful
unkindly	unlikely	dishonestly
disagreeable	repayable	unkindness

The experience that the child gains from exercises to improve his visual analysis of words must be used right away in meaningful settings. The child should be asked to put these words in sentences immediately or tell the derived meanings. This sort of drill should not be used in isolation but as a reinforcement of a broader program of word recognition. The words in these exercises should be ones familiar to the child or ones that soon will be introduced in the basic reading program.

Flexibility and the habit of dividing the words into the largest usable elements should be stressed. The program should teach the child to avoid faulty approaches to word recognition, such as letter-by-letter spelling or sounding. Sounding of individual letters, for example, may help a child to recognize a small word, such as *cat,* but it would be extremely confusing in recognizing longer or more complicated words, such as *telephone* or *impatient.* Yet many children do this letter-by-letter sounding of all unfamiliar words, because an isolated sounding method was used in their early reading instruction.

Many children have difficulty in word recognition because they are too dependent on one technique or because they do not use the most efficient ones. For example, they may have the habit of searching for known little words in larger words. This technique is helpful in identifying compound words or affixed words, but it is detrimental to recognizing many other words. Finding *ear* in *bear* is of doubtful help, as is finding *to—get—her* in the word, *together.* The exercises must encourage a diversified and flexible attack on words. They also must emphasize orderly progression through the word from its beginning element to its end.

Excessive Word Perceptual Errors

Some children's word perceptual difficulties are different from those just discussed. Their mispronunciations tend to form a consistent pattern that can be readily diagnosed. These errors are classified in many ways by different workers in the reading field. They are best thought of as word-perception errors. In general, the classifications are based on where the errors are in the words in which they occur. For example, a child may make an excessive number of errors in the initial part of words, such as calling *house, mouse.* Another child might cluster his errors around the middle of words. He might call *house, horse.* A third child may make an unusually high percentage of errors at the end of words. He might call *house, hour.*

For a certain child, these errors tend to be most frequent in a specific part of the word, because his word perception consistently neglects that part of the word. Roughly, these perceptual errors can be classified as Initial Errors, Middle Errors, and Ending Errors. The child also can confuse the order of word parts and make Orientational Errors.

Locational errors are diagnosed in two ways. First, a sample of errors made in word pronunciation can be assembled and classified. Second, the errors a child makes in multiple-choice test items, in which the distractors are selected to represent error types, can indicate error patterns. The *Gates-McKillop Reading Diagnostic Tests,* for example, utilize the first method of diagnosis, while the Bond-Balow-Hoyt *Silent Reading Diagnostic Tests* use the second. The diagnostician also may collect a sample of errors to classify informally. The disadvantage of this is that he cannot know the number of possibilities present in the sample he takes, nor can he judge how frequently a certain type of error typically occurs.

Initial errors indicate that the child, as he inspects words, neglects to notice the beginnings of words closely enough. He makes errors, such as calling *his, this* or *the, he.* Another type of initial error is calling the word *tall, fall* or *when, then.*

The remedial procedures used for correcting initial errors are similar to those for better visual analysis of words and knowledge of initial elements. The difference is emphasis. For the child who makes an undue number of errors in the initial part of words, even though he knows initial elements, the exercises focus his attention more directly and systematically on the beginning of words. Building a picture dictionary will force the child to look systematically at the words. Exercises in alphabetizing words will make him pay greater attention to word beginnings. Sorting labeled pictures for filing will also help. The child should be shown the nature of his errors and the difference between the word he pronounced and the way it actually appeared in print. For example, if he calls *cat, eat,* he should be shown that he got the word almost right, but that he must pay closer attention to the beginning of the word. This sort of encouragment should be maintained. All exercises on initial consonant blends and digraphs will help to overcome a child's tendency to neglect the beginnings of words. The following exercises also are good:

1. Multiple-choice questions in which the child is forced to differentiate among initial elements.

              boat.
    a. The man put on his goat.
              coat.

            way.
    b. The dog ran away.
            play.

2. Classification exercises that emphasize initial sounds and word meanings.

    a. Find every word that starts like *crack* and is something we can eat.

crab	candy	cranberries
apple	crown	cradle
cracker	bread	crumbs
creep	cried	cream

3. Multiple-choice exercises in which the initial blend is given.

    a. The car went down the str_____.
        strange   road   street

Middle errors result from insufficient inspection of words. These are caused by two factors. First, the child may hurry his inspection of unfamiliar words to a point he neglects the middles of words. Second, it may be the result of limited knowledge of vowel sounds. Exercises that teach the sounds of vowels will be helpful. Methods that encourage the child to inspect words in an orderly fashion will help to correct any tendency to neglect the middle of the word. Copying some of the words that cause difficulty may help, as would tracing the words. Using context as a check on accuracy will encourage the child to reinspect the words missed. A child using context clues, for example, could not very well call *cat, cot* in the sentence, "The cat climbed the tree," without rereading to find out what was wrong. He should be told why he needs to make a closer inspection of the middles of words and what the difference is between the error made and the printed word. Multiple-choice exercises are helpful in correcting this difficulty by forcing the child to differentiate the middle parts of words.

pen.
1. The pig was in the pan.
pin.

children.
2. The egg was laid by the citizen.
chicken.

Ending errors are made frequently; good readers make a higher percentage of these errors than do poor readers. An overemphasis on word endings may cause a neglect of the very important initial elements, and it also may cause reversals and other orientational confusions. The mature reader starts at the beginning of an unfamiliar word and works systematically along it from left to right until it is completely inspected. All the exercises designed to increase knowledge of variant endings, families of words, and suffixes will help to eliminate errors in the final elements of words. If the exercises are in contextual settings, the child must differentiate both beginnings and endings of words. These exercises are helpful in calling attention to the final element without creating more difficulties than are corrected. One exercise frequently used by teachers is harmful. Finding words in a list that belong to a *word family,* such as the *at* family or the *ay* family without using meaning as a check is detrimental because the child selects the words by the endings alone without recognizing what the words are. This forces the child to neglect the important initial element of the words and encourages him to avoid an orderly inspection of each word. Another precaution is to avoid overreacting to ending errors in oral reading by children who have perfect understanding but whose mispronunciations simply reflect dialect differences.

Exercises that may be used safely are:

1. Finish the word. It should rhyme with *call*.
   The boy was playing with a b_____.
   tall   back   ball

2. Find the word that ends like *coat*, which you would like to play with.
   goat   doll   float
   gloat   boat   clock

Orientation confusions are among the most troublesome perceptual errors made by disabled readers. All types of orientational problems will be discussed in the next chapter, which deals with the extremely disabled reader.

Overanalytical Habits

The overanalytical reader is produced from too early an introduction of detailed oral-phonetic instruction in word recognition or from too much emphasis on the establishment of word-recognition techniques. This overemphasis results in a lack of balance between building a sight vocabulary and word analysis. Then the child either fails to build a sight vocabulary and must attack each word he meets, or he acquires the habit of analyzing all words, even those he knows at sight. Another condition that predisposes a child to become an overanalytical reader is overusing artificial or isolated exercises for developing word-recognition techniques. An overemphasis on instruction with letter-by-letter sounding methods or other methods which encourage piecemeal observation of words also makes overanalytical readers. A fourth cause is too heavy a vocabulary burden through failure of the reading program to use a basal reader with carefully controlled vocabulary.

Overanalysis takes two forms. The child may analyze words he knows at sight. This is not only slow and impedes thoughtful reading, but also it may lead the child to make unnecessary errors in word recognition. Some children have so thoroughly established the habit of analyzing known words that they make more errors when allowed unlimited time to pronounce a list of words than they do when the same list of words is flashed before them by a tachistoscope forcing them to read the words at sight. It should be remembered that word-recognition techniques should be so engrained that the child will identify known words without detailed study, and that he will recognize rapidly the words he knows in any of their variant forms. He will resort to time-consuming, analytical procedures only when he is working out words he has not met previously. A good reader inspects a word in only as much detail as is required for its recognition. The overanalytical reader reverses this process. He approaches most words as unfamiliar. He studies them in detail, isolates elements within them, applies his knowledge of word elements, and then synthesizes the elements back into a word only to find that it is familiar. This pattern is harmful both to reading fluency and to comprehension. The child is so concerned with analyzing known words that he has no time to understand content. It takes him so long to recognize each word that he cannot group them into thought units. Both his comprehension and his speed of reading of connected material suffer.

The second type of overanalytical reader is the one who breaks words into too many parts. Instead of using large elements known to him, he resorts too early and too often to a study of individual letter sounds. This habit of recognizing words is extremely inefficient and often confusing. For most words, letter-by-letter sounding precludes recognition. Take the words in the previous sentence, for example, and try to sound each letter in the words and then blend them into the words. Only a few of the words could be recognized in this way, and even for those few that could, it would be a time-consuming and inefficient method. It is foolish, for example, for a child who knows the word *talk* to resort to a letter-by-letter sounding of the word *talking*. Yet many overanalytical readers do this. It would be equally foolish and totally ineffective for the child who knew *tion* in *action* to try a letter-by-letter sounding of that element. Yet many children who have had drill on isolated letter sounds do just that. This is not to imply that they did not need such training, but it does mean that care must be taken to maintain proper balances in word recognition.

Some children who are overanalytical go to the extreme of a "spelling attack" on words. They try to remember each new word by spelling it out. For example, they encounter the unknown word *donkey,* and try to learn it by naming each letter. It is impossible for a child to remember all of the words he is expected to learn by trying to recall the sequence of letters through spelling. There are many children who, when asked to work out an unknown word aloud, will name each letter in turn and sometimes, after calling the letters, can say the word. For example, a child will see the word *horse,* which he doesn't identify. When asked to try to pronounce it, he will say, *"h—o—r—s—e, horse."* This type of word recognition is detrimental to reading growth. It results from two conditions. First, the child is taught by a spelling method, in which he learns the names of the letters and then is expected to recognize the words by spelling them. The second condition is too early an emphasis on spelling.

The overanalytical reader can be detected by studying his relative effectiveness on timed and untimed word-recognition tests. He also can be identified by asking him to work on words orally when he gets into difficulty. A third way of detecting this type of difficulty is to note children who rank relatively high on tests of word elements, but who are low on tests of word recognition. They also tend to be slow readers with poor comprehension.

The remedial treament for children who tend to analyze words that are already known as sight words, is to give more training with the exercises discussed above for increasing sight vocabulary, associating words with meanings, and using context clues effectively. Flash techniques, such as a tachistoscope or an overhead projector are helpful. Rapid exposure of word cards is useful, too. All these exercises should be used just to reinforce the emphases that should be applied to the child's other reading experiences. Reading material with few if any word difficulties, for purposes that require rapid reading, such as reading to get the general significance of a paragraph, scanning to find a specific bit of information, or reading to predict outcomes, will help overcome overanalytical tendencies.

The overanalytical reader who breaks words up into too many parts is corrected by emphasizing structural analysis and knowledge of the larger elements. Stress on syllabication rather than on sounding each letter is desirable. Noting root words, prefixes, suffixes, and variant endings will give the child the habit of analyzing words into larger elements. Instruction in word recognition should encourage him to select as large elements as he can when he is working out the recognition of words not known at sight. In remedial work, weight should be put on exercises for developing effective visual analysis that teach the child to isolate the larger structural and visual elements within words. In addition, it should be stressed that wide reading of relatively easy material will help the child who tends to resort to piecemeal observation of words.

LIMITED KNOWLEDGE OF WORD ELEMENTS

The child who is to become a capable, fluent, and independent reader must develop an extensive knowledge of word elements. There is no point for the child to be skillful in visually analyzing words unless he knows what the parts say. It does not help, for example, for the child to separate visually the word *spring* into *spr—ing* unless he knows what the initial blend *spr* and the ending *ing* say. The child needs to learn a vast number of word parts. The larger the elements he can use in recognizing words, the more fluent and understanding his reading will be. The more he uses context and meaning clues, the less he will need to analyze the words. It often will be necessary for a child to break a word into small parts in order to recognize it. This will not aid him if he does not know the small elements. The child must master the knowledge of many phonic, structural, and visual elements in words.

The diagnostician has several ways of detecting limited knowledge of word parts. Most diagnostic reading tests sample the more useful phonic, structural, and visual elements. Any weakness on these tests in comparison with the child's general reading capability indicates that he may be limited in the number of elements with which he is familiar. Another means of spotting this weakness is difficulty in associating sounds with word elements when the child is working out the pronunciation of words orally. If the child uses reasonable visual analysis of a word but does not know letter sounds, common phonograms, or visual elements, he is limited in his knowledge of word parts. If he seems to be able to break a word into syllables but cannot pronounce many of them, he is limited in his knowledge of important word parts and should be given remedial training to increase his phonic, structural, and visual knowledges.

When the teacher or remedial worker points out to a child the similarity between a new word and other words he knows, he is receiving instruction in word-element knowledge. Manuals accompanying basic reading programs offer many suggestions for introducing new vocabulary to the child before he reads a selection. In presenting the new words, the teacher is supposed not only to make the meaning clear but also to show the child the most efficient visual analysis of each word and compare it, when necessary, with known words which contain the element which might cause the child difficulty. If, for example, the new word is *trouble,* the teacher might say that it begins like *train* and ends like *double.* The three words would be written on the chalkboard. The teacher also might say it is something we would rather not have. The teacher would have given some instruction in the knowledge of how *tr* and *ouble* sound.

Many exercises in manuals of basic readers give direct instruction in knowledge of word parts. These are especially good for the child limited in this area, because the basic vocabulary in these readers is well controlled and the authors of the manuals know the words taught previously. They can use known words to teach the elements needed for recognizing new words. The authors also can keep an account of the word elements they are teaching so that they can develop the knowledges gradually with ample reinforcement to ensure that they will be learned. It is recommended that a child limited in word-element knowledge be given instruction in basal reading materials at the appropriate level of difficulty. The teacher should emphasize the introduction of new vocabulary and the word-recognition exercises suggested after reading each selection. Word-recognition exercises in workbooks accompanying readers should be used to the fullest.

If other materials are used, the remedial teacher should use words that might cause trouble or illustrate an important word element. These words should be introduced as new words, as suggested in *teaching a selection,* described in chapter 8.

Some remedial teachers report success in using a linguistically regular approach as described by Fries (77) and Bloomfield and Barnhart (20). Programmed materials with a linguistically regular vocabulary, such as *The Programmed Reading Series* (201), have proved effective in training children seriously confused in distinguishing the phonemic and print signal relationships described by linguists.

All the exercises suggested in the above section for improving visual analysis of words aid in teaching knowledge of visual, structural, and phonic elements. Reinforcement exercises like the following will be beneficial to the child limited in his knowledge of word parts. The words used should have been or will soon be introduced in his basic reading book.

1. Exercises to teach initial consonant sounds.

   a. Say the words *can* and *come*. Put *C* before all the words that start like *can* and *come* and that also name an animal.

——cat	——candy	——cow	——cookies	——chicken
——duck	——eat	——chair	——elephant	——cake
——eel	——camel	——canary	——calf	——cub

   b. Make a word naming something to eat by putting the first letter of a word on the left in the right blank. The first one is done for you.

1. soon	——eaches	4. but	——ake
2. cook	—s—oup	5. people	——utter
3. puppy	——ookies	6. come	——eanuts

   c. Write the first part of the word in the space. It starts like one of the words below the sentence.

   (1) The dog ran ——ome.
   son   hope   cone
   (2) The cat wanted some ——ilk.
   pig   like   mill

   d. Draw a line to show which words start with the same sound as the thing in each picture. The first one is done for you.

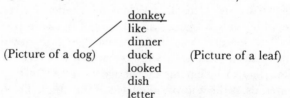

   (Picture of a dog)   donkey
   like
   dinner
   duck
   looked
   dish
   letter   (Picture of a leaf)

2. Exercises to teach initial blend sounds.

   a. Write in the blank the word that begins with the same blend as the word underlined.

   (1) The branch soon ——.
   bring   fell   broke
   (2) The block was painted ——.
   brown   blue   green
   (3) There was plenty to do at the ——.
   playground   school   park
   (4) The brown string was ——.
   street   strong   splashed

b. Draw a line to show which words start with the same sound as the things in the pictures.

<table>
<tr><td></td><td>truck</td><td></td></tr>
<tr><td></td><td>string</td><td></td></tr>
<tr><td>(Picture of a train)</td><td>tried</td><td>(Picture of a street)</td></tr>
<tr><td></td><td>tree</td><td></td></tr>
<tr><td></td><td>straight</td><td></td></tr>
</table>

c. Draw a line under the right word. It must start with the same blend as the key word.

(1) *clap*

	feet.
The cat has	claws.
	close.

(4) *smile*

	brown.
The puppy	small.
was	smoke.

(2) *flap*

	flat.
Away the bird	flew.
	sailed.

(5) *strap*

	rope.
The kite was	string.
on a	straw.

(3) *plan*

	plate.
We like to	sing.
	play.

(6) *tree*

	deed.
He did a	true.
good	trick.

The disabled reader, limited in this area, may be taught other important blends, such as: *bl, br, cr, dr, fr, gl, gr, scr, sk, sl, sn, sp, st,* in exercises such as presented above.

3. Exercises to reinforce knowledge of digraph sounds.

a. Finish the words. They begin like one of the words below the sentences. The first one is done for you.

(1) That cat can run.
Boy   This   Sing
(2) _____ere will we go?
What   Hear   Play
(3) The _____est was full of gold.
toy   boy   chair
(4) We get wool from _____eep.
ducks   ships   sleds
(5) His brother was only _____ee.
where   thread   see

b. Draw a line around the right word. It must start with the same digraph as the key word.

(1) *church*

	chimney.
We make butter in a	pail.
	churn.

(2) *ship*

	coat.
She put on her new	shoes.
	sharp.

(3) *they*

	there.
We will soon be	thing.
	back.

(4) *thick*

	home.
He was safe on	third.
	thin.

(5) *three*

	truck.
The king was on the	threw.
	throne.

(6) *whale*

	white.
The paper was	wheel.
	warm.

4. Exercises to teach vowel sounds.

   a. The vowels *a, e, i, o, u* say their names in many words. This is their long sound. Write the vowel that is long after each word. Then use the word in a sentence.

   age _____   dine _____   vase _____
   like _____   cave _____   use _____
   alone _____   home _____   rope _____
   bite _____   white _____   mane _____

   Call attention to the fact that each word has one consonant between the vowel and the final *e;* that usually makes the first vowel have a *long* sound. Some exceptions may be given, as:

   give   love   come   where
   some   live   whose   were

   b. Write the vowel that is *long* after each word. Then use the word in a sentence.

   peach _____   snail _____   heel _____   mail _____
   reach _____   road _____   keep _____   trail _____
   tease _____   bead _____   leaf _____   people _____
   plains _____   boat _____   mean _____   praise _____

   Call attention to the fact that many times when two vowels come together the first vowel takes the long sound and the second vowel is silent. Some exceptions may be given, as:

   bread   heavy   meant   poem
   break   great   house   piano
   chief   head   piece   moon

c. Put in the right word. It must have a short vowel.

The boy ran after the ———
boat   game   cat

Other exercises using context clues can be used, because it is only by context clues that the child can tell whether a vowel is long or short in an unknown word.

5. Exercises to teach hard and soft consonant sounds.

a. When *C* has the sound of *S* it has a soft sound. When it sounds like *K* it has a hard sound. Put *S* after the sentences in which *C* is soft and *H* when it is hard. The first one is done for you.

(1) We went to the camp. H
(2) I saw his face.———
(3) We rode on a camel.———
(4) It sold for ten cents.———
(5) The calf was brown.———
(6) We eat our cereal.———
(7) It was a new act.———

b. Similar exercises can be used to teach the other hard and soft consonant sounds.

6. Exercises using syntactical clues to teach variant endings.

a. Draw a line under the right word.

(1) The cat drink / drinks her milk.

(2) Now she wanted / wanting to run away.

(3) The boys plays / played ball.

(4) He wishes / wishing to go.

(5) Let us go in swim / swimming.

7. Exercises using context clues to teach common word elements.

   a. Put in the right word. It must end like the key word.

     (1) *talk*
       We had a brisk _____.
       chalk   walk   run

     (2) *light*
       It was a dark _____.
       right   room   night

   b. See how many words you can make that rhyme with the following words. Use each of them in a sentence.

bat	street	bright	bank
ball	house	sand	like

The exercises designed to increase knowledge of visual, structural, and phonic elements as often as possible should be put in contextual settings. This is desirable because many times the true sound of an element can be known only from its use in context. For example, the vowel sound in *read* cannot be known out of context. Context also stimulates more rapid recognition of the parts being taught, and it offers an immediate and independent check on the accuracy of the associaton of the printed symbols with the pronunciation. There are certain drill devices used to increase the disabled child's knowledge of word parts. They should be used sparingly, and the words drilled should be read in context so that the elements learned have a reasonable chance of being transferred into actual reading.

These devices are mostly adaptations of devices developed by Durrell (61). The following often are used:

1. Word wheels
2. Word slips
3. Word tachistoscopes

Word wheels are constructed by cutting two disks. One should be about five inches in diameter and the other slightly smaller. On the larger disk, words are printed with the initial element missing. These words all should start at the same distance from the center (about one inch) and progress toward the outer edge like the spokes of a wheel. Only words that begin with the same word element should be used on one disk. The initial element should be omitted. For example, if the initial blend *str* is to be taught, words such as *strap, strong, straw, string, strip, stream,* and *strange* could be used. The word endings only are printed on the larger disk (see figure 6). In the smaller disk, a radial slit of the proper size and position is cut to expose one word ending at a time. The initial blend *str* is printed just to the left of the slit (see figure 6). The two disks are fastened together at the center with a paper fastener (A), with the smaller disk on top. As the lower disk is rotated, the *str* on the smaller disk will make a word as it is combined with each ending on the larger disk (see figure 6).

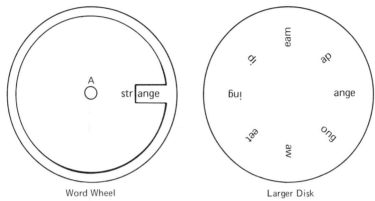

Word Wheel   Larger Disk

Fig. 6. *STR WORD WHEEL.*

Other word parts may be taught this way. With word endings, such as *ing, ake,* or *alk,* the word wheel will need to be changed so that the ending is printed at the right of the slit cut in the smaller disk, and the word beginnings are printed on the larger disk (see figure 7).

Fig. 7. *ING WORD WHEEL.*

Word slips may be constructed to practice the various word parts. They have an advantage over word wheels because they are easier to make. A manila folder can be used to make the removable faces and slips. Figure 8 illustrates the use of a word slip. The removable faces and slips can be varied in order to drill on any particular word part. The word slips and faces are made by typing the word part to be drilled at the appropriate place on the face (see figure 8, faces, 1, 2, and 3). The remaining parts of the words can be typed or printed at intervals on the slip. A permanent poster-board back can be used for all exercises, since the face is removable.

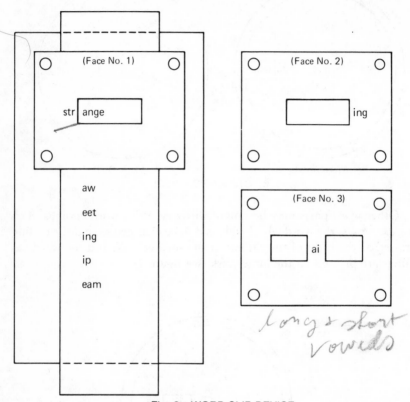

Fig. 8. *WORD SLIP DEVICE.*

Word beginnings that could be typed on word slips to use with the *ing* ending on removable face no. 2 are: *th, s, br, r, str, wr,* and *k.* The following words also could be used with this face: *walk, talk, sing, jump, build, play, say, feed, hear,* etc. Root words ending in *e* or those that double the final conso-nant could also be used with face no. 2.

Slips and faces, such as face no. 1, could be made for all the important initial consonants, blends, and digraphs. No. 2 faces and slips could be made for all the important variant endings and phonograms. No. 3 faces and slips could be made to teach long and short vowels and vowel combi-nations. The words used in these exercises should be those taught in the basal readers or from lists of common words as compiled by Dale, Dolch, Gates, and Thorndike.

The word-slip devices can be used as a tachistoscope by moving a small card up and down to expose quickly each new word to be studied. This is sometimes advisable for the child who has a tendency to dawdle or who tends to break words into too many parts. The word-slip device also can be used for drill on sight words if another face, with just an exposure slit without any letters, is made. In this case, the words on the typed slip should be spaced farther apart with a heavy black line between them. The teacher would show the black line and then say, "ready" and expose the word for an instant, and then move the word slip to the next black line while the child responds.

Although drill on word parts with devices like those discussed above has some merit for children limited in knowledge of visual, structural, and phonic elements of words, it is better to teach these in contextual exercises. Even these are best when teaching the elements in words that come from a basic reading program. Under such circumstances, the child not only will be taught the elements in contextual settings in which he associates the printed symbols with oral pronunciation, but he also will get adequate review of the words introduced, so that they can become a part of his permanent sight vocabulary. A more detailed way of teaching the child to relate word elements to sounds is in methods like those recommended by Monroe (141), good for extremely disabled readers. These methods are individual and time-consuming, but they do help the child severely limited in knowledge of word parts. Sound-tracing methods will be discussed in the next chapter on the extremely disabled reader.

LACK OF FLUENT ORAL AND VISUAL SYNTHESIS

The child must be able to reassemble a word after he has visually separated it into parts and recognized them. Effective and rapid synthesis of the parts into the whole word is essential to word recognition. Many children have difficulty with their reading, because they lack ability in word synthesis. This ability is called auditory blending. In actual reading, the word parts are neither thoroughly sounded nor auditorily blended. It is relatively infrequent that a mature reader resorts to auditory blending. He usually perceives the larger elements within a word visually and then synthesizes it visually without resorting to oral pronunciation at all. In the word *anytime*, for example, the able reader would see the words *any* and *time* in the larger word. He would not pronounce these parts nor would he pronounce the word as a whole, but he would see immediately that it was a compound word made up of two, well-known words. The mature reader would identify the word *anytime* by visually synthesizing the known parts and would know the meaning of the compound word. This form of visual analysis, perception, and synthesis takes place so rapidly that the mature reader is rarely aware of such perceptual acts. He immediately senses the meaning of the printed symbol without reflecting on the symbol itself.

The mature reader, while reading silently, does not even sound out the parts of a broken word at the end of a line of print. He just looks at the part of the word on the upper line and then quickly glances down to the remainder of the word on the next line. He immediately identifies the word and its meaning. No oral pronunciation or auditory blending takes place.

The child who is beginning to learn to read or the child who is disabled in word synthesis cannot so readily synthesize words visually. Indeed, he often finds it difficult to blend a word auditorily once he has pronounced it part by part. In his early reading instruction, the child often is required to sound out words part by part and then blend the sound elements together. Sometimes he makes too great a separation of the parts when orally studying the word, and he cannot auditorily reassemble it. The difficulty that children sometimes have in either auditory or visual synthesis of words is caused by too early and too much phonetic sounding of words. Other children may have difficulty with word synthesis because they lack the capacity to blend sounds orally. The latter group of children constitute a troublesome problem to the teacher. They are, for example, unable to tell what word an examiner is saying when he pronounces the word part by part. If he says the word *drink* as *dr—ink,* with about a second of time between the parts, the child cannot tell what the word is. In some cases, the child cannot even tell that the examiner is saying *drink* if he pronounces it normally a second time after he has dissociated it. Bond (22) has shown that a child who is limited in this ability is much more likely to become a disabled reader when taught by methods requiring him to use auditory blending than he would be if visual recognition and synthesis were emphasized.

Many children have difficulty in blending because the word parts were learned in isolation rather than in words, or they were taught too often in drill exercises rather than in contextual settings. In such situations, the child learns to lean too heavily on oral pronunciation and auditory blending of word parts. Often the oral pronunciation of words, part by part, leads the child to pause between each part making blending difficult if not impossible. Frequently, the child who resorts to letter-by-letter sounding has forgotten the beginning of the word before he has completed the parts. This does not indicate necessarily that the child has a synthesis difficulty, but rather, it suggests an erroneous technique of word recognition which should be corrected.

The diagnosis of inability to synthesize words is somewhat complex.

Three judgments must be made: (*a*) Is the child's problem really one of poor synthesis, or is it the result of ineffective analytical techniques? (*b*) Is the child's problem one of poor auditory blending, or is it poor visual synthesis? (*c*) Is the child's difficulty the result of faulty learning, or is he auditorily handicapped? These can be decided by studying the results of the reading diagnostic tests. In the *Gates-McKillop Reading Diagnostic Tests* (described in chapter 7), the results of the tests of Recognizing and Blending Common Word Parts, Visual Perception Techniques (blending letter sounds) and Auditory Techniques (blending letter sounds) will indicate whether the child has a real deficiency in visual or auditory synthesis and whether he is auditorily handicapped.

The diagnostician also may observe the child's ability to reassemble words that have been correctly analyzed and pronounced, part by part. If the child is unable to blend words analyzed, he lacks ability in auditory blending. The diagnostician can pronounce some words, part by part, to see if the child can blend the sounds he hears. If the child is able to blend a large percentage of the words and recognize them, the diagnostician can be sure that the child's difficulty is due to imperfect learning and not to an auditory handicap.

The remedial work that should be given to a child poor in the visual synthesis of words is to have him recognize words presented to him by rapid-exposure techniques. A spaced slip of words correctly analyzed into syllables could be exposed in the word slip tachistoscope and the child could tell some fact about each word. For example, the following list could be used and the child could tell if the word named an animal or a food.

ba	boon			chip	munk	
but	ter			don	key	
buf	fa	lo		choc	o	late
ce	re	al		cook	ies	
bum	ble	bee		lem	on	ade
car	rot			let	tuce	
mon	key			rob	in	

Any of the word-slip exercises, developed for teaching the child with limited knowledge of word elements, can be used also for rapid exposure exercises to sharpen visual synthesis. This tachistoscopic type of rapid exposure also is helpful in overcoming the overanalytical reader's problems. It is useful as a quick-exposure technique for developing quick recognition of sight words, as described above.

Typed exercises with many words broken at the ends of the lines read under timed conditions will help in developing rapid visual synthesis of words.

For the child who lacks ability in auditory blending, any sounding out of words should be done in a smooth rather than in an interrupted fashion. He should have much experience in blending two-syllable words, and he should have oral blending training. The teacher could pronounce words with the syllables only slightly separated, and the child could say the parts and blend. It would be best to start with two-syllable words and gradually build up to longer words. Then single syllable words could be separated and blended. For children with difficulty in blending, because they have learned to separate the words so distinctly that they are unable to synthesize them, there should be more exercises for developing sight vocabulary, for associating meanings with words, and for using context clues. Children with this type of difficulty also should read a lot of relatively easy material.

CASE STUDY

When Allan was referred to the Psycho-Educational Clinic for study, he was an attractive boy from a fourth-grade classroom. He was large for a boy ten years and six months old. He had puzzled his teacher for some time. His discussions of class enterprises and his way of expressing his ideas were very good. In certain class activities he was an eager participant, while in others he tended to withdraw. His teacher was well aware that there was a relationship between Allan's tendency to lose interest in an activity and the amount of reading involved in it. She also understood that he had to gather most of his information from class discussions, but once he had it, his reasoning and judgment about what he just had learned were mature. She knew that Allan was a disabled reader. She had watched the difficulties he experienced whenever he was asked to read something aloud.

From an examination of Allan's cumulative record card and recent test scores, his teacher had made the general diagnosis that his reading disability called for more detailed study. The general diagnosis showed that Allan had a reading score of 2.5. His arithmetic grade score was 3.5 for problem solving and 5.2 for computation. His score on a group intelligence test indicated that he had an I.Q. of 98. His previous school record showed that Allan had repeated the third grade and that during the second year in that grade, less reading growth took place than in the previous year.

Allan's teacher did not think that the 98 I.Q. represented his true intelligence, even though it was in keeping with the level of his general school achievement. She based this judgment on the quality of his discussions of a topic he knew something about and on his score in the computation section of the arithmetic test. She also had noticed that when problems were read to him, his arithmetical reasoning seemed competent. From all of this information, she felt that a thorough study of Allan's educational problem was required. Since she had no specialized training, she referred Allan to the Psycho-Educational Clinic.

The clinic made a more analytical diagnosis as the first step in studying Allan's problem. This phase of the diagnosis consisted of giving a revised *Stanford-Binet Mental Test* and *The Developmental Reading Test—Advanced Primary.* The mental test indicated that Allan had a mental age of 13-0 and an I.Q. of 124. The examiner stated that the true intelligence of this boy might be even somewhat higher since he would have based at year ten, had he not missed item 3, reading and report. At the eleven-year level, he missed only item 3, abstract words; and at the twelve-year level, items 1, vocabulary, 5, abstract words, and 6, Minkus completion. At year thirteen, the only item missed was number 5, dissected sentences. Allan received eight months credit at year fourteen and four months credit at the "average adult" level. All the items missed early in the test had a relationship to reading, so it was the examiner's judgment that Allan was a very able child with a severe reading disability. While it was suspected that Allan was considerably brighter than the 124 I.Q. indicated, all that could be said was that Allan had a mental age of at least 13-0 and that he should be expected to read, if everything else were normal, at $(4.5 \times 1.24) + 1.0$, or 6.6 grade level. (The grade expectancy was computed by the formula explained in chapter 3.) A comparison between the scores obtained thus far showed that Allan was a bright boy who should be reading at about 6.6 level of difficulty. His arithmetic scores of 3.5 for problem solving (written problems) and 5.2 for computation (no reading involved) showed that he was doing reasonably well in an area not directly related to reading. *The Developmental Reading Test* scores showed the following:

Vocabulary	2.3
General Comprehension	2.5
Specific Comprehension	2.7
Average Reading Score	2.5

Allan's average reading achievement of only 2.5 showed that he was seriously disabled in reading. The pattern of scores in the three areas of reading measured indicated that his problem was a basic one. A study of the comprehension sections of the test revealed accurate performance on the simple items of these power tests but such slow speed that the boy did not get very far through the tests, even though the time limits are ample for the ordinary child. These reading scores were checked by informal measurements made with basic readers. It was found that Allan could read comfortably material no higher than beginning second-grade level, and that he was frustrated by material above halfway through the second-grade level. At this level of difficulty, Allan started to skip words and his frequency of errors increased as he continued to read. It was felt, from all the information thus far obtained, that Allan was a case of *limiting disability* and his area of difficulty was in word recognition. A thorough case study was made.

We now must answer the questions raised in chapter 6.

1. Is ALLAN CORRECTLY CLASSIFIED AS A DISABLED READER? The case study showed that he was indeed a disabled reader, and that there was not the slightest indication of any physical, mental, or neurological condition to alter his classification to anything other than disability in reading. Even when Allan was tense and became blocked when reading aloud, there was no evidence of any basic emotional problem. However, there seemed to be an emotional involvement with respect to his reading and some accompanying rejection of reading activities.

2. WHAT IS THE TRAINING NEEDED? This is the essential question in reeducating a child who has been classified correctly as a disabled reader. Allan's reading pattern on the *Gates Diagnostic Tests* and on the *Silent Reading Diagnostic Tests* showed his limiting conditions. He could not be expected to become a good reader until his basic reading problems were corrected. Allan's reading profile, obtained by using the *Silent Reading Diagnostic Tests,* is shown in figure 9. A study of Allan's profile indicates the following facts:

a. Allan was an extremely able boy who had a basic word-recognition problem.

b. The comparison between Allan's total items right, total errors, and total omitted on Tests 1 and 2 showed that he attempted to recognize words but was ineffective. He was more than a grade higher in the tendency to omit words (3.0) than he was in number of errors made (1.8). Even though he was not beyond the lines of importance in either of the above, the difference showed that he was attempting the items but was inaccurate.

c. The fact that his score (2.6) on Test 1, Words in Isolation, was higher than his score (2.0) on Test 2, Words in Context—though the difference was not great enough to guarantee its significance—does suggest that he was ineffective in using context clues.

d. The Error Analysis showed that Allan had a tendency to neglect the initial part of the word (1.5). In fact, this was significant as it was outside of the lines of importance as described in the manual for this test. Allan made a score of 2.6 on ending errors, which showed that he paid more attention to word endings compared to word beginnings. This is always an unfortunate pattern. He also showed some tendency toward orientation errors in these tests. The amount of

Name _Allan_ _____ School _____ Grade _4_ Date _____

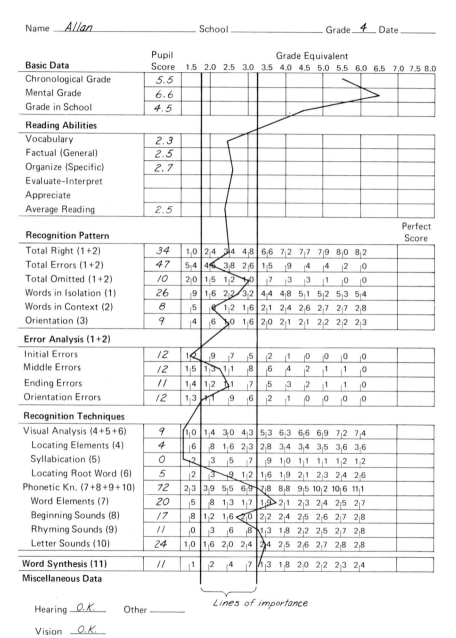

Basic Data	Pupil Score	Grade Equivalent (1.5 2.0 2.5 3.0 3.5 4.0 4.5 5.0 5.5 6.0 6.5 7.0 7.5 8.0)
Chronological Grade	5.5	
Mental Grade	6.6	
Grade in School	4.5	
Reading Abilities		
Vocabulary	2.3	
Factual (General)	2.5	
Organize (Specific)	2.7	
Evaluate–Interpret		
Appreciate		
Average Reading	2.5	

Recognition Pattern — Perfect Score

Recognition Pattern	Pupil Score	Values
Total Right (1+2)	34	1,0 2,4 3,4 4,8 6,6 7,2 7,7 7,9 8,0 8,2
Total Errors (1+2)	47	5,4 4,5 3,8 2,6 1,5 ,9 ,4 ,4 ,2 ,0
Total Omitted (1+2)	10	2,0 1,5 1,2 1,0 ,7 ,3 ,3 ,1 ,0 ,0
Words in Isolation (1)	26	,9 1,6 2,2 3,2 4,4 4,8 5,1 5,2 5,3 5,4
Words in Context (2)	8	,5 ,8 1,2 1,6 2,1 2,4 2,6 2,7 2,7 2,8
Orientation (3)	9	,4 ,6 ,0 1,6 2,0 2,1 2,1 2,2 2,2 2,3

Error Analysis (1+2)	Pupil Score	Values
Initial Errors	12	1,? ,9 ,7 ,5 ,2 ,1 ,0 ,0 ,0 ,0
Middle Errors	12	1,5 1,3 1,1 ,8 ,6 ,4 ,2 ,1 ,1 ,0
Ending Errors	11	1,4 1,2 1,1 ,7 ,5 ,3 ,2 ,1 ,1 ,0
Orientation Errors	12	1,3 1,1 ,9 ,6 ,2 ,1 ,0 ,0 ,0 ,0

Recognition Techniques	Pupil Score	Values
Visual Analysis (4+5+6)	9	1,0 1,4 3,0 4,3 5,3 6,3 6,6 6,9 7,2 7,4
Locating Elements (4)	4	,6 ,8 1,6 2,3 2,8 3,4 3,4 3,5 3,6 3,6
Syllabication (5)	0	,2 ,3 ,5 ,7 ,9 1,0 1,1 1,1 1,2 1,2
Locating Root Word (6)	5	,2 ,3 ,9 1,2 1,6 1,9 2,1 2,3 2,4 2,6
Phonetic Kn. (7+8+9+10)	72	2,3 3,9 5,5 6,9 7,8 8,8 9,5 10,2 10,6 11,1
Word Elements (7)	20	,5 ,8 1,3 1,7 1,9 2,1 2,3 2,4 2,5 2,7
Beginning Sounds (8)	17	,8 1,2 1,6 2,0 2,2 2,4 2,5 2,6 2,7 2,8
Rhyming Sounds (9)	11	,0 ,3 ,6 ,8 1,3 1,8 2,2 2,5 2,7 2,8
Letter Sounds (10)	24	1,0 1,6 2,0 2,4 2,4 2,5 2,6 2,7 2,8 2,8

| Word Synthesis (11) | 11 | ,1 ,2 ,4 ,7 1,3 1,8 2,0 2,2 2,3 2,4 |

Miscellaneous Data

Hearing _O.K._ Other _____   *Lines of importance*

Vision _O.K._

Fig. 9 *ALLAN'S PROFILE*

orientational confusion could be explained readily by his tendency to study the ends of words and to neglect their beginnings.

e. The section of these tests dealing with recognition techniques revealed an interesting and important condition. Allan was extremely poor in those phases of word recognition involving visual analysis of words into their larger, more useful elements. He was, however, extremely strong in phonics. His knowledge of word elements, for example, was at the 3.8 level, or over a year higher than his reading in general. In fact, Allan's phonic knowledge (3.5), compared with his visual analysis (1.5), showed that he was two years more advanced in his knowledge of word parts than he was in locating these elements within words. It also should be noted that his knowledge of beginning sounds (2.7) was more than a year behind his knowledge of word elements (3.8).

f. His word synthesis score of 3.4 indicated that there was no defect here.

g. In summary, this detailed study of Allan's reading pattern revealed that he needed the remedial training described in this and the preceding chapter, under four headings: (a) ineffective visual analysis of words, (b) failure to use meaning clues, (c) the second type of overanalytical reader, i.e., the reader who breaks words into too many parts, and (d) wrong beginnings.

Parts of the *Gates-McKillop Reading Diagnostic Tests* also were given to this boy. A study of the tabulated results of Allan's diagnosis indicated that this test verified the conclusions obtained from the *Silent Reading Diagnostic Tests.* It added the information that Allan had a relatively good sight vocabulary (3.1) and also that when he was given more time to study words, his overanalytical tendency got in his way. This was shown by comparing the score of 2.5 on the untimed word-perception test with the score of 3.1 on the flash word-perception test.

3. WHO CAN GIVE MOST EFFECTIVE REMEDIAL WORK? From recommendations made after the clinical diagnosis was completed, it was decided that Allan could be treated best in the school reading center, since his case of limiting disability needed only well-defined instruction and there was only a minor emotional rejection of reading.

4. HOW CAN IMPROVEMENT BE MADE MOST EFFICIENTLY? Allan was given remedial work in the school reading center for an hour each day in a basic reader at the beginning of second-grade level of difficulty. Workbook exercises and those suggested in the reader manual for using beginning elements, larger elements of words, visual analysis of words, and context clues were emphasized. Short selections were used for rapid reading. He was also given pertinent reinforcing exercises, such as those described in this and the preceding chapter.

5. DOES THE CHILD HAVE ANY LIMITING CONDITIONS THAT MUST BE CONSIDERED? Allan had no visual or hearing difficulties and no other limiting condition was identified.

6. ARE THERE ANY ENVIRONMENTAL CONDITIONS THAT MIGHT INTERFERE WITH PROGRESS IN READING? His parents were very concerned about Allan's reading, as well they might be. His mother had given him some reading instruction at home. She had sat with Allan every day after school for a period of three months, helping him with his reading. After that she had felt that she and the boy were not progressing, so she discontinued the instruction. The help she gave him was sounding out unknown words. This is just what Allan did not need, as he already had too much of a tendency to break words apart and sound each letter. His mother thought there was something wrong with Allan's memory because the words they worked out one day were forgotten the next. She was eager to cooperate. She accepted the clinic's suggestion to help him by discussing with him what he was reading at home and telling him words he did not know. The more technical teaching was left to the remedial teacher.

Allan's classroom teacher also was told the nature of his reading difficulty. She already knew that he was a slow reader and an ineffective one. She was interested in the findings of the complete diagnosis and readily fell in with the idea that she could make adjustments to his level of reading capability in the regular classroom work.

At the end of six months of instruction in the reading center, Allan was measured again. His reading ability, as tested by the *Gates Reading Survey*, showed gratifying results.

Vocabulary	4.5
Speed	4.4
Level of Comprehension	4.9
Average	4.6

The average gain was more than two years. At this time, it was felt that Allan could soon discontinue work in the reading center. He was still disabled in reading, but he had overcome much of his basic difficulty. It was felt that the classroom teacher could give him the additional instruction and experience he needed.

SUMMARY

Word recognition is difficult and complex to learn. It requires a highly integrated and flexible set of skills and abilities. To avoid some of the more serious types of word-recognition difficulties, well-organized instruction must be given at all levels. The child must be started by teaching him the habit of trying to recognize words as words. The early training includes the use of context clues, picture clues, and teacher's questions. Then the child is taught to note similarities in initial elements and gradually to acquire the whole hierarchy of word-recognition techniques. These skills and knowledges fall roughly into five types: (*a*) the ability to recognize many words at sight and to associate meanings with printed symbols; (*b*) skill in using context clues and other meaning aids to anticipate the words to be recognized and to check on their accuracy; (*c*) skill in using flexible and efficient, perceptual techniques in visually analyzing words into usable recognition elements; (*d*) knowledge of a wide variety of visual, structural, and phonic elements; (*e*) skill in both auditory blending and visual synthesis of word parts into word entities.

The major source of difficulty in word recognition is the failure to establish these basic learnings and the failure to maintain a balance among them. The best method for correcting difficulties in word recognition is to have the disabled reader develop these skills and knowledges in the course of reading meaningful material in a basal reading program. The remedial teacher should take great care in the methods she uses to introduce new words, so that the child's strengths may be utilized and any limitations in recognition may be corrected while the proper balances are maintained. The exercises suggested in the teacher's manuals stressing the skills needed by the child should be emphasized.

Workbook exercises that accompany basic readers are among the best sources for developing word-recognition skills and knowledges. Besides these, the remedial teacher will need to devise supplementary exercises. Various reinforcing exercises helpful in correcting limitations in word recognition have been described in this chapter. They should be used with caution and be recognized as drill devices rather than as a complete solution to the disabled reader's word-recognition problems. The disabled reader needs more than the usual amount of reinforcement in those areas which he has failed to learn sufficiently to maintain a balance among the word-recognition skills.

SELECTED READINGS

Bush, C. L., and M. H. Huebner, *Strategies for Reading in the Elementary School*, Chap. 4. New York: Macmillan, 1970.

Deboer, J. J., and M. Dallmann, *The Teaching of Reading* (rev. ed.), Chaps. 6A, 6B. New York: Holt, Rinehart and Winston, 1964.

DURRELL, DONALD D., *Improving Reading Instruction,* Chaps 10–12. New York: Harcourt Brace Jovanovich, 1956.

HARRIS, A. J., and E. R. SIPAY, *How to Increase Reading Ability* (6th ed.), Chap. 14. New York: David McKay, 1975.

HEILMAN, ARTHUR W., *Principles and Practices of Teaching Reading* (3rd ed.), Chap. 7. Columbus, Ohio: Charles E. Merrill, 1972.

KENNEDY, E. C., *Classroom Approaches to Remedial Reading* (2nd ed.), Chaps. 9, 10. Itasca, Ill.: F. E. Peacock Publishers, 1977.

OTTO, W., R. A. MCMENEMY, and R. J. SMITH, *Corrective and Remedial Teaching: Principles and Practices* (2nd ed.), Chap. 7. Boston: Houghton Mifflin, 1973.

SMITH, NILA B., *Reading Instruction for Today's Children.* Chap. 8. Englewood Cliffs, N. J.: Prentice-Hall, 1963.

WILSON, ROBERT M., *Diagnostic and Remedial Reading for Classroom and Clinic* (3rd ed.), Chap. 8. Columbus, Ohio: Charles E. Merrill, 1977.

Treating the Extremely Disabled Reader

eleven

Reading disability varies in degree. Some disabled readers have learned practically nothing; others read poorly, but at a level barely below what is reasonable to expect of them based on their reading expectancy. Disability in reading between these extremes may be graded in very small steps. Extreme disability cases, sometimes called nonreaders, dyslexics, or symbol association dysfunction cases are simply at the low end of the range. They are merely the most stubborn cases of disability who have failed to learn even after fairly extended instruction. They all are not alike. Extremely disabled readers differ in background, attitudes, perceptual competencies, special difficulties, and other respects. It is necessary to recognize individual differences among extremely disabled readers in organizing effffective remedial instruction. No single method or formula of remediation can possibly work for all extremely disabled readers.

METHODS OF TREATMENT

Teaching skill is very important to helping these extreme cases. Besides understanding the reading process, the teacher should be familiar with a variety of diagnostic and remedial procedures. She must be versatile in adapting these, both to accurate diagnosis of difficulties and to planning appropriate instruction for each particular case. Patience, sympathetic understanding of the pupil's difficulties, and skillful guidance throughout the instructional program are the key to aiding these extreme cases.

Certain methods of remedial instruction have been notably successful in teaching extremely disabled readers to read. Three of these general approaches are outlined briefly in the following sections.

Kinesthetic-Auditory-Visual Emphasis Methods

This method, sometimes called the Fernald-Keller kinesthetic method, described in detail by Fernald (75), was designed originally for and used successfully with extremely disabled readers. The features of the technique are to teach the child to write words correctly, to motivate him to do this, to have him read the printed copy of what he has written, and to move on eventually to extensive reading of materials other than his own. The program consists of four stages which are modified and summarized here:

STAGE 1: THE CHILD LEARNS BY TRACING WORDS. The essence of this first stage is to have the child learn words through finger tracing of written copy while pronouncing each part of the word as he traces. This is repeated until the child *can write the word without looking at the copy.* Clinical experience shows it is best if the words are written in large letters. They may be written for the child with crayon on paper or with chalk on the chalkboard. Some teachers even have the child trace in the air with his eyes closed after having traced on paper or chalkboard. Cursive writing is preferred, but many teachers feel that it is best to use manuscript writing with young children. Words learned through tracing may be used in stories a child wishes to write and may be filed according to alphabetical order. Points stressed in this first stage are that finger contact is important in tracing, words must be written without looking at the copy, words should always be written as units, and words should always be used in context. This means that the child must use the words in meaningful groups in sentences.

DURATION OF TRACING PERIOD. The length of the tracing period varies greatly from child to child depending on individual need for tracing to retain the word. Usually the tracing period continues for about one or two months.

MATERIAL USED. In the Fernald method materials are not simplified either in vocabulary or subject matter. Any word or sentence the child is capable of using properly in oral language can be learned so that it can be written and read. Clinical experience shows that when children learn using tracing methods, longer words are often retained better than are shorter ones.

STAGE 2. This is similar to Stage 1 except that the child no longer needs to trace. Rather, the child is able to learn a new word by looking at it, saying it to himself as he looks at it, and then writing it without looking at the copy. He says each part of the word as he writes it in multisyllabic words, stresses the syllables. Using new words for writing activities and filing them is continued. In all activities, pronouncing words as whole, unbroken units is emphasized.

STAGE 3. This stage dispenses with the use of specially prepared copy. The child now learns directly from standard printed words. He still must look at a printed word, say it to himself, and then write it. He may read from ordinary books with the teacher telling him words he does not know. Upon the conclusion of reading, the aided words are learned by the child following the look-say-write method described above. Many teachers choose to select the books children read in this stage so as to minimize the number of unknown words a child will encounter.

STAGE 4. The child is able to recognize some new words from their resemblance to words or word parts he remembers and on the basis of context clues. As in the previous stage, the teacher tells the child all words he cannot recognize. Difficult words are looked at, said, and then written from memory. Retention of words learned in this way is reported to be eighty to ninety-five percent.

During remedial instruction the child is not required to sound out any word when he is reading, nor is any word sounded out for him by the teacher. Nevertheless, children taught by this method do acquire phonics skills through the tracing-sounding and writing-sounding training. Although Fernald's children knew no phonics at the beginning of instruction and were given no formal training in phonics, they were able at the end of instruction to pass phonics tests at their age level. For a much more complete description of the Fernald method, consult Fernald (75, chapter 5).

Many teachers have reported great success in having children trace troublesome words in the air with their eyes closed. This modification emphasizes kinesthetic and auditory clues to word recognition while reducing the role of vision. For some children with severe visual-perceptual problems, tracing in the air with eyes closed seems to enable them to acquire an organized percept of the word which eludes them when vision is involved.

SUCCESS OF THE METHOD. Fernald (75) reports phenomenal success with her tracing method. Other clinicians have found the method successful but are more moderate in their views. There is little doubt that application of the method by a well-trained remedial teacher will achieve success in many extreme cases. Clinically, the method has been found to be most effective with visually handicapped children, certain neurologically impaired children, and children with visual-perceptual or visual-processing problems. Often these children have been unable to profit from the ordinary forms of classroom instruction, especially from those methods which depend largely upon visual presentation. Fernald considers the best way to overcome this extreme reading disability is to use the kinesthetic method described above. This kinesthetic activity involved in the tracing and writing, combined with saying the word, constitutes the core of the technique.

EVALUATION. When used by experienced clinicians, the Fernald method is undoubtedly successful. In the early stages it tends to be time-consuming. In an extreme case, the tracing may continue for eight months, although the average is only two months. But other methods require long periods of instruction also when dealing with extreme disabilities. So the time factor hardly can be termed a drawback. When the instruction is given properly, the pupils can be as well motivated as by any other method.

It is worthwhile inquiring into why this method is successful. Fernald considers the *kinesthesis,* coupled with enthusiastic and efficient teaching, the keys to its success. It should be noted that in addition to kinesthesis, other important features are included in proper teaching of the method: (*a*) The child learns effectively the left-to-right sequences of perception by his simultaneous tracing-sounding and writing-sounding of words. (*b*) The visual structure of the word is associated with sounding the pronounceable units of the word. (*c*) Skill in phonics is learned without being taught formally. As part of this sounding, the child learns what is equivalent to consonant substitution in recognition of new words. After recognizing a familiar element in a word, the child attaches the proper beginning or ending sound. Meanings supplied by the verbal context are used to choose the proper ending or beginning to recognize the new word. In the sentence "Mary *took* the kitten home," the element *ook* may be associated with or recognized as part of the familiar word *book* or *look.* The context then helps to give the proper word *took.* Also through tracing-writing-sounding, many initial and final elements become familiar to the child so that he makes the substitution readily. (*d*) The very nature of the program leads to skill in syllabication. (*e*) The Fernald method teaches left-to-right direction of word perception, the visual form of words, skill in phonics (including syllabication and the equivalent of consonant substitution), and use of context clues for identification and recognition of words. Added to all this, the child is strongly motivated by working with materials interesting to him. Although the kinesthetic aspects of this method may be very important for certain visually handicapped and neurologically impaired children, and for certain children with visual-perceptual or visual-processing difficulties, it should be noted that the emphasis on left-to-right perception, visual structure of words, skill in phonics, skill in syllabication, and use of context are inherent to the method when properly taught. It is doubtful that kinesthesis alone is responsible for the success of the method, but rather kinesthesis in combination with a sound, well-balanced program for teaching word perception in remedial instruction. Besides word recognition, the Fernald method stresses vocabulary and concept development, and comprehension.

Auditory (Sound-Blending)-Emphasis Methods

A strong phonics approach has been incorporated into a number of remedial procedures. One of the most comprehensive programs which have been successful in teaching excessively disabled readers is Monroe's. Her techniques are essentially phonics-based with emphasis upon patient, repetitive drill work, but include sufficient variety to retain the learner's interest without sacrificing the fundamental purposes of the drill. Such remedial programs must be prescribed in detail by the teacher for each reading disabled child. It is essential that known phonics elements be passed over very lightly and that unknown elements receive heavy emphasis in order to ensure maximum benefit to each child. The fundamental features of the Monroe method will be described here, although the other successful phonics-based programs generally are quite similar. To use any phonics-based remedial approach, it is imperative that the teacher be familiar with the details of the program. When using the Monroe approach, the teacher should read Monroe's book (141).

FAULTY VOWELS AND CONSONANTS. In extreme cases, these are major sources of difficulty. Although exact remedial needs differ from child to child, many who are severely disabled need instruction in discriminating specific speech sounds, in associating visual symbols with letter sounds, in observing that words with the same sounds often have the same letters, and in coordinating the temporal sequence of sounds with the left-to-right sequence of letters in a word.

One of the first steps is to strengthen the ability to discriminate speech sounds. Pictures of several objects beginning with the same consonant, or containing the same vowel are mounted on cards. The pictures may be obtained from magazines or old books. Examples of typical initial consonants used are:

b as in boy, book	*m* as in man, moon
c as in coat, cat	*t* as in tiger, table, etc.

As far as possible, words which contain a vowel immediately after the initial consonant are chosen for this early drill. Single consonant sounds are learned more readily than consonant blends. Thus the *s* sound is learned more easily in *seed* than in *store*.

Cards with pictures are arranged similarly for the vowels, such as:

a as in man, cat   *o* as in box, top
e as in pen, hen   *i* as in fire, kite, etc.

To develop discrimination, the instruction is started with unlike sounds, as *m* compared with *s*. The cards for *m* and *s* are arranged in a row in mixed order:

man   soap   moon   seed

The child is instructed to sound the *m* and then name the object in the picture. After he succeeds with unlike sounds, the more difficult discriminations are taught as *s* and *sh* in *seed* and *shell*. These drills are varied by asking the child to give words beginning with a certain sound. A similar procedure is followed in the drills on vowels.

The next step is associating the letters with their most frequent sounds. Tracing is introduced as a reinforcement when necessary. The child traces a letter written by the teacher. He sounds it as he traces. This is repeated until he can look at the letter and sound it correctly without tracing. Ordinarily, five or six consonant sounds can be learned at one sitting. After learning several consonant and vowel sounds, the child is taught blending letter sounds into words. The sounding-tracing method is an important aid in this. The sounding becomes a slow distinct articulation of the word as a unit while being traced. Monroe (141, pp. 121–123) gives a series of word lists to be learned in this manner. Recall is tested by presenting the words printed on cards. With this the child is encouraged to articulate the separate letter sounds and blend them. The phonics skills the child acquires gives him a feeling of mastery in word recognition.

The child next progresses to reading specially prepared phonetic stories. The child soon is able to handle stories in ordinary primers and first readers. Nonphonetic words are learned by tracing-sounding. As the child gains in vocabulary and reading ability, the nonphonetic words often are identified from context.

REVERSALS. Monroe found it necessary to give the child a definite motor cue to the correct direction for left-to-right sequence in perceiving words. This is accomplished by tracing-sounding as practiced by Fernald (see above). Monroe's adaptation of the method is described in detail in her chapter 6.

ADDITION OF SOUNDS. Failure to discriminate consonant blends and failure to discriminate word forms accurately, frequently leads to adding sounds. The sounds more frequently added are *r* and *l*. When this tendency ·

persists, drills are given on lists of words which are alike except for the presence of *r* or *l.* Examples are: *bed* and *bread; pan* and *plan.*

OMISSION OF SOUNDS, SUBSTITUTION OF WORDS, REPETITION OF WORDS, ADDITION OF WORDS, and OMISSION OF WORDS. Errors of these types are usually the result of the lack of accurate word recognition or an overemphasis on speed. Reading aloud by teacher and child together helps, as does more emphasis on developing better word-analysis skills, and going back to easier reading materials. If any of these errors remain, the teacher should call them to the attention of the disabled reader so that he may try to avoid them. An emphasis on context clues also is helpful.

SUCCESS OF THE METHOD. The Monroe method is particularly successful with extreme disability cases. For the twenty-seven children in her group whose reading ability would place them less than half-way through the first grade (1.0-1.4), the average gain was 1.3 grades after approximately twenty-six hours of remedial instruction over a period of about eight months. Her control group of fifty cases who received no remedial instruction gained only 0.14 of a grade in eight months. In other words, the children who had no remedial training made practically no gain, while those with instruction by her method gained over a year in reading.

EVALUATION. The Monroe method is a definite, somewhat rigid, drill program taking much time. The progress is from letter sounds to words in sentences. It delays reading of words longer than in the Fernald method. However, the teaching of extremely disabled cases to read will take time whatever the method used. The Monroe method probably takes no more time to get results with these cases than would other methods. Monroe has worked out an effective combination of the tracing-sounding method with phonetic training. She recognizes that drill in her method is somewhat mechanical and laborious in the early stages. But as the child progresses, much of his reading takes on the characteristics of normal performance, except when he encounters an unknown word. He then may use tracing or sounding, or both, until the word is recognized. He then proceeds with his reading. The view taken in this book is that the Monroe technique is good for some severely retarded readers. Although it also is successful with less severely retarded cases, other methods tend to get quicker results.

Visual-Structural Emphasis Methods

These approaches, as originally described in detail by Gates (83), are similar to those used in good classroom teaching, but consist of an enriched program. The approach to word study emphasizes visual-structural inspection and widely uses worksheet exercises. The child is encouraged to recognize words as entities, and in word study, to inspect the word carefully part by part from left to right. At the same time, the child notes similarities and differences, including minimal differences in words, with early emphasis on word beginnings and then on the overall structure of the words. In this way, the child establishes a knowledge of word elements in the actual process of contextual reading. Knowledge of phonic, structural, and phonemic elements is not neglected, but is taught so closely with actual reading that the transfer of the skills into total word-recognition capabilities is accomplished. When successful, this method helps to make fluent, thoughtful readers. It is true that some children need more diversified programs, with added intensive drill on the word elements themselves.

Remedial instruction for extremely disabled readers is like that for normal pupils except that the program of instruction is managed more carefully. Its adjustment to individual needs and individual instruction is emphasized. The teacher must be flexible in selecting just the technique or approach for the particular case. This requires intensive study of each child's abilities, difficulties, and needs. The teacher will have to spend more time and exercise more care in demonstrating and explaining the techniques. Additional explanations and suggestions are given as needed. She is careful that the pupil moves ahead at just the proper pace. When a method or device does not appear to help, the teacher shifts to some other devices or form of help.

If the more individualized teaching of the commonly used procedures is not successful, the teacher may resort to some of the techniques ordinarily used only with excessively disabled readers. First, the customary methods of observing words, using context clues, visual and auditory analysis, and development of appropriate left-to-right orientation in word perception are given a fair trial. If the child's responses then reveal inadequate progress in learning to read, the teacher may resort to tracing and writing techniques. Even in this case, the tracing and writing is not continued for weeks and months. It is to be used merely as a means of getting the child started, so he will consistently maintain the left-to-right progression in reading words. Once the child has begun to make headway in the tracing-writing technique, he should be shifted back to a program which covers the full range of reading activities for a normal child.

Gates claims that his procedure is used more widely with extreme disability cases than any other method. As evidence of its success, he cites the city-wide program carried out in the New York City schools, beginning in 1934. The instruction was individual and intensive but was by no means a narrow drill program. Many gadgets and special devices were invented and used by the teachers. They made special efforts to ensure that each pupil had large amounts of interesting reading material and an opportunity to use his artistic, dramatic, exploratory, constructive, and other interests in relation to his reading. Most teachers considered that best results were obtained with all types of cases, including extreme cases, by an intensive application of the same methods recommended for ordinary classroom use. A few felt that success with extremely disabled readers was obtained by spending some time in tracing-writing as in the Fernald method. Still other teachers considered that a phonics approach similar to Monroe's program produced the best results. Many felt that a more intensive use of either the tracing or the phonetic procedure was best for *certain cases but not for others.* Gates states that intensive use of tracing and phonics was a last resort when satisfactory progress was not made through a more comprehensive program.

SUCCESS OF THE METHOD. The results of the New York City remedial program undoubtedly were good. With two months of training, the average case gained over four times normal expectancy. Less than five percent failed to make normal progress. Later results were even more promising.

It should be noted that Gates admitted, although with some reluctance, that certain extremely disabled readers need special procedures such as tracing-writing. However, he insists that such procedures and other special devices should be abandoned as soon as possible.

EVALUATION. Visual-structural emphasis methods have certain advantages: (*a*) They tend to be flexible. Provisions are made for shifting temporarily to more rigid drill techniques when needed, such as tracing-writing approaches or phonics drills. (*b*) Many excessively disabled readers should achieve the characteristics of normal performance sooner with the visual-structural methods than with those with more rigid drill. (*c*) It would seem desirable to start the extremely disabled reader with a visual-structural program. If, after a fair trial, progress is not satisfactory, the teacher can turn to one of the other techniques. Tracing-writing approaches seem to benefit most the child who has difficulty forming an organized percept of whole words, and auditory (sound-blending) methods seem to help most the child who is notably stronger in auditory than in other learning abilities. After some progress is made with highly specialized, fixed procedures, a gradual transition can be made toward the broader and less mechanical instruction used with typical readers.

GENERAL STATEMENT. Almost any expert remedial teacher may be able to teach many of her extremely disabled children to read by any of the methods discussed here. To be really expert, she should be able to use each of the methods effectively. Then, after a thorough analysis of a case, she can apply the method most suitable for remedying the difficulties it presents.

There is no single, "sure-fire" method for teaching every extremely disabled reader and the same is true even for cases with less severe retardation.

Probably the reason for the success of these methods used with extreme disability cases is that a high percentage of them would be classified after an adequate diagnosis as word-recognition cases. Because these methods are successful in general does not mean that any one of them might not prove very detrimental to an occasional individual case. In the opinion of the authors of this book, the best approach to extreme cases appears to lie in making an exact diagnosis and then applying the indicated remedial work, which in some cases might well be a tracing-writing or a phonics drill program. In most cases, however, the balanced word-recognition attack described in chapters 9 and 10 should be used.

TREATING ORIENTATIONAL DIFFICULTIES

Word-orientation confusions are among the most troublesome errors made by extremely disabled readers. The problems of full reversals, part reversals, axial rotations of letters, and other orientational confusions in word recognition interfere with successful reading development. Any child who makes an extreme number of such errors has a limiting condition which must be corrected before continued growth in reading can be expected.

The term "reversals" is used to describe different kinds of errors in orientation. These errors are in observing letters in reverse orientation, as *d* for *b* when reading *dig* for *big*, or perceiving letters in reverse order or partial reverse order. Examples of complete reversals are reading *saw* for *was*, or *no* for *on*. Partial reversals are illustrated by reading *own* for *now*, or *ate* for *tea*. Also, there may be reversals of the order of words in a sentence, as "The rat caught a cat" for "The cat caught a rat."

During the preschool years, the child has learned to recognize people, landscapes, animals, and objects, both from firsthand visual experience and from viewing pictures and diagrams. In all this, the direction of the perceptual sequences, as revealed by eye movements, is neither orderly nor oriented to a specific direction. Rather, they are a series of brief glances while the eyes move in an irregular pattern of fixations over the object or picture. The direction of the movements is just as likely to be from right to left as left to right, or upward as downward, or obliquely in any direction. As the child looks over an object, noting points of interest or searching for familiar items, the direction of the eye movements is not only irregular but also unpredictable to a large degree. These habits of perception are established before entering school. Unless systematic instruction is given by the time the child begins to read words and sentences, he is likely to continue the habit of examining objects with irregular directional sequences in viewing words. To be efficient, the child must read words in a sentence, one after another from left to right. Unless a word is recognized at a glance, he must proceed along the word from left to right to identify it correctly.

Development of proper directional habits in reading requires two related instructional tasks. The first is acquisition of the left-to-right sequence of eye movements along a line of print. This is a somewhat gross orientation which nonetheless must be learned. The second task is establishment of the left-to-right direction of attack required for proficient word identification and recognition. This is a more precise and difficult skill. Contrary to one's first impression, these two aspects of sequential orientation in reading are related only roughly. It is true that both involve beginning at the left and progressing toward the right. But a child may have learned to begin at the left end of a line of print and, in general, move his eyes toward the right without having mastered proper directional orientation within particular words. Extensive and continuing training is needed for the latter.

Word Perception

As noted above, the wrong orientation in perceiving words results in reversal errors. Both diagnosis and remedial instruction for reversals are necessarily more elaborate than for directional habits in reading lines of print. The most satisfactory diagnosis of reversal tendencies is obtained through the use of standardized tests. Several of these were described in chapter 7. The parts of these tests which are used to detect and evaluate reversal errors are listed below:

1. *Durrell Analysis of Reading Difficulty:* Word Recognition and Word Analysis Test detects reversals of *b* and *d*, *p* and *q*, and of the sequences of letters within words.

2. Monroe *Diagnostic Reading Examination:* Oral Reading Test, Iota Word Test, and Word Discrimination Test detect reversals of *b* and *d*, *p* and *q*, *u* and *n*, and of the sequences within words and reversals of the order of words.

3. *Gates-McKillop Reading Diagnostic Tests:* The Oral Reading Test and Word Discrimination Test detect reversals of *b* and *d*, *p* and *q*, and of the sequence of letters in words.

4. Bond-Balow Hoyt *Silent Reading Diagnostic Tests:* Recognition of Reversible Words in Context Test and the error classification in the Word Recognition Tests detect reversal of the sequences of letters in words.

It already has been noted that it is normal for beginners to make some reversals and that these gradually are eliminated by most children as they progress in reading. For each pupil with a reading problem, therefore, it must be seen whether reversals are common enough to cause trouble rather than being merely occasional incidents in ordinarily adequate reading. In other words, it is necessary to decide whether the frequency of reversals is a sign merely of immature reading or is a genuine reading handicap. This evaluation is made by consulting the norms which accompany the Gates-McKillop, the Monroe, and the Bond-Balow-Hoyt tests. In each instance, the frequency of reversals which constitutes a reading handicap and which must be corrected is indicated.

As soon as children begin to read words and lines of print, proper directional orientation must be stressed. Effective reading is achieved only when perceptual sequences, largely guided by eye movements, move from left to right. Except for sight words, those which are recognized at a glance, the children must be instructed to examine a word from left to right in working out its recognition. It will be necessary for the teacher to demonstrate repeatedly the proper directional orientation in perceiving words. She should be sure, before using these terms, that all pupils have learned through preliminary and partly incidental training, the meaning of left and right.

The left-to-right habit is by no means confined to beginning instruction in reading. The training is continued, more or less, throughout instruction for development of the word-recognition techniques. Such training is constructive only when done correctly and systematically. Working out word identification through attention to initial consonants, consonant substitution, phonetic analysis, structural analysis, syllabication, and use of the dictionary requires constant attention to left-to-right orientation. Many pupils with proper directional habits in the early stages of reading will drop the habit at later stages unless additional instruction is given.

Remedial Procedures

In general, significant degrees of reversing the order of letters in words occur more frequently among the more severely retarded readers. This is not surprising when one refers back to the causes of reversals in word perception discussed above. The child who has severe eye defects, who has received inadequate training in left-to-right orientation, who has been taught to emphasize word endings rather than beginnings, or who has been exposed to an improper program of phonics training, not only develops reversals but also seldom progresses far in learning to read. Any analysis of the methods successfully used to instruct nonreaders or severely retarded readers reveals that much emphasis is given to orderly, left-to-right inspection of words, with an emphasis on developing an adequate apprehension of words as entities, and with instruction in the proper blending of letter sounds into word units.

The remedial teacher must not assume that correction of reversal tendencies is the entire instruction program for any reversal case. Ordinarily, other difficulties are present and must be remedied. But when reversals exist in significant numbers, as will be found in about ten percent of the disability cases, they are very important and require carefully organized and sometimes prolonged treatment.

At first, the teacher explains the necessity of viewing words from left to right. She accompanies this explanation with a demonstration. After writing a word on the chalkboard or on paper, she moves a pointer or her finger along the word as she pronounces it slowly. To emphasize the procedure when a restudy is needed, she then moves back her finger quickly to the very beginning of the word, and progresses to the right again as she reads it a second time. The second time, the teacher should stress the desirability of grasping the word as a unit after the difficult part is worked out. Next, the method of recognizing an unfamiliar word found in the context of a sentence is explained and demonstrated in a similar manner. The finger underlines the words as they are read. After a slight pause on reaching the unfamiliar word, the teacher moves her finger slowly along the word, pronouncing it as she did with the isolated word. The explanations and demonstrations are repeated as often as necessary while the pupil is practicing the left-to-right orientation in perceiving words. It is desirable for the pupil to practice with words in sentence context as soon as possible so that he may use context clues as much as possible in word recognition. In practicing sentences he will become accustomed to using the left-to-right progression along lines of print and to identifying unknown words in actual reading situations. Guided practice is transferred to sentences and paragraphs in book materials as soon as possible. It is important for the teacher to make sure that skill in proper perceptual orientation in reading isolated words and words in isolated sentences does transfer to book reading. For some children, this transfer is difficult and they need much directed practice.

Although a child may be encouraged at first to use his finger or a manila marker to guide his perception along the lines of print and along the successive letters in an unknown word, certain precautions are necessary. This is definitely a crutch and gradually should be eliminated when no longer needed. Some teachers feel that use of a marker is better because it is easier to eliminate than is finger pointing. Whether the child uses his finger or a marker, the teacher should instruct the pupil so that the perceptual aid is used properly, i.e., the child should not point at one word after another with stops, but use a consistent and *continuous* sliding movement from left to right to guide sequences of perception. Otherwise the finger or marker may be used only to keep the place rather than to promote left-to-right progression. It accomplishes nothing if the finger or marker is moved forward and backward along a line or a word, or if it is held in one place while the reader examines a word in random order. Using the finger or marker as a pointer will produce proper directional movements in reading and will correct reversal tendencies only when carefully supervised by the teacher.

Other Motor Aids

Use of the tracing-sounding-writing approach, described in detail earlier in this chapter, is one of the most useful procedures with persistent reversal cases. A modification of phonics emphasis and sounding-tracing is also effective. The procedure is illustrated by the following example: The word *man* is written in large, cursive writing on a piece of paper. Attention is directed to the word and its pronunciation. The child is asked to say *man* as slowly as possible, as demonstrated by the teacher. He then takes a pencil and traces over the word while saying *man* slowly. He is encouraged to trace quickly and speak slowly, so as to come out even. The aim of this is to pronounce the word distinctly and slowly enough so that its sequence of sounds becomes evident. Further training teaches the knack of sliding the voice from one sound to the next so that the word is pronounced as a unit.

A sound-dictation method has been substituted as a variation of the tracing method. Here the child writes the words as the teacher dictates their sounds slowly, first having told the child he would hear the separate sounds, and having asked him to say them slowly as he writes the letters for each sound. Thus, she pronounces *man,* first having asked the child both to say and to write whatever word she says. For *man,* the child is told that the *a* is short by hearing the teacher sound it that way. In this method, the child must have learned the letters that correspond to the letter sounds and know how to write them. Children with second- and third-grade achievement usually do well on such drills. According to Monroe, writing from dictation with these directions is as helpful as the tracing, and some children prefer to write. Both the tracing-sounding and the writing-sounding techniques encourage discrimination of sound sequences in words and the coordination of these with visual sequences. Detailed exercises for doing this are given by Monroe.

WRITING WORDS. Many children with reversal problems already have had some experience in writing by the time they reach the reading clinic. The remedial teacher can make good use of writing to promote correct orientation in dealing with words. When writing, it is necessary to begin at the left and move to the right. So when it is used to develop left-to-right orientation, it should be free writing rather than copying material from a chalkboard, a chart, or a book. The latter tends to become a piecemeal operation rather than a continuous sequence. The training can be started with simple words and sentences. Some polysyllabic words should be used as soon as the child can handle them. He should be encouraged to observe and pronounce aloud to himself each word as he writes it. This will call attention to the sequence of the word elements needed for correct perception. To become effective in correcting reversals, the child must observe the correct order of letters and letter sounds in the words he is writing. Whether the writing used is cursive or manuscript, the same precautions should be given to the child.

If there is any tendency to use mirror writing, which can occur in writing from right to left, it immediately will be obvious. Ordinarily, this reverse writing can be corrected by explaining to the child the need to move from left to right and by having him start writing words at the extreme left of the paper or chalkboard. He then will move readily in the only direction possible, which is to the right. In extreme cases, the child may be told when writing sentences, to write the separate words underneath each other, each word starting at the left margin of the paper. Or the teacher may make a short vertical line at which the first letter of each succeeding word in a sentence is to begin. This special procedure can be eliminated after some practice.

TYPING. Typing has been suggested as a technique for developing correct orientation in word perception. Presumably, the child is forced to observe the proper sequence of letters in words as he types them. It is true that he will get some practice in noting the beginning of words on the copy as he types the first letter, then the second, then the third, and so on through the word. But if he is just learning to type, he is merely typing series of letters that happen to be in groups. He will be so engrossed in selecting and pressing each key, that he is unable to use the correct techniques of word perception either on the copy or in what he types. Studies of typewriting reveal that words are typed as units only after a typist becomes fairly skilled. This certainly would not be the case with most young children. Furthermore, if it is beginning typing, there likely is little understanding of what is being typed. The beginner's attention is devoted to the mechanics of typing letters, not to word units and meanings. Moreover, it is possible to type words and not recognize them. Left-to-right progression along a word must be combined with identification of the word in order to be effective in developing correct orientation in word perception. The teacher will find it very difficult to teach proper orientation for word perception through typing. Other methods are better and less cumbersome.

CHORAL READING AND MOTION PICTURE AIDS. In choral reading, each member of the group and the teacher have copies of the reading material.

All read aloud in unison, led by the teacher. This should help develop consistent progress along lines of print but has little value in promoting correct orientation within words. Special motion pictures composed completely of lines of print, such as the Harvard Films developed by Dearborn and Anderson (55), also foster left-to-right progression along lines of print. Films could be devised with a moving spot of light to guide the eyes along each successive line of print. Actually, choral reading and the motion picture devices now available are more useful for phrasing than for left-to-right orientation.

Other Procedures

There are several other procedures for teaching the correct directional orientation in perceiving words. Of primary concern is developing the habit of initial attention to beginnings of words. Familiarity with and proper *use of initial consonants and consonant blends* as explained in the previous chapter are extremely important. Many children with reversal problems do not have this ability. While deficiencies in knowledge of initial consonants are being remedied, there are a variety of exercises for teaching the child to notice word beginnings first of all. The following are examples:

1. TO DIRECT ATTENTION TO THE INITIAL SOUNDS OF WORDS AND AT THE SAME TIME TO ENSURE THAT THE WHOLE WORD IS READ. Sentences are arranged with one word missing like those below. Beneath each are listed three words, only one of which may be used correctly to complete the sentence. Another of these three words besides the correct choice begins with the same sound as that underlined in the sentence. To choose correctly, the child must note both the beginning sound and the meaning of the right word. The items should be words that have been used in the reading lessons. The child is instructed to read each sentence, to note the beginning sound that is underlined in one word of the sentence, and then to draw a circle around the word below the sentence that correctly completes the sentence. He is told that the correct word will begin with the same sound as that underlined in the sentence, and he is warned that this is true also of one other word below that is incorrect.

> John wet his feet in the _____.
>   wall   step   water
>
> They shall go to see a _____.
>   catch   show   shook
>
> Mary's kitten likes to drink _____.
>   milk   make   cotton

2. TRAINING IN CONSONANT SUBSTITUTION may be used to teach the child to notice word beginnings. A few samples are given below:

a. For contextual meaning, first show the child a sentence such as: "He came to see the new game." Ask him to read the sentence and find two words that look alike except for the first letter. Pronounce *came* and have the child point to the letter that stands for the first sound. Do the same for *game.* Then write the letters *t, s, n, g, c,* and have him give the sounds of the letters. Then write the word *came.* After the beginning letter is located correctly, erase *c* and substitute *t.* Pronounce the new word. Continue with the word *game.* Interchange initial consonants *s, n,* and and *c* again, emphasizing the role of the initial letter and its sound in pronouncing the words.

b. Present to the child a word such as *may* or *last* or *pig.* Then ask him to tell you a word that looks and sounds like *may* except at the beginning. When he mentions a word like *day,* erase the *m* in *may* while he watches and substitute the initial consonant of the word mentioned. Ask the child to pronounce the new word and to note how changing just the first letter makes a new word.

c. We should insert a word of caution here. When using consonant substitution to accustom a child to notice word beginnings, it is advisable always to stress initial letters and sounds. Try to avoid calling attention to rhyming ends and ending families of words, like groups of words ending in *-at* or *-all.*

For instance, in choosing one word out of two to complete a sentence, emphasize that the sound of the first letter in pronouncing the word will tell which is correct. Thus, if working with consonants *t* and *w,* say "which of the two words after the sentence should be used in the blank?"

Mary likes to _____ in the snow.   talk   walk

3. VARIOUS GAMES may be played for informal training in using initial consonants to direct attention to word beginnings. *Consonant Lotto* and the first part of *Group Sounding Game* in the Dolch materials (The Garrard Press, Champaign, Illinois) are designed for this purpose.

Word wheels and the other devices described in the previous chapter may be made for drill on initial consonants in emphasizing word beginnings. In using a word wheel, words having the same ending are used, like: *throat, coat, goat, boat, float, gloat.* On the bottom disk, only the word beginnings are typed or printed, and placed so that they would show through an opening in the top disk, on which the ending, *oat,* is printed to the right of the opening. (See word wheels in the previous chapter.) The two disks may be rotated so that the child will see that by changing the initial elements, new words are made. This will force the child to pay attention to the word beginnings in order to recognize the words shown.

In a similar manner, a column of initial elements of words having the same ending, can be typed or printed, using triple spacing, on a slip cut from a manila folder. Then an exposure card can be made by cutting a slit in a piece of manila folder. The word ending should be typed or printed just to the right of the slit. (See the word-slip device in the previous chapter.) When the slip is moved into position, the various initial elements are exposed, one after another, for the child to use in making the words. He is forced to notice the changing elements, since they will determine what the words will be.

In all this work, the teacher should present the exercise so that the child always sees the initial consonant as the word is exposed. This is done by going at a leisurely pace, by pointing to the initial consonant, and by having the child sound the consonant and blend it with the word ending. If this is not done, the child may remember the initial sound and look first at the ending. The purpose is to teach the child always to notice first the beginning of the word. Noticing the beginning of a word first, must become an ingrained habit.

4. IT HAS BEEN SUGGESTED THAT A DEMONSTRATION OF REVERSAL ERRORS is valuable in discussing directional orientation in word perception. The purpose of this is to show a child what will happen when he starts reading at the end or the middle of a word rather than at the beginning. For instance, the teacher can write *war* and *raw,* one above the other. She then points out that the same letters are in both words, but they are different words so that he always should start at the left end of a word in reading it. Similarly, she calls attention to *left* and *felt,* or other partial or complete reversals.

5. ALPHABETIZING AND DICTIONARY EXERCISES promote left-to-right orientation in perceiving words. For early practice in alphabetizing, the child should have a file box or folder with the alphabet marked on the dividing cards. A single word that has been learned is written on a slip of paper. The word then is filed by its initial letter. When the order of the alphabet has been learned, several words beginning with the same letter can be filed according to the sequence of letters within the word. All this develops the habit of looking first at the beginnings of words, and then progressing from left to right. Exercises for developing skill in alphabetizing and using the dictionary are given in teachers' manuals and workbooks accompanying basic reader series.

A picture dictionary can be made for a relatively immature reading level. This will teach a child the alphabet as used for classification. Also, when he is writing a word for his dictionary, it will give him practice in going through a word from left to right.

Preventing Reversals

It is desirable to teach elementary reading so that severe reversal tendencies are not created. From the start, proper orientation in word study should be stressed, as discussed in the early parts of this chapter and in the previous chapter. This becomes particularly important in teaching the various aspects of word analysis such as initial consonants, initial phonograms, and blending letter sounds into proper sequences. The first letter or letter group in a word should be sounded first, followed by an orderly progression to the right. A well-organized program of teaching word analysis (see preceding chapter), with attention to individual needs should help to establish the normal left-to-right progression needed to prevent regressions.

SUMMARY

The extremely disabled reader is the child who has learned little or no reading during several or more years in school. Three types of remedial methods have proved to be especially successful in teaching these children to read. A tracing-sounding-writing method, such as was suggested originally by Fernald has been effective in developing left-to-right orientation in word perception, in directing attention to the visual characteristics of words, in developing skill in phonics, syllabication, and in the use of context in recognizing words. Such teaching also emphasizes developing vocabulary, concepts, and comprehension, but it is detailed, time-consuming, and must be done on an individual basis. The method often is successful with extremely disabled readers, but requires an unusually great amount of teacher time.

Phonics (sound-blending) methods, such as those developed by Monroe, have been successful with certain cases of extreme disability. These methods are phonics-based and emphasize the patient repetition of the necessary drill and have a program for introducing variety without losing sight of the fundamental purposes of the drill. Special procedures are used for correcting particular difficulties such as faulty vowels, consonants, reversals, and others. Tracing-sounding is employed when necessary. This method is very useful for many children, though it should not be used with those who are already overanalytical.

Another highly successful method, advocated by Gates, is one which embodies all the procedures and techniques taught to typical children in good classroom programs. This method works when children receive intensive instruction based on an accurate understanding of their needs.

The expert remedial teacher should be familiar with all these methods so that she will use just the right procedure in each case. The present writers suggest that a careful diagnosis usually can specify the area of difficulty and indicate the type of remedial instruction needed. Such a diagnosis shows which approach or combination of approaches would be best.

A special problem which most beginning readers experience and soon eliminate, but which remains a genuine reading handicap for a few, is difficulty with left-to-right word perception.

Many methods to eliminate reversal tendencies in word perception have been described. The more important include: (*a*) explanation and demonstration of the left-to-right progression in studying unknown words, (*b*) the Fernald tracing-sounding-writing method, (*c*) the Monroe combined phonetic and sounding-tracing method, (*d*) writing words, (*e*) training in use of initial consonants and consonant substitution, and (*f*) alphabetizing and dictionary exercises.

Remedial instruction includes methods which direct the pupil's attention to the beginning of a word and which lead to a consistent left-to-right progression in studying a word. These will encourage the habit of noticing the beginnings of words and then a visual left-to-right survey of word elements followed by sounding and blending of these elements into word entities. The particular methods used will depend upon the nature and severity of the difficulties as revealed by diagnosis.

SELECTED READINGS

FERNALD, GRACE M., *Remedial Techniques in Basic School Subjects,* chap. 5. New York: McGraw-Hill, 1943.

GATES, ARTHUR I., *The Improvement of Reading* (3rd ed.), chap. 10. New York: Macmillan, 1947.

HARRIS, A. J. and E. R. SIPAY, *How to Increase Reading Ability* (6th ed.), chap. 15. New York: David McKay, 1975.

MONROE, MARION, *Children Who Cannot Read,* chap. 6. Chicago: University of Chicago Press, 1932.

MYERS, P. I. and D. D. HAMMILL, *Methods for Learning Disorders* (2nd ed.), chap. 9. New York: John Wiley and Sons, 1976.

ROSWELL, FLORENCE and GLADYS NATCHEZ, *Reading Ability: Diagnosis and Treatment* (2nd ed.), chap. 5. New York: Basic Books, 1971.

Adapting Instruction to the Handicapped Child

twelve

Teachers must be aware that some children with reading difficulties also have special learning handicaps. Complex disability cases not only need expert remedial reading instruction but also must have instruction modified according to the characteristics of their specific handicapping conditions.

Many atypical children find complex learning such as reading, confusing and frustrating. Others with similar and equal handicaps learn to read exceedingly well despite these handicaps. For example, many hearing-impaired children derive great satisfaction from reading. Therefore, if their skills are well developed, these children become avid readers and demonstrate better than average reading abilities. But if an atypical child becomes a disabled reader, his remedial problem becomes complex. Atypical conditions which may contribute to and complicate the correction of reading difficulties include poor eyesight, defective hearing, speech defects, emotional problems, neurological limitations, and the like. The diagnostic and remedial methods described in previous chapters lack the details needed to solve the learning problems of handicapped children.

In some instances, the educational program for any specific group of handicapped children may be conducted in special classes using methods and equipment designed to meet their particular instructional needs. In other instances, these children are taught in the regular classroom and perhaps in the resource room with procedures adapted as needed to enable handicapped children to progress effectively. Appropriate educational adjustments are treated well in books dealing with the psychology and education of exceptional children and youth. In this chapter, we discuss the special modifications of remedial procedures needed for dealing with the added complications a handicapping condition causes in coexistence with reading difficulties.

Throughout this book, the emphasis has been on adapting instruction to the requirements of the individual as ascertained by a careful diagnosis. When dealing with disabled readers complicated by handicaps, there is need for even more individualized treatment. For the best results, there must be a more careful and thorough probing of each individual's needs, and a more continuous and usually prolonged application of individualized remedial instruction. The fundamental principles of remedial instruction needed for the specially handicapped do not differ basically from those discussed earlier. However, much depends upon skillful guidance. The fullest measure of success is achieved when an alert teacher senses every aspect of a pupil's difficulty and has at her command just the right procedures, demonstrations, materials, and instructional techniques to overcome or at least to alleviate the discovered difficulty. She must know just what materials and procedures to select for a particular difficulty, and when to shift from one procedure to another in order to keep the pupil moving in the right direction. In other words, the teacher must be flexible in organizing her remedial programs, in beginning at the right point, and in introducing new materials and techniques to promote continuous progress toward learning to read better.

Especially relevant is the personality of the teacher, who must be willing to work patiently to gain and to maintain good rapport with the child. For success, the child must like his teacher and expect that she is going to help him. Only when there are close personal relations between pupil and teacher will it be possible for the teacher to provide the incentives which will maintain the level of motivation necessary to achieve lasting improvement in reading. Besides being well trained, the teacher must like children and be enthusiastic about her work. It is not too much to say that success in teaching handicapped children depends largely upon the teacher.

It is inconceivable that any single, narrow, or limited approach to reading will be found adequate for helping complex reading disability cases become effective readers. The very nature of the learning adjustments atypical children must make in order to learn to read successfully varies from one type of handicap to another. The programs for these children have to be devised to foster the adjustments in learning that the children must make in order to be effective learners.

Handicapped children with reading difficulties especially need to feel successful in the remedial venture. Teachers must be flexible in their methods in order to sustain positive attitudes. They must remember that the basic task in teaching a reading-disabled handicapped child is to modify the teaching procedures used to correct the diagnosed reading problem in light of the unique adjustments that must be made in order to overcome the additional learning problems raised by the nature of the child's handicap.

The following general types of handicapped children for which the teacher must modify remedial methods warrant attention:

1. The visually deficient child
2. The auditorially limited child
3. The neurologically impaired child
4. The emotionally disturbed child
5. The mentally handicapped child
6. The speech defective child

THE VISUALLY DEFICIENT CHILD

Many visual defects such as ordinary myopia, hyperopia, astigmatism, and muscular imbalance can be remedied by properly fitted glasses or other medical means. Children with fully corrected vision suffer no visual handicap when they learn to read.

Every child should have visual screening and, when needed, adequate follow-up, eye examination before he receives any instruction in reading. Any treatment or correction necessary must be provided. There should be periodic visual examinations throughout the school years to identify and correct any significant defects which may develop later. Methods for diagnosing visual defects were discussed in chapter 4.

A small number of children have visual deficiencies which cannot be corrected completely by glasses. Accompanied by consultation with a competent eye specialist, educational adaptations are necessary for children with low visual acuity.

The main objective in teaching children with low visual acuity to read is to make as much progress in reading as possible without tiring them unduly or harming their eyes. Reading periods should be brief; the doctor should specify how much time the child should devote to reading activities.

Typography and illumination also must be considered. There is ample evidence that both normal and visually deficient readers find that words in large type sizes are easier to perceive correctly. Children with low visual acuity prefer eighteen-point or even larger type sizes. It also is advisable to use material printed in a line length of about twenty-four to twenty-seven picas (four to four and one-half inches) with ample leading or space between lines. Supplementary material can be prepared for these children using typewriters with primer-sized type. Visually handicapped children should have an ample amount and variety of reading material.

The visually deficient child needs abundant illumination. This means at least fifty foot-candles of light in any area where visually demanding activities such as reading, art and craft work, chalkboard work, or writing are performed. Felt-tipped pens and pencils which produce thick black lines should be used.

Reading should be coordinated with other means of learning. Learning through listening and discussing should be emphasized, and creative activities, such as creative dramatics are beneficial. The teacher must assume responsibility for encouraging learning through listening and doing. This entails much teacher discussion, reading aloud, story telling, guidance of student discussion, and supervision of creative activities. Audio-visual instruction, such as audio tapes, sound motion pictures, tape-slide presentations, video tapes, and television, all are beneficial.

According to Gates (83), these children are at no disadvantage in the auditory discrimination of words. Phonics emphasis in beginning reading instruction is helpful for many visually deficient children. However, care must be taken that letter-sound associations must not be overemphasized and as soon as possible, the children's attention must be directed to whole-word recognition and to perceiving the larger pronounceable units of words such as syllables, word roots, prefixes, and suffixes. This will enhance effective visual perception and minimize the need for minute examination of letter detail in working out words. Context clues should be stressed as an aid to word recognition and to recognition of words in thought units. Any procedure which leads to perceiving groups of words, whole words, and to larger parts of words in word attack, will help to reduce the detailed visual work in reading.

Many children suffer from a mild degree of visual deficiency, making their handicap less serious. These children can participate in the regular reading program. The teacher should select recreational reading materials with good print, see that there is adequate illumination in the classroom, and encourage these students to rest their eyes frequently. Some children benefit greatly from being taught to use paper or tagboard markers to isolate the line of print they are reading and thus to minimize visual distraction. Speed of reading should be de-emphasized, and accurate word recognition and close attention to meaning should be stressed. As with the more serious cases of visual deficiency, they should be taught to recognize words by the use of phonics, combining this with attention to larger units and relying heavily on context.

THE AUDITORIALLY LIMITED CHILD

Adaptations for the auditorially limited child differ, since hearing deficiencies occur in varying degress. The deaf are those whose hearing loss is so severe and is acquired so young that it precludes the normal development of spoken language. Other children are classified as partially hearing. They are able to use spoken language, but their auditory handicap limits their language learning and use of language. Auditory limitations range from slight to profound.

The sooner the hearing loss is detected the better, because appropriate help in the early years enables children to use their hearing as effectively as possible and to acquire language as fully as possible. All children should be given an adequate hearing screening before entering school. The measurement of hearing has been discussed in chapter 4.

SLIGHT HEARING DEFICIENCY. Moderate educational adaptations will help the child with a slight hearing deficiency to succeed in the regular classroom. Such a pupil should be given a favorable seat close to where the teacher usually talks to the class. Speech always should be enunciated clearly whenever the hearing-handicapped child is involved. He will be able to follow oral discussions more accurately if he watches the lips of the person speaking. Some training in speech reading is helpful. To avoid embarrassing the hearing-handicapped child, discussion groups should be arranged so that he can watch the lips of each speaker without obviously turning his head. Seating the children in a semicircle or around a table does this nicely.

The child with a hearing handicap is bound to have more or less difficulty in auditory discrimination. Because of this, the teaching of word perception should emphasize the visual approach to word identification and word recognition rather than phonics. This does not imply that word sounds should not be taught. The auditorially limited child needs a great deal of emphasis on auditory discrimination as an aid to speech and as an aid to reading. However, depending upon the exact nature of the auditory handicap, this child will not be able to use phonics as an aid to word recognition as easily as a child with normal hearing. For this reason, more attention than usual should be paid to the visual characteristics of words and to the use of visual analysis along with context clues for recognizing words previously met and for identifying unfamiliar words. The degree of this emphasis will depend upon how much difficulty the child has with auditory discrimination. If these precautions are taken, the child with a relatively slight hearing defect should be able to make normal progress in learning to read.

MILD AND MARKED HEARING DEFICIENCY. Hard-of-hearing children are under a severe handicap in learning to read in classes in which oral reading and phonics are stressed. They will need more emphasis upon silent reading and a visual approach to word perception. It is important that they be given many opportunities to show what they know through action. Much reliance on work-sheet activities is important. Language difficulties may preclude a clear understanding of words read, unless the teacher provides many opportunities for the hard-of-hearing child to demonstrate understanding. These children should receive special speech-reading and language instruction.

The hard-of-hearing child may experience adjustment difficulties unless special care is taken. Such a child easily can feel alienated from his peers. Every effort should be made to make the child feel that he belongs to the group in his class work and his play activities.

SEVERE AND EXTREME HEARING DEFICIENCY. There is great difficulty teaching reading to children with severe and extreme hearing deficiencies, especially for those children who have not developed language concepts. Thompson (205), under the direction of Gates, carried out a successful experiment in teaching beginning reading to deaf children who had not as yet learned to talk. Gates (83) described in some detail the procedures she used. This program depended entirely upon visual teaching materials. Words were introduced in a variety of contexts, most of which included some connection with real concrete objects, and by actions and demonstration. Extensive use was made of pictures accompanying the words and picture dictionary material. Mastery of each step was required before going on to the next. Progress was gradual from words to phrases to sentences to paragraphs. This method, or a modification of it, might be used well with children with severe or extreme hearing defects.

Teaching children with serious auditory handicaps to read is a highly specialized task which the ordinary remedial teacher will not encounter. Those who teach such children should consult such references as Hart (101), McLeod (137), and Thompson (205).

THE NEUROLOGICALLY IMPAIRED CHILD

There are a limited number of reading disability children who, after carefully planned and thoroughly implemented programs of reeducation, fail to show the desired progress. Some of these children may be handicapped by neurological impairment. This conclusion should never be assumed unless supported by expert medical evidence. Neurologically impaired children are classified medically in categories according to whether the disorder can be prevented or cured. Of course, whatever can be done medically to improve the learning ability of these children should precede or accompany any attempt at reading-improvement programs.

Remedial-reading programs for the children who have a neurological problem should take into account the behavioral characteristics of each child. Response patterns which suggest neurological impairment include: visual perception and synthesis problems, auditory discrimination and blending difficulties, symbol-sound or symbol-meaning association problems, and motor-coordination limitations. These anomalies necessitate two types of adaptations in remedial reading instruction. *First,* training to improve the child's visual, auditory, associative, or motor skills is indicated. *Second,* adaptations must be made in the methods of remedial instruction so as to use the child's strengths and to avoid his weaknesses in direct application to reading tasks.

VISUAL PERCEPTION AND SYNTHESIS PROBLEMS. The abilities to perceive differences in word configurations and to note the fine distinctions within the printed symbols are necessary for effectiveness in word recognition and for success in learning to read. The child who cannot visually distinguish rapidly between word patterns such as *fall* and *fell; learn* and *lean;* or *stop* and *tops* will have trouble in acquiring even the beginning reading skills. Many children start learning to read with just such limitations. For the neurologically impaired, these problems of visual perception may be even more troublesome. Direct training in noting likenesses and differences may be given in much the same way that they are developed in reading-readiness materials. The teacher dealing with a child with such neurological impairment will find the materials developed for typical prereading children who are immature in visual perception and synthesis, to be effective in teaching the handicapped child. For all but the most severely handicapped, the exercises which deal with actual similarities and differences in printed symbols are more useful than those using geometric designs. Matching exercises involving individual stimulus cards prompt close visual attention and reduce distractability. Tracing exercises greatly benefit some neurologically impaired children especially if they are encouraged to trace large figures or symbols. During the school day, these children should be encouraged to participate fully in appropriate art, craft, and physical education activities. Children with poor visual perception often have difficulty with these activities; and yet with sensible adaptations, such pursuits help strengthen visual perceptual abilities. In dealing with the disabled reader who has such a visual-neurological impairment, the paramount remedial reading task is to teach him to attend to word patterns as effectively as his limited perceptual capacity will allow.

Reading-readiness books contain exercises which are carefully scaled in difficulty. These exercises are designed to develop the perceptual skills needed in reading and give varied experience and practice in visual perception and synthesis. The remedial teacher can use such exercises as models for making additional exercises, since the neurologically limited child will require considerably more training to develop perceptual skills. Caution should be exercised in the length of the practice periods used for such training. These periods should not be extended to the point of fatigue. It should be pointed out also that this training can continue along with regular remedial teaching designed to improve word-recognition skills. Much of the ability in visual discrimination, as applied to words, is developed in the actual process of learning the word-recognition techniques.

In teaching the child with limited visual perception, the remedial program should lean more heavily upon methods that emphasize auditory sound-blending approaches to reading. For children who still do not make progress, kinesthetic-auditory-visual training may be needed. The periods of visual perceptual activity should be of short duration and well spaced. Sometimes it is necessary to break the reading material into single sentences or short paragraphs. These are read and discussed one at a time, thus giving the child frequent intervals of visual relaxation. As he matures in reading and perceptual skills, the segments of reading can be lengthened. Even then, the child should be encouraged to look up from the print to relax and to think about the content he has read. Uses of context clues should be developed as an aid to recognition.

AUDITORY DISCRIMINATION AND BLENDING DIFFICULTIES. Children who cannot detect the differences in spoken words that sound somewhat alike, who are not able to select which one of two words completes a rhyme, or who cannot discriminate well enough to select which one of a group of words starts with the same sound as a given spoken word do not have the auditory capabilities necessary to learn to read by certain methods of instruction. Such word-discrimination skills must exist in order to profit from oral word study and phonetic training. The ability to blend letter sounds or phonemes into whole words when given orally is required for oral-phonetic training methods to succeed.

Auditory skills can be developed by having the child learn to listen more carefully to word sound patterns than he has in the past. The materials are as extensive as the rhymes and words that are found in children's literature and in the spoken language of the children being taught. As in visual skills, the remedial teacher can find many excellent suggestions from prereading materials and oral games used in kindergarten. Each of these sources will provide the teacher with models of exercises that she can develop. The neurologically limited child who has auditory discrimination and blending deficiencies will need a more extensive program of training than will the usual child. The auditory training might well start with distinguishing between gross sounds such as crumpling paper, running water, shutting doors, typewriting, and so forth. Then it might progress to noting which of two out of four orally presented words sound the same; first using words that have markedly contrasting patterns, such as *make, want, make, have;* and then progressing to finer discriminations, as *roam, room, ram, roam.* The child should be able to make these auditory discriminations with his eyes closed or when his teacher is not in view to ensure that he has heard the differences rather than read his teacher's lips. Auditory training periods should be short to ensure attention, and because such training tends to be tiring. Picture cards may be used for the child to perform such activities as naming the pictures and then sorting the cards according to the beginning sounds of the picture names. These children like visual clues, occasionally need practice in recalling the names of common objects pictured, and should be able to distinguish clearly sounds in words based on their own as well as on other people's pronunciations. To specifically enhance sound-blending skills, the teacher may ask the child to hand her the picture of the c--ar or of the b--oa--t. Many exercises designed to develop auditory skills are included in reading-readiness materials.

SYMBOL ASSOCIATION PROBLEMS. The abilities needed to make instant and accurate associations between printed symbols and spoken sounds, and between printed symbols and meaningful words are necessary for effective reading. The child who cannot make these associations instantly will be a faltering reader, and the child who cannot make them accurately will be unable to make much progress at all. For most children, these difficulties signal that the pace of reading instruction has been too fast and that they have not been given enough opportunity for review. For the neurologically impaired, symbol association problems may be much more severe.

Direct training in symbol-sound and symbol-meaning associations may have to be given in a manner similar to that used in beginning reading instruction. Some neurologically impaired children require so much practice that the remedial reading teacher may have to find or design many supplementary materials to maintain interest. Gamelike activities can make repetitive practice seem more enjoyable. Sorting word cards into categories by meaning gives good practice in symbol-meaning associations. The teacher of such children must be able to judge when to practice further and when to move on. Enough practice is essential, but too much only causes the child to fall farther behind. The issue is complicated further by the great variability in associative abilities which some neurologically impaired children demonstrate from one day to the next. The willingness to make appropriate instructional adjustments and to at all times emphasize what the child has done well, will maximize instructional effectiveness in this type of case.

MOTOR COORDINATION LIMITATIONS. The major area of limited motor coordination related to reading is oculomotor coordination. The child with an oculomotor control problem has difficulty in focusing on the printed page and in coordinating the two eyes during the reading act. He also has trouble in following the line of print rhythmically as he progresses along the line. Kephart (121) gives suggestions for improving such oculomotor coordination.

It is enough to state here that methods using markers as aids to maintaining line location, sweeping below the line of print with a marker, and emphasizing left-to-right progression will be helpful. The section dealing with orientational problems in word recognition, discussed in chapter 11, should help the child to overcome oculomotor problems in reading. Kinesthetic methods often are suggested to supplement adequate oculomotor control in reading. Clinical workers giving remedial training to severely handicapped children may find the methods suggested by Fernald (75) helpful.

Correcting the reading disabilities of the neurologically impaired child is difficult and usually time-consuming. But if training and adjustments are made, even these children can develop reading capability. Additional suggestions for teaching children with learning disorders associated with neurological impairment are described by Cruickshank (48), Kephart (121), and Myers and Hammill (145).

Teachers and clinicians working with reading disability cases should be aware that many symptoms of neurological impairment are shown by the typical reading disability case, and a child should not be assumed to have a neurological problem unless it is confirmed by a medical examination.

Normal children with perceptual and motor problems should have training similar to that just described in this section. The training need not be as intensified, and progress would be expected to be more rapid than it is in the case of the neurologically impaired child.

THE EMOTIONALLY DISTURBED CHILD

The role of emotional disturbances in reading disability was discussed in detail in chapter 5. There it was noted that most reading cases show some emotional maladjustment. Some children are maladjusted when they first arrive at school. Others develop emotional disturbances when frustrated in their futile attempts to learn to read. Whatever the roots of the trouble, it is certain that the remedial teacher has emotional maladjustment to deal with in most of her disability cases.

Reading disability cases often are characterized by lack of persistence, tendencies to withdraw from the group, daydreaming, inattentiveness, fear, anxieties, overdependency, submissiveness, and overdemanding behavior. These emotional reactions may range all the way from severe functional disorders to mild rationalization. The authors even have encountered disabled readers who have had nausea any time they were expected to read, and others who made such statements, as: "I can read perfectly well at home when I have on my father's glasses, but my own glasses don't seem to help"; or, "I don't want to read about a boy that has a boat. I want to have one myself."

Inasmuch as reading ability is so necessary for success in school, even the otherwise emotionally secure child who has persistent reading problems finds adjustment difficult. If he comes to school with emotional problems, he finds reading disability even more troublesome. In such cases, a minor difficulty in learning to read can seem an almost insurmountable discouragement which can start the child into a downward spiral of frustration.

In many instances, the emotional maladjustment clears up when the child has succeeded through remedial reading instruction. With the few who have deep-seated adjustment difficulties, better-defined therapy is necessary. Besides remedial instruction for correcting reading difficulties, the therapeutic role of the remedial teacher also is important in correcting reading disability. It is desirable that in every instance a therapeutic relationship between teacher and pupil should be developed. According to research reports, psychotherapy offers increased progress in reading, a more flexible approach to learning, and improvement in personality. Further, the therapy appears to have a lasting effect. Roswell and Natchez (165) have made some excellent suggestions concerning the psychotherapeutic principles that underlie instruction in remedial reading, pages 63–77.

Fisher (76) tested the hypothesis that psychotherapeutic procedures will help to remove reading disabilities in which emotional adjustment is involved. Twelve boys in an institution for delinquent boys were divided into two matched groups of six each. All were retarded more than three years in reading. They all had the same classroom teacher and all received remedial instruction for three hours per week given by the same remedial teacher. One group of six participated in nondirective or group-centered therapy for one hour per week. The other group received only the remedial instruction. The members in the therapy group and at the therapy meetings were encouraged to speak freely about their feelings, attitudes, and experiences. The program was continued for six months. Final testing revealed that the nontherapy group gained on the average 8.25 months in reading; those who had therapy gained 11.5 months, or 39.4 percent more than the nontherapy group. It was concluded that the psychotherapeutic relationship established by the training was an important factor in the correction of reading disabilities in these delinquent boys.

Although the numbers in Fisher's groups were small and they were delinquent cases, the results appear to emphasize an important aspect of remedial instruction, particularly for cases with marked emotional maladjustments. In working with emotionally disturbed, reading disability cases, psychotherapy is important. It is probable that all skillful remedial teachers bring some psychotherapy into their relations with disability cases. The teacher gradually breaks down the resistance to learning as she emphasizes achievement. In this way the child feels supported by the teacher's interest in his work and the acceptance of him and his reading problem.

The child soon gains confidence in his own possibilities as a result of his teacher's confidence in him, and in the demonstration that he is improving. He also soon recognizes, through working in small groups with other disabled readers, that his own difficulties are not unique and that other children, who are capable in many other ways, have similar reading difficulties. He no longer feels alone or ashamed of his reading limitation. As he gains stature in reading, he is led to take a more responsible and self-directed role in his reading assignments. Gradually he is taught to work cooperatively in small groups, helping other children and accepting help from them.

Through the optimistic confidence of the teacher and the well-planned, carefully programmed remedial lessons attuned to the child's specific rate of learning and instructional requirements, the teacher is able to build up his feeling of security. As he gains power in reading, his confusions diminish, his interest expands, and he appears to be a happier, better-adjusted person. His confidence has been reestablished, and other evidences of personal and social.well-being become apparent. Care must be taken to ensure his continuing success, but from time to time he must be given material difficult enough to challenge his growing capability. He must, of course, have a reasonable chance of being successful, and the teacher should be at hand to give him any needed assistance if he is not yet ready to take this next step. With the more severely maladjusted cases, an organized program of psychotherapy, in addition to reading instruction, very likely will promote more rapid and lasting gains in reading. Furthermore, there will be more improvement in emotional adjustment than from reading instruction alone. Psychotherapy is sometimes needed before any systematic reading instruction. For some of the severely maladjusted children, psychiatric help will be needed.

A number of writers concerned with emotionally disturbed children, including Hewett (106), have stressed the importance of the emotionally disturbed child's behavior. Besides helping an emotionally disturbed child with a reading problem to gain confidence in himself as a learner, the teacher often must help the child learn to behave as a learner. This is necessary because some emotionally disturbed, reading-disabled children exhibit certain specific behaviors which interfere with reading progress. These behaviors include inattention to reading tasks, lack of active response to reading, and inability to complete work.

To help children attend to reading, the teacher first of all should consider the physical environment. It should be free from distraction. Many children can attend to their reading better when allowed to work in a carrel or study booth. For others it is helpful to remove all unnecessary materials from work surfaces as these materials often are distracting. Short, definite units of work are an aid to the child who has difficulty attending to his reading. Tokens for paying attention such as those made of plastic, colorful stickers, or simple check marks can be awarded to a child for attentive behavior. Charts or other records of progress in paying attention to reading often help children learn to increase their attention to reading.

In the clinic, teachers have noticed that jewelry such as dangling beads or brightly colored pins distract certain students. Teachers also have observed that a soft voice and short, simple, direct instructions help children who have difficulty attending. Gamelike, supplementary reading activities often help children attend to reading tasks, because of the added incentive of wanting to win. Very few children will attend to reading when they have no purpose for reading, or when the reading seems uninteresting to them, or when it is too difficult.

Clinical cases of complex disability are seen who refuse to read at all or respond only minimally to reading tasks. There are children who read orally so slow and hesitantly and in such a muffled tone that they cannot be heard, or they stop at every difficult word and refuse to try, or they rush rapidly through all reading with little thought of the meaning, thinking only of finishing. It also is easy to find children who spend their reading time trying to converse with the teacher about any conceivable subject other than reading, and also those who are perpetually late and frequently absent. To help such children to respond to reading, teachers can reduce the level and amount of reading the child must do until he can see that it can be accomplished easily. Instructions for reading should be specific, not vague and openended, because vague and openended reading tasks appear to these children to be without end. The teacher should guarantee the child success by having him compete against himself, not against others. As an example, she might have him see if he could do better today than he did yesterday. Charts of the child's work are helpful for comparison. Reading selections closely tied to the child's own interests will help to kindle enthusiasm for reading.

Children having difficulty completing their work can be helped if the teacher carefully prepares and organizes their work. Often teachers find that they must plan in stages what must be done to finish a worksheet or reading selection and then help the student by these same stages finish the work. Often children who have difficulty completing their work are not aware of time. Therefore, it is essential to give them ample time to complete their reading and must be given time reminders. It also is important to reward and praise them for completing their reading. Hewett (106) gives more suggestions for teaching emotionally disturbed children.

THE MENTALLY HANDICAPPED CHILD

Children with below-average intelligence commonly are classified into the following groups according to Gillespie and Johnson (91): (1) slow learners (I.Q. 68–84), (2) educable mentally retarded (I.Q. 52–68), (3) trainable mentally retarded (I.Q. 36–52), (4) severely mentally retarded (I.Q. 20–36), (5) profoundly mentally retarded (I.Q. 0–20). People with I.Q.s in the trainable mentally retarded range can learn to read on a word-by-word basis when given intensive instruction and massive review. For those with I.Q.s of about 50 to about 70, although progress in reading is extremely slow, with superior extended reading instruction, the expected reading grade of a child with an I.Q. of 70 is 5.2 at age sixteen (Brueckner and Bond, 32). Ordinarily children with I.Q.s of about 50 to 70 receive reading instruction in a special education class or resource room. Children with I.Q.s above 70 usually are able to achieve more, and if given excellent instruction, may be expected to achieve reading grades at the 6.0 to 7.5 grade level (32) by the age of sixteen. It is the reading instruction of the children with I.Q.s between 68 and 84, who are taught in regular classes, that we will consider in our discussion of slow learners. In general, slow learners can, with proper instruction, make progress up to the grade level corresponding to their mental age. The consensus of educators is that mentally retarded children should be started on a systematic reading program only when they reach a mental age of at least six years. As noted by Kirk (122), slow learners differ from normal children in learning to read because they cannot be expected to begin learning to read at the chronological age of six, and even thereafter they naturally learn at a slower rate. They become discouraged in regular classrooms because of continued failure. This and their usually somewhat impoverished environmental and experiential background are reflected in poor language usage.

The slow learners will need a prolonged prereading and reading readiness period. On entering school, they will be more retarded than the normal child in the abilities and skills which form the basis for success in beginning reading. According to Gates (83), the readiness program for slow learners should be broader and richer than normal so as to reduce to a minimum the new learnings required when the pupil actually begins to read. The general aspects of reading readiness have been discussed in earlier chapters. Details of such programs may be found in Bond and Wagner (26), Tinker and McCullough (212), Monroe (141), and Hildreth (107). During the prereading training and when the child's mental age is between five and six, he will be able to learn to recognize his name and a few words used as labels and signs. Before reaching at least six years mental age, systematic reading instruction as is ordinarily given will result only in a tremendous waste of time and energy on the part of the teacher, because so little is learned from it. Nevertheless, if special instructional methods (described later) are employed, these children can be given profitable reading instruction before six years mental age. Otherwise some of these children would not begin to read until they are eight or nine years old.

The mentally retarded child differs from the normal one in his reading progress, mainly by being a slower learner. He is ready to begin formal lessons at a somewhat later chronological age and he progresses at a slower rate. This means that at each succeeding level in the developmental program, he should have more materials and more individualized guidance than the normal child. Gates (84) has shown that the slow learner needs many more repetitions of a word in the context of basic reading materials before he can learn it. This is in addition to his encounters with such words in appropriate supplementary reading. The reading materials used are the same as those which have proved satisfactory with regular normal pupils. But there is more of the material, and the instruction is more individualized and more intensive. Repetition, explanation, demonstrations, provision of experience units, and amount of recreational reading should be extensive. In short, the program for the slow learner is broad, detailed, simplified, and *slow-moving*. In other respects, the program of reading instruction is the same as that for normal children. Programs devoted largely to drill exercises with little recreational reading tend to be less effective than the richer program just described. The interest and attention of slow learners is held and their motivation made greater by exposure to large amounts of interesting and exciting material pitched at an appropriate level of difficulty. Gates (84) and Huber (109) have shown that slow learners enjoy approximately the same kind of reading material as average and superior children of their age.

Reading Disability

When classroom reading instruction and materials are not adjusted to the slow learner, he may become a reading disability case. Other causal factors described in chapters 4 and 5 also may be involved. If a mentally retarded child fails to learn to read at the level indicated by his capacities, he should be considered to be a disability case. The diagnosis of the extent and nature of his disability rests on the use of the techniques described for normal children in earlier chapters. According to evidence cited by Kirk (122), between five and ten percent of mentally retarded children are educable reading disability cases. Coincidentally, this is about the frequency of disability cases among mentally normal children.

Remedial Instruction

Results cited by Kirk (121) and Featherstone (73) demonstrate beyond doubt that slow learners who become reading disability cases profit significantly from remedial instruction. For instance, in a group of ten children, with mean C.A. of 12-9 and mean I.Q. of 75, an average gain of 1.2 grades was achieved by sixty-eight standard lessons, each thirty minutes long, over a period of about five months. This rate of progress was five times that of one hundred unselected children of similar mental ability. Furthermore, five months after the remedial training ceased, these cases continued to progress in the regular classroom situation at a rate twice that of the one hundred children who had not had the remedial instruction. Most of the ten remedial cases also showed better general adjustment and improved attitudes and behavior as they became more proficient in reading. Other data cited revealed similar gains. It was concluded that significant and satisfying results can be obtained from remedial instruction with slow-learning children who are retarded in reading.

The Hegge-Kirk remedial method was devised primarily for mentally retarded and dull-normal children. The details of this method are given in *Remedial Reading Drills,* by Hegge, Kirk, and Kirk (102). The method in its initial stages is primarily a phonic method. It is more complete than most phonic systems. There is much drill and an emphasis on certain principles of learning, such as the concrete associative aids used to help the child learn a new sound. Retention is aided by having the child say the sound, write it, and then blend the sounds into words. Sentence reading, story reading, and teaching words as entities are introduced at the appropriate places as the child progresses. *This method is successful.* Any teacher who plans to use the method should consult Kirk (122) and the pamphlet by Hegge, Kirk, and Kirk (102) for more complete details. On the basis of his experiments with slow learners in the New York schools, Gates (83) suggests a broader program of instruction. Although more inclusive and more individualized, his plan approximates the regular basic program used for normal pupils. Significant features are its informality, its wide range of approaches, and its freedom of activity according to individual interests. Gates and Bond (87) offer evidence of this method's success. They show that classes of twenty-five children taught by this approach gained 1.2 years in reading during a five-month training period. For details of the method, see Gates (83), pages 503–509.

The following suggestions, adapted from Brueckner and Bond (32, pages 188–190), give proven procedures for teaching slow-learning children to read:

1. Instruction in reading should begin later than for normal children. Due to limited intelligence, slow-learning children have not acquired the experience necessary for initial instruction in reading by the age of six years or six years and six months. Although it is not wise to wait for a mental age of six years and six months, initial instruction should be deferred as long as is required to make some progress in the prerequisite learnings.

2. Slow-learning children develop reading ability in much the same way as normal children, but at a somewhat slower pace. This is true for their capability in word recognition, vocabulary readiness, and the setting of purposes. Any modifications in instruction necessary are more in a changed emphasis rather than in a drastically different program.

3. A large amount of carefully controlled material must be used with slow learners. To make new words a permanent part of the child's sight vocabulary, he must be introduced to them more slowly than are brighter children. That is, vocabulary development is more gradual.

4. Slow-learners require more review of basic words. This is achieved by use and reuse of workbook material, and by rereading a selection several times for different purposes, and by reading much additional material with the same vocabulary.

5. The slow-learning child has to be given more detailed and simplified explanations and simpler techniques. Frequently, he finds directions in workbooks or in informal exercises difficult to grasp. The teacher must be sure that each child understands what is expected of him in all his reading assignments.

6. More concrete illustrations of the things about which he is reading are needed. In contrast with the average child, the slow learner is handicapped in generalizing and in thinking abstractly about what he is reading. He should be given every opportunity, therefore, to come into direct contact with the things about which he is studying.

7. Reading goals should be relatively short-range, i.e., reached rather quickly. The slow learner cannot work effectively upon projects of long duration.

8. The slow learner requires more rereading before he can grasp the different purposes of what he reads. For example, if he is to read about a buffalo hunt, the first reading may be only to find out that the Indian boy shot a buffalo, the second reading to discover how the tribe prepared for the hunt, the third time to find out how the hunt actually was conducted, and so on. Although the brighter child could achieve most of the purposes

listed by just one reading, the slow learner cannot. Furthermore, the latter does not mind rereading because each new time helps him get a fuller understanding of the story.

9. There should be more experience and more guidance in exploring the visual and auditory characteristics of words. For word-recognition skills to operate effectively, they must be applicable to a wide variety of words. These skills are difficult for slow learners to acquire. They profit from additional drill in analyzing words and in learning the sounds of different word elements. Since rapid reading is not important to slow learners, a moderate degree of overanalysis is of little consequence provided it does not interfere with comprehension.

10. It is advisable to use more oral reading and oral prestudy in instructing slow-learning children. Many of them need to vocalize what they are reading before they can comprehend it well. The fact that vocalization slows the reading rate is of little significance for these children.

11. Slow-learning children should do more building models, cutting out pictures, and the like, in connection with their reading than the brighter children do.

12. Finally, slow-learning children profit from being in the same classroom with average and superior children, provided the instruction is adjusted somewhat to their special needs. Although the slow learner will not be able to read much above his mental level, in many other respects his learning experiences may be similar to those of other children.

Brueckner and Bond (32, p. 187) provide data on the reading grade that may be expected of slow-learning children at age sixteen, under both average and superior instruction:

Stanford Binet I.Q.	Expected Reading Grade Under Average Instruction	Estimated Reading Grade Under Superior Instruction
85	7.0	7.5
80	6.2	6.7
75	5.4	5.8
70	4.8	5.2

These data for estimated reading grade at age sixteen with superior instruction represent what may be expected when the instruction is adjusted to the needs of the slow-learning child. The above results, derived from a follow-up study, indicate that those children who were given special instruction could not maintain reading ability very far in advance of their mental grade. However, in *individual* follow-ups of the slow learners, it was found that some were able to acquire reading ability somewhat in excess of their mental level.

The remedial teacher who works with slow learners should be familiar with the procedures and general approach to the problem recommended by Kirk, Brueckner and Bond, Gates, and Featherstone. The Monroe (141) procedure, which places great emphasis on phonics drills, was found also by Monroe and Backus (142) to be effective in remedial work with slow-learning school children. The well-trained remedial teacher is versatile in selecting and applying the most appropriate of these techniques for adjusting instruction to the needs of each child.

THE SPEECH-DEFECTIVE CHILD

Speech defects occasionally are present in reading-disabled children. The role of such defects as causes of difficulties in reading were reviewed in chapter 4. Speech defects which interfere with clear enunciation may be associated with inadequate auditory discrimination and thus may lead to difficulty in word recognition. For children with these defects, the use of phonics as a major aid to word recognition should be minimized. Rather, emphasis should be placed on study of the visual characteristics of words, especially during the early stages of learning to read. Also, silent rather than oral reading should be stressed.

Some children with speech defects are embarrassed when asked to read aloud or to take part in discussion. To avoid bruising the child's sensitivities, the teacher should be sympathetic and tactful. But it is not wise to excuse the child altogether from oral work. The problem of balancing oral and silent work is delicate.

A first step is to give the child proper speech training with a speech teacher. As the child progresses toward smoother and more fluent speech, he gains self-confidence. One way of correcting speech difficulties is reading aloud. At first, the pupil should read some well-prepared selection aloud to his teacher in private. As the speech difficulty is overcome, the child will be ready and perhaps eager to do some oral reading in class. The teacher should encourage but not force the child to do this. At the same time, as the child becomes more sure of himself, remedial measures for correcting specific reading difficulties may be undertaken.

CASE STUDY OF AN UPPER ELEMENTARY
STUDENT WITH A BASIC WORD RECOGNITION
PROBLEM AND AN AUDITORY LIMITATION

Paul, a fifth-grade student, was referred to the Achievement Center for help in reading during an eight-week summer period. He came from the Achievement Center service area, where he had attended school during the previous school year. Before that he had attended a school in a district approximately one hundred miles away.

SCHOOL HISTORY. When Paul was admitted to the center, he was eleven years and five months old. His school referral form showed that he had had a slight hearing deficiency which first was diagnosed in the first grade. The child had received no type of special services before his fifth grade year. He was referred for resource room services by his fifth-grade teacher who also requested Achievement Center services because of her concern for the child's reading difficulties.

SCHOOL BEHAVIOR. According to the referral information, Paul was described as having an excellent attitude toward school, peers, and teachers. His classroom behavior was characterized by his fifth-grade classroom teacher as normal in all ways, except that he "always seemed unusually attentive." The classroom teacher's interpretation was that the child was straining to listen due to his auditory impairment.

ABILITIES. According to the *Wechsler Intelligence Scale for Children—revised,* his ability to learn was found to be above average with a full-scale I.Q. of 114. The difference between his verbal I.Q. and performance I.Q., however, was large. His verbal I.Q. was found to be 98 and his performance I.Q., 130. This would place his reading expectancy at 6.6. However, in view of the thirty-two-point discrepancy between verbal and performance I.Q., the clinician noted that had his reading expectancy been based on his verbal I.Q. alone it would have been 4.8, and had it been based on his performance I.Q. alone, it would have been 7.4. The clinician felt that under the circumstances, it was difficult to conclude definitely what was reasonable to expect of this child in reading, but chose 6.6 as the best of the three alternatives.

Paul was given the *Peabody Individual Achievement Test.* His grade scores were:

Name of Subtest	Grade Equivalent	Standard Score
Mathematics	6.4	103
Reading Recognition	3.9	85
Reading Comprehension	5.3	97
Spelling	4.2	89
General Information	5.8	100
Total Test	5.0	97

OBSERVATION OF BEHAVIOR DURING TESTING: Paul was cooperative during testing. He showed some signs of nervousness on the reading subtests. He ran his fingers through his hair and glanced around the room frequently.

INTERPRETATION OF TEST RESULTS: Paul scored below his estimated potential in all areas tested except mathematics. Mathematics vocabulary and reasoning appeared to be adequate.

The clinician decided to test him further in reading and spelling to determine his strengths and weaknesses in those academic subjects, but noted that mathematical computation was not adequately screened by the diagnostic instrument. The clinician noted that Paul's spelling was at a 4.2-grade level on a test which required him to pick the correctly spelled word from four visual presentations. To prevent a superficial diagnosis, the clinician administered the spelling subtest of the *Wide Range Achievement Test.* Paul achieved a grade equivalent of 2.9, with a standard score of 77, and a percentile rank of 6. The discrepancy was sufficient to cause suspicion that the difference was due to the different tasks that the child was expected to perform. Although the *Peabody Individual Achievement Test* required a highly visual form of spelling, the *Wide Range Achievement Test* required Paul to spell words from dictation.

DIAGNOSTIC ACHIEVEMENT TESTS:

A. *Durrell Analysis of Reading Difficulty* (selected sections)

Name of Subtest	Grade Equivalent	Comprehension
Oral Reading	4L	Good
Silent	4L	Fair
Listening Comprehension	3	—
Flash Words	3H	—
Word Analysis	4H	—

OBSERVATION OF BEHAVIOR: Paul appeared to be nervous during testing. He moved a great deal in his chair and ran his fingers through his hair. He appeared to be trying very hard to do well.

INTERPRETATION OF TEST RESULTS: On this test, the oral and silent reading were at the same grade level and well below his estimated reading potential. The low scores appeared to be due to slow reading time. Comprehension was better in oral reading, when compared to silent reading. Both flash words and word analysis scores were below his estimated level with flash words being significantly lower. From the results of these four subtests, it appeared that Paul had difficulty in immediate recognition of words which seemed to result in accurate but slow and inefficient reading at a fourth-grade level.

Paul's score on the listening comprehension subtest showed this skill to be one of significant weakness for him. This very important skill necessary for school success required remediation.

B. Silent Reading Diagnostic Test

Name of Subtest	Grade Equivalent
Word Recognition Skills	
Total Right	3.6
Words in Isolation	3.8
Words in Context	3.1

Error Patterns	Clinical Interpretation
Recognition Techniques	
Total Right	6.2
Visual Structural Analysis	6.8
Syllabication	6.0
Word Synthesis	4.5
Phonic Knowledge	
Total Right	3.9
Beginning Sounds	4.0
Ending Sounds	4.0
Vowel and Consonant Sounds	3.0

OBSERVATION OF BEHAVIOR: Paul appeared to try very hard. He showed some signs of nervousness: tapping pencil on table, running his fingers through his hair, and asking when the test would be over.

INTERPRETATIONS OF TEST RESULTS: Paul's weaknesses on the *Silent Reading Diagnostic Test* were in the areas of Word Recognition Skills and Phonic Knowledge. He showed strength in the Recognition Techniques, mostly in visual analysis; and weakness in his knowledge of phonics, especially in isolated single-letter sounds. His error pattern showed strength in proper left-to-right visual inspection of words, free from reversals or orientation difficulties.

Further informal testing in phonics knowledge revealed secure knowledge of CVC words and common vowel teams in reading, insecurity in application of phonics knowledge to spelling, and great difficulty in giving the sounds of isolated letters, especially short vowel sounds and *r*-controlled vowel sounds.

The answers to the chapter 6 diagnostic questions are:

1. IS PAUL CORRECTLY CLASSIFIED AS A DISABLED READER? Yes, although he possessed some well developed skills in visual analysis of words, his overall level of functioning in reading was well below what was reasonable to expect of him. He had a limiting condition complicated by a slight hearing deficiency.

2. WHAT IS THE NATURE OF THE TRAINING NEEDED? The remedial plan for Paul included: (*a*) phonics worksheet activities stressing visual associations among word elements, larger word parts, and their sounds. Paul completed this work silently. (*b*) Games using word and phrase cards designed to exemplify various phonics generalizations were used. Paul was required to respond orally. (*c*) He also was taught to

make visual-mental pictures to aid himself with certain difficult sounds. For example, he chose to think of a view of a city to help himself with the soft sound of "c." (d) Paul was encouraged to read during reading instructional time and especially at home from several high-interest, easy-reading level books which were chosen to be at a recreational reading level. He also did some prepared oral reading. (e) There were exercises in which Paul listened to short, simple stories about subjects interesting to him and then paraphrased the story, answered questions about it, or drew an illustration of it. He also followed increasingly complex oral directions.

3. WHO CAN MOST EFFECTIVELY GIVE THE REMEDIAL WORK? Paul received forty hours of direct one-to-one instruction during the summer and returned to his school in the fall where he received daily, small-group instruction. Diagnostic findings were shared with the concerned teacher.

4. HOW CAN IMPROVEMENT BE MADE MOST EFFICIENTLY? Aside from encouraging Paul to do a lot of recreational reading, the rest of the educational program emphasized overcoming auditory difficulties by using visual means and emphasizing worksheet activities and games. Although much of his work was done silently, he did respond orally in game-like situations, in prepared reading situations, and in response to short stories read to him.

5. DOES THE CHILD HAVE ANY LIMITING CONDITIONS THAT MUST BE CONSIDERED? Paul was a friendly, likeable, well-mannered boy. But because he was hearing-handicapped, he was uneasy and insecure in situations in which he had to listen carefully. It seemed to be important in teaching him, to use visual examples and to help him to see what was wanted. Once he knew what was expected, he worked well. He enjoyed activities in which he could express himself through drawing and he was able to draw fairly well.

6. ARE THERE ANY ENVIRONMENTAL CONDITIONS THAT MIGHT INTERFERE WITH PROGRESS IN READING? The parents were completely supportive of Paul and of the reading program. They were interested in the books he brought home for reading and showed obvious delight in his progress.

RESULTS. After the summer instruction period, Paul demonstrated mastery of all letter sounds in reading. His silent and oral reading speed became more typical of a fifth than of a fourth-grade student. His listening improved to the point where he could obey a series of five complex commands with one hundred percent accuracy. As Paul progressed in the program, it was noted that he became less tense when he read. His mother also remarked that, at home, she noticed he was beginning to enjoy reading. Paul continued to make gains in subsequent small-group instruction during his sixth-grade year. Then the instructional emphasis was changed and letter-sound associations were no longer stressed. Rather, instruction was directed toward helping Paul develop his knowledge of word meanings, increase his fund of sight words, utilize context clues, and rely heavily on his visual abilities in reading. Although during his sixth-grade year, Paul had not as yet reached his expectancy level in reading, his classroom work reflected improvement in reading and was comparable to that of his classmates.

SUMMARY

In this chapter, we have considered the modifications of remedial instruction that are necessary for correcting reading disabilities made more complex because of limiting conditions within the child. Children who have reading problems and who are also learning under other handicaps are encountered by every remedial teacher. Frequently, the overall education of these children is directed by specialists who have been trained to teach children with the various handicaps discussed in this chapter. The remedial reading teacher can obtain many helpful suggestions and insights into the particular adjustments needed for a specific child by discussing the child's problems with the special-education teacher. The responsibility of the remedial teacher is to diagnose the reading problem, locate the nature of the confusions in reading, and suggest modifications in reading methods needed for correcting the disability. The classroom teacher, working cooperatively with the remedial-reading teacher, should be aware of the child's reading program so that other phases of his education may be coordinated with the reading-improvement program. What these children need most is an adequate diagnosis of the nature of their reading disabilities and a well-planned program of remedial instruction, modified to take into account their learning handicaps.

Among the children with complex reading disabilities, are those visually deficient, auditorially limited, neurologically impaired, emotionally disturbed, mentally handicapped, and speech defective. Individualized treatment is necessary for all of them. The teacher is especially important in dealing with handicapped children. She must be patient, understanding, and skilled and versatile in remedial reading. A narrow or limited approach for all cases will be inadequate.

Most children with reading disabilities show some symptoms of emotional disturbance or behavioral disorder. For the more severe emotional cases, some psychiatric therapy may be necessary. The children experiencing behavioral disorders benefit from close management coupled with reasonable goals.

Mentally handicapped children who can profit from reading instruction also can be reading disabled. The proportion of reading disability cases in this group is about the same as among children with average and above-average intelligence. With proper instruction, the mentally retarded can learn to read and to maintain their reading competence at a reasonable level. A modified phonics approach stressing drill has been used successfully in remedial work with slow-learning children. The Hegge-Kirk method, which is slow-moving and repetitive and which involves much phonics drill, represents a method which has worked well with many educable children. A broader method, similar to good, developmental reading instruction, but highly individualized, seems appropriate for nonremedial, mentally handicapped children in the regular classroom.

Children with moderate visual deficiencies should be taught by methods which emphasize auditory approaches. Those with severe visual handicaps should avoid severe visual fatigue. They need ample light, large print, and short reading periods. Learning activities which do not require close visual work should be stressed.

Children with mild hearing deficiencies get along well in normal classroom activities which emphasize visual approaches to reading. Over-reliance on phonics should be avoided in teaching hard-of-hearing children. For them, visual techniques of word recognition should be stressed even more than for children with milder hearing deficiencies. Children with severe and extreme hearing deficiencies should be taught to read by specialists in deaf education. Emphasis should be upon sight words, the visual characteristics of words and upon silent reading.

The few disabled readers who also have neurological impairments constitute some of the most complex remedial cases. These children require carefully arranged training programs, designed to develop their impaired perceptual and motor skills to the fullest extent possible. They also require remedial reading instruction that is modified to use their areas of strength and to avoid their weak perceptual and motor skills.

Children with speech difficulties should have corrective work in speech given by a specialist. As their speech becomes better and more fluent, they may be reintroduced to regular methods of remedial instruction.

SELECTED READINGS

Cruickshank, W. M., and G. O. Johnson, *Education of Exceptional Children and Youth* (3rd ed.), chaps. 5, 6, 7, 9, 10, 11. Englewood Cliffs, N.J: Prentice-Hall, 1975.

Dechant, E. V., and H. P. Smith, *Psychology in Teaching Reading* (2nd ed.), chaps. 6, 8. Englewood Cliffs, N.J.: Prentice-Hall, 1977.

GILLESPIE, P., and L. JOHNSON, *Teaching Reading to the Mildly Retarded Child,* chaps. 7, 8, 9. Columbus, Ohio: Charles E. Merrill, 1974.

KEPHART, N. C., *The Slow Learner in the Classroom* (2nd ed.), chaps. 8–13. Columbus, Ohio: Charles E. Merrill, 1971.

KIRK, S. A., *Educating Exceptional Children* (2nd ed.), chaps. 5, 6, 7, 9, 11. Boston: Houghton Mifflin, 1972.

MANN, L., and D. A. SABATINO, *The Third Review of Special Education,* chaps. 2, 6, 10. New York: Grune and Stratton, 1976.

ROSWELL, FLORENCE, and GLADYS NATCHEZ, *Reading Disability: Diagnosis and Treatment* (2nd ed.), chap. 4. New York: Basic Books, 1971.

Correcting Basic Comprehension Deficiencies

thirteen

At all grade levels reading instruction should serve to develop comprehension. The fundamental goal in seeking to produce effective readers is to enable them to comprehend whatever printed materials will serve their purpose, no matter how difficult these materials may be. The acquisition of a sight vocabulary and skill in recognizing words, and of verbal facility in general, all are aimed at achieving adequate understanding and interpretation of the meanings embodied in printed symbols. The extent to which these meanings are clearly and accurately understood and interpreted by the reader represents the degree to which he has become a good reader.

Comprehension depends on the background the reader brings to the reading, his vocabulary development, and his ability to interpret the author's words into concepts. Through constant attention to words and their use, the child builds a meaning vocabulary. He attends to words, phrases, and sentence structure because he finds them useful in getting along in his environment. There is a wide variety in the vocabulary, the use of sentence structure clues (*syntax clues*), and the use of significant meaning clues (*semantic clues*) that children bring to reading. They possess various language components because of the differences in the pre-school learning environments they have experienced. Even their language patterns may be quite different one from another.

It has been emphasized that true reading is reading with understanding or comprehension. Comprehension depends on facility in using concepts or meanings evolved through experience. To be of use in reading, the concepts acquired through experience must be attached to words or groups of words as symbols of their meanings. These words become a part of one's understanding and speaking vocabulary. Then, when a reader recognizes a word or group of words, perception of the printed symbol stimulates recollection or construction of meanings for which the symbol stands. Obviously, the meanings recalled are those possessed by the reader and necessarily must have evolved through past experience. The meaning may be derived directly from those past experiences, or it may consist of a newly constructed meaning which results from combining and reorganizing meanings already possessed by the reader. The author brings known ideas together in such a way that the reader senses a new relationship and therefore gains a new idea, concept, or sensory impression. Take for instance, the meanings aroused when a fourth-grade city child reads the sentence "The tired rider drooped in his saddle as his spotted horse walked along the mountain trail." Since the reader has not seen such a rider, he may organize the meaning of the sentence from a variety of remembered visual experiences such as: (*a*) his father napping with his head bent forward as he rests in an easy chair; (*b*) a bridle path through the park; (*c*) a mounted policeman sitting erect on his black horse; (*d*) a spotted black and white dog; and (*e*) the scenery during an auto trip through hilly country. By combining these concepts, the child may achieve an approximation of the meaning intended by the writer of the sentence. So one reads primarily with his experiences which are based upon sensory impressions such as hearing, seeing, tasting, smelling, and touching. Also involved is one's behavior in adjusting to all kinds of situations, including the accompanying emotional reactions and imagination.

The development of concepts which carry meanings begins early in a child's life. Activities at home, hearing the talk of parents and other children and adults, listening to radio and viewing television, trips around the neighborhood, and sometimes more extended travel all are involved in developing a hearing-meaning vocabulary. Concepts are acquired. The child begins to use words and, later, sentences correctly. Using oral language forms precisely is acquired gradually. For use in reading, a meaning must be attached to a word, for it is only by the use of words that meanings can be recalled. If the recalled meanings are to be precise, the words which stand for those meanings must have been in the usage vocabulary of the reader. The degree to which he is able to use a word in his language and thinking determines to a large extent how effectively he will be able to use it in reading.

In normal development, a child's experiences will lead him to use sentences for verbal communication. Sentences are groups of words organized in meaningful relationships. Nearly all reading matter is in the form of sentences. How well a reader understands sentences and how skillful he is in using sentence forms determines how well he will be able to read print organized into sentences. The precise meanings of certain words in a sentence are comprehended from the context of the sentence.

The comprehension of sentences is facilitated when reading is done by thought units. A thought unit is a group of words which make up a meaningful sequence in a sentence. For instance, in the sentence "One of the men / saw the bricks / start to fall," there are three thought units as the spacings indicate. Verbal facility in oral communication leads to phrasing into thought units. Growth in reading sentences by thought units, however, is relatively slow. It is dependent on increased efficiency in the recognition of single words. Only when the child has developed an adequate sight vocabulary, can he group words into thought units. Some grouping (two-word units) occurs during the latter part of grade one. Progress is more rapid from the third grade on. The average reader is fairly proficient in reading by thought units by the time he reaches the sixth grade.

The child with good verbal facility is able to organize his ideas into thought units, which are reflected in his spoken sentences. A similar trend is found in reading. The child who is a word-by-word reader seldom grasps the meaning of a sentence as a whole. But when a child is reading by thought units, the resulting organization of the material aids comprehension. Proficiency in perceiving words in thought units usually is accompanied by understanding of the material being read.

Attention also must be directed to comprehension of paragraphs and larger units. To comprehend the material in a paragraph requires an understanding of the relations between the sentences in that paragraph. This involves identifying the topical sentence containing the key idea and understanding its relation to the explanatory or amplifying sentences.

We also must note the relation between paragraphs in longer selections. In a well-written story or article, the paragraphs will be arranged in an orderly manner. The introductory paragraph or paragraphs usually briefly present the plan, central theme, or purpose of the story or article. Succeeding paragraphs, arranged in logical sequence, carry the story through its principal points and on to the ending. In expository material, the paragraphs follow one another in orderly sequence providing the details to explain the event, process, or activity outlined in the introduction. For comprehension of larger units, the pupil will need to understand this relation between the introductory and subsequent paragraphs.

Essentially the same processes are involved in comprehending printed material and in understanding spoken words. In both, perception of words provokes meanings which lead to comprehension. The meanings provoked by the perceived words depend mainly on two factors: (*a*) the learner's or the reader's entire background of experience, and (*b*) his facility in language usage for purposes of communication. Children show marked differences in the length and complexity of a selection which they can comprehend. If a child has made normal progress in the mechanics of reading (word recognition, etc.) he should be able to comprehend just as long and complex a unit he reads as he can if the same words are spoken.

During the primary grades, when pupils are in the process of mastering the mechanics of reading, listening comprehension tends to be reading comprehension. It must be kept in mind that when a child begins grade one, there is a six-year lag between reading comprehension and listening comprehension. From birth on, the child has been developing listening comprehension. Furthermore, at the first-grade level, a child normally would hear more running words in two days than he reads in the entire first-grade program. Word repetition and vocabulary control in first-grade materials are advantageous to rapid development in reading comprehension.

As soon as there is progress in mastering the mechanics of reading, occurring sooner for the more able child, the two modes of comprehension become equal. Then, as greater proficiency and maturity are reached, reading comprehension may become more proficient than listening comprehension. In the primary grades, considerable time must be devoted to developing word-recognition techniques and to building a sight vocabulary. As these skills improve, there is greater opportunity for the pupil to concentrate on comprehension. Then, with a richer background of reading and other experiences, with increasing maturity and improved reading proficiency through the upper grades, reading comprehension becomes superior to listening comprehension. This is because the reader can stop and reflect, evaluate or debate, or reread parts of the material.

The implication of these trends, for instruction to improve reading comprehension, seems clear. Though word-recognition techniques and other mechanics should be emphasized in the early grades, so that they may become as automatic as possible, comprehension should not be neglected. With the mastering of the mechanics, the major portion of the pupil's attention during reading can be devoted to comprehension. This, with the teacher's guidance, will become more and more proficient. Thus, the well-balanced program of instruction through the grades is dominant in developing reading comprehension to a level that is as good as or better than listening comprehension. This balanced program also will, of course, give appropriate emphasis to oral language and usage, which play an important role in improving reading.

This development of reading comprehension to a high level of proficiency should be stressed through the grades. As the child progresses, his acquisition of information depends more and more upon what he reads. It is desirable, therefore, for reading comprehension to become as good as or better than listening comprehension.

There is a distinct need for improving the ability to comprehend a wide variety of materials for many purposes. If the purposes for which people read were analyzed and if the types of reading abilities employed in meeting these purposes were listed, it would be found that certain abilities, in varying combinations, were used to meet certain reading purposes and that other combinations of abilities were used to meet other reading purposes. For example, if the purpose of the reader were to choose between two courses of action, he would be likely to use the following types of reading: reading to draw inferences, and reading to predict outcomes. Or again, if his purpose were to estimate the quality and relevance of a textbook, his types of reading might be: skimming material for the general impression, and reading to note details of organization, quality, interest value, and validity of content. Finally, if his purpose were to read for enjoyment, his types of reading might be to sense the main idea and form sensory impressions.

Overcoming specific comprehension defects will be discussed in the next chapter. The disabled reader who is low in all types of comprehension, is limited in either suitable word-recognition skills, discussed in chapters 9 and 10, or in one or more of the basic comprehension abilities. This chapter will be devoted to a discussion of remedial teaching of the basic comprehension abilities, under the following headings:

1. Limited meaning vocabulary

2. Ineffective use of sentence sense

3. Insufficient comprehension of longer units

LIMITED MEANING VOCABULARY

The acquisition of word meanings is fundamental to all comprehension in reading. When word meanings are ample, precise, and rich, and when semantic variations are understood, there are adequate concepts for the pupils to draw upon to do effective reading. Without satisfactory word meanings, comprehension of either spoken or printed language is impossible. Comprehension of sentences and paragraphs naturally requires an understanding of their words.

There are four classifications of vocabulary: listening, speaking, reading, and writing. When a child enters school, his listening vocabulary far exceeds the other three. While estimates of the size of the listening vocabularies of first-grade children vary considerably, the concensus is that the average is nearly 20,000 words. Whatever the actual number, authorities agree that the listening vocabularies of first-grade children are extensive, and that the size has increased in recent years because of television, motion pictures, travel, and more reading aloud to children by their parents.

Entering first-grade children's average speaking vocabularies, around 6,000 words, are their second largest one. Their reading and writing vocabularies are little more than their own names. Within a few years, the typical child's reading vocabulary will exceed his speaking vocabulary and for some, their reading vocabulary will surpass the listening vocabulary.

Some children will not have developed meaning vocabularies large enough to read and understand materials above the third-grade level. These children should be classified as disabled in one of the basic comprehension abilities, namely, limited in meaning vocabulary. There are two tasks in remediation. First, the meaning vocabulary must be increased, and second, the habit of paying attention to words and their meanings must be established.

It must be recognized that word meaning has several aspects which are not discrete but overlap both in their importance and development. The teaching of vocabulary entails more than merely teaching the child to recognize words. It comprises, in addition to recognition, enriching new words and extending their meanings. Strang, McCullough, and Traxler (199) say that the further the sense of a word is from its usual meaning, the more difficult it is to understand.

The nature and accuracy of the meaning depends upon several factors:

1. The extensiveness of meaning depends upon the number and kinds of situations in which the word is met.

2. The accuracy depends upon the skill with which the reader relates the new understanding to previous backgrounds.

3. The vividness depends upon the emotion, interest, acceptance, and purposefulness of the reader.

4. Retention depends upon the usefulness of the word to the reader.

General Remedial Approaches to Limited Meaning Vocabulary

There are general approaches to vocabulary development used by the classroom teacher from the first grade on, that should be emphasized further for the disabled reader who has shown limited growth in learning word meanings and who has failed to establish the habit of attending to their meanings. These approaches include the use of firsthand experiences, wide reading, and audiovisual aids.

Firsthand experiences offer many opportunities for building understanding of words and for acquiring the habit of learning their meanings. Reading disability cases frequently are deficient in those experiences which furnish a supply of word meanings sufficient to ensure reading with understanding. The remedial teacher should provide the needed experiences as much as possible. The procedures are essentially the same as in any good instructional program. The only difference is that the instruction is more individualized. Part of the time the teacher will be concerned with a single child. At other times she may deal with a small group of children with similar deficiencies. Furnishing the desired experiences should be integrated with the rest of a well-coordinated program of remedial instruction.

To gain the most from an experience, careful planning is necessary. As noted by Dolch (58), experience alone does not educate. Without proper guidance, a child may go to a museum, a concert, or a botanical garden, and return without any new words to think or talk about.

Since the meanings a child learns from reading are determined by the nature and clearness of his concepts, these experiences should yield as varied and accurate meanings as possible. Acquiring experiences should be a purposeful activity. Children should be prepared beforehand so that they may look for and understand as many of its features as possible. They should know what to look for and what questions they would like to have answered.

If experiences are to be profitable, the child must think about them, seek out their meaning and use them in subsequent speaking, listening, and reading. For motivation toward this end, there must be an opportunity both before and after an experience, for discussion guided by the teacher. During this exchange of ideas and the answering of questions, there will be opportunity to define purposes, extend information, clear up misconceptions, and clarify and enrich meanings. This preparation for experience and the discussion following it, tends to be highly profitable whatever the nature of the experience. Development of word meanings and concepts also is promoted by the exchange of experiences in informal discussion. In all this planning and discussion, children should be encouraged to seek meaning in everything they encounter and to ask for additional explanations and further clarification of whatever they do not understand.

Growth in word meanings comes with use. Having acquired new "labels" or words through experience, opportunity should be provided for prompt use of the new vocabulary in speaking, listening, writing, and reading.

Wide reading is another way in which word meanings and the habit of attending to them may be built. Many remedial teachers select a book highly interesting to a disabled reader and read it aloud to him as a motivating device. They show the child some of the rewards that come from being able to read. These remedial teachers also use the content of the book to teach word meanings and the habit of studying them. The teacher discusses the story with the child, pointing out the well-chosen words and picturesque connotations the author used. She also shows the disabled reader ways in which the content defines the meaning of words, and how the author defines words for the reader. Both the teacher and the disabled reader are aware that his problem is one of building vocabulary. A disabled reader should be shown how a mature reader uses these aids for vocabulary development. This is applicable to the intermediate-grade child, and even more to the high school and adult disabled reader. It is at these levels that lack of vocabulary growth becomes most evident.

The disabled reader should be encouraged to note, by himself, words that are attractive to him, or those that have unusual meanings, or are especially descriptive. In this way, the habit of attending to word meanings is developed and vocabulary-building skills are gained. The disabled reader who is limited in vocabulary also should do extensive independent reading both during reading sessions and at home.

The extension and enrichment of word meanings are aided by wide reading of interesting and relatively easy materials. For such reading, not more than one unfamiliar word should appear in one hundred to two hundred running words. Ordinarily each new book, story, or article that is read will introduce new words to the reader and repeat words previously encountered. The use of old words in a variety of contexts broadens and clarifies their meanings. The more important new words will be seen enough to acquire more and more meaning. It is unrealistic to expect that a clear meaning for every new word will be learned right away. This does not mean that unfamiliar words should be ignored. It is particularly important that the reader should pay attention to whatever unfamiliar words he meets in context. Eventually, many of these words will become commonplace. Motivation is maintained by guiding children to material which catches their interest and has just the right amount of difficulty so that the context will yield the most intelligible clues to the meaning of any new words.

In any wide reading program, the proper use of clues from their contexts is essential if the concepts or meanings of the new words are to be learned satisfactorily. The remedial teacher, therefore, will need to test the child's skill in the use of various context clues and structural aids and to give whatever instruction is necessary, using methods described later. For best results, this checking and training in the use of clues must be a continuing program with each disabled reader since this skill is ordinarily slow to develop.

The acquisition of verbal meanings alone is not enough. In any program for developing word meanings through reading, the goal should be to go beyond mere verbal meanings. As pointed out by Dolch (58), one way to do this is to appeal to realistically conceived imagination. If the child is helped to use his imagination to extend his verbal understanding of words to concrete pictures, instead of being satisfied with a synonym, he will try to recall some of the sensory impressions, emotional reactions, ideas, and events suggested by each word.

Many samples may be found in the teacher's manuals and workbooks of basic readers. When using them, many associations can be made by discussing the items and the correct answers with the children. All these exercises provide opportunities to develop further the attitude of demanding that meanings be found in everything read. Another approach is to ask the child to tell everything a word, a phrase, or a symbolic expression makes him think of. Skill in getting him to extend meanings from mere words to reality through using his imagination may develop slowly. However, once he gets the knack of doing this, the wide reading program will pay big dividends in developing his understanding of what words mean.

The disabled reader should be encouraged to discuss his independent reading with his remedial teacher. The discussion should include new words he has found useful and should include using them in his own speech. He also should report on the aids to meaning he used in enlarging his vocabulary. This can be done because the disabled reader helped in formulating the *plan of his remedial program.*

Audiovisual aids can be used to build clear, precise, and extensive meanings of words. It is not feasible, and frequently not possible, to develop word meanings by direct experience alone. Much worthwhile experience can be provided to pupils through secondary media. Among these are visual and auditory aids, such as models and construction projects, dramatization, pictures, exhibits of materials related to a new topic, motion pictures, filmstrips, chalkboard sketches, charts, maps, slides, recordings, radio and television programs and educational talks by outsiders.

In using these vicarious aids to build word meanings, the remedial teacher should recognize that vocabularies are built to the extent that these aids are used properly. It is inefficient merely to present such experiences without first preparing the students for them and without following the presentation with discussion. The preparatory work should set purposes for viewing or listening. These purposes should include the idea that vocabulary growth is one outcome of the experience. The preparatory work should indicate the way in which the audiovisual material may best be studied. During the discussion following the presentation, the students should be encouraged to use the new vocabulary and even to explain the meanings of the terms used. The fundamental steps in teaching a reading selection, discussed in chapter 8, could well be used in teaching audiovisual material. It is obvious that the teacher should preview the material in order to prepare for using it in the classroom.

Formal Methods of Enriching Word Meanings

The teaching of word meanings is valuable only when it is done properly. We have emphasized that direct, systematic, well-planned drill on words in context increases knowledge of vocabulary, but that teaching of words in isolation is usually wasteful and ineffective. The correct meaning of a word frequently depends on its context. Often, familiar words are used in an unfamiliar sense. Teaching these new meanings of old words and the relation of the particular meaning to context is a considerable part of vocabulary training. (The teaching of word meanings for technical terms found in the content fields is a topic to be taken up in the next chapter.)

In the present discussion, the authors defend the view that word study can be profitable in developing meanings only to the degree that it consists in using each word in various contexts, in associating it with concrete experiences, in giving it a sufficient number of oral and written repetitions in a varied program of wide reading. First of all, word study should deal with new words met in context. Learning a word's meaning will then fulfill the child's immediate need, his present desire to understand the passage. This should be followed by using the word in discussion and in oral and written reports. Finally, he should read several materials in which the word occurs frequently.

Since many words have several meanings or shades of meaning, the initial contact with a new word in context can provide it with only a limited meaning. To extend and enrich the meaning of a new word, the word should also be presented in various contexts selected to bring out and emphasize different shades of meaning or different meanings. Exercises of this kind may be followed by discussions and other exercises designed to point up the different shades of meaning. It also is helpful for the remedial teacher to introduce activities which apply meanings of the word to such concrete situations as demonstration and use of equipment, giving titles to pictures or drawings, and writing of letters. These concrete activities are useful techniques for extending and enriching the meaning of a word through association with doing something that is not strictly limited to talking and reading. Besides these, more formal reinforcing exercises are helpful in overcoming limited vocabulary difficulties. These will be discussed under the following headings:

1. Role of the basic sight vocabulary

2. Use of context clues and authors' definitions

3. Use of structural aids

4. Use of the dictionary

ROLE OF THE BASIC SIGHT VOCABULARY. As already implied, the child can make little progress in reading without a basic sight vocabulary. This becomes especially important for the disabled reader. The Dolch basic sight vocabulary (57) of 220 service words contains about sixty-five percent of all the words in the reading material of the primary grades and nearly sixty percent of those in intermediate grades. With normal progress, the child will have mastered these 220 service words during his third year in school.

Many disabled readers are particularly deficient in recognizing and understanding the proper use of these words. When recognition of these words is being taught, emphasis should be on developing an understanding of their meaning when used in context. One way to do this is to organize exercises like the following:

Directions: Read the sentence on the left and then underline the word at the right that gives the idea or meaning of the word underlined in the sentence.

1. He sat <u>under</u> the tree.   (*a*) when   (*b*) where   (*c*) how   (*d*) why
2. He left <u>on</u> July 6.   (*a*) when   (*b*) where   (*c*) how   (*d*) why
3. He ran <u>because</u> he was late. (*a*) when   (*b*) where   (*c*) how   (*d*) why
4. Jack has a <u>brown</u> coat.   (*a*) color (*b*) wood   (*c*) cloth (*d*) straw
5. Ann has the <u>right</u> box.   (*a*) odd   (*b*) wooden (*c*) correct (*d*) small

The meanings of some of these service words can be taught best in terms of usage in context rather than as defining words. For instance:

1. When John and Bill reached home, mother gave <u>them</u> some cookies.

Children are taught that *them* means the persons, animals or things talked or written about.

A variety of sentences to illustrate this meaning should be presented to the disabled reader. Similar treatment should be given to the meanings of such words as *they, could,* and *what.*

Many of the basic sight words are particularly difficult for disabled readers to learn and retain. It is a cardinal principle that those words which carry the most meaning are remembered best. This stresses the need for developing as much meaning as possible for the words in the basic vocabulary (or for any other words, for that matter). Without the teacher's guidance, such words as *where, their, by, myself, which,* and the like do not have much meaning to many disabled readers.

Use of context clues and authors' definitions. The meaning of a new word frequently can be derived from its context. To do this, the child will need to comprehend the rest of the words in the sentence or passage. Many disabled readers make little or no use of context in trying to discover the meanings of unfamiliar words. They should be given practice in "guessing" the meaning of unknown words as they occur in context. They should be taught to read the rest of the sentence or passage and then look back and try to decide what the unknown word probably means. For instance, note the sentence:

The Indians in the canoe were from a <u>reservation</u>, the land set aside for Indians who still lived in the northern part of the state.

The word *reservation* acquires meaning from the context which follows in the rest of the sentence. Take another example:

Although Mary was surprised when Jack <u>glared</u> at her, she was not disturbed by his angry look.

If a sentence is part of a story, other sentences may amplify and clarify the meaning. Although some guesses may be wrong, this training usually builds considerable skill in deriving meaning from context.

Context clues to word meanings frequently come from the author's definitions. Such a definition may be the explanation given in the rest of the sentence, or it may come from another word or phrase in the sentence. Sometimes it is in a separate sentence. A few examples follow:

1. When Mother did not like the retort Harry made, she asked him to answer her more politely.
2. The boys were delighted with the summer cruise—a voyage by steamship on the Great Lakes.
3. Just after we got on the train the conductor gave the engineer the signal to start. In addition to directing the trainmen, the conductor also collects the passengers' tickets.

Another difficulty which disabled readers have is in choosing the correct meaning of a word that has several meanings. For instance, the correct meaning of *paid* in the following sentence depends on the context of the complete sentence: "Jack paid dearly for his mistake." In fact, the correct meaning for such words is sensed *only* in terms of the context. Many and varied examples of exercises to train pupils in use of context clues as aids to working out word meanings are given in workbooks and teachers' manuals.

USE OF STRUCTURAL AIDS. Direct, systematic, well-organized drill on words is valuable for the disabled reader in developing word meanings when this drill is on words in context or is related to the usage of words in context. When the remedial teacher produces sufficient motivation to lead to a general interest in words, she will find it profitable to devote some study to the meanings suggested by common prefixes, suffixes, and word roots, and to synonyms and antonyms. This approach to word study should be used when a word that lends itself to analysis is met in context. A few examples will illustrate:

1. The sailors aboard the ship (prefix and word root).
2. He has a kingly appearance (word root and suffix).
3. The army was undefeated (prefix, root, suffix).

In addition to identifying the root word and prefix or suffix with their meanings, the possibility of making other words by adding other prefixes or suffixes may be explored at appropriate times. The meanings of the more common word roots, prefixes, and suffixes may be worked out in this manner. The disabled reader will be helped by such reinforcement training in identifying and understanding word roots, prefixes, and suffixes by using the following types of exercises:

1. Draw a line under the root word in each of the following and tell what the root word means:

   worker   untie   kindly

2. Draw a line under the prefix in each of the following and tell how the prefix changes the meaning of the root word:

   unlike   return   displace

3. Draw a line under the suffix in each of the following and tell how the suffix changes the meaning of the root word:

   slowly   worker   doubtful

After roots, prefixes, and suffixes have been identified, their uses in developing meanings should be brought out through discussion and supplementary exercises. One way of doing this is to rewrite sentences. The disabled reader is given a sentence containing words with prefixes. He is asked to identify the word with a prefix and then told to rewrite the sentence with a new word or phrase that will replace it without changing the meaning of the sentence. Example:

Your bicycle is unlike mine.

Your bicycle is different from mine.

Training in structural aids to meaning should be given in context, such as illustrated in the following exercises:

The prefix *un* can mean (a) not, (b) opposite action, or (c) something was removed. Show which meaning is implied by putting the appropriate letter before each sentence.

_____1. The boy untied the horse.

_____2. The man was unkind to the horse.

_____3. The rider was unhorsed.

Complete the following sentences:

1. A snowball is a ball made of _____.
2. A steamboat is a boat run by _____.
3. A flowerpot is a pot for _____.
4. A fireplace is a place to have a _____.

USE OF THE DICTIONARY. Proper use of a good dictionary can be an important aid to the disabled reader in developing word meanings. Few children acquire the dictionary habit or know the wealth of fascinating information that can be found in a dictionary. Development of the dictionary habit depends upon a well-organized program of instruction carried out by a skilled and enthusiastic remedial teacher. No child will enjoy using a dictionary to get word meanings until he has become skillful in finding a desired word quickly. After finding a word, the child must know how to select from the several meanings listed, the one that fits the context from which the word came. This means that he must have a grasp of the meaning of the rest of the sentence or paragraph in which the unknown word occurs. Considerable training is required to develop skill in choosing correct dictionary meanings. Exercises such as those found in workbooks are easily constructed. An example follows:

Directions: Several numbered definitions are given for the word in heavy black type. Read the word and its definitions. Next read the sentences below the definitions. Write the number of the definition in front of the sentence in which the meaning of the word is used.

grate (1) grind off in small pieces   (2) rub with a harsh sound   (3) have an annoying or unpleasant effect

_____ Please grate the cheese to put on the salad.

_____ Mary's manners always grate on me.

In addition to developing skill in using the dictionary to find word meanings, this type of exercise provides further training in deriving meanings from context clues and in noting different meanings for the same word.

Experience with synonyms and antonyms enriches word meanings when the words are in context. Some dictionaries for children give synonyms for certain words but not antonyms. Ordinarily, exercises like those given above or like those below are used for choosing words of like or opposite meanings.

Directions (synonyms): Read each sentence and note the underlined word in it. Select from the list of words below the sentences the word that means the same or nearly the same as the underlined word. Write the word selected on the line after the sentence.

Father had no reason to doubt Jim.   _____

The automobile repair man needs many implements.   _____

trucks   tools   avoid   mistrust

In a similar way, exploring synonyms (words of like meaning) and antonyms (opposites) of words in context enriches the meaning of words. Supplementary exercises like the following may be used:

1. Underline the word that means the same as beautiful:
    pale   pretty   lonely   thoughtful
2. Underline the word that means the opposite of noisy:
    boastful   tiny   quiet   rosy

Informal Methods of Enriching Vocabulary

There are many creative approaches to enriching and expanding the vocabularies of disabled readers. These approaches also develop the word-study habits necessary for continuing growth in the reading vocabularies of intermediate, high school, and adult readers. The following activities are merely suggestions from many possible ones. The Cloze technique, often used in testing comprehension, can be used as an imaginative use of word meanings. A sentence like:

As the horse approached his stable, he _____ ahead, but his rider _____ _____ in the saddle.

The student is to think of as many groups of words as he can to complete the sentence in order to change the picture the sentence paints. The student might think of groups such as:

galloped, slumped over

trudged, sat erect

walked, felt insecure

stumbled, sat confidently

The disabled reader might help his remedial teacher by writing exercises for younger readers. Multiple-choice exercises using antonyms, synonyms, or semantic variations could be constructed. A dictionary could be used to find the choices. This would be both a creative and a useful dictionary activity.

Another dictionary exercise which would be both instructive and motivating would be for the disabled reader to make his own dictionary of new words that he found interesting. He would see his list of interesting words grow, and he would discover new meanings for many of them.

Encouraging the disabled reader to write stories about events for his parents to read is another good activity. He should use the new words he has found interesting. Experience charts are an especially effective and creative activity in building vocabulary when groups of disabled readers work together. The group should discuss the choice of words while making the experience chart, and decide why one word expresses an idea better than another.

INEFFECTIVE USE OF SENTENCE SENSE

Besides knowing the meanings of words, there are many other basic comprehension skills needed to understand sentences. The basic comprehension skills needed in sentence comprehension are reading in thought units, using punctuation as aids to meaning, interpreting connectives, identifying pronoun-antecedent relationships, and adjusting to varied sentence structures. To comprehend the increasingly more complex sentences the student will meet in intermediate grades, high school, and adult reading, he must be able to understand the relationships among the various parts of sentences. These skills must continue to develop, for complete comprehension. The disabled reader who is weak in one or more of these basic skills will be discussed under the following headings:

1. Inability to group words into thought units

2. Ineffective use of punctuation

3. Limited skill in interpreting connectives

4. Confusion in identifying pronoun-antecedent relationships

5. Ineffective use of syntax

6. Inability to adjust to varied sentence structures

INABILITY TO GROUP WORDS INTO THOUGHT UNITS. It already has been noted that reading by thought units promotes comprehension of sentences. Many disabled readers are either word-by-word readers or they tend to group words inappropriately so that clear comprehension of the sentence as a whole is impossible. At the start of instruction in reading, the child must recognize each word separately. In the beginning, he is required by his immaturity to study each word closely in order to identify it at all, so there is little likelihood that he will be able to group several together for recognition as a thought unit. As the child becomes more adept at word identification and as he builds a stock of words that he can recognize at sight, he is able to group some together.

The first grouping by thought units rather than by individual words is in two-word combinations, as: "the cat"; "Daddy said"; or "to ride." Such grouping of words takes place only after the child is very familiar with each of the words and only when they are set off together by the typography. For example, in the sentence "Daddy said, 'We can stop,'" the punctuation makes the grouping of "Daddy said" a natural and easy thing to do. Later, at the primer level, when two-line sentences begin to appear, additional help is given to the child in order for him to learn to read in thought units. A sentence would be printed like the following:

Judy said, "Put the duck
in the water."

The child would almost be forced, by the format, to read by thought units. Still later, he is expected to be able to analyze a sentence into thought units rapidly as he progresses along the line of print. This is a mature sort of reading that must be predicated on recognizing the words and phrases at sight.

Inability to read in thought units can be diagnosed in several ways. The simplest method is to listen to the disabled reader read easy material orally. If he reads in a word-by-word manner or if he clusters words in meaningless groups, he is probably ineffective in recognizing thought units in his silent reading and he is certainly not reading orally by thought units. Another method of diagnosing this ability is to flash phrases before the child for recognition. If he reads the phrases significantly less well than does the usual child of equal general reading ability, it is safe to assume that he has limited ability in recognizing thought units in isolation. It is then probable that he cannot pick out and recognize thought units in a sentence. Such a test does not give any indication of ability to analyze sentences into thought units. Therefore, both oral and flash appraisals should be made.

There are techniques for appraising eye movements in silent reading which also are useful in diagnosing the ability to read in thought units. Pictures of eye movements, like those made by the ophthalmograph, have been used. However, it is questionable whether the additional information obtained by using this device is worth the expense. In all probability, a pocket mirror would give almost as much information with practically no expense. If a pocket mirror is placed on the table between the child and the examiner, the eye movements can be observed as he reads. The number of fixations he makes while reading each line of print can be observed and recorded. The examiner will not be able to tell whether the fixations the child makes are reasonable stops, i.e., whether a stop is made for each thought unit, but he can tell whether or not the number of fixations is the same or more than the number of thought units. Gates and Cason (88) have shown that the oral reading diagnosis and the flash presentation of phrases are among the most practical and accurate appraisals of ability to read by thought units.

Remedial methods for the child who has been diagnosed as disabled in reading thought units must be based on the premise that ultimately he will have to learn to recognize meaningful groups of words as he silently reads consecutive printed matter. He will be reading sentences, not isolated thought units. Skill in reading by groups of words is dependent in part on the ability to analyze the sentences into reasonable units. It is also necessary for the disabled reader to encompass the group of words he separates into single ideas. The remedial work must teach the child to recognize rapidly thought units of several words and also to spot such groups of words in the sentences he reads. Many disabled readers are able to recognize isolated thought units flashed before them, but still they are incapable of reading silently or aloud by thought units. Since they cannot readily divide a sentence into proper clusters of words, they must read each word separately.

Remedial instruction designed to enable a child to read in thought units should be done in context or the phrases learned in isolation should be read immediately in complete sentences. The following exercises will give instruction and experience in reading by thought units:

1. Whenever the remedial teacher introduces new words in a selecton, it is desirable to have them read in the phrases in which the child will see them.

2. After the selection has been read, the child can reread to locate certain expressive phrases suggested by the teacher.

3. Preparing material to read orally provides excellent experience in reading by thought units.

4. Multiple-choice exercises in which phrases are used as answers and distractors may be used.

   a. Draw a line under the correct phrase to complete the sentence.

                    over the fence.
     (1) The ball sailed down the hole.
                   under the water.

                   flew away.
     (2) The dog talked softly.
                   ran fast.

   b. Quickly find the phrases on the pages given to answer these questions.

     1. On the page I tell you, find the phrases that answer the following questions:

Question	*Phrase*
(*a*) Where was the rooster?	(near the barn)
(*b*) What did John see?	(a pink light)
(*c*) Who was happy?	(the white bear)
(*d*) When did the boys swim?	(one summer day)

   c. Mark off the thought units in the following sentences and tell the *who,* or *what, did what, where, why* questions they answer.

     1. The large truck went slowly down the street.
     2. Billy and Frank quickly made a snow fort to hide behind.

   d. Draw a line from the phrase to the word that has a similar meaning.

a big meal	stroke
to rub softly	feast
away from everybody	chop
to cut down	alone

   e. Find these phrases in your book on the page I give, and tell what they mean.

her grandson's father	with a splash
answer the knock	cry for help
bright as stars	pulls us out
break the horse	fine fishing country
white as snow	gift of sight

 f. On the pages I tell you, find a phrase that makes you:

hear something	(the screaming gulls)
feel something	(the cool breeze)
see something	(colored autumn leaves)
smell something	(sweet-scented flowers)
taste something	(a sour apple)

5. The use of rapid exposure techniques, such as the tachistoscope described in chapter 10, will aid in teaching disabled readers to recognize a phrase or thought unit with one eye fixation. For group work, the Minneapolis North High School Reading Committee found that an opaque projector can be used as a tachistoscope. A piece of cardboard is placed before the lens and moved up and down to expose thought units for about one-half a second. The phrases for this work should be in the form of sentences, such as the following:

A brown beaver	at the bottom
was at work	of the pond.
near the island.	He swam
He was making	under the water
a tunnel	again and again.

 a. Sentences may be separated into thought units to be read by the children:

The old man	with the angry face	was happy now.
He had found	the one thing	he liked.

INEFFECTIVE USE OF PUNCTUATION. Inadequately interpreting punctuation or ignoring it altogether also may hinder sentence comprehension. Possibly the most common difficulty with punctuation among disabled readers is the failure to learn the more common uses of the comma, i.e., to separate words and groups of words written as a series in a sentence, to set off an appositive, or to set off a parenthetical expression in a sentence. This and other punctuation necessary for comprehension are listed by McKee (136, pp. 282–285).

Informal procedures must be used to find out if a child is using punctuation properly. For instance, commas properly used should aid in grouping words into thought units. Much is learned about commas by having the pupil read sentences aloud. If commas are not used to guide inflection and emphasis in phrasing, it is likely that the child does not understand the function of the punctuation marks in what he reads. Under these conditions, he will have difficulty in comprehending the full meaning of a sentence. Test sentences like the following may be taken from reading textbooks and used to illustrate the use of commas.

1. Deer, too, were there.
2. They stood still, heads up, listening.
3. Mary said, "Now we can go home."
4. After dark, when all was quiet, he slowly walked down the street.

A few children will need supervision to recognize that a capital letter is a clue to the beginning of a sentence and that a period or question mark signals the end of a sentence.

Remedial training in the use of punctuation to facilitate comprehension will involve at least two things: (*a*) by discussion, attention of the pupil is directed to the punctuation within a sentence as indicating the relation between what has just been read and what follows; and (*b*) the pupil is given ample practice with sentences from the context of his reading. The training should start with relatively simple sentences and gradually progress to more complex ones. In all cases, the sentences should be made up of words the child knows and can pronounce. In general, simple explanations and supervised practice will lead to improvement.

In a similar manner, as the child progresses in his reading, he may need help in the interpretation of semicolons, colons, and dashes. This training is necessary for sentence comprehension and for oral reading. In fact, interpretive oral reading helps to develop these skills.

LIMITED SKILL IN INTERPRETING CONNECTIVES. The disabled reader who is weak in sentence comprehension must be taught how a sentence is unified. Remedial teaching should begin with direct sentences whose parts are found easily. Then more complex sentences should be introduced. Finally, the disabled reader should be taught the importance of learning connectives. He should be shown that they can change the anticipated flow of the thought or qualify it in some way. This is a problem often found in social studies material. Teaching the role of connectives should start out with relatively simple illustrations and then provide some examples, taken from one of the student's social studies textbooks. A sentence like the following might be used:

> We were going swimming, but a thunder storm began, so we decided to watch television instead.

After the sentence is read, the disabled reader can be asked if the people went swimming, what words show that they did not go, and why they changed their minds.

CONFUSION IN IDENTIFYING PRONOUN-ANTECEDENT RELATIONSHIPS. Sometimes difficulties arise when the thing or person referred to by a pronoun is not grasped readily. Disabled readers often have this kind of difficulty. The following type of exercise may be used for remedial instruction.

Directions: In the following sentences, the underlined word is used in place of the name of a person or thing already mentioned. Draw a circle around the word or words that tell who or what is meant by the underlined word.

1. After <u>he</u> arrived home from school, Jack shoveled the snow off the walk.
2. As the horses were freed, <u>they</u> galloped across the field.

3. Mary and Jane went to the store after <u>they</u> finished lunch.
4. Henry looked on with interest as <u>his</u> sister, Jane, rode toward <u>him</u> on <u>her</u> new bicycle.

INEFFECTIVE USE OF SYNTAX. Understanding word order within a sentence is vital to sentence comprehension. For example, the sentence, *Only Tom went to the store,* has a meaning different from *Tom went to the only store.* The disabled reader who cannot use syntax to grasp meaning while reading often will not comprehend what is read. The child should practice reading exercises which reinforce his knowledge of sentence relationships, such as: the actor, the action, and the object of the action. Exercises designed to bring together knowledge of spoken language and reading comprehension, are helpful:

1. Read this sentence:

   The big grey elephants at the zoo wanted more roasted peanuts.

   a. Put "C" before the three most important words in the sentence.

   _____ zoo roasted peanuts
   _____ peanuts wanted elephants
   _____ elephants wanted peanuts

   b. Put "C" before the words that show the elephants had already had some peanuts.

   _____ wanted zoo peanuts   _____ wanted more peanuts
   _____ wanted roasted peanuts   _____ elephants roasted peanuts

2. Read this sentence:
   The boys ran to the circus to see the clowns do funny tricks.
   a. Who did tricks?
   _____ the boys   _____ the clowns   _____ the circus
   b. Why did the boys run to the circus?
   _____ to see the clowns   _____ to do some tricks
   c. Where did the boys run?
   _____ to see the clowns   _____ to the circus
   d. What was funny?
   _____ the tricks   _____ the boys   _____ the clowns

INABILITY TO ADJUST TO VARIED SENTENCE STRUCTURES. The inability of disabled readers to sort out and properly relate the meanings in different parts of a sentence sometimes is complicated by sentence structure. For instance, difficulties may arise when the subject is last, or between two parts of the predicate rather than at the beginning. Informal exercises for diagnosing such difficulties and for remedial instruction are similar to those described above for developing sentence comprehension. For example, what word answers the question "who" in each of the following sentences?

"Hearing the low, rumbling sound again, Jack suddenly remembered something." "Then into the cool water went John."

Writers themselves are to blame for hindering sentence comprehension. Too frequently, sentences are excessively long and too complex for clear understanding. Sometimes they are just poorly written, but the reader must learn to make the adjustment if he wishes to read these materials.

The following types of exercises may be helpful in developing flexibility in adjusting to sentence structure:

Directions: Read each sentence. Then decide whether the underlined part tells when, why, how, what, or where. Draw a line under the right one of the words which follow the sentence.

1. The large farm belongs to father.   when   why   how   what where

2. Because John was ill, he did not go to school.   when   why   how what   where

3. Uncle John went into the big barn.   when   why   how   what where

4. All the children came on the run.   when   why   how   what where

5. Mary's train will arrive at six o'clock.   when   why   how what   where

A variation of the above is to find and copy the word or words that answer the question, "who" or "where." After informing the pupil that the sentences answer the questions "who" and "where," he is directed to write below the sentences the word or words that answer the question:

1. The boy went to the chalkboard to write the word.
2. From school to the park is only one-half mile, explained the teacher.

Words that tell

Sentence Number	Who?	Where?
1	——	——
2	——	——

The responses may be made by having the child draw a line under the words that answer the question, "where," and the like.

In a similar manner, exercises may be constructed that answer the questions "when" and "what," or "why" and "how." They may be varied by using sentences or unusual structural patterns. The sentences may be taken directly from books or made up from words in the reading vocabulary. Sample items may be found in Russell and Karp (167) and in workbooks accompanying basic readers.

INSUFFICIENT COMPREHENSION OF LONGER UNITS

Frequently, disabled readers are unable to understand the meaning of a paragraph. These children tend to consider each sentence as a separate unit unrelated to the other sentences in the paragraph. It is possible for them to read and understand words, thought units, and sentences and yet not comprehend fully the connected material in a paragraph. Similarly, some pupils are unable to sense the relation between paragraphs in stories and various expository materials. Comprehension of paragraphs and development of story sense will be considered in this section. The next chapter will cover specific comprehension defects.

LIMITED KNOWLEDGE OF PARAGRAPH ORGANIZATION. Comprehension of a paragraph requires an understanding of the relationships between sentences in that paragraph. Many readers, disabled in all types of comprehension, need guidance in identifying the topical sentence containing the key idea and in interpreting its relationship to explanatory or amplifying sentences.

Remedial teaching of paragraph organization centers on understanding the interrelationships among sentences. Exercises requiring the disabled reader to find which one of several statements best represents the general meaning of a given paragraph are helpful. Calling attention to various types of paragraph organization is even more important in increasing paragraph comprehension. This instruction should start with the simplest type, that in which the topic sentence is the first presented and the following sentences expand the main idea. The second type of paragraph presents a series of related facts and concepts, and the topic sentence comes last in the form of a generalization. This type of paragraph is used frequently in scientific writing. Finally, the disabled reader should be taught to recognize a third type of paragraph organization, the one in which introductory concepts are presented initially, followed by a summary topic sentence, and then concluded with sentences which modify or limit the general idea. This type of paragraph often is found in social studies materials.

To develop skill in finding the topic sentence, the child is given illustrations and explanations. After the examples and explanations, he is asked to find and underline the topic sentence in other paragraphs. Besides finding the topic sentence, the pupil should be guided to understand how the other sentences in the paragraphs develop the idea presented in the topical sentence: by details, by emphasis, by explanations, by contrast, and by repetition of the same idea in other words. One technique of doing this is to number the sentences in a paragraph. Then through questions and analysis, the role of each sentence in relation to the others is discussed.

A well-written paragraph is concerned with one central idea. Training to grasp this idea may be carried out in various ways: A paragraph is given, followed by three phrases, one of which is the headline or title that best expresses the topic of the material in the paragraph. The disabled reader is to indicate which one is best. He may be asked to write a headline (topic) for the paragraph, or to write a sentence expressing the topic; or he may be given a topic sentence and asked to write a short paragraph with supporting and amplifying sentences; another device is to give him a paragraph which is good except for one sentence. The child is asked to underline the topic sentence and then to cross out the sentence which does not belong.

Although the comprehension of paragraphs is important in all reading, it is absolutely essential for clear understanding as the disabled reader moves into reading the content subjects. Some training for understanding paragraph unity usually is introduced when third-grade reading ability is reached. More formal training to develop paragraph comprehension becomes a regular part of reading instruction at the intermediate grade levels.

INABILITY IN INTERRELATING THE PARTS OF A TOTAL SELECTION. For full comprehension of longer units, the child should be taught to sense the relation between the paragraphs which make up the unit. In good expository writing, the introductory paragraphs usually state the reason for the piece, or what is to be described or explained. The following paragraphs give the details of the explanation in logical sequence. The final one or two paragraphs ordinarily state the outcome or conclusion, or they summarize what has been said. In stories, there are ordinarily three parts: (*a*) the beginning gives either the time or the place of the story, or both, and sometimes also the characters; (*b*) this introduction is followed by the body of the story which tells what happens; and (*c*) the final paragraphs usually relate the conclusion of events.

The remedial teacher aids in developing story sense so that the disabled reader understands better the relation between paragraphs and is able to identify the three main parts of stories and expository materials. In teaching the relation between paragraphs, the following may be helpful: (1) Explain the three main parts of a story, point out these parts in an example, and formulate a set of questions for each part. The questions should be organized to show the content of each part (introduction, body, outcome). (2) teach the disabled reader to recognize the transitional expressions that often start a paragraph. These expressions precede the main idea or topic of the new paragraph. They begin with such phrases as: (*a*) *But something else has happened . . . (b) Then he turned to John . . . (c) When this was done, he turned . . .* (3) Give the child practice in writing one sentence to express the main idea in each paragraph of a story or an article. Then have him link these sentences together in a coordinated pattern of thought, using transitional words or phrases when needed.

With expository materials, it would be profitable to have the student try to make an outline of the main and subordinate ideas.

SUMMARY

To read means to read with understanding. To accomplish this, there must be comprehension of words, thought units, sentences, paragraphs, and longer units. Instruction for developing comprehension coordinates all these into an integrated sequential program.

Listening comprehension runs ahead of reading comprehension in the early grades. As the mechanics of reading mature, reading comprehension catches up with and soon equals listening comprehension. With still further progress in reading, reading comprehension becomes superior. The aim in reading instruction is to reach this level as soon as possible.

Comprehension depends upon a group of concepts or meanings evolved through experience. Deficiencies discovered should be remedied as much as possible in the school. Firsthand experience is best, supplemented by vicarious or secondhand experience. The aim of such experiences is to form concepts tied to words which can be used by the disabled reader in thinking, speaking, listening, writing, and reading.

Instruction techniques for teaching word meanings include pointing out the use of context clues, ensuring wide reading, encouraging the attitude of demanding understanding of words read and noting authors' definitions, studying words systematically, and using the dictionary. To be effective, all word study must use each word in context.

To comprehend sentences, the child must understand the words and the relations between these words and groups of words. He also must be able to read by thought units, interpret punctuation, and understand figures of speech, symbolic expressions, and semantic variations. Remedial instruction for sentence comprehension is based on informal exercises.

Paragraph comprehension depends on comprehension of the sentences and on understanding the relation between these sentences. Similarly, the comprehension of larger units is based upon paragraph comprehension and understanding the relations between the paragraphs involved.

SELECTED READINGS

CUSHENBERY, DONALD C., *Reading Improvement in the Elementary School,* chap. 6, West Nyack, N. Y.: Parker, 1969.

DEBOER, JOHN J., and MARTHA DALLMANN, *The Teaching of Reading* (rev. ed.), chaps. 7A, 7B. New York: Holt, Rinehart and Winston, 1970.

DECHANT, EMERALD V., *Improving the Teaching of Reading* (2nd ed.), chaps. 12, 13. Englewood Cliffs, N. J.: Prentice-Hall, 1970.

DURKIN, DOLORES, *Teaching Young Children to Read* (2nd ed.), Boston: Allyn and Bacon, 1976.

HARRIS, ALBERT J., and E. R. SIPAY, *How to Increase Reading Ability* (6th ed.), chap. 16. New York: David McKay, 1975.

———, and EDWARD R. SIPAY, *Effective Teaching of Reading* (2nd ed.), Chaps. 10, 11. New York: David McKay, 1971.

SPACHE, GEORGE D., and EVELYN B. SPACHE, *Reading in the Elementary School* (3rd ed.), chaps. 13, 14. Boston: Allyn and Bacon, 1973.

TINKER, MILES A., and CONSTANCE M. MCCULLOUGH, *Teaching Elementary Reading* (4th ed.), chap. 9. New York: Appleton-Century-Crofts, 1975.

WILSON, ROBERT M., *Diagnostic and Remedial Reading for Classroom and Clinic* (3rd ed.), chap. 9. Columbus, Ohio: Charles E. Merrill, 1977.

ZINTZ, M. V., *The Reading Process* (2nd ed.), chap. 11. Dubuque, Iowa: Wm. C. Brown Co., 1975.

Overcoming
Specific
Comprehension
Limitations

fourteen

The preceding chapters of this book have considered the limitations in reading abilities affecting the disabled reader's entire reading achievement. Deficiencies in basic comprehension and in word recognition prevent effective reading of all types of materials and unless corrected, preclude future reading growth. Ths disabled readers so far discussed are those classified as having *limiting* or *complex disabilities*. They often have difficulties in reading so severe or so complicated by various handicaps that they require extensive remedial adjustments.

This and the following chapters will consider the disabled readers who are classified as having a *specific disability*. They need corrections in reading patterns that must be made if maturity in reading and satisfactory communication between author and reader is to be achieved. The disabled readers to be discussed are basically good readers, but have specific problems that must be corrected if full realization of their reading potential is to be achieved. The disabled reader with a specific disability can and should receive corrective training in the classroom or school reading center.

Remedial teaching, discussed in the remaining chapters, is of special importance in the intermediate grades, high school, and adult educational programs. The students with difficulties in these types of reading growth often are unable to progress in their entire education as well as they should because of a readily correctable reading problem.

Among the more frequent areas of specific difficulties in comprehension abilities, basic study skills, and reading materials of the content fields are the following, which will be discussed in this chapter:

1. Limitations in specific comprehension abilities.
   a. Inability to locate and retain information read.
   b. Inadequate sense of organization of material.
   c. Limited ability in evaluating what is read.
   d. Immaturity in ability to interpret content.
   e. Lack of appreciative abilities.

2. Insufficient development of basic study skills.
   a. Lack of skills needed to locate sources of information.
   b. Inefficiency in using basic references.
   c. Limited skill in interpreting pictorial and tabular materials.
   d. Lack of diversified techniques of organizing information.

3. Deficiencies in reading content materials.
   a. Social Studies
   b. Science
   c. Mathemetics
   d. Literature

LIMITATIONS IN SPECIFIC COMPREHENSION ABILITIES

Comprehension is made up of a number of basic abilities, including skill in recognizing words and their meanings, grouping words into thought units, and giving the proper emphasis to the thought units so that the sentences may be understood. Moreover, it is the ability to ascertain the relationship between the sentences that enables the reader to understand the paragraph. When the relationship between paragraphs is understood, the reader arrives at the meaning of the total passage.

Although these basic comprehension abilities underlie the communicative act of reading, they alone are not sufficient. The reader needs a group of diversified comprehension abilities with flexibility in their use. Unfortunately, there are many adults for whom the reading program did not develop flexibility in the use of specific comprehension abilities. Some people read all material as though each illustrative detail were to be retained forever. They have not developed such higher-order comprehension abilities as the ability to organize facts so that generalizations can be made, the ability to evaluate, or the ability to reflect. Other people read primarily for appreciation, and retain little of the content in material that should be read for more specific purposes.

Inability to Locate and Retain Information Read

This category of specific comprehension abilities requires exact, careful reading. The various comprehension abilities included are: recalling specific items of information, noting the details within a passage, retaining fundamental concepts, using facts to answer specific questions, and finding statements to prove a point or to answer a question. These specific comprehension abilities begin their development in the child's early reading assignments and are continued as goals of instruction as long as systematic training is given. Many children, however, fail to establish a high degree of accuracy in the various ways of locating and retaining factual information. On the other hand, numerous other children are found to be overly exacting. These latter should be encouraged to read relatively easy material for the purpose of enjoyment, for predicting what is going to happen next, or to get the general gist of a story or passage.

Children who are not exacting enough in their reading or who cannot remember details within the passage when this is what is demanded by the purposes for reading, should be given reading that requires the collection of factual information with close attention to detail, and then requires that this factual information be used. The material for children with a limited capacity for locating and retaining specific items of information should have considerable factual content. For this, science material is better than narrative; something from social studies is good provided it is designed to give information rather than an overall impression. In other words, the material that will be found most useful in developing ability to read for informational purposes will be material that contains plenty of facts.

A chart should be kept showing the disabled reader's percentage of correct responses. Children at all levels of general reading competency may be inexperienced or ineffective in this type of reading comprehension. The exercises and materials in which the disabled reader is expected to get practice in attending to specific details should be at a level somewhat below his general reading capability, but it does not have to be as simple as indicated by his measured score in this type of reading. By this we mean that if a disabled reader of fifth-grade age and mental ability has a general reading capability of 4.0 and measures 2.5 in reading to recall items of specific information, the remedial work ordinarily would not need to use material of 2.5 level of difficulty, though it ought to be somewhat easier than 4.0 in difficulty.

A few samples of reading purposes that will give experience in reading to locate and retain factual information are:

1. Read the story to see what facts it tells about robins.
2. Read the selection to find all the things a beaver uses in making his home.
3. Read the selection to find how the Plains Indians made use of buffaloes.
4. Reread the selection to find additional facts about the animals discussed to add to your list.
5. Find and read sentences to prove or disprove these statements given orally.
    a. A big sea lion weights about six hundred pounds.
    b. A big elephant may be eight feet high.
    c. A baby kangaroo sleeps in its mother's pouch.
    d. A full-grown kangaroo weighs more than a sea lion.
    e. Baboons like to swim.
6. Read to learn about the former home life of one of the major Indian groups in America: where they lived; what they ate; how they prepared their food; what they wore; what tools they used.

Inadequate Sense of Organization of Material

The specific types of comprehension included in this category have as their major distinguishing characteristic the ability to sense order or relationship among the facts read. They include abilities such as: classifying and listing facts in a sensible manner, establishing a sequence of events, following a series of related directions, sensing relationships, and distinguishing between the major ideas and the related facts. These are exacting sorts of reading but they are important. Reading to organize information begins in children's prereading exercises when they classify pictures of animals, for example, into those they would see on a farm and those they would see in a forest; or when the child arranges a series of pictures in an orderly sequence of events. Some fail to develop the ability to sense the organization and relationship among the ideas they are reading, and this is a severe handicap in using printed material. These children need remedial work to become proficient in this area of comprehension abilities.

The material for developing ability to organize and sense relationships among facts, naturally must contain plenty of facts to organize and relate one to the other. The best materials are those units in some of the modern basic readers included to show the disabled reader how to read science and social studies materials. The sections of the manuals related to these units of content matter will be found to contain many examples of exercises for developing ability to sense organization and relationships among the facts read. Other science and social studies materials at the proper level of difficulty can be used to develop these abilities. The remedial teacher must use reasons for reading which require the child to organize, and she should check on his effectiveness in carrying these out. Below are some specific purposes that will help to teach sensing the organization of ideas and information:

1. Read about animals to make a summary chart showing: where they live; what they eat; how to recognize them; how they protect themselves; who their enemies are; how they get ready for winter.
2. Read to make a list of: (*a*) the kinds of damage done by floods; (*b*) means that are used to prevent damage.
3. Read to make an outline of three types of soil conservation problems discussed in the selection.
4. Read to summarize the information given about petroleum under the following headings: how petroleum was formed; how oil wells are located; how oil is obtained from below the ground; uses of petroleum; how we can conserve our petroleum resources.
5. Read the selection to find what is done first, second, and third in making a print of your hand.
6. Read to find and list in order the steps taken by Charles Hall in his experiments to find a quick and inexpensive way of changing alumina into aluminum.
7. Read to find out in what ways the life of a boy who lives by the sea in Brittany is the same and how it is different from that of a boy who lives in Bora Bora.

Limited Ability in Evaluating What Is Read

This group of comprehension abilities involves not only reading and understanding what the author said, but reflecting on it so that critical judgments may be made. It includes such specific types of comprehending as differentiating between fancy, fact, and opinion; judging the reasonableness and relevancy of ideas presented; sensing implied meanings; establishing cause-and-effect relationships; making comparisons; judging the authenticity of materials read; and critically appraising the validity of the author's presentation. Like all other comprehension abilities, these have their start in early reading lesssons and develop as long as growth in reading continues. The time at which a child is asked if a fanciful tale really could have happened is the start of such instruction. Reading to evaluate includes some of the most important types of reading. The person who is taught to read, but not to reflect on what is read, frequently is in danger of coming to faulty conclusions. The child who is unable to read critically and to judge the reasonableness of material at his level of advancement should be given remedial instruction to overcome this deficiency. Reading to evaluate what is read is gradual in development and should not be left to chance learning.

The material best for learning how to evaluate is that written to influence people's opinions. During the early elementary school grades, such material is not readily available. Nevertheless, even there, certain types of evaluative reading can be done. Often ideas are implied rather than directly stated. Frequently there are cause-and-effect relationships, even in first-grade material, and often statements of fact and opinion can be compared. Any material that is at the child's general reading level may be used to increase his ability to evaluate what is read. Many of the comprehension exercises in basal readers have the child reread material in order to evaluate it in a wide variety of ways. Some exercises that teach the child to judge, reflect on, and evaluate are illustrated by the following:

1. Have the child, after reading a somewhat fanciful story about animals, reread it to distinguish between the realistic and the fanciful statements.
2. Have the child decide from the titles of stories whether they are likely to be real or fanciful.
3. Have the children discuss whether a story read could have happened and give their reasons for their opinions.
4. Ask a child to judge which of given paragraphs in a fanciful story could have happened and which could not.
5. Ask him to judge the reasonableness of statements by indicating which probably are true and which probably are not true.
6. Have the child find and read aloud just the part that proves a point and no more.
7. Have the children come to such conclusions from their reading as why pioneers might prefer to be paid in corn or other goods rather than in money.
8. Have the child judge the point of view of two people about a common event.
9. Have him find facts that are relevant to a topic.
10. Have the children read to find statements which characters make that they know to be true and those that are their opinions.

Immaturity in Ability to Interpret Content

This category of comprehension abilities is composed of types of reading that project the understanding of the selection beyond the statements of the author. It differs from organizing what is read in that it requires a child to derive new ideas from what he reads. Reading to interpret includes understanding the significance of a selection read, drawing an inference or conclusion not expressly stated, predicting the outcome of given events, forming one's own opinions, and inferring time and measurement relationships. These comprehension abilities require the reorganization of information and ideas expressed so that new relationships can be understood. In the prereading lessons, the child may be asked to study a set of related pictures and to select, from the two final pictures, the one that would best complete the series. Or, he may have to form an opinion about what he should do when a pet dog digs up the garden. From this meager beginning, the child gradually develops the ability to make judgments like the importance of the Constitution and the Bill of Rights to our way of life.

Some children who have good general reading ability find it difficult to interpret what is read. This type of reading ability is best developed in material that requires careful, considered judgments. It also is developed by setting purposes for reading that necessitate reflecting upon what is read. The child must learn to take the facts and ideas presented, reorganize them, and recognize relationships among them that he did not find on the surface. Social studies and science lend themselves to these sorts of reasoning, but well-written narrative material and essays also are useful in developing the ability to interpret.

The main requirement of remedial instruction for the disabled reader who is otherwise a capable reader, is to have him read for purposes that force him to reflect upon what he reads. The following purposes illustrate the nature of reading assignments that will encourage interpretive reading:

1. Have the children anticipate the ending of the story.
2. Have the children read to find out why the signing of the Magna Carta is important to them.
3. The children may read to find which colony in America they would have preferred to live in, and why.
4. Have the children form an opinion about which of the two people they have read about they would prefer to have as a friend.
5. Have the children form opinions about effects of various inventions such as movable type, electric light, and the reaper.
6. Have them form conclusions about how climatic conditions have affected the ways in which people live.
7. Have them read to draw conclusions and form generalizations from the facts given in science.

Lack of Appreciative Abilities

This set of comprehension abilities is somewhat different from the others. The four types of specific limitations discussed previously dealt with noting and retaining factual information, organizing information, judging the authenticity of information, and interpreting it. Appreciation abilities deal more with the aesthetic qualities of reading. Reading abilities such as understanding the feeling expressed by the author; recognizing the plot, humor, and action; forming various sensory impressions; and understanding the personal qualities of the characters are essential for appreciating what is read. The basic reading program and the program of guided literature reading are designed to build these capabilities.

The child who cannot visualize the scene described, or sense the feeling of aloneness experienced by an early explorer, or appreciate the humor of an absurd situation, is in reading difficulty, although he may be able to do all of the factual types of reading. The materials best for developing reading to appreciate are the best literature, short stories, anthologies, and the like. The child must read for reasons that encourage appreciation. It would be unfortunate to force the factual types of reading, required for other comprehension abilities, on the child when he is reading material that should be read for personal development, appreciation, or for its own beauty.

An example of the effects of pursuing the wrong purposes at the wrong time can be seen in the quotation from Bond and Handlan (25):

> An extreme example of formal recitation was observed in a class in which the children had read Alfred Noyes' romantic poem, "The Highwayman." For thirty-five minutes the teacher stood before the class and asked questions: "What was the girl's name? What color was her hair? What did the Highwayman wear?" More times than not, each question demanded only one or two words in response. If she failed to get the exact answer after four or five trials, she answered the question herself and went on to the next. Some of the period was spent in scolding the children for inattention and in moving two or three who grew restless under the barrage of questions. At no time during the lesson did the children have a chance to see that the rhythm of the poem showed how "the Highwayman came riding"; at no time did they have a chance to enjoy the story or to appreciate the beauty of some of the especially effective bits of description. It was difficult to see how this formal recitation helped the children either understand or enjoy the poem.

To cultivate appreciation, the teacher first must find material that the child in difficulty can read and that will be interesting to him. Fortunately, when the lack of ability to read for appreciation is a specific limitation, the child has capability in the basic skills and abilities and is generally a competent reader. He can read material at a level of difficulty that is near his level of general growth and development, but he does need special help in appreciating the tone, plot, or action; in appreciating a characterization; or in visualizing a description. He can be taught the abilities necessary for appreciation, using material that is suitable to one of his age and in accordance with his interests. He is not limited in reading in general and he has no basic defects in his skills and abilities. If he were so limited, these basic defects would be his primary problem and would receive first attention.

Although guiding children to read quality materials is essential in improving reading to appreciate, there are certain other things that can be

done to encourage it. The following illustrations indicate the kinds of experiences that improve appreciation:

1. Read a story to obtain the visual background needed to represent it on
   a mural.
2. Read a story to participate in a creative dramatic representation of one
   of the characters.
3. Read several stories to select one that would make a good play. (In
   order to do this, the child must sense the action, visualize the scenes,
   and understand the characters.)
4. Read to prepare a story for *interpretive oral reading* in book-sharing time.
5. Read to plan a radio or television presentation of a story.
6. Have the child discuss how he thinks someone in the story felt.
7. Have the child describe the sights, sounds, and smells encountered by
   the boy in the story who was adrift in New York harbor.
8. Locate some descriptive words within a story.
9. Read to share an adventure.
10. Read for the enjoyment of a good story.

INSUFFICIENT DEVELOPMENT
OF BASIC STUDY SKILLS

There are specific limitations in the basic study skills. The child can be an
excellent reader in general, but at the same time be unable to (*a*) locate
sources of information; (*b*) use basic references; (*c*) interpret pictorial and
tabular materials; or (*d*) set findings down in a usable form of organization.
A child who is limited in any of these skills has a specific difficulty in reading which should be corrected if he is to use the printed page effectively.

Two steps are needed to obtain the desired diagnostic information
about a particular pupil. The first is to use a standardized test. Some of the
more useful standardized tests are described in chapter 7 and others are
listed in Appendix V. For the most part, these tests will indicate only in
which of the above areas his difficulty lies. They will define neither the nature of the problem nor the remedial work needed to correct it. The child
may show, for example, that he is ineffective in locating sources of information, but this will not tell whether his difficulty lies in inability to alphabetize, inability to select key words, or inability to judge in which book he
might find a certain subject. A test of the basic study skills will give only a
general diagnosis, revealing the skill that needs further analytical exploration by the diagnostician.

Each of the four categories of basic study skills listed above is composed of many parts. The teacher must know just where a child's difficulty
lies if remedial treatment is to be effective and not waste time on elements

already mastered. It would be wasteful to spend time teaching a child who is weak in locating sources of information to alphabetize if he already knows how to alphabetize. It would be equally undesirable to spend time and effort teaching him key words, when his real difficulty is that he does not know in which type of book he can find the information he wants. He is competent in selecting the key words, once he locates a book likely to contain the information.

The second step is to study the disabled reader as he works in the area of his weakness. This requires sampling his performance in that area. For example, if he is weak in the use of basic references, it may be that he does not know whether the types of information he desires can be found in an encyclopedia, a dictionary, an atlas, an almanac, a telephone book, a standard text, or just where. By studying the selections he makes when answering questions such as "Where would you be likely to find information about: the time of the monsoons in India, the definition of a word, the address of another school, the population of a town, or the location of a country?" the diagnostician can narrow the problem.

A study of the disabled reader's efficiency in using the basic study skill in question also is needed. He may know which reference to use, under which heading to look for the information he wishes to find, and how to estimate pages within the reference, but still he may be slow and inefficient in using what he knows. The work sample will also give this necessary information.

Which remedial methods are proper is usually obvious when the nature of the difficulty is thoroughly diagnosed. The teacher needs to teach the child to do the things in which he is limited. If he does not know how to alphabetize, it is relatively easy to teach him the order of the letters and the fact that words are arranged in lists in this order by their first letters, then by the second letters, and so on, and that it is always done in this way. This is a different and much simpler type of learning than is, for example, word recognition, in which few such rules apply.

Lack of Skills Needed to Locate Sources of Information

Skill in finding sources of information is helpful to most study activities. The child who knows how and when to use the table of contents, the index, and the card catalogue is better equipped for independent study than is the one who does not think of doing these things or is not as skillful at them. Among the most frequent limitations in this skill are: (*a*) inability to decide which books contain the information wanted; (*b*) not knowing how to use such tools as the index, the table of contents, the card catalogue, the reader's guide, and the like; (*c*) limited skill in estimating the probable key words under which the information is classified or inflexibility in selecting other references when the first one does not contain the information wanted; (*d*) inefficiency in finding words in an alphabetical listing, especially in those lists with major and subordinate subdivisions; (*e*) inability to find pages in a book; (*f*) little skimming ability, making it hard to find exact information.

The teacher must establish in which of these skills the child is behind and then give him reading assignments requiring their use in finding the information for a definite purpose. If he shows poor judgment as to which book might contain the information that he desires, the teacher can teach him how to choose a good source by asking him questions. If his weakness is in not knowing whether to use the table of contents or the index, she can explain the use of each and give him experience in using them. If use of key words is the difficulty, several topics can be chosen to show how they are listed, from general to specific, from common to unusual, from major to related headings.

If the child's weakness is in finding words in an alphabetical list, he must be drilled on the alphabet, on estimating how far through the alphabet one of the letters is, and on placing words in alphabetical order. The child who has insufficient skimming ability can be given many exercises that require the rapid location of specific facts within a page or a few pages on which the fact is known to be discussed. It might be well to start such exercises with the location of a date, since numbers on a page of print can be found readily.

Inefficiency in Using Basic References

The child who is capable of finding information in general may find using basic reference material confusing. His difficulty usually is not knowing what kind of information each reference contains. He does not know to which book he should refer for the kind of information he desires. The teacher should find out which of the references the child is unfamiliar with and give him experience in using them. Many adults, for example, do not know all of the types of information that can be most readily found in the telephone book. The child is often uncertain about the difference between an encyclopedia and a dictionary and which should be used to get a specific bit of information. He may be equally confused about what can be obtained from other reference books. After the teacher pinpoints the nature of the problem, an explanation of the contents of the different basic references and some experience in using each usually will correct the difficulty. At times it will be necessary to have the child tell in which of the common reference books he would look to find such things as the facts about Columbus, the meaning of the word *Tory,* the amount of wheat grown in Kansas last year—each time checking the accuracy of his answer by looking up that topic.

Limited Skills in Interpreting Pictorial and Tabular Materials

Skill in reading maps, graphs, charts, and tables is becoming increasingly important to understand printed material. The child who fails to develop such skills will be handicapped in his reading in the content fields during his school years and also as an adult. If standardized tests show that he is weak in this group of skills, the teacher should make a more analytical diagnosis to find which kinds of pictorial and tabular aids are causing him difficulty and to determine the exact nature of his trouble.

Again, as in most of the study skills, once the nature of the difficulty is known, the remedial work to be undertaken is definite. The child who has a disability in map reading, for example, may be in difficulty for a variety of reasons. He may be unaware that different maps use different scales. A map of his city may, for example, be larger than a map of his state, so he is troubled about distances and comparative sizes. He may get erroneous notions because he does not know that a flat map of a vast area must distort some things in order to show others. Many maps of the United States show Maine closer to the top than the state of Minnesota. Therefore many people think that Maine extends farther north than Minnesota, but in reality it does not. Because wall maps always have north at the top, many children think rivers flow downhill to the south and so they are surprised to learn that some rivers flow north and empty into Hudson Bay. There are many such faulty concepts established in trying to read maps.

In reading other types of pictorial and tabular materials, there also are many kinds of confusion. The diagnostician should first find the source of the difficulties and then give the child systematic instruction and purposeful experiences in order to overcome the weakness. The corrective work is best accomplished in the science and social studies units of those basic readers which systematically teach the study skills. They contain specific exercises to develop skill in interpretation of pictorial and tabular presentations. The principles these illustrate can be reinforced by the reading assignments in science and social studies classes. Krantz (127) has shown that each of these fields has its own specific study skills. The main feature of remedial instruction is that it is based upon a careful diagnosis which has determined the exact kind of instruction needed. It must be realized that these skills begin to form early in the child's reading experience. Map reading may be started by interpreting a map which the teacher has made to show the children safe ways to go home from school. A chart showing daily temperatures at noon is often one of the child's early school experiences.

Remedial instruction for those children who are weak in these skills must progress from simple illustrative maps, graphs, charts, and tables to more complex ones. It will prove helpful to progress from representations of things that the child has experienced to more remote illustrative materials.

Lack of Diversified Techniques in Organizing Information

Skill in organizing information so that it can be understood and retained is essential. Many techniques are necessary in order to relate the facts learned from reading so that their interrelationships can be studied. The comprehension abilities required in classifying, recognizing relationships, understanding major concepts and subordinate ideas, and establishing a sequence are related closely to the basic study skills of organization. Without these comprehension abilities, the child would find it difficult to learn the skills of organization. The child, for example, who cannot detect the difference between a major concept and the subordinate ideas will find outlining difficult. The one who does not have the ability to sense a sequence of events will find making a time-line a confusing enterprise. If a child is unable to classify ideas into reasonable groupings, he will run into trouble trying to tabulate information for further study on a two-way chart.

The difference between the comprehension abilities involved in sensing the organization of information and the basic study skills of organization is that the former is reasoning and restructuring information, and the latter is just the mechanics of ordering the information for further study.

In studying a science unit dealing with conservation of mineral resources, for example, the child may need to isolate and classify those ideas that deal with each of the resources discussed. He also must understand certain relationships between the nature of the mineral and the problem of conserving it. Uranium, coal, and petroleum are chemically changed in use, while aluminum, copper, and iron are not necessarily altered. The child may reason from these facts to certain generalizations concerning the conservation of each. This would be a high level of comprehension ability in the area of organization. The basic study skill may be arranging his findings in a two-way chart with each of the metals listed along the side and the various facts concerning it listed across the top, such as: where it is found, how it is mined, the way it is changed by use, and other facts. Then each bit of information may be put in its proper cell for future study. Skill in making such a chart is a basic study skill. The generalizations made from studying the chart, as well as gathering the information to make the chart, would be the result of what we have throughout termed *comprehension.*

The child needs to develop many ways of arranging his information, if he is to think effectively about the ideas involved. Basic study skills are taught in some reading programs from the start. When a child is told to record only the most important ideas for presentation to the class, he is making a rudimentary outline. He is making a two-way chart when he lists some animals he has read about in a third-grade reader along one side of his paper, while across the top of the paper, he puts such headings as: who its enemies are, how it protects itself, how it gets ready for winter, and what it eats. When the children list the order in which pictures for a box movie will be shown, they are establishing the forerunner of a time-line graph.

The remedial teacher who finds a disabled reader limited in this area of basic study skills needs only to suggest reading purposes that require organization and then show the child the most efficient mechanical methods to follow in recording his findings. He should be taught how to indicate major and subordinate areas in an outline, how to make a time-line, how to make a classification chart, and the like. There is no doubt that much of the instruction will be in the selection of the most efficient organization tool for the type of reasoning involved.

To summarize, the major problem for the remedial teacher when correcting a limitation in the basic study skills is to find exactly the skill in which the child is not sufficiently proficient and then give him the specific training he needs through instruction. Care must be taken to follow a reasonable sequence in developing the skill. Most basic study skills can be taught only in material that is written in a style and is read for purposes that the study skill serves. It would not, for example, make sense to ask a child to make an outline of a poem. It would be unwise also to try to teach the study skills of science using a fanciful tale. Probably many teachers will find in some of the modern basic readers with true content units the best material available for developing diversified basic study skills. Some teachers may prefer to use texts from the content fields as materials. In either approach, the teacher must teach the child the skills and give him enough practice in using each of them so that they become a permanent part of his reading equipment.

DEFICIENCIES IN READING CONTENT MATERIALS

In the intermediate grades and at more advanced educational levels, some students are found to lack the flexibility necessary to adjust reading procedures and abilities to the distinct purposes and materials of each content field. By *content field,* we mean any field that uses a specific type of material which requires unique language structures, vocabularies, or purposes; for example, shop manuals, scientific or arithmetical materials, poetry, or even cookbooks, and so forth. The adjustments are numerous and often subtle. Nonetheless, when the specific problem or problems are pinpointed, direct instruction focused on the problems will correct the lack of proficiency in a given field. Diagnoses of poor reading within a content field are accomplished best by informal procedures and on-the-job observation. Once the problem is located, the remedial work is done best by the teacher of the specific content field, with supportive help by the reading center, when needed.

The curricular materials of every field the child meets impose their own specific and unique demands upon his reading capabilities. Each field has unique reading problems. A fourth-grade child, for example, who has been reading stories for most of his three years of reading experience is confronted suddenly with a geography book. He has always read a story from the top of the first page on through several pages, uninterrupted. In the geography book, he starts at the top of the page in the customary manner. He reads about ten lines and then is told to look at figure 1 on page 12. He looks at figure 1 on page 12, and returning to the page he had just left, starts at the top of the page again. He has always done this. He reads ten lines that seem familiar and is asked to look at figure 1 on page 12. He says to himself that he has already looked at figure 1 on page 12, so he goes on reading down the page. Somewhat later he reads, "You noticed in figure 1 that. . . ." He had noticed no such things. No one had told him to look for them and he was unfamiliar with the ways of the geographer. These episodes are, of course, minor misunderstandings, but many reading disability cases are caused by an accumulation of such misunderstandings or faulty learnings, each small in itself.

The first indication that a student is having trouble in reading the materials in a specific subject usually comes from the teacher's observation of his classroom performance. She should check to see that the problem is not due to general reading disability but is limited to difficulty in reading the materials of the specific content area.

Strang (195) has outlined certain diagnostic procedures common to all content areas. Some of her material is summarized below in modified form:

SELF-APPRAISAL. To a large degree, responsibility for improvement rests with the pupil. Initiative to help himself is promoted by self-appraisal. When a pupil realizes the reading potentialities and reading goals that are possible and desirable for him, he tends to change his behavior so as to achieve them.

The teacher, acting as a sympathetic consultant, can aid the pupil in his appraisal. She raises questions about the pupil's reading tasks, his dissatisfactions with procedures, what reasons may exist for his inefficiency, and the ways to reach the desired improvement. The pupil is urged to discuss such questions freely with the teacher and to seek her aid in working out his reading problems. A frank discussion of the reading difficulty with an understanding listener usually clarifies it for both the pupil and the teacher. The best approach for beginning a face-to-face conference with a pupil is determined by what the teacher already knows about the child. The preparation for such a conference is important. To listen with understanding and to provide guidance when requested, the teacher should have organized all available relevant information about the pupil: school records, developmental history, school adjustment, test scores, interests, and so forth. The more complete the teacher's understanding is of the pupil's abilities, needs, and interests, the more helpful she can be in guiding him to analyze his reading difficulty.

OBSERVATION OF CLASSROOM ACTIVITIES. In any content field, diagnosis and remediation are intimately related to the instructional procedures. There is opportunity in nearly every class period to detect and correct reading difficulties. A well-conducted class period may reveal one or more of the following: (*a*) whether the relevant reading was done with a well-defined purpose; (*b*) the degree to which the essential vocabulary is understood; (*c*) whether the discussion shows that the concepts incorporated in the reading are clearly comprehended; (*d*) difficulties in applying comprehension abilities and study skills to the particular subject matter; (*e*) difficulties in interpreting pictures, charts, graphs, and tables; (*f*) difficulties with symbols or abbreviations; and (*g*) whether proper adjustment in reading procedure was made to the specific organization of the subject matter. As each difficulty is discovered, suggestions are made by the teacher and by the pupil for overcoming it. At times, there will be evidence indicating a need for individual corrective work with some pupils.

COMBINATION OF METHODS. Information from one or more diagnostic procedures is used by the teacher to guide her day-by-day instructional program and to obtain a comprehensive picture of an individual pupil's difficulties. Both the pupil and his reading teacher can learn much more about the reading process he uses in a content field by the following procedure: A passage is chosen from a textbook or reference book in the field. The teacher sits beside the pupil and observes his methods and notes his spontaneous comments. The meaning of the passage is discussed. When errors are made, the pupil is urged to try to recollect where and how he went wrong in comprehending the material. As Strang (195) notes, the pupil's suggestions on how to surmount his difficulty often are sound and practical. Also, having made the suggestions himself, the pupil generally is motivated to carry them out. In this kind of diagnostic procedure, the teacher can do much to guide the pupil toward insight into his difficulty through unobtrusive shaping of the discussion and by suggesting questions he might ponder. This technique, applicable to any subject, can be one of the best sources of diagnostic information.

GENERAL NATURE OF REMEDIAL INSTRUCTION. Certain principles are basic to successful remedial reading instruction in all the various subjects. An interest and purpose for reading in each field must be developed. When interest is keen and purpose is clear, the pupil will be motivated to understand his difficulties and to undertake with some enthusiasm the practice necessary for improvement. The remedial instruction should begin at the child's present level of proficiency. Practice materials should be a regular part of the reading assignments in the field. From the beginning, the teacher should make sure that the reading procedures used are appropriate for the material and the purposes for which it is read. Motivation for improvement is increased when the pupil cooperates with the teacher in planning the remedial work. Motivation is maintained more easily when the child sees his own day-by-day progress.

Some of the major difficulties encountered by the disabled reader are described in the sections that follow. The teacher should study the student's performance and determine which of these stumbling blocks is at the root of the problem. Then, working cooperatively with the disabled reader, a plan for correcting the problems should be formulated. The specific content fields to be discussed are the social studies, science, mathematics, and literature. These fields give a sampling of the diversified types of reading to which a student must be able to adjust.

Social Studies

Relatively many severe reading problems are encountered in the social studies. The pupil's understanding of historical, civic, economic, and geographic realities ordinarily must be gained through reading, since his direct experience in these areas tends to be restricted. The variety and amount of reading required is great. Some of this reading may be done rapidly for the main idea. Other materials and purposes demand slow, careful reading with attention devoted to closely packed, sometimes intricate, details. The degree of precision required for satisfactory results from much of the reading will fall between these two extremes.

SPECIAL VOCABULARY. Commonly encountered stumbling blocks in reading social studies material are the specialized terms and their accompanying concepts. These include unique words such as *cuneiform, plateau,* and *integration,* as well as proper names of people, places, and events. There also are words with specialized meanings when they occur in certain contexts. These include *mouth, cape, run, court,* and *balance.* Especially difficult are abstract terms such as *democracy, culture,* and *civilization.* Although a pupil may be able to pronounce some of these words without help, many of the meanings are learned only gradually and with the teacher's aid.

COMPLEX CONCEPTS. The concept gives meaning to an item of vocabulary. Consequently, the development of vocabulary meanings and the development of concepts progress hand in hand. In the social studies, many concepts, and consequently the word meanings, are very complex and difficult to learn. Extensive reading of appropriate materials helps this, but the number of topics to be covered should be restricted. Incentives to dig out meanings, clearing up misconceptions, and developing effective methods of procedure are given largely by the teacher.

SELECTION, EVALUATION, AND ORGANIZATION. The wide and extensive reading to achieve satisfactory progress in the social studies requires application of various kinds of comprehension and study skills. The student must be acquainted with source materials and their use in selecting pertinent information, be able to read critically and evaluate the selected materials, and be skillful in organizing the information to use in reports or discussions. These special skills were considered in detail earlier in this chapter.

READABILITY. The style of writing used in social studies textbooks frequently puts many obstacles before the reader. One instance of this is the many facts and ideas which are packed into a relatively small space without enough organizational clues in the form of headings, subheadings, and boldface or italic type to bring out clearly the relative importance of the different facts and ideas. Hence, there is little or no indication of which are worth learning. Yet to memorize all the details is neither possible nor desirable. Under such conditions, the pupil is inclined to stumble along, learning indiscriminately some facts and ideas, or even learn nothing at all.

In addition, the writers of social studies books frequently introduce specialized words without defining them. Too often they inject new ideas without clarifying them. It should be noted, however, that in some recently published texts, there has been distinct progress toward overcoming many of these shortcomings.

CONTENT AND SKILLS. Is it the teachers' responsibility to teach content or skills in the social studies? It is assumed that the teacher will provide practice on the skills needed along with instruction in social studies content. Too frequently this does not happen. The survey by Austin and Morrison (3) showed that teachers reported that they do not have time to teach everything. They felt it more important to cover subject matter than to teach the reading skills needed in the content areas. Herber (104) points out that this dichotomy of either content or skills is not necessary if the skills are taught as they are needed to read the assigned selections in the required textbook, and "if the skills are taught functionally *as* students read the required text, using the text as the vehicle for skills development" (p. 95). If this is done, content and skills are taught simultaneously. Skills should not be pulled out of context and taught separately.

HISTORY. Certain reading problems in the social studies are particularly apparent in the field of history. Three are of prime importance: *First,* the materials in history usually do not consider that the temporal order of events is not sensed readily by many pupils. *Second,* writers do not seem to appreciate that pupils tend to interpret everything in terms of present-day conditions. Consequently, it is difficult for pupils to see historical events in relation to the period when or the place where they occurred. This happens most frequently with the treatment of the historical predecessors of modern methods of communication, transportation, science, or living conditions in general. Good instruction requires that the pupils be furnished with as adequate a background as possible for interpreting past events in relation to the time and conditions in which they occurred. *Third,* the reading and interpretation of pictures, charts, maps, and related materials are specialized kinds of reading which develop relevant word meanings and concepts as well as provide information. Details for developing these skills were given earlier in this chapter.

GEOGRAPHY. The reading problems common to the social studies also occur in geography. Others more specifically related to reading geographical materials should be noted briefly. *First,* to understand geographical material requires appreciation of such human conditions as housing, clothing, food, occupations, and traditions; of such material conditions as the physical features of landscapes, climate, and vegetation; and of the relation between the two sets of conditions. *Second,* it is necessary for a pupil to maintain his geographic set in absorbing the contents, in verbal or quantitative form, which are relevant to a geographical unit. This set is made through preparation of the unit and definition of its purposes. *Third,* there is a problem in teaching the child to think concretely in terms of geographical location as he reads about different places and what goes on in them— such as methods of housing, transportation, and industry. *Fourth,* there is the problem of interrupted reading, as a geography text is organized so that it refers the child to material on other pages.

Science

For the child to understand the world in which he lives, he must learn some science. The variety of purposes for which science is read ranges from reading to gain general impressions and grasp relationships to reading to learn in detail the consecutive steps in an experiment, or to evaluate the conclusions arrived at in a class discussion. Many of the difficulties of reading science are due to the inherent difficulty of this material. Many of the problems encountered in reading science are similar to those met in the social studies. Others are unique to the science material, such as its purposes and emphases. Because of this, somewhat different reading abilities, skills, and techniques are required.

VOCABULARY. The language of science is precise and specific. Each branch of science—chemistry, biology or physics, etc.—uses its own vocabulary terms, as well as the basic vocabulary used in more general reading. Since these terms embody scientific concepts, it is necessary for the pupil to learn the essentials of scientific vocabulary in any area if he is to comprehend the material. Examples of rather highly specialized scientific terms are *electromagnet, molecule, gravity,* and *lever.* The pupil also must learn specialized meanings of general words used in a scientific context. Examples from physics are *scale, charge,* and the verb *conduct.*

CONCEPTS. Even the elementary concepts in science are sometimes complex and difficult to understand. Two examples are the concepts represented by the terms *magnetism* and *photosynthesis.* The degree to which concepts in science are grasped will depend upon the capabilities of the individual pupils, the clarity of the context in which the unfamiliar items of vocabulary occur, and the skill of the teacher in demonstrating and explaining them. Many reasonably concrete scientific concepts are readily demonstrated, explained, and understood, such as *electromagnetism* and *surface tension.* Many other scientific concepts are not subject to direct demonstration and therefore must be handled by means of verbal description and abstract explanation. These are difficult for the pupil to understand. Diagrams and similies sometimes are helpful in explaining or clarifying such concepts.

PICTURES AND DIAGRAMS. The reading and interpretation of pictures and diagrams in science tends to be inadequate without some form of systematic instruction. Ordinarily, an explanation of these pictures and diagrams is supplied in the accompanying legend as well as in the textual discussion of the facts and principles. Some children fail to relate this verbal discussion properly to the diagram or pictures. Abstract schematic diagrams themselves are still more difficult to read and interpret.

FOLLOWING DIRECTIONS. The directions to be followed in carrying out experiments in science are specific. Both children and adults seem to have much difficulty in following these printed directions. Yet the successful performance of the experiment requires that they be followed very carefully. This reading should therefore be done slowly, meticulously, and thoughtfully in order that the sequential order of the steps described may be followed. Ordinarily, difficulty does not arise because the pupil cannot read and understand the words and sentences, but rather because he does not follow them correctly, omits steps, or does them in the wrong order. Training in doing this better should receive more emphasis in instruction.

COMPREHENSION ABILITIES AND STUDY SKILLS. Remembering facts encountered is, on the whole, a minor aspect of reading science materials. More important is the recognition of relationships and the formulation of generalizations. The higher levels of comprehension in reading science materials can be achieved only when the pupil has learned to perceive the proper relationships among the pertinent facts. When this has been acquired, the pupil then can proceed to formulate his own statement of these relationships, i.e., to make a generalization. To achieve these ends, it is particularly important that the child learn to think while reading scientific materials. Skill in doing this is developed relatively slowly.

The abilities needed for comprehension and study are more or less constantly used in reading science materials. The particular skills employed in this will depend upon the nature of the material and the purpose for the reading. The pupil must be prepared to vary his procedures for the most effective reading. For instance, when working on a topical unit in science, he must read to select, evaluate, and organize, and this he cannot do unless he can grasp relationships and make generalizations.

Mathematics

Reading mathematical material presents a variety of problems, some of them highly specific. Frequently, there are more reading problems per page in mathematics than in any other subject. As noted for science, mathematics, too, has its own technical vocabulary (*numerator, quotient,* etc.). It also uses common words with a special meaning (*product, dividend, power*), employs complex concepts, and involves the study of relationships and the making of generalizations. Pictures and diagrams must be read and interpreted. Much of this reading is concerned with the exposition of processes, procedures, solving illustrative problems, and giving directions for assignments.

MEANING OF SYMBOLS. In arithmetic and other forms of mathematics, pupils must learn to attach meanings to highly abbreviated symbols such as $+$, $-$, $\div$, $=$, $\times$, $\sqrt{}$, and many others. At first the reading dealt with words as symbols; now they are condensed to "shorthand" signs. Thus, "is equal to" is represented by the symbol $=$. Also, pupils need to learn to recognize promptly many specialized abbreviations such as *lb., ft., yd., pk., min.,* to mention only a few. Meanings must also be assigned both to numbers encountered in verbal contexts and to those same numbers isolated in columns (problems in addition, subtraction, and multiplication). In this the pupil must comprehend the place value of numbers such as 429, the significance of 0 in such numbers as 30 and 0.4, and the meaning of common and decimal fractions. One prerequisite for a pupil to solve a mathematical problem is that he have as accurate a command of all the technical symbols it uses as if these concepts were expressed uneconomically in words. Without systematic instruction, many pupils make slow progress in acquiring sufficient skill to understand and properly manipulate these symbols, abbreviations, and numerals.

VERBAL PROBLEMS. The statement of a verbal mathematical problem is ordinarily extremely compact, divorced from concrete context, and involves complex relationships. Satisfactory reading of such a problem is achieved by slow, careful, precise progress, together with rereading and thinking. Besides a clear understanding of words and phrases, relevant facts must be selected and relationships between the pertinent words and phrases must be weighed in the whole problem. Reading verbal mathematical problems is one of the most difficult reading tasks encountered in the content areas. There will be little success without intensive concentration. The teacher should realize fully the reading difficulties the child faces. A good method for handling verbal problems is to encourage the pupil to adopt a pattern of procedure. The problem should be read to determine its nature and what processes should be used to solve it. Then it should be reread to select the relevant information and the processes to be used. The problem then should be solved and the answer checked for accuracy. To use this study procedure successfully the pupil must understand the number system and know the basic arithmetic facts discussed above. He also must possess a vocabulary foundation for quantitative reasoning and clues for the use of mathematical processes.

Literature

Unlike such areas as science, mathematics, and social studies, literature lacks a regular methodical sequence of content. Literary materials can be stories about men and women as well as animals, or are historical novels, poetry, plays or essays. To a considerable degree, the primary concern of teaching literature has been the development of reading interests and tastes. These will be considered in a later chapter. There are, however, certain problems in the reading of literary materials that are discussed here.

Ability to read literary materials profitably depends upon proficiency in many reading abilities. Smith (179) has emphasized that a major function of teaching literature is to develop the reading skills necessary for intelligent interpretation of an author's meaning, for sharing the moods he wishes his readers to feel, and for entering imaginatively into whatever experience he creates. These capabilities usually are those emphasized in the basic developmental reading program. They are refined, expanded, and perhaps supplemented with the teacher's guidance while reading literary materials. Proficiency in general reading ability is intimately related to success in literary achievement. The fundamentals of general reading ability as measured by standardized reading tests are concerned mainly with comprehension and vocabulary. Elden Bond (21) found that general comprehension (combined score from four tests) and general vocabulary (combined score from five tests) were related closely to literary acquaintance. In fact, this relationship (r = about .70) was much closer than that between literary acquaintance and any of the specialized reading abilities measured. We can state with confidence that the better a pupil's proficiency in general reading comprehension and the larger his vocabulary is, the more success he will have in reading literary materials. This is because both the tests and the books previously read have been primarily narrative, and literature is primarily narrative material.

BASIC READING ABILITIES. In a way, general comprehension and vocabulary knowledge are products of progress in the reading abilities developed in the basic reading program. As the program unfolds, pupils will progress in acquiring word-recognition techniques, reading by thought units, and in techniques for increasing word knowledge, basic comprehension abilities, and special comprehension abilities. To read literary materials well at any grade level, the pupil should have made normal progress in acquiring these fundamental reading abilities taught in the basic course. In other words, the pupil will be able to read literary material satisfactorily at the reading level he has reached in the basic abilities, but not much higher.

ENRICHMENT OF MEANINGS. The profit gained from reading literary materials is in great part dependent upon the enrichment of meanings it brings. Important ways of enriching meanings are to be found almost anywhere in literature. One of these is a full appreciation of descriptive words, especially words associated with sensory impressions, with sights, sounds, taste, touch, and smell. Meanings also are enhanced through skill in interpreting figures of speech and symbolic expressions. The reader may need to draw upon his previous experience to interpret an illusion and to gain deeper insight into what is presented. Frequently the effects of writing depend on the reader's imaginative penetration into mere hints and suggestions. Another aspect of reading literary material is the provocation of moods. Smith's (180) example illustrates this:

> Alone in the night
> On a dark hill
> With pines around me
> Spicy and still.

Here the reader is asked to respond to the author's mood.

GENERAL COMMENT. The foundations for successful reading of literature consist of the basic reading abilities and comprehension abilities presented in a broad developmental reading program. These are refined, expanded, and supplemented in reading literary materials. Only as children learn the techniques of reading literature under a teacher's skillful guidance, can they be expected to read literature with understanding and pleasure.

In addition to the general level of reading ability, there are specific types of comprehension closely related to continued growth in reading literature. The two specific comprehension abilities, discussed earlier in this chapter, essential to success in reading the various types of materials in literature, are *reading to interpret* and *reading to appreciate*. The teacher must check these two specific types of comprehension when diagnosing the student with difficulty in reading and enjoying literature. These two types of comprehension are needed to read poetry, narratives, drama, or essays. The authors suggest that the readers of this book review the suggestions for correcting weaknesses in these two comprehension abilities.

No other field has as big a problem in diversifying approaches to reading its materials as does literature. The skills needed for reading a drama are different from those needed for reading poetry, although both include sensory impressions, mood, and imagination. Both are related to proficiency in oral reading. Neither drama nor poetry should be read at a constant or rapid rate. For example, in the phrase, "the murmuring pines and the hemlocks," the reader should pause and let his imagination take over. He should sense the movement of the trees, smell the aroma, feel the rug of needles under foot, hear the gentle wind, see the sunlight breaking through the branches, and see the pattern of shadows on the ground.

The next two chapters will deal with three specific reading difficulties directly related to problems faced by literature teachers. One of these is a deficiency in the general rate of comprehension and the flexibility of rate needed. Another problem especially related to drama and poetry is deficiency in oral reading. The third deals with the student who does not have lasting interest in reading or who is a reluctant reader. These three reading disabilities must be corrected if reading literature is to become a permanent accomplishment for personal development and enjoyment.

SUMMARY

Three major groups of specific remedial problems are discussed in this chapter: the disabled reader who is limited in one or more types of comprehension, the one who has failed to develop some of the basic study skills, and the one who is an ineffective reader of content materials but who is in all other respects a competent reader. Each of these disabled readers needs remedial help to overcome a specific defect.

The usual method of correcting a specific type of comprehension difficulty is to have the disabled reader read material in a well-graded, basic reader at the appropriate level of difficulty for him. The purposes for reading the material should be such that the ability in which he is limited is stressed. The reasons for reading should be understood by the child before the reading is done and there should be checks on the accuracy of the reading at the end. These check questions should reflect the specific comprehension ability being emphasized. The specific comprehension abilities discussed here were reading to retain factual information, reading to sense the organization of information, to judge the authenticity and relevance of information, to interpret the information given, and to appreciate.

The methods suggested for correcting limitations in basic study skills were to find exactly the skill in which the disabled reader was ineffective and then to teach that skill and give him enough practice to make it permanent. The basic study skills discussed were location of sources of information, use of basic references, interpretation of pictorial and tabular materials, and methods of organizing information.

Reading skills and abilities need to be adjusted to each subject matter field. The comprehension abilities employed and the rate of reading depend on the nature and organization of the material, its difficulty, and the purpose for which the reading is to be done.

Social studies, science, mathematics, and literature are the four content fields considered. They involve a wide range of materials to be read, and somewhat different reading abilities are required in each field. Problems that arise in each were considered briefly.

SELECTED READINGS

BURMEISTER, L. E., *Reading Strategies for Secondary School Teachers,* chaps. 7, 8, 9. Reading, Mass.: Addison-Wesley, 1974.

CUSHENBERY, DONALD C., *Reading Improvement in the Elementary School,* chap. 7. West Nyack, N. Y.: Parker, 1969.

EARLE, R. A., *Teaching Reading and Mathematics.* Newark, Del.: International Reading Association, 1976.

GRAY, LILLIAN, *Teaching Children to Read* (3rd ed.), chap. 12. New York: Ronald Press, 1963.

HARRIS, ALBERT J., and EDWARD R. SIPAY, eds., *Readings on Reading Instruction* (2nd ed.), chap. 11. New York: David McKay, 1972.

————, *Effective Teaching of Reading* (2nd ed.), chap. 12. New York: David McKay, 1971.

HERBER, H. L., ed., *Developing Study Skills in Secondary Schools.* Newark, Del.: International Reading Association, 1965.

————, *Improving Reading in Science.* Newark, Del.: International Reading Association, 1976.

KALUGER, GEORGE, and CLIFFORD J. KOLSON, *Reading and Learning Disabilities,* chap. 14. Columbus, Ohio: Charles E. Merrill, 1969.

MILLER, WILMA H., *Diagnosis and Correction of Reading Difficulties in Secondary School Students,* chap. 8. New York: Center of Applied Research in Education, 1973.

ROBINSON, H. A., *Teaching Reading and Study Strategies,* chaps. 6, 7, 8, 9, 10. Boston: Allyn and Bacon, 1975.

SMITH, HENRY P., and EMERALD V. DECHANT, *Psychology in Teaching Reading* (2nd ed.), chap. 12. Englewood Cliffs, N. J.: Prentice-Hall, 1977.

SPACHE, GEORGE D., *Toward Better Reading,* chap. 16. Champaign, Ill.: Garrard, 1968.

TINKER, MILES A., and CONSTANCE M. MCCULLOUGH, *Teaching Elementary Reading* (4th ed.), chaps. 10, 13. Englewood Cliffs, N.J: Prentice-Hall, 1975.

Correcting
Reading Rates
and
Oral Reading
Difficulties

Two reading difficulties related to reading comprehension concern many people. Adults and students alike wonder how fast they can or should read. There also are many adults and students who feel uncomfortable in oral reading situations and often rightly so, in view of their lack of skill. Both of these reading difficulties often persist, even though the reader so disabled is mature in all other aspects of reading growth. Of course no one can be a rapid reader or an effective oral reader if he does not have the basic word-recognition skills and the basic comprehension abilities. Correcting inefficient rates of comprehension and overcoming ineffective oral reading is discussed in this chapter.

CORRECTING INEFFICIENT RATES OF COMPREHENSION

In recent years, much attention has been devoted to rapid reading in magazine articles and newspapers and on radio and television programs. The unsophisticated individual gains the impression that all he has to do to improve his reading is to read faster. Thus speed reading courses have become profitable business. Such courses are advertised widely in newspapers, magazines, and television and radio commercials. Concern for rate of reading also is reflected in the writings of professional educators. Public interest is heightened by enticing promises to teach people to read 1,000 or even up to 20,000 words per minute with good comprehension.

Since there is so much to read today and so much pressure to keep informed, the ability to read rapidly is a valuable asset. Increasing one's reading speed by twenty-five to fifty percent will save much time. Some readers can improve their rate by fifty to one hundred percent.

Most people read unnecessarily slowly. It is best to read any material, whether a novel, business report, medical journal, textbook, or other material, as rapidly as possible with understanding. As we shall see below, it is possible to increase one's rate of reading by a considerable degree without loss of comprehension, but not from 12,000 to 20,000 words per minute. These claims are unrealistic. The question, "How fast should I read," can have no single answer. But it is safe to say that most of us should read much faster than we presently do. We will discuss what is involved in becoming a rapid reader.

Certain writers seem to believe that speed of reading is a valid measure of reading performance in itself, even when it is divorced from comprehension. The fact is that a measure of the rate in which words are recognized as words, with no reference to apprehending their meanings and relationships, yields a score of little or no significance in real life. Put plainly, "reading" without comprehension is not reading. The only practical and adequate definition of rate of reading is to redefine it as the *rate of comprehension* of printed and written material. This is the definition followed in this book. To measure speed of reading, therefore, one must measure the rate with which material is comprehended. We also must bear in mind that comprehension itself is always to be considered in relation to the purpose for which the reading is done. In practice, it becomes important to know the rate at which a particular pupil grasps the general ideas in a story, or the rate at which he comprehends an exposition of history or science material, or the like. In tests, rate of reading is rate of comprehending as measured in the particular test. In consequence, standardized tests for speed of reading have certain limitations. The materials in such tests provide inadequate samples of all the different materials pupils must read; the speed of reading is measured for one only.

In some discussions it is assumed that speed of reading is a general ability that somehow transfers readily to the reading of a wide variety of materials. There is no such general speed of reading ability. Even for the proficient reader, the rate of reading is fairly specific to a particular reading situation.

Every teacher must realize that rapid reading in itself does not produce better understanding. A fast rate of comprehension is possible only if the pupil possesses the abilities necessary for clear and rapid understanding.

An uninformed person is likely to believe that a fast reader is inaccurate and poor in comprehension while a slow reader is accurate and comprehends better. Research on this question emphatically fails to substantiate this belief. There is the contrasting opinion that fast reading is good reading and that slowness makes for poor reading. Although some fast readers do comprehend better than slow readers, there are many exceptions: Fast readers are not always good readers.

In evaluating the data on rate related to comprehension, one should keep in mind that there is no general speed of reading skill nor any one comprehension skill. These skills are specific, varying with the kind of material and purpose of reading (Tinker, 210; Pressey and Pressey, 157; Gates, 81; Shores, 175; Spache, 186). Improvement in rate in one type of reading is not likely to transfer to any significant extent to all reading. It probably operates only in the particular type of material employed for the training. For example, improvement in rate of reading literature will not necessarily transfer appreciably and automatically to reading science.

The teacher should realize that neither slow nor fast reading by itself produces proper understanding. Accelerating reading in itself does not improve comprehension. For some pupils it may even decrease it. The best rate for a particular child to read a specific set of material is pretty much an individual matter to be determined by individual diagnosis. Although the fast readers among mature readers usually comprehend better, there are exceptions. The best indications are that a program to improve speed of reading would be advantageous to most pupils who are advanced in the basic reading abilities, provided speed is not pushed to where adequate comprehension is impossible. Any general program for accelerating speed of reading for all pupils in a class is inadvisable. Finally, the true relationship may be that the child who has the necessary akills and abilities to comprehend well also has those necessary to read faster. So drill on speed of reading per se cannot be expected to be worthwhile. There are students, however, who have habits in silent reading that prevent them from adjusting their rate to the purpose and difficulty of the material. They always read at an undesirably slow rate.

Diagnosing Inefficient Rates of Comprehension

Taking into account what has been said above makes it appear hazardous to specify average rates of comprehension for the different grade levels. In a given grade, the average rate may be 290 words per minute for reading in one situation and only 140 words in another. It should be remembered that when average rates are given, they are for reading a specific kind of material for a set purpose. The published averages are usually for relatively easy materials in some reading test. They are not to be interpreted as norms for all kinds of material read for different purposes. While standardized tests with norms give some information, most of the diagnosis must be gained from informal appraisals.

STANDARDIZED TESTS. Standardized tests designed for measuring reading ability in the primary grades ordinarily are not concerned with speed. In fact, it is unwise to stress speed of reading during the first three years in school. The emphasis should be on developing such things as sight vocabulary, word-recognition techniques, reading by thought units, vocabulary knowledge, and comprehension. Any attempt to measure speed at these levels might lead to misplaced pressure on speeded reading, before acquiring the basic techniques upon which smooth, rapid reading depends.

Most standardized tests are designed to measure speed of reading of relatively easy materials for a set purpose. The vocabulary concepts and sentence structures are simple. These tests should provide an opportunity for pupils to show their maximum speed of reading *specific, easy materials.* When the purpose is varied, as in the four types of *Gates Basic Reading Tests,* the speed scores will reveal, to some degree, the pupil's versatility in adapting speed to purpose when the material is easy.

Measures of speed of reading on standardized tests have specific limitations. As noted above, the tests use very simple specific materials, and the purpose for which the reading is done is limited. Earlier discussion has indicated that speed on such tests is not closely related to speed in reading other kinds of materials. These tests are useful, therefore, only to gain some preliminary information about speed of reading. They are not appropriate for finding out the speed at which material in basic or supplementary texts will be read. Informal tests will be needed for this.

INFORMAL DIAGNOSIS. For the most part, informal tests of reading rate are more useful for diagnostic purposes than standardized tests. When the test results are used to guide instruction, the teacher will want to know the rate at which a pupil can read material in the basic text or in units on history, or science, or geography, or another field. She also will want to know how versatile the pupil is in adapting his speed to changes in difficulty and to the varying purposes for the reading. These objectives can be reached only through informal tests.

Informal rate-of-reading tests are constructed easily. The teacher merely selects from a text, supplementary reader, or a book employed in a unit, a series of consecutive paragraphs of the difficulty and complexity desired. The length of the test will vary with the type of material, the child's reading level, and the difficulty of the material. Ordinarily, the selection will contain from about 400 to 800 words. The longer selections may be used for more mature readers and for less exacting reading tasks.

There should be a set of comprehension questions for the child to answer when the reading is completed. These questions may be modeled on those in workbooks. The nature and number of the questions should be determined by the purpose for the reading. When reading is for getting the main idea, the pupil may be asked to check the correct answer out of five listed. When reading to answer specific questions, there may be six or eight questions. If the purpose is to note important details, there may be ten or twelve questions. Unless comprehension is checked, a child may skip through the material to make a good record and not understand it adequately.

The purpose for the reading should be understood by the pupil before starting to read a selection. If individual testing is done, the child may read directly from a book. The number of words read per minute for two or three minutes of reading is computed.

If an entire class is to be tested at the same time, the selection should be mimeographed. A definite time limit, short enough so that the fast readers cannot quite finish, is set. Each pupil marks where he is when time is called and then counts the words read. Or, all the pupils may be allowed to finish the selection. Each student copies down the last number, indicating elapsed time, that the teacher has listed on the chalkboard. The teacher changes the figure on the board at the end of every ten seconds. This method of timing is preferred, since the questions to be answered cover the entire selection.

INTERPRETATIONS OF DIAGNOSIS. Grade or centile norms are usually given for standardized tests. By consulting these, the teacher is able to discover whether the pupil is reading unduly slowly for the type of material used and for the purpose set by the test. The scores identify pupils who are fast and accurate, fast and inaccurate, slow and accurate, slow and inaccurate, and so forth.

In using the informal rate tests, the teacher also can take into account both rate and degree of comprehension. After testing several children, both good and poor readers, the teacher will have data to show whether a particular child reads relatively slowly or fast in a specific reading situation. From the scores on comprehension she also will be able to note accuracy of comprehension. Good comprehension is represented by about eighty-five percent accuracy; average comprehension by about seventy percent; and poor comprehension by about fifty percent or less.

Diagnosis always should consider comprehension along with rate. If the rate is high and comprehension low, or both rate and comprehension are low, exercises to increase rate are *not indicated*. But when rate is average or low and comprehension high, the pupil undoubtedly will profit by a program to increase his speed of reading.

As already indicated, the proficient reader will adjust his rate to the difficulty of the material, to the nature of the material and to the purpose of the reading. The pupil who uses only one rate will encounter many difficulties. If the habitual rate is fast, it is not suitable for reading difficult materials in content areas; if it is a slow, plodding rate, it is not suitable for story reading and other easy materials. Similarly, when the purpose is to grasp the main idea, the rate should be faster than when it is to note the important details.

Degree of versatility in adjusting rate may be ascertained as follows: (*a*) by use of informal tests, as described above, the rates for reading materials at several levels of difficulty and complexity may be determined; (*b*) the rates for reading a single selection for different purposes may be measured. First, have the pupil read it for the general idea, then reread it to find the answers to certain questions, then read it again to note the important details. If about the same rate, either fast or slow, is used in all reading, remedial instruction to develop the ability to adjust speed of reading to fit the situation is indicated.

General Remediation for Inefficient Rates of Comprehension

To be effective, a program for increasing speed of reading must be organized carefully and must be temporarily the major instructional objective. The program should be confined to those pupils who show prospects of improving. Any attempt to increase the reading speed of mentally dull children or of those with a limiting or complex disability, will lead to confusion and discouragement rather than to more efficient reading.

MATERIALS. Relatively easy material should be used, particularly in the early stages of the program. It should contain *very few* if any unfamiliar words. The difficulty level of the material should be one to two grades below the average reading grade level of the pupil. In general, the material should be selected from books other than the basic texts. Temporarily, other kinds of reading should be curtailed or eliminated, such as reading to study, and especially oral reading. Only when there is considerable improvement in speed of reading the easy materials is it safe to introduce *gradually* the more difficult types of reading. It is important to make this transition in order to get the transfer to appropriately rapid reading of regular classroom materials. The transition should be made under the teacher's observation and guidance, otherwise it may be only partial or nonexistent. It is possible for a child to learn to read easy material rapidly but not transfer this to other instructional materials.

In the early stages of the speeded program, there should be little emphasis on comprehension checks. The comprehension exercises should not be such that they delay rapid perception or interrupt the flow of ideas. It is enough in the early stages of the program merely to ask the pupil what a story is about. When rapid recognition of words and smooth phrasing become habitual, comprehension will improve. It then will be safe to place more emphasis on comprehension checks. Each exercise can be followed by five or six questions on its content. Rapid reading with adequate comprehension is, of course, the goal sought.

MOTIVATION. In any program for increasing speed of reading, a variety of incentives is necessary if the pupil is to be motivated. Without motivation, a pupil will not feel any urgency to read faster and is not likely to do so. Proper incentives include the following: (*a*) The reading material used should be interesting *to the pupil.* The interested child is a motivated one. Other things being equal, he will be anxious to reach quickly the end of an interesting story to find out what happened. (*b*) A daily record of results should be kept. The teacher should greet any evidence of improvement with enthusiasm. Gains that are seen and appreciated will motivate the child to even greater effort. (*c*) Avoid fatigue and boredom. The exercises should be introduced with zest and in such a manner that the child will wish and expect to improve. Any sign that he is tired or annoyed call for discontinuing the exercises until he shows a more positive attitude. (*d*) The teacher's cheerful and sympathetic guidance will help maintain motivation. At times, this will mean working alone with a pupil to provide just the help and encouragement he needs. This is particularly important during the periods when no discernible gains can be observed, and the child becomes discouraged. (*e*) Allowing the child to participate with the teacher in organizing his remedial program will aid his motivation. The benefits he will enjoy when he can read faster are discussed with him. His special difficulties are talked over, and the plans for improvement are worked out jointly by teacher and pupil. As obstacles arise or old habits crop up, procedures for eliminating them also are worked out together. The more clearly the pupil understands his difficulties and the more he participates in the remedial planning, the better his motivation will be for overcoming the handicaps. (*f*) The purpose for each exercise should be understood. Reading without a purpose—and this means a clearly understood purpose—cannot be well-motivated reading. Sometimes pupils may be reading with more attention to details than is necessary. A talk about this with the pupil will show him what he is doing wrong and how to correct it. (*g*) When improved speed has been acquired through special exercises, incentives should be provided to motivate a transfer of the faster reading to leisure reading and to school subjects. All sorts of encouragement should be used. Examples are, praise for the number of stories or books read for enjoyment, discussion of the benefits of fast reading, and emphasis on doing class assignments speedily. The carry-over of the new habits to all types of reading will be promoted by training in flexibility. (*h*) After the special instruction for increasing rate of reading is completed, the teacher must be alert to relapses to the old slower rates. Motivation to maintain fast reading may be provided by special speed tests at periodic intervals, together with class discussions on the importance of adjusting speed to purposes and materials.

WORKING AGAINST TIME. Practically everyone can read faster if he is inclined to, or if he has an incentive to do so. As already noted, most pupils coast along at a comfortable rate in their reading. With the proper setting which encourages a pupil to step up his speed of reading and with well-organized practice day by day, real progress can be achieved.

An effective and much-used technique for increasing speed of reading is to work against time. Relatively easy material, a grade or so in difficulty below the pupil's grade placement, for example, is selected for the beginning exercises. These early exercises should be about 350 to 400 words in length. They may be mimeographed on one page. When the teacher is working with a single pupil, his reading may be done directly from a book or magazine. Five or six comprehension questions are arranged on a separate sheet. These questions should be relatively easy, dealing with the general ideas in the story. Thus, for a story about certain animals seen on a trip through the woods: "What did Mary see in the woods?" "What were they doing?" After the story is finished, it is taken away and the questions are answered. Comprehension probably will suffer during the early exercises but will improve as time goes on.

Each exercise should be introduced under as favorable conditions as possible. The purpose of the reading is made clear to the pupil. The setting should be such that the pupil will be eager to read as fast as possible with understanding. He should expect to improve over previous exercises. The teacher times the reading and computes the number of words per minute as his score. The pupil should be shown how to plot his scores on a simple graph so that he will see his gains. When little or no gain is achieved for a time, the teacher should be sympathetic and encouraging. If several pupils are tested together, the teacher can mark the time on the chalkboard every ten seconds. As each pupil finishes, he notes on his paper the time shown on the board.

Two exercises per day will provide enough pressure for this kind of work, and they should be separated by an hour or so. This *spaced learning* will be more effective than several exercises, one after another. After the first few exercises, comprehension should be adequate. As the program gets well under way, no pupil should be pushed to read faster than he can comprehend.

As the program continues and the pupil has gained speed in reading easy material, the teacher must help him make the transfer to regular school materials and to recreational reading. Gradually, more and more of the materials for the exercises are taken from books comparable to those used in class work. The exercises should become longer. At the same time, standards of comprehension are stepped up but always should remain appropriate to the purpose of the reading. The pupil also should be urged to do all his reading at a faster pace, whether in school books, newspapers, magazines, or story books.

MECHANICAL DEVICES. A number of mechanical devices have been developed and promoted for increasing speed of reading. One which has found wide usage is the Harvard Reading Films (or adaptations of the principle). It is a motion-picture method in which phrases, grouped in thought units, appear on a screen in bold-faced type on a faint printing of the whole page of connected material. The rate at which the phrases succeed one another can be varied by adjusting the speed control of the projector. A variety of other mechanical devices are available to pace the reader by moving a shutter, line by line, over the material being read. Or, a moving slot travels across the lines of print from left to right, covering and uncovering material as it goes. The reader is expected to keep up with the shutter. The rate of moving the shutter may be varied from slow to fast. In one machine, a shadow from a wire moves down the page of print. The reader tries to keep ahead of the shadow. The trade names of some of these machines are Controlled Reader, Reading Accelerator, Reading Rate Controller, Rate Reader, and Reading Board. The same goal may be reached by a push-card method described by Blair (18). The teacher pushes a large card from the top to bottom of a page while the reader is supposed to keep ahead of the card. The rate of moving the card can be varied to suit the needs of the particular pupil.

The Flashmeter and other short exposure devices known by the general name, tachistoscopes, are used to flash number series and words upon a screen for a brief interval. The aim of this technique is to develop quick perception and to increase the span of recognition, and hence the speed of reading. Flash cards may be used instead of a tachistoscope. However, Anderson and Dearborn (1) are doubtful that tachistoscopic training increases speed of reading. They conclude that the time might be spent better on promoting growth in comprehension. But Brown (31), on the other hand, describes and supports the alleged advantages of using the tachistoscope to improve reading, including rate. His report, and others like it, fail to take into account the role of other factors in an experimental test program, such as motivation to improve vocabulary, comprehension training, and the like. In a carefully controlled experiment, Manolakes (139), checked the influence of tachistoscopic training on improvement of eye movements and hence on speed of reading. When the effects of other factors were isolated, he found that the use of the tachistoscope had no effect upon reading performance. In a more recent study, Bormuth and Aker (28) using sixth-grade pupils, investigated the influence of tachistoscopic training on reading performance. All other factors in the experiment were controlled carefully. They found that the tachistoscopic training over a period of twenty weeks was ineffective in improving rate of reading, comprehension or vocabulary. Jones and Van Why (117) also found that tachistoscopic training over a period of three months had no effect on reading rate and comprehension with fourth- and fifth-grade pupils. An evaluation of the entire body of relevant literature by Tinker (211) suggests that tachistoscopic training to improve rate of reading is of questionable value.

In every study evaluating the use of machines, it has been found that they are no more effective in increasing speed of reading than are less complicated but sound classroom procedures. Cason (37), working with third-grade children, found significant gains: (*a*) by use of Metronoscope, (*b*) by well-motivated free reading in the library, and (*c*) by use of special exercises marked up into phrase units. The gains proved to be just as good by one method as any other. Her analysis indicated no benefit from the machine. Westover (225) found that college students who used ordinary materials and methods in a well-motivated, speed-up program made just as large gains as students using a modified Metronoscope.

One argument for use of machines is that pupils are interested in the use of the device and thus highly motivated. This is true. But even so, such children make no greater gains than those taught by regular methods. There is always a possibility that some child will improve with machine training but not by ordinary methods, though no investigation has shown this to be so.

In general, it seems that programs for improving speed of reading can be just as satisfactory without use of elaborate machines. This assumes that the materials are carefully selected, the program of training properly organized, and the instruction effectively carried out. If the teacher is able to provide the incentives which will motivate the pupil, machines or other gadgets are not necessary to achieve satisfactory gains in speed of reading. In other words, use of certain machines does increase speed of reading, but their use is not necessary to get equivalent gains.

There are two other drawbacks to mechanical gadgets to increase speed of reading: (*a*) the machines are expensive; (*b*) the use of machines too often becomes a ritual and overemphasizes the mechanical aspects of speeded reading over the more important processes of comprehension and thinking that results from reading.

Remediation for Specific Types of Inefficient Rates

Disabled readers deficient in the basic word-recognition skills and basic comprehension abilities are classified as having limiting or complex disabilities. These basic problems, which preclude all types of further reading growth, must be corrected before using any exercises to increase rate of reading. The remedial training needed for *basic word-recognition difficulties* is discussed in chapters 9 and 10. The correction of *basic comprehension deficiencies* is discussed in chapter 13.

There are two basic problems included in the discussion of remediation of specific types of rate problems, the overanalytical reader and the word-by-word reader. Both will profit from programs to increase rate, and therefore the correction of these two types of disabilities and improvement in rate can be done concurrently. The remediation of these disabilities includes rapid-exposure techniques and rapid-reading exercises. For this reason, these disabilities are included in the following list of specific types of inefficient rates of reading to be discussed:

1. The overanalytical reader

2. The word-by-word reader

3. The reader with faulty habits

4. The reader with faulty eye movements

5. The reader with excessive vocalization

6. The inflexible reader

THE OVERANALYTICAL READER. There are two types of overanalytical readers. One has a tendency to analyze words he already knows as sight words. The second type of overanalysis is a tendency to break words into too many parts. Such a disabled reader, for example, may use a letter-by-letter sounding technique or he may not use the rapid technique of recognizing the largest known parts within the word he is trying to identify. The remedial treatment for both types of overanalytical problems should be the training given in the section on treating *overanalytical habits* in chapter 10 and also, the *general remediation for inefficient rates of comprehension* given in this chapter. For this type of slow reader, tachistoscopes or other rapid-exposure devices are useful.

THE WORD-BY-WORD READER. The word-by-word reader is one who has failed to learn to read in thought units. He may not be able to recognize a group of three or four words at a glance. If so, the rapid-recognition training with rapid-exposure techniques is useful. But he may not be able to group the words into thought units as he reads connected material. In this case, he should be given the training suggested under the heading, *thought units,* in chapter 13. He also should be given the training suggested under the heading, *general remediation for inefficient rates of comprehension,* in this chapter. It should be noted that in chapter 13, the use of rapid-exposure techniques is recommended for reading in thought units.

THE READER WITH FAULTY HABITS. Some children have the habit of moving the finger or pointer along the line of print to guide their reading. Although justified with some children in early stages of learning or remedial work, the practice should be discarded as soon as feasible. Continued habitual use of such crutches will hinder development of rapid reading.

The best remedial technique to use with this habit is to discuss the problem with the student and then require him to hold the book with both hands. Continuing to point, while holding the book with both hands will then be awkward for him, and to move his fingers along the print will remind him that he is pointing again.

Another faulty habit is one called head movements. Instead of sweeping along the line of print with appropriate eye movements, the student moves his head from left to right. This is stopped by explaining the problem to the student and then asking him to rest his chin on one hand as he attempts to read more rapidly. This practice will warn him if he moves his head again.

Many children develop a congenial, meandering way of reading that is considerably below the rate at which they might read with both understanding and pleasure. When this becomes habitual, as frequently happens, it is a handicap to proficient reading. This easygoing dawdling permits attention to wander and fosters daydreaming. In addition, the child covers an inadequate amount of material in an allotted time. When unduly slow reading is really dawdling, exercises to promote an appropriate faster rate should be provided. In any reading, the correct rate is the fastest for the situation which produces proper comprehension. The general approaches to increasing rate of comprehension usually will overcome habitual dawdling.

THE READER WITH FAULTY EYE MOVEMENTS. Much space in the literature has been devoted to the role of eye movements in reading, and the relation of eye-movement patterns to speed of reading. In particular, it has been pointed out that rapid reading is accompanied by a few fixations and few regressions per line of print. This has led to the use of many gadgets and techniques to train eye movements for increasing reading speed. The training is designed to produce reading with few fixations and no regressions on each line read. This is a misplaced emphasis, for "good" eye-movement patterns are symptoms of reading efficiency, not contributors to it.

Furthermore, exercises in "training" eye movements tend to be mechanical and emphasize speed of reading rather than rate of comprehension. In fact, when comprehension is improved by the procedures described in this book, it will be automatically reflected in improved eye-movement sequences and faster reading.

THE READER WITH EXCESSIVE VOCALIZATION. In the early stages of silent reading in the primary grades, many children tend to articulate words. At this level, vocalization does not slow down speed of silent reading for the child can read no faster than he can talk. Later, as reading skill develops, vocalization becomes a handicap to improving speed of silent reading. With some children, the habit of pronouncing each word is so strong that it persists to adulthood if not corrected. The words may be whispered, or the lips and vocal organs may form the words without any sound, or the words may be formed mentally as inner speech with little or no movement of the speech organs. Whatever form the articulation or inner speech takes, it is time-consuming. As long as the habit persists, silent reading can be no faster than the words can be articulated. Until vocalizing is eliminated at least in part, there can be little improvement in speed of reading. For most rapid reading, the vocalization must be either greatly reduced or eliminated.

The teacher may detect vocalization by *direct observation.* The pupil reads a story silently while the teacher observes the amount of movement occurring in the speech mechanism. The pupil may whisper loudly, whisper faintly, move lips with no sound, or neither move lips nor whisper, but have movements of the throat in the region of the vocal chords. The whispering or lip movements easily are noted. Some practice is required to detect vibration in the vocal cords. The teacher places the tips of her fingers against the child's throat about half way between the chin and collar bone. Then she has him read aloud and feels the movement. Then the child reads silently without vocalizing, this movement should become so slight that it cannot be felt. If there is no observable whispering, lip movements, or throat vibrations, ordinarily there is insufficient vocalization to interfere with development of a satisfactory rate of reading.

Proper silent reading must be something other than inaudible oral reading. One method of decreasing extreme vocalizing during silent reading is to make it impossible for the speech mechanism to pronounce words. If a child is required to hold an object between his teeth, it is very awkward and unnatural for him. It is much better to have the student place his hand against his throat so that he can feel any vocalization movement as he reads. Ordinarily, such devices are not necessary, or they may intefere rather than help. It is better to tell the child that saying words to himself hinders rapid reading, and that such verbalization can be eliminated. He is told that, to read faster, he must not say the words to himself or move his lips or tongue He must try to read fast.

A good technique for eliminating vocalization is to give the child reading material which is very easy and extemely interesting, with practically no unfamiliar words. If the material is interesting and exciting, there will be motivation for rapid reading. The motivation should be such that the child will want to tear through the story at a fast clip to find out what happens. He is urged to do this. Particularly at first, books with short stories or mysteries should be used. These materials are valuable in the early stages of using fast reading to overcome vocalization. When a satisfactory rate of reading becomes habitual, the child can be guided to more diversified materials.

A rapid reader cannot vocalize since it takes too long to articulate the words. When a child gets a good start in reading these easy stories, he should be encouraged in every way to race through them as rapidly as possible. For a while he may get little meaning, but at this stage this is unimportant. With the rapid reading, vocalization will diminish. When vocalization has been reduced to a minimum, better comprehension will return. Actually, vocalization during silent reading is oral reading without speaking the words out loud. In many cases it may be advisable to avoid regular oral reading while eliminating the vocalizing. This will help to de-emphasize articulation.

THE INFLEXIBLE READER. It already has been noted that *relatively* rapid reading is desired in any area of reading. That is, the reading should be at as fast a rate as the material can be comprehended. Although a properly fast rate of reading mathematical materials is relatively very slow, some pupils still read such materials at an undesirably slow rate. The same is true for areas such as science and social studies. Whatever the material and purpose, there can be unnecessarily slow or fast rate of progress. A rapid rate of reading in itself has no particular value. The proficient reader will have several speeds, each of which can be used as the occasion demands. An essential part of the instructional program is to see that pupils acquire these speeds and gain skill in using them appropriately. The emphasis should be on making pupils adaptable, versatile readers who are able to adjust their rates to the nature and difficulty of the material and to the purpose of the reading. The goal is to *comprehend* at as fast a rate as possible. The best way to teach a child to comprehend at an appropriate rate is to furnish him with the skills and concepts to understand properly what he is to read. When this is done, he will learn to understand rapidly what he reads. Several aspects of this problem need attention.

Braam (29) has shown that, in addition to increasing reading rate, it is possible to improve flexibility in reading. He used a group of seventy-one college-bound high school seniors (presumably gifted). They were given an intensive six-week program of training in speed and flexibility appropriate to five types of material: fiction, literature, science, history, and psychology. The measure of flexibility was time to read selections of 750 to 900 words, graded by the Dale-Chall readability formula. Pretesting revealed slow, inflexible readers, and post-testing showed "fast, flexible readers who not only read rapidly but also vary their rate as they read different kinds of materials." Apparently, familiarity with the content affected flexibility more than difficulty of the text as measured by the readability formula. It is possible that, for these subjects, familiarity with the materials determined to some degree the difficulty of each kind of content read.

To read effectively, rate must be appropriate to the nature and the difficulty of the material. The nature of materials varies widely. At one time, the pupils may be reading a fast-moving story, or an item of general interest in a newspaper. Here the appropriate rate of reading is relatively rapid. A short time later, the pupil may be reading geographic material concerned with the concept of erosion by wind and water. In this, a relatively slow rate of reading is necessary to grasp the ideas and relationships. Still later he may be reading the procedures for solving a mathematical or scientific problem which requires a very slow, analytical procedure and often rereading. The pupil needs to exercise discrimination in sizing up the nature of the materials so that he may adopt a rate appropriate to understand a particular kind of material.

Adjusting to variations in difficulty is similar. Variation in difficulty arises in many ways. Materials in some content areas have more facts than others, for example, science or mathematics compared to literature. At times, there is marked variation in difficulty within the same unit in a single area. These difficulties may occur when unfamiliar vocabulary terms and concepts are encountered, complex sentences and paragraphs, or any unusual construction. Increased attention to content necessitates slower reading for adequate understanding. The pupil should read just as slowly as is needed to grasp what is presented. Any pupil who attempts to read all materials at the same rate, despite their content or difficulty, will be in trouble. To read with understanding and at an effective rate, he must be able to modify his rate to fit both. Easy material should be read faster than difficult material, and familiar material should be read faster than unfamiliar material.

Perhaps most important of all is the adjustment of rate of reading to the purpose for which the reading is done. This has been stressed in earlier discussions. If the pupil needs to get only a general impression or idea, or if he merely needs to look up a given item on a page, the speed should be relatively rapid. But if he needs to grasp the concepts in a given selection thoroughly, his pace will be relatively slow. This emphasizes the importance of purposeful reading. Before reading any unit, the child should be clear as to the purpose for reading. The most satisfactory purpose is one stated by the pupil himself. When he cannot do this the teacher's guidance should help provide him with a purpose *acceptable* to him. To be a really good reader, however, he must have learned to set his own purpose. This requires discrimination and flexibility. The pupil must be able to size up the materials and clearly understand the purpose for reading them. Then he must be flexible in choosing the appropriate rate for him to read with understanding. In other words, *the proficient reader is the adaptable, versatile reader.*

To gain flexibility in rate of reading, the child must learn to choose the particular speed for a particular situation and to read at that rate with understanding. This requires the teacher's guidance because every pupil reads many kinds of materials for many purposes. The development of flexibility in speed of reading tends to be slow and difficult to learn. It is a perennial problem at all levels from the third grade on. The teacher should not attempt to develop flexibility at just one specific grade level. Training to develop flexibility must continue throughout the school years. For the majority of pupils, flexibility in adjusting rate of reading is acquired slowly. But the pupil who achieves it possesses a fine asset.

Opportunities for guidance in adjusting speed of reading to the kind of materials are abundant in teaching units in the content areas. Preparation for every unit should include discussion of the right reading procedures.

Another strategy is to have pupils read the same material several times, each time for a different specific purpose such as: (*a*) to grasp the main idea, (*b*) to note the important details, (*c*) to answer questions given in advance, and (*d*) to evaluate what is read. Witty (228) presents a useful outline of examples of reading purposes, reading materials, and reading methods. One column lists "why you are reading," in another, "what you are reading," and in a third, "how you should read." In most workbooks accompanying basic readers, there are exercises to develop flexibility in rate of reading.

There is always opportunity to guide the development of flexibility when teaching the specific comprehension abilities and study skills described in an earlier chapter. Any instruction designed to develop comprehension in reading will necessarily involve guiding the pupils to discover the most effective rate at which to read a specific set of material.

Gains to Be Expected

In the primary grades, while the mechanics of reading are being mastered and where much of the reading is oral, the rates of both silent and oral reading are about the same. But in the fourth grade, children are ready to learn to read silently faster than they can possibly read orally. Spache (183) states, "If given proper instruction, children show proportionately more growth in speed of reading at about the fourth grade than during any other period in their schooling" (p. 247). Since about 1920, the classroom has stressed improvement of the rate of reading. Often there has been an unfortunate emphasis upon increasing rate at the expense of the more fundamental reading skills.

As noted above, the first step in organizing a speed of reading program in a school is to reduce to a minimum any habits that may hinder or obstruct gains in speed. When this is done, a teacher can expect practically all her pupils to increase their rate with training. There will be individual differences in the amount of gain achieved. There is ample evidence that training produces greater gains among the more fluent readers than among the less able ones.

In a properly conceived and executed program for a group at any school level, a few children will achieve relatively small gains, many will make moderate gains, and a few will achieve large gains. An occasional child will make really exceptional improvement. Ordinarily pupils are given special practice periods of ten to thirty minutes each. The program usually extends over several weeks with a total of fifteen to eighteen hours of training. Representative average gains for groups vary greatly. Bird (12) reported a 17 percent gain: O'Brien (148), 30 to 35 percent; Brooks (30), 37 to 56 percent; and Harris (100), 39 percent. With an intensive nine-week program of training high school pupils, Engelhardt (68) obtained average group gains of about 45 to 110 percent. If a school training program extends over two months or so, the teacher may expect an average gain of 40 to 50 percent. There is little evidence concerning transfer of rate to other reading materials or the degree to which the gains are maintained after the training stops.

In most programs to improve rate, comprehension is maintained at an adequate level, seventy-five percent or higher. However, if speed alone is emphasized, comprehension may decrease. No pupil should be pushed to this stage.

How fast can a person be expected to read? Since many factors affect rate of reading, no single answer to this question can be given. The available data are usually for reading fairly easy material. With such material, 400 words per minute is very high for a seventh-grade pupil; 600 words per minute is very high and 850 exceedingly rare for college students. It is not uncommon for some well educated adults to attain rates of 500 to 600 words per minute. These rates are for superior readers. There is, however, a physiological limit beyond which rate of reading cannot go. Spache (183) points out that this limit is around 800 to 900 words per minute when one reads most of the words on a page. If we find reports of rates between 1200 and 1500 or more words per minute, they refer to partial reading, or skimming. Any claim that a person can be taught to read 10,000 or even 20,000 words per minute is unrealistic. Words simply cannot be seen at that rate.

As mentioned above, there should be no stress in the primary grades upon improving rate of reading. For a majority of pupils up through about the fifth grade, a satisfactory rate may be expected as a result of a good developmental program. But some pupils in the intermediate grades can profit by a program to improve their rate of reading. These include the dawdlers and those who persist in their habits of slow reading after the major causal factors (vocalization, poor recognition of words, small sight vocabulary, etc.) have been reduced or eliminated. Flexibility in reading rate should be taught also in the intermediate grades and beyond. In general, although sometimes attention is given to improving rates in the early intermediate grades, provisions for developing appropriate rates of reading seem desirable from the beginning of the sixth grade on through high school and into the early college years.

OVERCOMING INEFFECTIVE ORAL READING

Oral reading is a part of any well-rounded developmental program of reading instruction. There are close relationships between the development of oral and silent reading abilities, and as a result there is need for a careful balance between the two. If an undue amount of oral reading is used to teach silent reading in the early grades, growth in both oral and silent reading may be impeded. The child may become self-conscious about his oral reading and he may become an overvocalizer, one who pronounces every word to himself whenever reading silently. The tendency to have children read aloud from a basic reading book, one after another around the room, has little to justify it. A far better approach is to have the children first read silently—a paragraph, a page, or a selection—in order to find the answer to a specific question or for some other well-defined purpose, and then read aloud the part of the selection that answers the question or fulfills the purpose.

The development of oral reading is important enough to deserve a place in the program rather than to be the mere handmaiden of the silent-reading program. The reading curriculum should develop oral reading in a way that will produce competence in this area and does not harm silent reading. The ultimate aim of oral reading instruction is to enable the reader to interpret a passage for others. The effective oral reader learns to interpret printed material in a relaxed and fluent manner to an audience. At the start, all oral reading should be prepared oral reading, but as the child matures in both silent and oral reading ability, he will become more adept at reading orally at sight. There are, then, sight and prepared oral reading, both of which can be interpretive. The amount of preparation needed for oral reading depends on the circumstances and the maturity of the reader. The parent who reads a story to his child probably is reading it at sight. Sharing a book by reading it aloud, in the New England reading circle-manner, also is done at sight. In most other instances, oral reading is prepared, interpretive reading rather than sight reading. Both types of oral presentation should be outcomes of a reading program.

There are many adults who dislike to read orally. This probably is because of unhappy, early reading experiences and failure to develop oral reading ability. Just a few years ago, it was the custom for more of the child's reading time to be devoted to reading a selection orally at sight, while the rest of the class looked at it, each in his own book, than to any other phase of reading instruction. Unfortunately this method still persists in some classrooms. If a listening child lost his place because he got bored with the reader's slow pace and read ahead for himself silently, he was punished. Some teachers went to the extreme of binding the books with rubber bands so that the children could not turn the pages and read ahead. Meanwhile the poor reader stumbled along with each of his errors apparent to all. The good reader either thought about something else or followed along at the necessary slow pace hindering his own silent reading abilities. The results were both insecure and ineffective oral reading and slow and laborious silent reading.

Even though conditions have changed and oral reading is taught in a more effective way, there are still some children who are good silent readers and who have developed all the basic reading proficiencies but are retarded seriously in oral reading ability. These children constitute a group having a specific disability. If their poor oral reading is the result of some basic inadequacy, the major problem is correcting that difficulty. When there is no such underlying difficulty and the child is an ineffective oral reader, his problem should be diagnosed. The child who is poor in oral reading, but is otherwise an able reader for his general reading level, may suffer from one of the following difficulties: (*a*) he may have an inappropriate eye-voice span, (*b*) he may lack proper phrasing in oral reading, (*c*) his rate and timing in oral reading may be unfortunate, or (*d*) he may become emotionally tense while reading aloud.

Inappropriate Eye-Voice Span

Many children who are disabled in oral reading are in difficulty because their eye-voice span is inappropriate. They may be focusing their attention directly on the word they are speaking or they may be trying to maintain an eye-voice span that is too great for their general reading maturity. If it is the former, the child will read aloud in a halting and stumbling fashion with little expression and many pauses. He can not anticipate the meaning of what he is reading and therefore can not express it with his voice. He may very likely read in a monotone. Each word that he does not recognize at sight will cause him to halt for inspecting it, whereas if his eye-voice span were longer, he would have time to identify words before pronouncing them.

If the latter is the trouble, if the child is trying to maintain too great an eye-voice span in oral reading, then he probably is an exceptionally able silent reader who is transferring to the oral reading his silent reading habits. He is racing ahead silently, perhaps at the rate of 300 to 400 words a minute, but he can pronounce words orally at only 140 words a minute. Such a child may try to maintain an eye-voice span of 8 to 10 words. If he does this in his oral reading, he likely will omit many words or read so rapidly that he can give but little expression to what he is reading aloud. He may lower his voice, enunciate poorly, and show little concern for his audience.

The diagnosis of eye-voice span is easy for the diagnostician to make. The child is given a book at the right level of difficulty for oral reading—a level at which he will encounter few word difficulties. He is given time to prepare the material and then he is asked to read it aloud to the examiner, who is at the child's right As the child reads aloud, the examiner reads along silently with him. At intervals, the examiner covers the child's page with a three-by-five card in order to find out how many words the child is able to say after he can no longer see the print. This should be done three or four times before the examiner starts keeping the actual record. The examiner should cover the rest of the line of print when the child is pronouncing a word that comes about one-third of the way through it. This testing also should be done with unprepared or sight oral reading. In this way, the examiner will have information on the eye-voice span of a child in both prepared and sight oral reading. Children in the early grades, with first- or second-grade reading ability, cannot maintain an eye-voice span of more than a word or two in unprepared oral reading. In sight oral reading, they can be expected to be little more than oral word-callers. Instruction in sight oral reading should be delayed until they have greater competency in reading. They will, however, tend to have a longer eye-voice span when reading aloud material that they have prepared for oral reading and therefore can be expected to interpret more effectively.

Remedial instruction for the child with a narrow eye-voice span always should be done in the prepared oral reading situation. The child should not be allowed to do any sight oral reading. Conversational passages are best for developing fluent oral reading for such a child. The material should be easy, with few if any unfamiliar words. The child should be encouraged to try to look ahead. Special attention should be given to phrasing. In certain cases, it will be profitable to use the method of testing eye-voice span as a device for teaching the child to lengthen his span. The purpose for his oral reading should be real, such as preparing to read something aloud that he knows he is going to read to others. He should rehearse until he is satisfied that he is ready for the oral reading.

The child who is trying to maintain too long an eye-voice span needs to be taught to use one that is more appropriate to the oral reading situation. At the start of remedial training he should be given an opportunity to read prepared material before an audience. If a tape recorder is available, his oral reading should be recorded so that he can learn his oral reading pattern and think about how to improve it. He should be taught how to pause from time to time while reading aloud, and he should be encouraged to look at his audience frequently. The problem of teaching the child who has too long an eye-voice span, is in getting him to use his superior reading ability effectively in oral reading.

Lack of Proper Phrasing Ability

A pupil who is a poor oral reader may lack proper phrasing ability and tend to read aloud either word by word, or by clustering words into groups disregarding the thought units involved. In either circumstance, attention to the meaning of what is read is neglected. The word-by-word reader can be detected immediately as he reads orally. Each word is pronounced as an unrelated entity. The words are read much in the manner that a mature reader might read a grocery list. When a child reads in this way, he may be directing his attention to the meaning of each word, but he is paying little attention to the interrelationships among them. The child who clusters words without regard to the real thought units is more difficult to detect when listening to his oral reading. What he reads may seem rather fluent, but it does not seem to make sense. This kind of oral reading sounds as though someone were trying to read a grocery list four words at a time, and putting in expression not warranted by the dissociated content.

The remedial training for children who lack proper phrasing in oral reading is the same for both types. The word-by-word reader was brought about in the first place by his having to read material with too large a vocabulary or by using content that repeated words in a mechanical and more or less senseless way. Early books should introduce words at a slow rate and they should be used frequently, but always in meaningful content, without needless repetition. Beginning reading books that say, "Make, make, make it, John," or "See, see, oh, see," or "Look, look, oh look," are giving what is probably the best possible training in word-by-word reading.

The material used to correct the tendency to use inappropriate phrasing in oral reading should be easy for the child, avoid inane repetition, and include a considerable amount of conversation. Dramatic readings, tape recordings, dummy or live microphone readings, and other such activities encourage proper phrasing. No sight oral reading should be attempted until growth in phrasing is well established.

Unfortunate Rate and Poor Timing in Oral Reading

Many children who lack ability in oral reading attempt to read too rapidly or have a poor sense of timing. They may start out reading at a reasonable rate but go continually faster until little of what is read can be understood. The good oral reader, at any level of advancement, reads at a rate that is relatively slow. He has a moderate degree of flexibility in his rate so that he may express different moods by altering his rate of reading. He learns to use pauses effectively to hold the attention of his audience and also to emphasize important points.

One of the most helpful means of aiding the poor oral reader is to devote attention to his rate and timing. The child will profit from listening to good oral readers on the radio or on television and trying to emulate their performances. Tape recordings of the child's own reading will demonstrate his present pattern to him. The expert reader will set the child's goals. Oral reading situations best suited to the child's needs are those in which he shares findings related to class enterprises. Having him be the news commentator during sharing periods is excellent because the news is made up of short paragraphs giving accounts of different unrelated events. Each one is read and then the child pauses before going on to the next. The pauses are short enough so that he does not accelerate his reading. Reading long selections from a story should be avoided until the child has his speed and timing under control.

The Emotionally Tense Oral Reader

Some children who have had frequent unfortunate experiences in oral reading become insecure or even frightened in such situations. The child who is experiencing emotional tensions with his oral reading can be detected by noting changes in the pitch of his voice while he reads. If his voice gets increasingly higher as he reads, he is becoming more and more tense. If his errors increase as he reads, he probably is becoming emotionally blocked. There are few situations more highly emotionally charged than is oral reading for the poor reader. Everything that can be done to relieve his tension in oral reading situations should be done. Two things that will help is to have him read material that is free from difficulties and that he has prepared so well that he can feel confident. Another aid to the emotionally tense reader is having the teacher near at hand and ready to prompt him if he gets into difficulty. Having the child read out of the sight of his audience seems to lessen some of his tension and will help him to establish confidence. Reading offstage as a narrator in a play or reading behind the screen for a shadow show often will help the tense reader. A microphone placed in another room over which an announcement or a news report is read offers a good opportunity for the child to read, free from self-consciousness. If, under these conditions, the reading is well prepared and the material is relatively easy to read, great progress can be expected. As soon as possible, the child should discard these devices and learn to read before his audience.

In working with the emotionally tense oral reader, certain precautions should be taken. His early oral reading experiences should grow out of a desire to share a story with others. He should be encouraged to tell the major part of the story in his own words and read orally only a small section, a paragraph or two is enough. He should select the part that he would like to read and have it prepared in advance, even rehearsing it aloud with the teacher. Then, when he does read it aloud to the group, if he gets into difficulty with a word, the teacher should supply it immediately. If, while reading, the child uses a high pitched or strained voice, reads at an unusually rapid rate, or shows any other sign of emotional tension, he should finish by telling the rest of the story. Gradually he can increase the length of the selection he prepares for oral reading. Only after he becomes confident in situations to which he comes prepared to read orally to the group should he attempt to read aloud at sight. In all oral-reading, the material should be relatively easy and free from words that the child is likely to find difficult.

Desire for Self-Improvement of Oral Reading Should Be Used

There is much in common among the four types of poor oral readers discussed above. As soon as the children recognize their problem and are eager to improve their oral reading, a self-check list of questions can be used. Each child will check his progress in the phase of oral reading upon which he is working. One may be working on his rate of reading, another may be working on phrasing, and a third on accuracy. The children may, under proper circumstances, judge the oral reading of one another. When this is done, they should tell what they liked, how well they think a child did in respect to what he was working on, and name any ways in which they think he might do still better. Such a list as the following adapted from Bond and Wagner (26), will prove helpful:

1. Did he select material that is of interest to his listeners?

2. Was he well enough prepared?

3. Did he read loud enough for all to hear?

4. Did he read as though he were telling the story?

5. Was he reading at a pleasant rate?

6. Did he express the meaning well?

7. Was he relaxed and did he have good posture?

8. Did he use the punctuation marks to help him?

9. Did he make us feel he wanted to read his story to us?

When oral reading is taught properly, not only is interpretive reading enhanced, but also oral language patterns are improved and better silent reading results. The child who is accustomed to reading aloud with pleasure will use some of the expressions he likes in his spoken language. He will gain feelings of confidence before groups and will sense the importance of adequate preparation. His silent reading will improve because, in his preparation for oral reading, he will be concerned with the meaning, the characterizations, and the action which he is to interpret to others. His concern with thought units in oral reading will teach him to cluster words together properly in his silent reading. Modern programs of oral reading appear to be vastly superior to the "round-the-room" reading of bygone days which produced the many insecure oral readers among the adults of today.

CASE STUDY OF A HIGH SCHOOL STUDENT WITH A BASIC COMPREHENSION LIMITATION AND POOR RATE OF READING

Albert, a ninth-grade student, was referred to the Psycho-Educational Clinic for work in reading during a ten-week summer period. He came from a distant state and stayed with his grandparents during his remedial work. He also registered in a summer reading improvement class at University High School. He had attended a school system in one of the mountain states during his elementary and junior high school years.

SCHOOL HISTORY. At the time Albert was admitted to the clinic, he was fifteen years, seven months old. His school record showed that he had repeated the second grade because of an illness which kept him out of school for the last two months of the school year. Albert's work up until that time seemed to be progressing well, except for a notation that he was having some difficulty in oral reading.

The rest of the elementary-grade years of the record showed that he was progressing with somewhat below-average success in social studies and reading, but because of his good work in arithmetic and science, he was not considered an educational problem. Albert was known to be a bright boy and he was cooperative, although his teachers noted that he was shy and withdrawn. His teachers had made a special effort to get him to participate in class activities. During the junior high school years, Albert continued to do reasonably well in mathematics courses, somewhat poorly in science, and just passed social studies and English.

As a result of a conference with Albert, it was found that he had been given some work at a reading center during the preceding year, in order to increase his speed of reading. He said that he had improved a little, but try as he would, he could not seem to read fast enough to keep up with his assignments. Albert indicated that he took his books home and read his regular texts with great care, but could not find the time to do the extra reading required in the English and social studies courses. He found the mathematics and science courses easier to cover. He also said that he did not like to participate in class discussions, bringing the clinician to conclude that he was somewhat of a "loner" in school.

PHYSICAL STATUS. Albert's physical status was excellent and there was no indication of any sensory limitation. He liked to go hiking in the mountains and was very fond of skiing, which he did often with his father. His shyness seemed to be limited to the classroom, since he participated in skiing, swimming, and tennis with other children and adults. The clinician felt that he was quite superior in these sports.

ABILITIES. Albert was found to be an intellectually able boy. He was measured on the *Wechsler Adult Intelligence Scale,* and was found to have a verbal I.Q. of 114, a performance I.Q. of 126, and a full scale I.Q. of 120. This would place his reading expectancy at the equivalent of a beginning college freshman $(1.20 \times 10) + 1$, or grade 13 reading expectancy. It was felt by the examiner that the verbal rating may have been somewhat depressed because of his reading difficulty, and that his actual I.Q. was higher than the 120 indicated by the total score.

Albert was given *The New Developmental Reading Tests, Form A,* with the time limits indicated in the manual. His grade scores follow:

Basic Reading Vocabulary	10.6
Reading for Information	4.4
Reading for Relationships	5.1
Reading for Interpretation	4.1
Reading for Appreciation	3.9
Literal Comprehension	4.5
Creative Comprehension	3.9
General Comprehension	4.4

These results show that word recognition was not Albert's basic problem. In fact, the 10.6 grade score in reading vocabulary was exceptionally high in comparison with his total score of 4.4. Because all types of comprehension were low, some form of difficulty in basic comprehension or rate of reading was judged to be at the root of the reading problem of this capable boy. The test pages were studied further, and it was found that Albert had a high degree of accuracy (one-hundred percent) in reading for information (grade score 4.4) and reading for relationships (grade score 5.1), but he was only sixty percent accurate in reading for interpretation (grade score 4.1), and eighty percent accurate in reading for appreciation (grade score 3.9). He appeared to have more trouble with the creative types of reading than with the literal types. This might have been anticipated because he had had relative success in mathematics and science.

As the manual for *The New Developmental Reading Tests* suggests, alternate test, *Form B,* was given without time limits. Albert did somewhat better in the untimed situation on these power tests, but not enough better to indicate that his rate of reading was his only, or even his basic, problem. His grade scores on *Form B,* untimed, were:

Basic Reading Vocabulary	10.9
Reading for Information	5.0
Reading for Relationships	5.6
Reading for Interpretation	4.5
Reading for Appreciation	4.4
Literal Comprehension	4.2
General Comprehension	4.7

These results showed that Albert had a reading problem which influenced both his rate of reading and his general comprehension. It was felt by the examiner that the differences in types of reading could be explained by Albert's greater satisfaction in reading science and mathematics, and by his tendency to avoid reading literature and social studies.

Albert's oral and silent reading ability was then appraised by informal techniques (Chapter 7). He was found to read orally and silently at approximately the same rate—about ninety words a minute. He could read seventh-grade material aloud without excessive word-prounuciation errors; but when he answered questions about the content, even of fourth-grade material, he was inaccurate and asked to be allowed to reread to find the answers. This he could do reasonably well. Albert was a word-by-word reader, who gave no indication of reading in thought units and had little sense of sentence organization. His eye-voice span was limited to one or two words.

In silent reading, Albert could be seen to make many eye fixations per line of print, and he made many large regressions. This indicated that in silent reading, Albert was using much the same single-word techniques that he had used in oral reading. The examiner also noted that while Albert was reading silently he was, in fact, reading aloud to himself. This showed up in lip movements and other indications of excessive vocalization. Albert was reading silently, word-by-word, vocalizing what he read, and then rereading to understand the meaning of what he had read. He was using second-grade reading techniques. Using these reading patterns, Albert could be expected to understand but little more than the literal meaning of what he read. His span of recognition for phrases, flashed by means of a tachistoscope was limited to two words, and often the second word was wrong.

The answers to the diagnostic questions raised in chapter 6 indicated the following:

1. IS ALBERT CORRECTLY CLASSIFIED AS A DISABLED READER? The results of the diagnosis showed that he was definitely a disabled reader. Albert had a limiting condition that would have to be overcome before he could become an able reader and achieve educationally in keeping with his intellectual capacity. Albert's tendency to withdraw in the schoolroom was felt to be a symptom, and not the cause, of his problem. Rather, it led one to believe that he was aware of his reading inadequacy.

2. WHAT IS THE NATURE OF THE TRAINING NEEDED? The remedial program designed for Albert had the following components: (*a*) Practice in rapid recognition of phrases, including flash drills, as discussed in chapter 13. (*b*) Prepared oral reading, with emphasis on proper phrasing and oral expression of sentence meaning to improve reading in thought units. (*c*) Steps to overcome the vocalization Albert used in all other reading activities. (*d*) Use of context clues and other meaning clues as an aid to comprehension (see chapter 13). (*e*) Provision of increased experience in interpretive and appreciative types of reading throughout the training period (see chapter 14).

3. WHO CAN MOST EFFECTIVELY GIVE THE REMEDIAL WORK? On the basis of the diagnosis, it was decided that work with an individual remedial teacher, plus a reading-improvement class, was the best arrangement that could be made for Albert during the summer period.

4. HOW CAN IMPROVEMENT BE BROUGHT ABOUT MOST EFFICIENTLY? At the start, the material selected by the clinician was the *Seventh-grade Classmate Edition of The Developmental Reading Series* and selected exercises from the accompanying skill-development book. This simplified seventh-grade basal reader requires reading ability of about the end of fourth-grade level, but has the interest level and format of a seventh-grade book. In addition, independent reading of suitable materials, such as those discussed in chapter 8, was encouraged. The remedial teacher gave Albert many opportunities to do prepared oral

reading with emphasis upon proper phrasing and oral expression of sentence meaning, both to improve oral reading and to develop phrasing. This was thought to be justified in spite of Albert's vocalization tendencies, since lack of reading by thought units and sentence meaning is more limiting to total reading growth than is vocalization. The remedial teacher developed exercises to help train him in locating thought units within sentences, as described in chapter 13. Flash drills, using both a tachistoscope and flash cards, were developed for rapid phrase-recognition exercises.

The teacher of the reading improvement class was informed of the findings of the diagnosis, and she adjusted her instruction for Albert in order to achieve the same remedial objectives. Her help was especially effective in providing experiences in reading for interpretation and appreciation, and in helping Albert to overcome his tendency to withdraw when working in groups.

Albert took home relatively easy books for independent reading. He was told to read these books as rapidly as he could for three, fifteen-minute periods, as measured by the timer on the electric stove. Then he was to note, for each fifteen-minute period, the number of pages read, such as: from the top of page twenty-one to the middle of page twenty-nine. He also was told to write, in not more than three short sentences, the major ideas presented. Each day he would bring the results of his independent reading to the remedial teacher. Using his "major ideas" sentences as notes, he would discuss the independent reading he had done at home the day before. He also kept a daily rate chart, calculated on the results of his final fifteen-minute, timed period of reading. Albert was, of course, free to read the books taken home for leisurely, untimed reading, and he was encouraged to do so. During his home reading, as in all other reading activities, Albert was told to try to limit vocalization. This home practice was reinforced by the flash drills used to develop phrase recognition which also help in overcoming vocalization.

5. DOES THE CHILD HAVE ANY LIMITING CONDITIONS THAT MUST BE CONSIDERED? Albert was not limited in any sensory or physical way that would contribute to the complexity of his reading problem. His tendency to withdraw in school situations and his lack of confidence, while thought to be a direct outgrowth of his reading frustrations, were taken into account in formulating the remedial plans. Albert's confidence was bolstered by the acceptance of himself and his reading problem by the remedial teacher. His withdrawal tendencies were recognized quickly by the high school corrective-reading teacher. At the very start of instruction, she provided Albert with a story to report on about delivering the mail on skis and encouraged him to tell about his

own skiing experiences. This approach quickly established Albert favorably among his classmates.

6. ARE THERE ANY ENVIRONMENTAL CONDITIONS THAT MIGHT INTERFERE WITH PROGRESS IN READING? The environment in which Albert was placed during this summer period was thought to be ideal. His grandparents were cooperative and knowledgeable. They made certain that he had an enjoyable summer vacation including opportunities to swim and play tennis with his classmates. They also provided Albert with a suitable place for leisure reading, and took a healthy interest in what he was reading.

Results. Albert was given remedial instruction as outlined above, and he also enrolled in the reading improvement class for the ten-week period. The results were thought to be outstanding. Of course, Albert was an able boy with no limiting physical conditions and was helped under ideal circumstances. His problems were of a type in which rapid correction often takes place. Nonetheless, the results were gratifying to all persons concerned.

The New Developmental Reading Tests, Form A, were repeated at the end of the ten-week period, with the following results:

Basic Reading Vocabulary	10.8
Reading for Information	9.4
Reading for Relationships	9.7
Reading for Interpretation	9.8
Reading for Appreciation	10.0
Literal Comprehension	10.4
Creative Comprehension	10.1
General Comprehension	10.4

The limiting condition of word-by-word reading and his excessive vocalization had been overcome. Albert now was able to couple his skill in word recognition and his large sight vocabulary with his able intellect, to read slightly better than a typical beginning tenth-grade student, even though he was still not reading up to his reading expectancy level. Albert also had overcome the insecurity in reading situations which previously had inhibited his performance. This gain in confidence undoubtedly helped to improve his measured reading capabilities. Albert's interest in reading and his ability to concentrate on what he was reading developed to the point that while reading a book on his way to school on the bus one morning, he missed his stop and rode all the way to downtown Minneapolis before he looked up from his book to check on his whereabouts.

An informal evaluation showed that Albert was able to read high school material for varied purposes at from 300 to 400 words a minute, with a high degree of accuracy. It was felt, at the end of the session, that his reading ability would no longer interfere with his future progress.

Albert has exchanged Christmas cards with his remedial teacher for four years and is now in college. He reports that he is enjoying his college work, that his major interest is still in the fields of mathematics and science, but that he likes to read for pleasure, too.

SUMMARY

A good speed of reading is that rate at which material is comprehended according to the purpose for which it is being read. For the proficient reader especially, speed of reading is fairly specific to the particular reading situation, materials, and purposes. In general, the goal is to comprehend at as fast a rate as possible. Some details discussed in achieving this goal are: (*a*) rate of comprehension that avoids dawdling; (*b*) rate to fit material read; (*c*) rate to fit purpose; (*d*) flexibility in adapting rate to materials and purposes; (*e*) relation of rate to comprehension; (*f*) role of eye movements in different rates; and (*g*) norms for speed of reading. General methods for determining deficiencies in rate of reading include standardized tests and informal tests. Each type of test should supplement the other in diagnosis.

A complete diagnosis of difficulties in speed of reading must include an analysis of possible limiting conditions, such as the basic word-recognition skills and basic comprehension abilities which preclude rapid reading. These must be corrected before the specific types of inefficient rates can be overcome. The specific rate problems discussed include: the overanalytical reader, the word-by-word reader, the reader with faulty habits, the reader with faulty eye movements, the reader with excessive vocalization, and the inflexible reader.

The program for improving rate of reading must include the following: (*a*) use of appropriate materials; (*b*) proper incentives to develop and maintain motivation; and (*c*) techniques for increasing rate.

Two general techniques are used to increase speed of reading. The first is working against time with proper materials and adequate motivation. The second is using various machines. Just as much gain in speed can be obtained by the well organized, less complicated, and less expensive procedures as by machines.

An essential part of any program for speeding up reading is to develop flexibility in adjusting rate to materials and purposes.

Ineffective oral readers need to be given material that is relatively easy for them to read and have ample opportunity to prepare it. The major problems in oral reading are: inappropriate eye-voice span, lack of proper phrasing, unfortunate rate and timing, and emotional tension.

SELECTED READINGS

BURMEISTER, L. E., *Reading Strategies for Secondary School Teachers,* chap. 10. Reading, Mass.: Addison-Wesley, 1974.

DURKIN, DOLORES, *Teaching Young Children to Read* (2nd ed.), chap. 8. Boston: Allyn and Bacon, 1976.

HARRIS, ALBERT J., and EDWARD R. SIPAY, *How To Increase Reading Ability* (6th ed.), chap. 19. New York: David McKay, 1975.

MILLER, W. H., *Diagnosis and Correction of Reading Difficulties in Secondary School Students,* chap. 9. New York: Center for Applied Research in Education, 1973.

TINKER, M. A., and C. M. McCULLOUGH, *Teaching Elementary Reading* (4th ed.) chaps. 11, 12. Englewood Cliffs, N. J.: Prentice-Hall, 1975.

ZINTZ, MILES V., *The Reading Process* (2nd ed.), chap. 14. Dubuque, Iowa: Wm. C. Brown, 1975.

Encouraging Continued Growth in Reading

sixteen

After a child has overcome a reading handicap sufficiently to allow him to discontinue the concentrated remedial program, he should be put into classroom situations where he will gain increasing independence in reading. He must be aided and assisted carefully by the classroom teacher. This child needs the support and encouragement necessary to ensure that he will continue to make reading gains, and he also needs opportunities to develop gradually real self-sufficiency and independence in reading.

If the results of remedial training are to become permanent and if continuous growth in reading is to occur in the classroom, the child should:

(a) develop a permanent interest in reading,

(b) establish independence in the use of reading, and

(c) continue to progress in reading after remediation.

These three essentials will be discussed in the following sections.

DEVELOPING A PERMANENT INTEREST IN READING

Throughout a remedial treatment program as discussed in this book, attention was given to the independent reading of the disabled reader. The development of reading interests and the desire to use reading as a source of information and enjoyment were considered essential to reading growth. If remedial instruction is to establish permanent learning, an appreciation of reading as a worthwhile activity must be cultivated.

Of great importance in establishing a continuing appreciation for and utilization of reading is to provide the child with selections and materials which appeal to his own interests. Whether in the remedial reading setting or in the classroom, nothing is more important to insuring continued growth in reading than maintaining strong motivation. There is ample evidence from both clinic and classroom to show that children make greater progress in their reading when they can read about things that are highly interesting to them. Larrick's (129) claim that under such conditions, half the battle is won, may well be an understatement.

Interest breeds motivation, the will to do something, including the drive needed for learning. This also is true for learning to read—the interested child becomes the motivated child, the habitual reader. This is why many authorities on reading stress the interaction among interest patterns, reading activities, and progress in reading.

Students' interests and reading preferences have been researched extensively. The results of several studies are listed here. Stanchfield (192) classified 153 boys in grades four, six and eight with I.Q.'s ranging from 90 to 120 into groups of superior, average, and poor readers. There were strong similarities among the interest preferences of all three grades, and also among the superior, average, and poor readers. The boy's first three choices were outdoor life, explorations and expeditions, and sports and games. Tied in fifth place were science fiction, sea adventure, and fantasy. Then came historical fiction, humor, adventures of boys in everyday life, and outer space. The boys were least interested in plants, music, plays, art, family and home life, and poetry. In general, the boys' interests turned toward unusual experiences, excitement, suspense, liveliness and action, but not toward anger, hate, cruelty, fighting or brutality, or familiar experiences.

Using 102 prose selections of about 400 words each, dealing with 30 different topics, Jungblut and Coleman (118) determined their appeal to pupils in grades six, seven, eight, and nine in 146 classrooms. The selections were written at different grade levels of difficulty, from 3.0 to 7.0, so that they also could be read by disabled readers. Topics in the selections were classified as biography, history, miscellaneous, narrative, science, and occupational. The authors concluded that twenty-four of the thirty topics would be interesting to disabled readers at the junior high school level.

Vaughn (215) determined differences in reading preferences by sex using an interest questionnaire given to 134 students in the eighth grade. In general, the boys preferred mystery and science, invention, history, and biography. The girls chose stories relating to home and school, novels, and mystery. Comics were chosen by about a third of both boys and girls, with the low-ability boys tending to rank them highest, the bright boys preferring science fiction. It appeared that above the primary grades, differences according to sex were more important than differences in intelligence in determining reading interests.

Norvell (147) studied the interests of 24,000 pupils in grades three through six. He found that boys tend to prefer prose, and girls, poetry. Changes of interests with age were prominent.

Other recent studies show similar trends. In general, during grades four to eight, boys tend to prefer reading about sports and games, outdoor life, exploration and expeditions, science fiction, sea adventures, physical struggle, animals, humor, heroism, courage, mystery, patriotism, fantasy, historical fiction, and outer space. Boys are least interested in plants, music, art, home life, description, fairies, romantic love, sentiment, poetry, and stories with girls or women as leading characters. Girls tend to prefer material on home and school life, human characters, domestic animals and pets, lively adventure, romantic love, sentiment, the supernatural, mystery, patriotism, and poetry. They do not like descriptions of violent action, instructional matter, fierce animals, and stories about younger boys and girls (except babies). Girls usually enjoy boy's books, but boys reject most girl's books. Mystery stories are liked by both boys and girls. This interest increases from grade four through twelve, but low-ability children care less for humorous items than brighter pupils do. During this same period, interest in cowboy stories and in fairy tales decreases. Books enjoyed do not vary much according to ability, but bright pupils tend to read three or four times as many books as those of average ability. Studies show that sex differences, not prominent during the early primary grades, become clear-cut by about age nine or ten. Although girls share the boys' liking for mystery and adventure, they do not usually like science and invention. Boys ordinarily avoid material that is considered feminine.

Identifying Specific Interests of a Disabled Reader

Studies of children's reading interests are valuable for suggesting what types of books might appeal to children of a certain age and sex, and also what books might appeal to a given child. However, in teaching an individual child, especially one who is resistant to reading, it becomes necessary to identify and evaluate his own particular interests.

QUESTIONNAIRES. Information may be gained from simple questionnaires. Often the best questionnaire is one devised by the teacher herself, for it can apply specifically to a particular child or group of children. A set of questions designed for a certain child or group of children should be modified before being used with other children. An interest questionnaire useful at the upper elementary level follows. The items were adapted from questionnaires by Witty and Kopel (231), Harris and Sipay (100), and Austin, Bush, and Huebner (2).

Sample Interest Questionnaire

NAME _____ DATE _____

GRADE _____ AGE IN YEARS _____ MONTHS _____

1. What do you like to do after school?
2. What do you like to do when it rains?
3. What do you like to do in the summer?
4. What programs do you like on television?
5. What games do you like to play?
6. What hobbies or collections do you have?
7. What books that you have read did you like best?
8. Do you own any books?_____What are some of them?
9. What kinds of things would you like to read about?
10. If you could have three wishes and they all might come true, what would you wish?
    1.
    2.
    3.

With reading-disabled children, the teacher often must read the items to each child and write in his responses.

INTERVIEW. As the remedial teacher works with a disabled reader, she should be alert to the child's interests. When the child seems to be comfortable in the remedial-reading setting, the teacher should have a relaxed interview with him.

This interview may supplement the questionnaire, or in some cases, substitute for it. During the interview, every effort is made to make the child comfortable so he will talk freely about his activities in and out of school, the kind of reading he likes, his favorite television programs, and so on. The teacher may use a mimeographed outline to guide her interview and to record the information. It should not be used if it breaks the rapport between teacher and pupil. Jotting down such items as favorite sports, movies, books, or suggestions for future reading ordinarily will not disturb a child. But sometimes the relaxed personal give-and-take of a quiet interview may be ruined by following a mimeographed schedule. Although an interview may be time-consuming, so much information is usually gained that it is worthwhile.

OBSERVATION. A relatively simple and effective way to find out what a child's interests are is to watch his daily activities in and out of school.

When children are free to express themselves in talk, play, drawing, and other activities, the alert teacher will find many opportunities to jot down an anecdotal note for later reference. The child who draws dogs probably is interested in reading about dogs. The girl who loves to play nurse usually enjoys reading about nurses. Many possible reading interests are discovered in this way.

METHODS FOR DEVELOPING THE DESIRE TO READ. Children with reading disabilities, nearly all of whom, at the start of remedial treatment, dislike reading, present special difficulties. The first problem is to identify the pupil's interest patterns as described above. His introduction to voluntary reading should be with a book on a topic of paramount interest to him. The book should be easy to read, short, well written, and have lots of pictures. More books are to be supplied as needed. The first several books all may be on one subject, perhaps animals, if they are what he likes. It is important to keep within the area of his known interests, until the habit of voluntary reading is established, even if they are very narrow. He may refuse to read anything but animal stories, or space stories, or gangster stories. But, in time, his interests may be expanded gradually. The main problem with disabled readers is to teach them to read at an appropriate level. Enrichment and expansion of interests can come gradually.

To develop an interest in reading, conditions in the classroom, resource center, clinic, and at home must be favorable to reading. Reading is encouraged at home by things such as (*a*) attitudes of parents supportive of reading, (*b*) available books and magazines of proper levels of difficulty and interest, (*c*) conversation with the child about books, magazine stories, and articles, and (*d*) story telling and story reading in the home. To be effective, these activities must be spontaneous, rather than staged in an effort to snare the child into reading. Many children want to be like their parents, in ways that are genuine and worthwhile. Under such favorable conditions, most children will lengthen their leisure-time reading and broaden their reading interests.

A favorable physical setting for the resource center or the clinic should include a reading corner just like that available in many classrooms. It should have a table or two with comfortable chairs, book shelves, and a great variety of reading materials. There should be attractive books, magazines, well-selected comic books, reference materials, and so on, chosen for the age of the children using the reading corner. The range of difficulty of the reading material should be great enough to cover the abilities of each pupil and have such variety of content that each child can find something interesting to read. Of course the reading corner should be used for browsing and independent reading. The displays of material should be changed frequently and always made attractive. This should be a reading corner for leisure reading. Even with little guidance from the teacher, the reading corner usually cultivates an appreciation of reading as a worthwhile activity.

Although the real motivation for reading must come from the child himself, the teacher, having appraised intrinsic motivations, can help the child pursue established interests and discover new ones. The child is not born with interests. They are acquired, including those in reading, and can be encouraged by training. One interest can lead to another. For example, a child may be interested in baseball. This may lead to reading newspaper accounts of baseball games, which in turn may lead to reading biographies of baseball heroes, which may lead to reading about—who knows what? Some suggestions for developing and extending permanent interests in reading are discussed in the following sections.

BUILD INTEREST BY READING TO DISABLED READERS. The remedial teacher who has a knack of reading stories aloud with real enthusiasm so that they fascinate the children will have little difficulty in stimulating interest in reading. An entertaining story which the teacher has read to a group will be reread by many pupils when it is placed in the reading corner and when attention is called to it. Similarly, some of the more advanced readers among the pupils may read aloud to the group a selection from a story which they have prepared to read. When this is done, the reader is motivated to do his best, and his listeners become interested in the story and will probably wish to read it all.

BUILD INTERESTS FREE FROM SKILL-DEVELOPMENT INSTRUCTION There should be a clear-cut distinction between reading done in the remedial program to develop skills and abilities and reading to expand interests, much of which is achieved during the time set aside for personal reading. McKee (136) emphasizes this point when he says "methods used to help children build an abiding interest in good reading material and a taste for such material must be inherently informal," enabling children to approach a selection as something to be enjoyed in its own right. There is no surer way to stifle expanding interests than to stop the ongoing enjoyment of a story or selection in order to engage in drill upon a fundamental of reading or to attempt to extract an analysis of content, plot, or characterization. It is unwise to probe and quiz, implying that nothing can be learned unless the teacher asks questions and the children answer them. When a child needs help in recognizing a word or comprehending a concept, it should be given freely and quickly so that he can continue to communicate with the author actively and with interest.

PRESENT SYSTEMATIC LESSONS. Lessons to expand reading interests should be planned carefully and systematically. Recommending systematic planning, Burton and Larrick (36) state: "Emphasis on the pleasures of reading in the elementary school does not mean a *laissez-faire* policy of 'surround them with books and sit back.' Instead, it means careful planning to provide for individual differences in an atmosphere that encourages children to wonder and to seek, to contemplate and to evaluate." Based upon knowledge of each child's reading abilities and interests, the remedial teacher can arrange experiences to expand interests. One way is to integrate the ideas found in reading with the children's daily experiences. Careful integration of ideas requires thought and attention. Any subject contains a potential for deepening and expanding reading interests. It often is assumed that the development of reading interests is limited to reading juvenile fiction. Such an assumption should not be made. It should be recognized that at the present time, children's interests are being expanded beyond juvenile fiction. It is equally important to recognize that children are interested in the wonders of the world about them. The concept of children's literature has broadened to include materials from many fields, both factual and fictional.

USE OF HOBBIES TO STIMULATE READING INTERESTS. Teachers have found that allowing pupils time in school to pursue hobbies is worthwhile. One child's enthusiasm may spark others' interest in a particular hobby. Often the teacher can suggest some type of related reading which will be valuable to the young enthusiasts. Especially at the secondary level, many students participate in optional after-school activities which stimulate strong interest in reading. Books directed toward specialized interests such as *How to Stay Alive in the Woods* or *Step-By-Step Jewelry,* often have great appeal to students who devote their time and energy to such areas.

Other methods to stimulate interest in reading include (*a*) displays of book jackets and book advertisements, (*b*) a book club with its own pupil officers, (*c*) carefully organized and regularly changed book exhibits in a corridor case, (*d*) an attractive wall chart on which each pupil can list books he has read, and (*e*) *very brief* book reports. In general, the enthusiastic teacher who plans systematically for developing interests just as for developing other aspects of reading, will find she is rewarded.

Perhaps the most effective incentives for broadening interests come from feeling the enthusiasm of the teacher and of other pupils for stories and books not dealing with what one thought was the only interesting area. Judicious use of all the methods discussed above may be used to expand reading interests as well as to deepen them. The alert teacher will know which method or methods to use with a particular pupil.

We have pointed out the strong influence of a teacher's enthusiasm. It is well known that the teacher who is most successful in developing an interest in reading in a specific area is one who herself is interested in that material, lives it, appreciates it, and shares her enjoyment with the children whom she teaches. It also should be noted that interaction among students often generates reading interests which are almost unlimited.

GENERAL STATEMENT. Encouraging continued growth in reading by a particular pupil will have been achieved when he has acquired broad and permanent interests and desirable tastes. Although growth in reading interests and tastes is gradual, proper guidance throughout the grades can accomplish much. Besides providing strong motivation for learning to read, interests determine what is read and how much is read voluntarily. To a large degree, taste in reading depends upon interest patterns. Reading instruction should therefore make use of the dynamic tendencies provided by a child's interests. Guidance can broaden these interests and stimulate new ones. In order to do something for a child's interests, it is first necessary to find out what they are at present. Information is available on which interests tend to be shared in common by many children of the same age and sex. To identify and evaluate a child's specific interest patterns, use may be made of questionnaires, interviews, and observation of his behavior.

At home, interest in reading is encouraged by favorable attitudes of parents, availability of books, conversation about books and reading, and story telling and story reading. At school, interest in books and reading is promoted by an attractive reading corner adequately supplied with books, by oral reading and story telling by the teacher, by free reading periods, by displays of book jackets and advertisements, and by pupil book clubs. Most important of all, perhaps, is the guidance provided by the enthusiastic and well-read teacher.

There is no such thing as a criterion of good taste which is applicable to all children. Improvement in taste is relative to the level of a particular pupil. Although improvement is slow, well-organized guidance can lead to discrimination and improved choice of reading materials for all children. The gains will be large for some pupils, small for others.

Factors which condition the development of tastes include reading ability, interest patterns, amount and variety of voluntary reading, availability of materials, time for leisure reading, and skill of the teacher. A program of guidance is essential. It has been demonstrated that well-organized and well-executed programs bring about remarkable improvement in reading tastes.

The reading of comics presents special problems in reading interests and tastes. Children who do practically no voluntary leisure reading except comics neglect reading the materials needed to enrich and extend their interests and cultivate taste. The teacher can provide guidance to instill some degree of discrimination toward comics so as to bring about a preference for the more acceptable ones. She can also guide pupils to similar subject matter in books of recognized worth.

A remedial program to broaden interests and cultivate tastes is essentially the same as the sequential program. The main difference is that the remedial program is more intensive and more highly individualized.

ESTABLISHING INDEPENDENCE IN USING READING

When a child begins remedial reading instruction he often is insecure, lacking self-confidence and independence. An important part of helping such a child improve his reading is to help him learn to become increasingly more independent.

Developing Initial Independence

In initial remedial-reading instruction, it often is wise to intersperse short, easily accomplished reading activities with other types of activities which are more appealing to reading-disabled children. However, eventually as a student gains in confidence and in reading skill, it becomes desirable to devote more of the instructional period to reading. In addition, the student should be asked to read increasingly longer selections and should be given less direct teacher assistance for the purpose of increasing the student's reading independence. Allowing a student to take an appropriate book home to read is a similar aid to independence. Although oral reading instruction is valuable for many reading-disabled children, silent reading must receive a good deal of emphasis in order to help establish skills for independence in reading. Allowing a student to make his own reading selections from among available choices fosters independence in reading, as does allowing him to use reading for his own reasons. The independent reader reads books of his own selection for such reasons as: for pure enjoyment, because his friends are talking about a certain book, or because he needs information for a project or activity.

The older student will benefit from some direct instruction in functional reading of such materials as: the newspaper, the telephone book, television guides, catalogs, and promotional pamphlets. Most students enjoy reading these materials, especially when they are allowed to read according to their own interests, and learn to use the materials in an independent manner to gather useful information.

Learning to Use Library Resources

Reading-disabled children often do not make successful use of the school library and therefore can profit from direct assistance in library usage as a part of their remedial instruction. The organization of the library and library procedures can be discussed with the disabled reader on an individual basis by the school librarian. The reading teacher can help the child successfully practice such procedures as using the card catalog, finding a book, and checking out books until the student becomes quite skillful and confident in obtaining books from the library.

Use of the public library also should be encouraged. Often, upon the remedial reading teacher's suggestion, parents will take their reading-disabled children to the public library and assist them in book selection and in obtaining a library card. With encouragement from the school and from the home, such children can become proficient in the use of both the school and the public library and begin to use both with independence.

Exploring Other Sources of Reading Material

When the other children in the school make purchases of inexpensive editions of well-liked books through the school book club, the disabled readers should be assisted to do so, too. The remedial reading teacher can compile an appropriate list of choices for the child who reads poorly and the parents can encourage him to choose a book or two.

In addition, parents can point out to their reading-disabled children the many displays of books or magazines which are sold in stores. If a child shows an interest in a magazine from a store display shelf, a parent should feel free to buy it for the child even though it may seem to be too advanced. Although the child may not be able to read every word or even to understand every idea in the magazine, it is a step toward independence in reading to have a magazine of one's own.

It is also beneficial for poor readers to be introduced to a book store and to see the many different books offered for sale such as attractive oversized picture books, inexpensive paperback books, and fat hardcover books. It is good for the child to observe that people come to the store to select and purchase books. Perhaps when looking through the books in the store, the child might decide that he wants a book of his own. Such a decision is part of reading independence.

CONTINUING PROGRESS IN READING AFTER REMEDIATION

When a child has shown sufficient growth in reading to enable him to discontinue remedial assistance, it is important that planning between the remedial teacher and the classroom teacher be done in order to accomplish a smooth transition for the child. During remediation a good deal of communication between the classroom teacher and the remedial reading teacher served to coordinate efforts on the child's behalf. At the termination of remediation, the remedial teacher will want to share some insights and suggestions with the classroom teacher in order to help her assist the child to continue to grow in reading.

The classroom teacher should support the child so he can maintain confidence in his reading now that he will be without the reassurance of the remedial teacher. The classroom teacher also should be alert to signs of difficulty in reading so that the child does not experience immediate frustration in classroom reading situations. In some instances, children may revisit the remedial reading teacher once a week or twice a month for the purpose of a little additional supportive attention. On occasion, these children benefit from being enrolled in a summer program designed to enhance reading improvement.

It also is important for parents to continue to be encouraging of their child's reading efforts and to continue to be aware of and supportive of their child's reading program. Communication with the classroom teacher is beneficial. Occasionally, parents can continue to provide home assistance in reading under the classroom teacher's guidance. Sometimes they will want to communicate to the teacher about signs of tension they detect in their child or to mention how much better their child seems to like school now that his reading is more successful.

When a disabled reader has overcome the reading difficulties that were impeding his reading and educational growth, when he has developed a real desire to read, and when he has established independence and self-sufficiency in the use of reading as a tool of learning at his level of reading expectancy, then his chances for continuing growth in reading become excellent. If, in addition, his teachers continue to give instruction suited to his individual learning characteristics, his successful reading development will be practically ensured. Such diagnostic teaching in classrooms and resource centers will make possible success for many students who otherwise would be unable to realize their complete educational potential. Such teaching takes the highest level of professional dedication, but therein lies the educational future of many children.

References

1. ANDERSON, I. H., and W. F. DEARBORN, *The Psychology and Teaching of Reading.* New York: Ronald Press, 1952.

2. AUSTIN, M. C., C. L. BUSH, and M. H. HUEBNER, *Reading Evaluation.* New York: Ronald Press, 1961.

3. AUSTIN, M. C., and C. MORRISON, *The First R.* New York: Macmillan, 1963.

4. BALOW, I. H., and B. BALOW, "Lateral Dominance and Reading Achievement in the Second Grade," *American Educational Research Journal,* 1 (1964), 139–143.

5. BALOW, B., R. RUBIN, and M. J. ROSEN, "Perinatal Events as Precursors of Reading Disability," *Reading Research Quarterly,* 11 (1975), 36–71.

6. BELDIN, H. O., *Differences Between Good and Poor Readers.* Paper presented at the annual meeting of the College Reading Association, October, 1976, Miami Beach, Florida.

7. BELMONT, L., and H. G. BIRCH, "Lateral Dominance, Lateral Awareness, and Reading Disability," *Child Development,* 36 (1965), 57–71.

8. BENDER, L., "Specific Reading Disability as a Maturational Lag," *Bulletin of the Orton Society,* 9 (1957), 9–18.

9. BENNETT, C. C., *An Inquiry into the Genesis of Poor Reading.* New York: Bureau of Publications, Teachers College, Columbia University, 1938.

10. BETTS, E. A., *Foundations of Reading Instruction.* New York: American Book, 1957.

11. BIRCH, H. G., and J. D. GUSSOW, *Disadvantaged Children: Health, Nutrition, and School Failure.* New York: Grune and Stratton, Inc., 1970.

12. BIRD, C., *Effective Study Habits.* New York: Appleton-Century-Crofts, 1931.

13. BIRD, G. E., "Personality Factors in Learning," *Personal Journal,* 6 (1927), 56–59.

14. BLACK, F. W., "Cognitive, Academic, and Behavioral Findings in Children with Suspected and Documented Neurological Dysfunction," *Journal of Learning Disabilities,* 9 (1976), 182–187.

15. ———, "An Investigation of Intelligence as a Causal Factor in Reading Problems," *Journal of Learning Disabilities,* 4 (1971), 139–142.

16. ———, "Neurological Dysfunction and Reading Disorders," *Journal of Learning Disabilities,* 6 (1973), 313–316.

17. ———, "Self-Concept as Related to Achievement and Age in Learning Disabled Children," *Child Development,* 45 (1974), 1137–1140.

18. BLAIR, G. M., *Diagnostic and Remedial Teaching* (rev. ed.). New York: Macmillan, 1956.

19. BLANCHARD, P., "Reading Disabilities in Relation to Maladjustment," *Mental Hygiene* (1928), 772–788.

20. BLOOMFIELD, LEONARD, and CLARENCE BARNHART, *Let's Read: A Linguistic Approach.* Detroit: Wayne State University Press, 1961.

21. BOND, E. A., *Tenth-Grade Abilities and Achievements.* New York: Bureau of Publications, Teachers College, Columbia University, 1940.

22. BOND, G. L., *The Auditory and Speech Characteristics of Poor Readers.* New York: Bureau of Publications, Teachers College, Columbia University, 1935.

23. BOND, G. L., and R. DYKSTRA, *Coordinating Center for First Grade Reading Instruction Programs.* Final Report of Project No. X–001, contract no. OE–5–10–264. Minneapolis: University of Minnesota, 1967.

24. BOND, G. L., and L. C. FAY, "A Comparison of the Performance of Good and Poor Readers on the Individual Items of the Stanford-

Binet Scale, Forms L and M," *Journal of Educational Research,* 43 (1950), 475–479.

25. BOND, G. L., and B. HANDLAN, *Adapting Instruction in Reading to Individual Differences.* Minneapolis: University of Minnesota Press, 1952.

26. BOND, G. L., and E. B. WAGNER, *Teaching the Child to Read* (4th ed.), New York: Macmillan, 1966.

27. BORMUTH, JOHN R., "Comparable Cloze and Multiple-Choice Test Comprehension Scores," *Journal of Reading* (Feb. 1967), 295.

28. BORMUTH, J. R., and C. C. AKER, "Is the Tachistoscope a Worthwhile Teaching Tool?" *The Reading Teacher,* 14 (1961), 172–176.

29. BRAAM, L., "Developing and Measuring Flexibility in Reading," *The Reading Teacher,* 16 (1963), 247–251.

30. BROOKS, F. D., *The Applied Psychology of Reading.* New York: Appleton-Century-Crofts, 1926.

31. BROWN, J. I., "Teaching Reading with a Tachistoscope," *Journal of Developmental Psychology,* 1, no. 2 (1958), 8–18.

32. BRUECKNER, L. J., and G. L. BOND, *Diagnosis and Treatment of Learning Difficulties.* New York: Appleton-Century-Crofts, 1955.

33. BRYAN, TANIS, and JAMES BRYAN, *Understanding Learning Disabilities,* chap. 7, 172–177. Port Washington, N. Y.: Alfred Publishing Co., 1975.

34. BUROS, OSCAR K., ed., *Reading Tests and Reviews.* Highland Park, N.J.: Gryphon Press, 1975.

35. _____, *The Seventh Mental Measurements Yearbook.* Highland Park, N. J.: Gryphon Press, 1972.

36. BURTON, DWIGHT L., and NANCY LARRICK, "Literature for Children and Youth," *Development in and through Reading,* Sixtieth Yearbook of the National Society for the Study of Education, part I. Chicago: University of Chicago Press, 1961.

37. CASON, E. B., *Mechanical Methods for Increasing the Speed of Reading.* New York: Bureau of Publications, Teachers College, Columbia University, 1943.

38. CLYMER, T. W., *The Influence of Reading Ability on the Validity of Group Intelligence Tests.* Ph.D. dissertation, University of Minnesota, Minneapolis, 1952.

39. COHEN, S. A., *Teach Them All to Read.* New York: Random House, 1969.

40. COHEN, S. A., and T. COOPER, "Seven Fallacies: Reading Retardation and the Urban Disadvantaged Reader," *Reading Teacher,* 1972, 38–44.

41. COHEN, A., and G. G. GLASS, "Lateral Dominance and Reading Ability," *Reading Teacher,* 21 (1968), 343–348.

42. COLE, L., *The Improvement of Reading.* New York: Holt, Rinehart, and Winston, 1938.

43. COLEMAN, R. I., and C. P. Deutsch, "Lateral Dominance and Right-left Discrimination: A Comparison of Normal and Retarded Readers," *Perception and Motor Skills,* 19 (1964), 43–50.

44. *The Cowboy Sam Series.* Chicago: Benefic Press, 1971.

45. CRANE, J. A., *Reading Difficulties as a Social Work Problem.* Master's thesis, McGill University, Canada, 1950

46. CRITCHLEY, M., *The Dyslexic Child.* Springfield, Ill.: Charles C. Thomas, 1970.

47. CROSLAND, H. R., "Superior Elementary-School Readers Contrasted with Inferior Readers in Letter-Position, 'Range of Attention' Scores," *Journal of Educational Research,* 32 (1939), 410–427.

48. CRUICKSHANK, W. M., ed., *Psychology of Exceptional Children and Youth,* (3rd ed.), Englewood Cliffs, N. J.: Prentice-Hall, Inc. 1971.

49. DALE, EDGAR, and JEANNE CHALL, "Formula for Predicting Readability," pp. 11–20 and 37–45. *Educational Research Bulletin,* 27. Columbus: Ohio State University, January-February, 1948.

50. DARROW, HELEN FISHER, and VIRGIL M. HAWES, *Approaches to Individualized Reading.* New York: Appleton-Century-Crofts, 1960.

51. DEARBORN, W. F., "Teaching Reading to Non-Readers," *Elementary School Journal,* 30 (1929), 266–269.

52. ———, "Ocular and Manual Dominance in Dyslexia," *Psychological Bulletin,* 28 (1931), 704.

53. ———, "Structural Factors Which Condition Special Disability in Reading," *Proceedings of the American Association of Mental Deficiency,* 38 (1933), 266–283.

54. ———, "The Nature and Causation of Disabilities in Reading,"

Recent Trends in Reading, Supplementary Educational Monographs no. 49. Chicago: University of Chicago Press, 1939.

55. DEARBORN, W. F., and I. H. ANDERSON, "Controlled Reading by Means of a Motion Picture Technique," *The Psychological Record,* 2 (1938), 219–227.

56. *The Deep-Sea Adventure Series.* Menlo Park, Calif.: Addison-Wesley, 1967.

57. DOLCH, E. W., *A Manual for Remedial Reading* (2nd ed.), Champaign, Ill.: Garrard, 1945.

58. ———, *Psychology and Teaching of Reading* (2nd ed.), Champaign, Ill.: Garrard, 1951.

59. ———, *Problems in Reading.* Champaign, Ill.: Garrard, 1948.

60. DOUGLAS, J. W. B., J. M. ROSS, and J. E. COOPER, "The Relationship Between Handedness, Attainment and Adjustment in a National Sample of School Children," *Educational Research,* 9 (1967), 223–232.

61. DURRELL, D. D., *Improving Reading Instruction.* New York: Harcourt Brace Jovanovich, 1955.

62. ———, *Durrell Analysis of Reading Difficulty* (rev. ed.), New York: Harcourt Brace Jovanovich, 1955.

63. DURRELL, D. D., and H. A. MURPHY, "The Auditory Discrimination Factor in Reading Readiness and Reading Disability," *Education,* 73 (1953), 556–560.

64. DYKSTRA, R., *Continuation of the Coordinating Center for First-Grade Reading Instruction Programs.* Final Report of Project no. 6–1651, contract no. OEC3-7-001651-0472. Minneapolis: University of Minnesota, 1967.

65. EAMES, T. H., "The Anatomical Basis of Lateral Dominance Anomalies," *American Journal of Orthopsychiatry,* 4 (1934), 524–528.

66. ———, "A Frequency Study of Physical Handicaps in Reading Disability and Unselected Groups," *Journal of Educational Research,* 29 (1935), 1–5.

67. EBERLY, D. W., *How Does My Child's Vision Affect His Reading?* Newark, Del.: International Reading Association, 1972.

68. ENGLEHARDT, R. M., "Speed Is Not a Nasty Word." *Journal of Reading,* 8 (1965), 330–331.

69. ENGLE, P. L., "Language Medium in Early School Years for Minority Language Groups," *Review of Educational Research,* 45 (1975), 283–325.

70. *Everyreader Series.* St. Louis: Webster Press, 1962.

71. FARR, ROGER, *Reading: What can be Measured?* Newark, Del.: International Reading Association, 1967.

72. FARRIS, L. P., "Visual Defects as Factors Influencing Achievement in Reading," *Journal of Experimental Education,* 5 (1936), 58–60.

73. FEATHERSTONE, W. B., *Teaching the Slow Learner,* (rev. ed.), New York: Bureau of Publications, Teachers College, Columbia University, 1951.

74. FELDHUSEN, J. F., J. R. THURSTON, and J. J. BENNING, "Longitudinal Analysis of Classroom Behavior and School Achievement," *Journal of Experimental Education,* 38 (1970), 4–10.

75. FERNALD, G. M., *Remedial Techniques in Basic School Subjects.* New York: McGraw-Hill, 1943.

76. FISHER, B., "A Psychologist's Evaluation of Teachers' Reports and Suggestions for Their Improvement," *Educational Administration and Supervision,* 38 (1952), 175–179.

77. FRIES, CHARLES C., *Linguistics and Reading.* New York: Holt, Rinehart and Winston, 1963.

78. FROST, B. P., "Some Personality Characteristics of Poor Readers," *Psychology in the Schools,* 2 (1965), 218–220.

79. FRY, E., "Programmed Instruction and Automation in Beginning Reading," *Elementary Reading Instruction.* Boston: Allyn and Bacon, 1969, 400–413.

80. GANN, E., *Reading Difficulty and Personality Organization.* New York: King's Crown, 1945.

81. GATES, A. I., "An Experimental and Statistical Study of Reading and Reading Tests," pp. 303–314; 445–464, *Journal of Educational Psychology,* 12 (1921).

82. ———, "Failure in Reading and Social Adjustment," *Journal of the National Educational Association,* 25 (1936), 205–206.

83. ———, *The Improvement of Reading* (3rd ed.), New York: Macmillan, 1947.

84. ———, *Interest and Ability in Reading.* New York: Macmillan, 1930.

85. _____, "The Role of Personality Adjustment in Reading Disability," *Journal of Genetic Psychology*, 59 (1941), 77–83.

86. GATES, A. I., and G. L. BOND, "Relation of Handedness, Eye-Sighting, and Acuity Dominance to Reading," *Journal of Educational Psychology*, 27 (1936), 455–456.

87. _____, "Some Outcomes of Instruction in the Speyer Experimental School (P. S. 500)," *Teachers College Record*, 38 (1936), 206–217.

88. GATES, A. I., and E. C. CASON, "An Evaluation of Tests for Diagnosis of Ability to Read by Phrases or 'Thought Units,' " *Elementary School Journal*, 46 (1945), 23–32.

89. GAVER, M. V., "Effectiveness of Centralized Library Services in Elementary Schools (phase 1)," *Library Quarterly*, 31 (1961) 245–256.

90. Geneva Medico-Educational Service, "Problems Posed by Dyslexia," *Journal of Learning Disabilities*, 1 (1968), 158–171.

91. GILLESPIE, P. H., and L. JOHNSON, *Teaching Reading to the Mildly Retarded Child*, Columbus, Ohio: Charles E. Merrill, 1974.

92. GLIESSMAN, D., "Understanding in Reading from the Viewpoint of Science Psychology," *The Reading Teacher*, vol. 13, 1959, pp. 22–28.

93. GOODGLASS, H., and M. BARTON, "Handedness and Differential Perceptions of Verbal Stimuli in Left and Right Visual Fields," *Perceptual and Motor Skills*, 17 (1963), 851–854.

94. GOODMAN, K. S., "Miscues: Windows on the Reading Process," in *Miscue analysis: application to reading instruction*, ed. K. S. Goodman. Champaign, Urbana, Ill.: ERIC Clearinghouse on Reading and Communication, National Council of Teachers of English, 1973.

95. GOODMAN, K. S., and CAROLYN BURKE, *Theoretically Based Studies of Patterns of Miscues in Oral Reading Performance*. Final Report, project no. 9–0375, grant no. OEG–0–320375–4269, U. S. Dept. of Health, Education & Welfare, 1973.

96. GOODMAN, YETTA M., and CAROLYN BURKE, *Reading Miscue Inventory-Manual*. New York: Macmillan, 1971.

97. GROFF, PATRICK, "Reading Ability and Auditory Discrimination: Are They Related?" *The Reading Teacher*, 28 (1975), 742–747.

98. HAEFNER, R., *The Educational Significance of Left-Handedness*. New York: Bureau of Publications, Teachers College, Columbia University, 1929.

99. HAMMILL, D. D., and S. C. LARSEN, "The Relationship of Selected Auditory Perceptual Skills and Reading Ability," *Journal of Learning Disabilities,* 7 (1974), 429–435.

100. HARRIS, A. J., and E. R. SIPAY, *How to Increase Reading Ability* (6th ed.), New York: David McKay, 1975.

101. HART, B. O., *Teaching Reading to Deaf Children,* in The Lexington School for the Deaf Education Series, Book IV. New York, N.Y.: Alexander Graham Bell Association for the Deaf, 1976.

102. HEGGE, T. G., S. A. KIRK, and W. D. KIRK, *Remedial Reading Drills.* Ann Arbor, Mich.: Wahr, 1945.

103. HENRY, S., "Children's Audiograms in Relation to Reading Attainment," *Journal of Genetic Psychology,* 70 (1947), 211–231; 71 (1948), 3–63.

104. HERBER, H. L., "Reading Study Skills: Some Studies," *Reading and Inquiry.* Newark, Del.: International Reading Association, 10 (1965), 94–96.

105. HERBERT, D. J., "Reading Comprehension as a Function of Self Concept," *Perceptual and Motor Skills,* 27 (1968), 78.

106. HEWETT, F. M., *The Emotionally Distrubed Child in the Classroom.* Boston: Allyn and Bacon, 1968.

107. HILDRETH, G., *Teaching Reading.* New York: Holt, Rinehart and Winston, 1968.

108. HILLERICH, R. L., "Eye-Hand Dominance and Reading Achievement," *American Educational Research Journal,* 1 (1964), 121–126.

109. HUBER, M. B., *The Influence of Intelligence upon Children's Reading Interest.* New York: Bureau of Publications, Teachers College, Columbia University, 1928.

110. HUELSMAN, C. B., Jr., "The WISC Subtest Syndrome for Disabled Readers," *Perceptual and Motor Skills,* 30 (1970), 535–550.

111. *Interesting Reading Series.* Chicago: Follett, 1961.

112. ISOM, J. B., "Neurological Research Relevant to Reading," in *Perception and Reading,* ed. H. K. Smith. Newark, Del.: International Reading Association, 1968.

113. JASTAK, J., "Interferences in Reading," *Psychological Bulletin,* 31 (1934), 244–272.

114. JENSEMA, C., *The Relationship between Academic Achievement and the Dem-*

ographic Characteristics of Hearing Impaired Children and Youth. Office of Demographic Studies, Gallaudet College, Washington, D. C., 1975.

115. JOBE, F. W., *Screening Vision in Schools.* Newark, Del.: International Reading Association, 1976.

116. JOHNSON, M. S., "Factors Related to Disability in Reading," *Journal of Experimental Education,* 26 (1957), 1–26.

117. JONES, R., and E. VAN WHY, "Tachistoscopic Training in the Fourth and Fifth Grades," *Journal of Developmental Reading,* 6 (1963), 177–185.

118. JUNGBLUT, A., and J. H. COLEMAN, "Reading Content that Interests Seventh, Eighth, and Ninth Grade Students," *Journal of Educational Research,* 58 (1965), 393–401.

119. KARLSEN, B., *A Comparison of Some Educational and Psychological Characteristics of Successful and Unsuccessful Readers at the Elementary School Level.* Ph.D. dissertation, University of Minnesota, Minneapolis, 1954.

120. KENNEDY, H., "A Study of Children's Hearing as It Relates to Reading," *Journal of Experimental Education,* 10 (1942), 238–251.

121. KEPHART, N. C., *The Slow Learner in the Classroom* (2nd ed.), Columbus, Ohio: Charles E. Merrill, 1971.

122. KIRK, S. A., *Teaching Reading to Slow-Learning Children.* Boston: Houghton Mifflin, 1940.

123. KIRK, S. A., and J. ELKINS, "Characteristics of Children Enrolled in the Child Service Demonstration Centers," *Journal of Learning Disabilities,* 8 (1975), 630–637.

124. KNOX, G. E., "Classroom Symptoms of Visual Difficulty," *Clinical Studies in Reading:* II. Supplementary Educational Monographs no. 77, pp. 97–101. Chicago: University of Chicago Press, 1953.

125. KOOS, E. M., "Manifestations of Cerebral Dominance and Reading Retardation in Primary-Grade Children," *Journal of Genetic Psychology,* 54 (1964), 155–165.

126. KOZLOWSKI, L. J., "Identifying Visual Problems by Teacher Observation," *Clinical Studies in Reading:* III. Suppl. Educ. Monog. no. 97. Chicago: University of Chicago Press, 1968, 117–121.

127. KRANTZ, LAVERN, *The Relationship of Reading Abilities and Basic Skills of the Elementary School to Success in the Interpretation of the Content Materials*

in the High School. Ph.D. dissertation, University of Minnesota, Minneapolis, 1955.

128. LADD, M. R., *The Relation of Social, Economic, and Personal Characteristics to Reading Ability.* New York: Bureau of Publications, Teachers College, Columbia University, 1933.

129. LARRICK, NANCY, "Making the Most of Children's Interests." *Education,* 73 (1953), 523–531.

130 LARSEN, J., C. E. TILLMAN, J. J. ROSS, P. SATZ, B. CASSIN, and W. WOLKIN, "Factors in Reading Achievement: An Interdisciplinary Approach," *Journal of Learning Disabilities,* 6 (1973), pp. 636–644.

131. LAZAR, M., MARCELLA K. DRAPER, and LOUISE H. SCHWIETART, *A Practical Guide to Individualized Reading.* New York: Bureau of Educational Research, Board of Education of the City of New York, Publication no. 40, October 1960.

132. LIN-FU, JANE S., *Vision Screening of Children.* U. S. Department of Health, Education and Welfare. Washington: U. S. Government Printing Office, PHS Publication no. 2042, 1971.

133. LLOYD, H. M., "What's Ahead in Reading for the Disadvantaged?" *The Reading Teacher,* 18 (1965), 471–476.

134. LORGE, IRVING, "Predicting Readability," *Teacher's College Record,* 45 (March 1944), 404–419.

135. LYLE, J. G., "Certain Antenatal, Perinatal, and Developmental Variables and Reading Retardation in Middle-Class Boys," *Child Development,* 1970, 41, 481–491.

136. McKEE, P., *The Teaching of Reading in the Elementary School.* Boston: Houghton Mifflin, 1948.

137. McLEOD, B., *Teachers' Problems with Exceptional Children, IV: Deaf and Hard-Of-Hearing Children.* Office of Education Pamphlet no. 54. Washington: U. S. Government Printing Office, 1934.

138. *The Macmillan Reading Spectrum.* New York: Macmillan, 1964.

139. MANOLAKES, G., "The Effects of Tachistoscope Training in an Adult Reading Program," *Journal of Applied Psychology,* 36 (1952), 410–412.

140. MARTYN, D. W., "Observations of an Itinerant Teacher," *Academic Therapy,* 7 (1972), 439–442.

141. MONROE, M., *Children Who Cannot Read.* Chicago: University of Chicago Press, 1932.

142. MONROE, M., and B. BACKUS, *Remedial Reading.* Boston: Houghton Mifflin, 1937.

143. *The Morgan Bay Mysteries,* Menlo Park, Calif.: Addison-Wesley, 1962.

144. MUEHL, S., "Relation between Word Recognition Errors and Hand-Eye Preference in Preschool Children," *Journal of Educational Psychology,* 54 (1963), 316–321.

145. MYERS, P. I., and D. D. HAMMILL, *Methods for Learning Disorders.* New York: John Wiley & Sons, 1969.

146. *The New Phonics We Use.* Ardmore, Pa.: Meredith, 1972.

147. NORVELL, G. W., *What Boys and Girls Like to Read.* Morristown, N. J.: Silver Burdett, 1958.

148. O'BRIEN, J. A., *Silent Reading.* New York: Macmillan, 1922.

149. OLSON, W. C., "Reading as a Function of Total Growth," *Reading in pupil development.* Supplementary Educational Monographs no. 51, Chicago: University of Chicago Press, 1940, pp. 233–237.

150. ORTON, S. T., *Reading, Writing and Speech Problems in Children.* New York: W. W. Norton, 1937.

151. *The Pal Series.* Middletown, Conn.: Xerox Education Publications, 1973.

152. PARK, G. E., and K. A. SCHNEIDER, "Thyroid Function in Relation to Dyslexia (Reading Failures)," *Journal of Reading Behavior,* 7 (1975), 197–199.

153. *Phonetic Reader Series.* Cambridge, Mass.: Education Publishing Service, 1962.

154. PIKULSKI, J. J., "Assessing Information about Intelligence and Reading," *The Reading Teacher,* 29 (1975), 157–163.

155. POLING, D. L., "Auditory Deficiencies of Poor Readers," *Clinical Studies in Reading,* II, 107–111, Supplementary Educational Monographs, no. 77. Chicago: University of Chicago Press, 1953.

156. PRENDERGAST, M. A., and D. M. BINDER, "Relationships of Selected Self Concept and Academic Achievement Measures," *Measurement and Evaluation in Guidance,* 8, (1975), 92–95.

157. PRESSEY, L. W., and S. L. PRESSEY, "A Critical Study of the Concept of Silent Reading Ability," *Journal of Educational Psychology,* 12 (1921), 25–31.

158. PUTNAM, LILLIAN R., "Controversial Aspects of Individualized Reading," pp. 99–100. *Improvement of Reading Through Classroom Practice,* International Reading Association Conference Proceedings, 9. Newark, Del.: International Reading Association, 1964.

159. QUANT, I., *Self-Concept and Reading.* Newark, Del.: International Reading Association, 1972.

160. RABINOVITCH, R. D., "Dyslexia: Psychiatric Considerations," pp. 73–79, in *Reading disability: progress and research needs in dyslexia,* ed. John Money. Baltimore: Johns Hopkins Press, 1962.

161. REYNOLDS, M., *A Study of the Relationships Between Auditory Characteristics and Specific Silent Reading Abilities.* Ph.D. dissertation, University of Minnesota, Minneapolis, 1950.

162. RIST, R. C., "Social Class and Teacher Expectations: The Self-Fulfilling Prophecy in Ghetto Education," *Harvard Educational Review,* 40 (1970), 411–451.

163. ROBINSON, HELEN M., "Visual and Auditory Modalities Related to Methods for Beginning Reading," *Reading Research Quarterly,* 8 (1972), 7–39.

164. ———, *Why Pupils Fail in Reading.* Chicago: University of Chicago Press, 1946.

165. ROSWELL, F., and G. NATCHEZ, *Reading Disability: Diagnosis and Treatment* (2nd ed.). New York: Basic Books, 1971.

166. ROURKE, B. P., "Brain-Behavior Relationships in Children with Learning Disabilities," *American Psychologist,* 30 (1975), 911–920.

167. RUSSELL, D. H., and E. E. KARP, *Reading Aids through the Grades* (rev. ed.). New York: Bureau of Publications, Teachers College, Columbia University, 1951.

168. RUTHERFORD, W. L., "Vision and Perception in the Reading Process," in *Vistas in reading,* ed. J. A. Figurel. Newark, Del.: International Reading Association, 1967, pp. 503–507.

169. RYSTROM, R., "Reading, Language, and Nonstandard Dialects: A Research Report," in *Language Differences: Do they Interfere?* Newark, Del.: International Reading Association, 1973, pp. 86–90.

170. SANDIN, A. A., *Social and Emotional Adjustments of Regularly Promoted and Non-Promoted Pupils.* New York: Bureau of Publications, Teachers College, Columbia University, 1944.

171. SARTAIN, HARRY W., "The Roseville Experiment with Individualized Reading." *The Reading Teacher,* 13 (March 1960), 277–281.

172. SEIGLER, H. G., and M. D. GYNTHER, "Reading Ability of Children and Family Harmony," *Journal of Developmental Reading,* 4 (1960), 17–24.

173. SEWELL, T. E., and R. A. SEVERSON, "Intelligence and Achievement in First-Grade Black Children," p. 112. *Journal of Consulting and Clinical Psychology* 43 (1975).

174. SHANNON, O. S., C. R. HORNE, G. B. JAMES, and B. F. JOHNSON, "Operation Head Start in the Memphis and Shelby County Schools," *The Reading Teacher,* 19 (1966), 335–341.

175. SHORES, J. H., "Reading of Science for Two Separate Purposes as Perceived by Six Grade Students and Able Adult Readers," *Elementary English,* 17 (1960), 461–468.

176. SIMONS, H. D., "Black Dialect and Learning to Read," in *Literacy for Diverse Learners.* Newark, Del.: International Reading Association, 1973, 3–13.

177. CAROLINE, SISTER MARY, *Breaking the Sound Barrier.* New York: Macmillan, 1960.

178. SLOVER, VERA, "Comic Books vs. Story Books," *Elementary English,* (May 1959).

179. SMITH, D. V., "The Goals of the Literature Period and the Grade Sequence of Desirable Experiences," *Improving reading in all curriculum areas.* Supplementary Educational Monographs no. 76, Chicago: University of Chicago Press, 1952, pp. 188–194.

180. ————, "Literature and Personal Reading," *Reading in the Elementary School.* Forty-eighth Yearbook of the National Society for the Study of Education, part II. Chicago: University of Chicago Press, 1949, pp. 205–232.

181. SMITH, N. B., *Reading Instruction for Today's Children.* Englewood Cliffs, N. J.: Prentice-Hall, 1963.

182. SORNSON, H. H., *A Longitudinal Study of the Relationship Between Various Child Behavior Ratings and Success in Reading.* Ph.D. dissertation, University of Minnesota, Minneapolis, 1950.

183. SPACHE, G. D., *Good Reading for the Disadvantaged Reader.* Champaign, Ill.: Garrard, 1970.

184. ———, *Investigating the Issues of Reading Disabilities.* Boston: Allyn and Bacon, 1976.

185. ———, "A New Readability Formula for Primary-Grade Reading," *Elementary School Journal,* 52 (March 1953), 410–413.

186. ———, *Toward Better Reading.* Champaign, Ill.: Garrard, 1963.

187. SPACHE, G. D., and E. B. SPACHE, *Reading in the Elementary School,* (2nd ed.), Boston: Allyn and Bacon, 1969.

188. SPACHE, G. D., and C. E. TILLMAN, "A Comparison of the Visual Profiles of Retarded and Non-Retarded Readers," *Journal of Developmental Reading,* 5 (1962), 101–109.

189. SPACHE, GEORGE D., and others, "A Study of a Longitudinal First Grade Reading Readiness Program," *Cooperative Research Project 2742.* Tallahassee, Fla.: Florida State Department of Education, 1965.

190. *Specific Skills Series.* New York: Barnell Loft, 1976.

191. *SRA Reading Laboratories.* Chicago: Science Research Associates, 1961.

192. STANCHFIELD, J. M., "Boys' Reading Interests as Revealed through Personal Conferences," *The Reading Teacher,* 16 (1962), 41–44.

193. STEVENS, D. O., "Reading Difficulty and Classroom Acceptance," *Reading Teacher,* 25 (1971), 52–55.

194. STONE, C. R., *Eye and Ear Fun.* St. Louis: Webster, 1943.

195. STRANG, R., "Diagnosis and Remediation of Reading Difficulties in Content Fields," *Improving Reading in Content Fields.* Supplementary Educational Monographs no. 62. Chicago: University of Chicago Press, 1947, pp. 197–201.

196. ———, *Diagnostic Teaching of Reading.* New York: McGraw-Hill, 1964.

197. ———, "Relationships between Certain Aspects of Intelligence and Certain Aspects of Reading," *Educational and Psychological Measurement,* 3 (1943), 355–359.

198. ———, *Reading Diagnosis and Remediation.* Newark, Del.: International Reading Association, 1968.

199. STRANG, RUTH, C. M. McCULLOUGH, and A. E. TRAXLER, *The Improvement of Reading* (4th ed.). New York: McGraw-Hill, 1967.

200. *Sullivan Associates Readers.* New York: McGraw-Hill, 1966.

201. Sullivan Associates, *The Programmed Reading Series.* New York: McGraw-Hill, 1973.

202. TAYLOR, E. A., *Controlled Reading.* Chicago: University of Chicago Press, 1937.

203. TEEGARDEN, L., "Clinical Identification of the Prospective Non-Readers," *Child Development,* 3 (1932), 346–358.

204. THAYER, J. A., "Johnny Could Read—What Happened?" pp. 501–506, 561. *Journal of Reading,* 13 (1970).

205. THOMPSON, H., *An Experimental Study of the Beginning Reading of Deaf-Mutes.* Bureau of Publications, Teachers College, Columbia University, 1927.

206. THOMSON, M., "Laterality and Reading Attainment," *British Journal of Educational Psychology,* 45 (1975), 317–321.

207. THONIS, E. W., *Literacy for America's Spanish Speaking Children.* Newark, Del., 1976.

208. TINKER, K. J., "The Role of Laterality in Reading Disability," pp. 300–303 in *Reading and Inquiry,* Conference Proceedings of International Reading Association. Newark, Del: International Reading Association, 10 (1965).

209. TINKER, M. A., *Preparing Your Child for Reading.* New York: Holt, Rinehart and Winston, 1971.

210. ————, "The Relation of Speed to Comprehension in Reading," *School and Society,* 34 (1932), 158–160.

211. ————, "The Study of Eye Movements in Reading," *Psychological Bulletin,* 43 (1946), 93–120.

212. TINKER, M. A., and C. M. McCULLOUGH, *Teaching Elementary Reading* (4th ed.), Englewood Cliffs, N. J.: Prentice-Hall, 1975.

213. TRAXLER, A. E., "A Study of the California Test of Mental Maturity: Advanced Battery," *Journal of Educational Research,* 32 (1939), 329–335.

214. VAN ALLEN, R., "How a Language-Experience Program Works," in *Elementary Reading Instruction,* pp. 361–368. Boston: Allyn and Bacon, 1969.

215. VAUGHN, B. I, "Reading Interests of Eigth-Grade Students," *Journal of Developmental Reading,* 6 (1963), 149–155.

216. VEATCH, JEANNETTE, *Individualizing Your Reading Program.* New York: G. P. Putnam and Sons, 1959.

217. VENEZKY, R. L., and R. S. CHAPMAN, "Is Learning to Read Dialect Bound?" pp. 62–69, in *Language Differences: Do they Interfere?* Newark, Del.: International Reading Association, 1973.

218. VERNON, MAGDALEN D., *Backwardness in Reading.* Cambridge, England: Cambridge University Press, 1957.

219. ———, *Visual Perception and Its Relation to Reading.* Newark, Del.: International Reading Association, 1969.

220. VICK, M. L., "Relevant Content for the Black Elementary School Pupil," pp. 14–22, in *Literacy for Diverse Learners.* Newark, Del.: International Reading Association, 1973.

221. WATTENBERG, W. W., and C. Clifford, "Relationship of Self-Concept to Beginning Achievement in Reading," p. 58, in *Childhood Education,* 43 (1966).

222. WEINTRAUB, SAMUEL, *Auditory Perception and Deafness,* in *Reading Research Profiles.* Newark, Del.: International Reading Association, 1972.

223. ———, "Eye Hand Preference and Reading," *Reading Teacher,* 21 (1968), 369–401.

224. ———, *Vision-Visual Discrimination,* in *Reading Research Profiles.* Newark, Del.: International Reading Association, 1973.

225. WESTOVER, F. L., *Controlled Eye Movements versus Exercises in Reading.* New York: Bureau of Publications, Teachers College, Columbia University, 1946.

226. WHEELER, L. R., and V. D. WHEELER, "The Relationship Between Reading Ability and Intelligence among University Freshmen," *Journal of Educational Psychology,* 40 (1949), 230–238.

227. WILKINS, S. V., "Personality Maladjustment as a Causative Factor in Reading Disability," *Elementary School Journal,* 42 (1941), 268–279.

228. WITTY, PAUL, *How to Become a Better Reader.* Chicago: Science Research Associates, 1953.

229. ———, "Individualized Reading: A Postscript," *Elementary English,* 31 (March 1964), 211–217.

230. WITTY, P., and D. KOPEL, "Factors Associated with the Etiology of Reading Disability," *Journal of Educational Research,* 29 (1936), 449–459.

231. ———, *Reading and the Educative Process.* Boston: Ginn, 1939.

232. ———, "Sinistrad and Mixed Manual-Ocular Behavior in Reading Disability," *Journal of Educational Psychology,* 27 (1936), 119–134.

233. WITTY, P., and H. S. SCHACHTER, "Hypothyroidism as a Factor in Maladjustment," *Journal of Psychology,* 2 (1936), 377–392.

234. YOUNG, F. A., "Reading Measures of Intelligence and Refractive Errors," *American Journal and Archives of American Academy of Optometry,* 40 (1963), 257–264.

235. ZIMMERMAN, I. L., and G. N. ALLEBRAND, "Personality Characteristics and Attitudes toward Achievement of Good and Poor Readers," *Journal of Educational Research,* 59 (1965), 28–30.

Appendixes

I. SELECTED SOURCES OF GRADED BOOK LISTS

A Basic Book Collection for the Elementary Grades (7th ed.), Chicago: American Library Association, 1960.

A Basic Book Collection for Junior High Schools (3rd ed.), Chicago: American Library Association, 1960.

CUSHENBERY, D. C., *Reading Improvement in the Elementary School,* pp. 165–192. West Nyack, N.J.: Parker Publishing Co., 1969.

GRAY, LILLIAM, *Teaching Children How to Read* (3rd ed.), New York: Ronald Press, 1963. List of graded books, pp. 409–410.

HARRIS, ALBERT J., *How to Increase Reading Ability* (6th ed.), Appendix B. A series of readers rated for reading grade level and interest grade level. New York: David McKay, 1975.

LARRICK, NANCY, *A Teacher's Guide to Children's Books.* Columbus, Ohio: Charles E. Merrill, 1963. Several graded book lists.

Reading Cumulative Record, Primary Grades. Fort Lauderdale, Fla.: The Mills Center (1512 E. Broward Blvd.), 1963.

SPACHE, G. D., *Good reading for Poor Readers* (rev. ed.), Champaign, Ill.: Garrard, 1974. Graded and classified lists.

STRANG, RUTH, *Helping Your Child Improve His Reading.* pp. 220–242. New York: E. P. Dutton, 1962. Graded lists of children's reading materials.

VAN ORDEN, P., *The Elementary School Library Collection* (10th ed.), New Brunswick, N.J.: Bro-dart Foundation, 1976.

II.   SOURCES OF MATERIALS

Adventures with Books: A Reading List for Elementary Schools. Chicago: National Council of Teachers of English, 1960.

Aids to Selection of Materials for Children and Young People. National Educational Association Journal, January, 1962.

ALLEN, PATRICIA H., compiler, *Best Books for Children—3,300 Selected Titles* (rev. ed.), New York: R. R. Bowker, 1964.

Basic Book Collection for High Schools. Chicago: American Library Association, 1964.

Best Books for Children. A Catalog of 4000 titles. Boston: Campbell and Hall, 1970.

Bibliography of Books for Children. Washington, D.C.: Association for Childhood Education. An annual pamphlet.

Booklist: A guide to New Books. Chicago: American Library Association. This bimonthly journal has a section devoted to children's books.

Books for Children, 1968–1969: Preschool through Junior High School. Chicago: American Library Association, 1970.

Books for Children. Chicago: American Library Association. Published annually.

Books of the Year for Children. New York: Child Study Association of America. A pamphlet dealing with books for boys and girls, published annually.

Bulletin of Children's Book Center. Chicago: Center for Children's Books, University of Chicago Library. Issued monthly.

BUROS, O. K., ed., *Reading tests and Reviews 2.* Highland Park, N.J.: Gryphon Press, 1975.

————, ed., *The Seventh Mental Measurements Yearbook.* Highland Park, N.J.: Gryphon Press, 1972. Reviews and evaluations of mental tests, reading tests, and machines used in reading. Also see previous editions.

Chicago Tribune, *Books for Children Supplement.* This supplement and those in other newspapers are printed as a children's book section, usually in October or November.

Children's Book Council. Twelve recommended book lists in *The World of Children's Books*. New York: Children's Book Council.

COOKE, D. E., chairman, *The Road to Better Reading*. pp. 77–83. Albany, N.Y.: New York Education Department, 1953. Films for reading improvement.

Coronet Instructional Films. 65 E. South Water St., Chicago, Ill. 60601. A wide variety of teaching films.

DEASON, H. J., compiler-director, *The AAAS Science Book List for Children*, (3rd ed.), Washington D. C.: American Association for the Advancement of Science, 1970.

DEVER, ESTHER, *Sources of Free and Inexpensive Educational Materials*. Grafton, W. Va. (P.O. Box 186): Published privately by the author, 1962.

DILL, B. E., *Children's Catalog* (13th ed.), New York: H. W. Wilson Co., 1976.

DOLCH, E. W., *Dolch Materials for Better Teaching of Reading*. Champaign, Ill.: Garrard. A variety of devices and other materials for developing word recognition, sight vocabulary, etc. Request catalog from publisher.

EAKIN, MARY K., *Good Books for Children* (3rd ed.), Chicago: University of Chicago Press, 1967.

Free and Inexpensive Learning Materials (12th ed.), Nashville, Tenn.: Division of Surveys and Field Services, George Peabody College for Teachers, 1964–1965.

FULLER, MURIEL, ed., *More Junior Authors*. New York: H. W. Wilson Co., 1963.

GOODMAN, YETTA M., and KENNETH S. GOODMAN, compilers, *Linguistics and the Teaching of Reading—An Annotated Bibliography*. Newark, Del.: International Reading Association, 1967.

Graphic Tools (3rd ed.), Austin, Tex. (841 Airport Blvd., Lot No. 7); Graphic Tools for Teachers, 1965.

GRAY, LILLIAN, *Teaching Children to Read* (3rd ed.), New York: Ronald Press, 1963. Various book lists and materials.

GREEN, RICHARD T., compiler, *Comprehension in Reading—An Annotated Bibliography*. Newark, Del.: International Reading Association, 1971.

Guide to Children's Magazines, Newspapers, and Reference books (rev. ed.), Washington, D. C. (3615 Wisconsin Ave., 20016): Association for Childhood Education International, 1964.

HILL, WALTER, and NORMA BARTIN, compilers, *Reading Programs in Secondary Schools—An Annotated Bibliography*. Newark, Del.: International Reading Association, 1971.

HOLLOWELL, LILLIAN, *A Book of Children's Literature* (rev. ed.). New York: Holt, Rinehart and Winston, 1966.

HORKHEIMER, MARY F., and J. W. DIFFER. *Educators' Guide to Free Filmstrips*. Randolf, Wis.: Educators Progress Service, 1963.

————, *Educators Guide to Free Films*. Randolf, Wis.: Educators Progress Service, 1963.

Horn Book Magazine. Boston: Horn Book. A monthly magazine devoted to books and reading material for young children.

Information Please Almanac. New York: Simon and Schuster. Revised yearly.

LARRICK, NANCY, *A Parent's Guide to Children's Reading* (rev. ed.), New York: Doubleday, 1969.

Let's Read Together (2nd ed.), Chicago: American Library Association, 1964.

Paperback Goes to School. New York: Bureau of Independent Publishers and Distributors (10 E. 40th St.), 1963.

Reader's Choice. A catalogue obtainable from Scholastic Magazines, 909 Sylvan Ave., Englewood Cliffs, N.J.

Reader's Digest Service. Pleasantville, N.Y.: Educational Division, Reader's Digest Services. A variety of books and learning aids.

ROSWELL, FLORENCE, and GLADYS NATCHEZ, *Reading Disability: Diagnosis and Treatment* (2nd ed.), New York: Basic Books, 1970, pp. 234–241. Games, devices, and workbooks.

SCHAIN, R. L., and M. PALMER, *How to Get and How to Use Free and Inexpensive Teaching Aids*. New York: Teachers Practical Press, 1963.

SEELS, BARBARA, and EDGAR DALE, compilers, *Readability and Reading: An Annotated Bibliography*. Newark, Del: International Reading Association, 1971.

SPACHE, G. D., *Good Reading for Poor Readers* (rev. ed.), Champaign, Ill.: Garrard, 1974.

————, compiler, *Sources of Good Books for Poor Readers—An Annotated Bibliography,* (rev. ed.), Newark, Del.: International Reading Association, 1969.

SPACHE, G. D., and EVELYN B. SPACHE, *Reading in the Elementary School* (3rd ed.), Boston: Allyn and Bacon, 1973. See *Selected Readings* following each chapter.

SPITZER, LILLIAN K., compiler, *Selected Materials on the Language-Experience Approach to Reading Instruction—An Annotated Bibliography.* Newark, Del.: International Reading Association, 1967.

TINKER, M. A., *Preparing Your Child for Reading.* New York: Holt, Rinehart and Winston, 1971. See *Appendix* for books to read together and list of teaching materials.

TOOZE, R., *Storytelling.* Englewood Cliffs, N.J.: Prentice-Hall, 1959.

TRELA, THADDEUS M., and GEORGE J. BECKER, compilers, *Case Studies in Reading—An Annotated Bibliography.* Newark, Del.: International Reading Association, 1971.

VERNON, M. D., *Visual Perception and Its Relation to Reading—An Annotated Bibliography* (rev. ed.), Newark, Del.: International Reading Association, 1969.

WEST, DOROTHY H., and RACHEL SHOR, eds., *Children's Catalog* (12th ed.), New York: H. W. Wilson, 1971.

World Almanac and Book of Facts. New York: New York World-Telegram and Sun, (revised yearly).

III. REPRESENTATIVE INTELLIGENCE TESTS

American School Intelligence Test. Bobbs-Merrill. Grades kgn–3, 4–6, 7–9, 10–12. Two forms. Time: not given. Group test.

California Short-Form Test of Mental Maturity. CTB/McGraw-Hill, Grades kgn–1.5, 1.5–3.5, 3–4, 4–6, 6–7, 7–9, 9–12, 12–16, and adults. One form. Time: 45–48 minutes. Group test.

California Test of Mental Maturity. McGraw-Hill. Grades kgn–1.5, 1.5–3.5, 4–6, 7–9, 9–12, 12–16, and adults. One form. Time: 48–92 minutes. Three scores: total mental, language, nonlanguage. Group test.

Chicago Non-Verbal Examination. Psychological Corporation. Age 6–adult. One form. Time: about 55 minutes. Group test.

Cooperative School Ability Test. Educational Testing Service. Grades 4–6, 6–8, 8–10, 10–12. Two forms. Group test.

Culture Fair Intelligence Tests. Institute for Personality and Ability Testing. Ages 4 to adult. Three scales: ages 4–8 (one form); ages 8–14 and average adult (two forms); ages 13–superior adult (two forms). Group tests not requiring reading.

Detroit Tests of Learning Aptitude. Bobbs-Merrill. Ages 3–adult. One form. Individual test.

Full-Range Picture Vocabulary Test. Psychological Test Specialists. Preschool to adult. Two forms. Individual test.

Goodenough-Harris Drawing Test. Harcourt Brace Jovanovich. Ages 3–13. Group test.

Henmon-Nelson Tests of Mental Ability, rev. ed. Houghton Mifflin. Grades kgn–2, 3–6, 6–9, 9–12, 13–17. Two forms. Time: 30 minutes. Group test.

Junior Scholastic Aptitude Test, rev. ed. Educational Records Bureau. Three forms. Time: 60 minutes. Group test.

Kuhlmann-Anderson Intelligence Tests, 7th ed. Personnel Press. Grades 1, 2, 3–4, 4–5, 5–7, 7–9, 9–12. One form. Time: 40–45 minutes. Group test.

Kuhlmann-Finch Tests. American Guidance. Grades 1, 2, 3, 4, 5, 6, 7–9, 10–12. Time 25–30 minutes. Group test.

Lorge-Thorndike Intelligence Tests, Multi-Level Edition. Houghton Mifflin. Grades 3–13. Verbal, nonverbal, and total scores. Group test.

Otis-Lennon Mental Ability Test (Revision of Otis Tests). Harcourt Brace Jovanovich. Two forms. Grades kgn., first half grade 1, 1.5–3.9, 4–6, 7–9, 10–12.

Otis Quick Scoring Mental Ability Tests. Harcourt Brace Jovanovich. Grades 1–4, 4–9, 9–16. Two forms. Time: 30–40 minutes. Group test.

Peabody Picture Vocabulary Test. American Guidance Service. Ages 2.5–18. Two forms. Vocabulary only. Individual test.

Pintner-Cunningham Primary Test. Harcourt Brace Jovanovich. Group test. Grades kgn–2.

Scholastic Mental Ability Tests. Scholastic Testing Service. Grades kgn–1, 2–3, 4–9. One or two forms at different levels. Time: 26–60 minutes. Group test.

Short Test of Educational Ability. Grades kgn–1, 2–3, 3–6, 6–9, 9–12. Group test.

Slosson Intelligence Test. Slosson Educational Publications. Ages 6 months–adult. No time limit. Individual test.

Revised Stanford-Binet Scale, 3rd ed. Houghton Mifflin. Ages 2–adult. No time limit. Individual test.

Wechsler Intelligence Scale for Children—Revised. Western Psychological Services. Ages 5–15. Verbal and performance scores. Time: 40–60 minutes. Individual test.

Wechsler Preschool and Primary Scale of Intelligence—Revised. Consulting Psychologists Press. Ages 4–6.5.

IV.   REPRESENTATIVE READING READINESS TESTS

American School Readiness Test, rev. ed. Bobbs-Merrill. Grades kgn–1. One form. Time: about 45 minutes. Vocabulary, visual discrimination of various kinds, recognition of words, following directions, memory for geometric forms. Group test.

Binion-Beck Reading Readiness Tests for Kindergarten and First Grade. Psychometric Affiliates. Grades kgn–1. One form. Time: about 40 minutes. Picture vocabulary and discrimination, following directions, memory for story, motor control.

Gates-MacGinitie Readiness Skills Test. Teachers College Press. Beginning first grade. Listening comprehension, auditory discrimination, visual discrimination, following directions, letter recognition, visual-motor coordination, auditory blending, word recognition. Individual test.

Harrison-Stroud Reading Readiness Profiles. Houghton Mifflin. Grades kgn–1. One form. Time: 79 minutes. Using symbols, visual discrimination, using the context, auditory discrimination, using context and auditory cues, naming letters.

Kindergarten evaluation of learning potential. McGraw-Hill. Included are provisions for evaluation of readiness by the teacher.

Lee-Clark Reading Readiness Tests, revised. McGraw-Hill. Grades kgn–1. One form. Time: about 15 minutes. Letter symbols, concepts, word symbols.

Macmillan Reading Readiness Test. Macmillan Publishing. Kgn. Quantified rating scale, visual perception, auditory perception, vocabulary concepts. Separate norms for disadvantaged children.

Metropolitan Readiness Tests. Harcourt Brace Jovanovich. Grades kgn–1. Two forms. Time: about 60 minutes. Reading readiness, number readiness, drawing a man.

Monroe Reading Aptitude Tests. Houghton Mifflin. Grades kgn–1. One form. Time: about 50 minutes. The 17 subtests include visual functions, auditory discrimination, memory for a story, motor control, vocabulary knowledge, length of sentences used, and laterality preferences.

Murphy-Durrell Diagnostic Reading Readiness Test. Harcourt Brace Jovanovich. Grade 1. One form. Time: parts 1–2, about 60 minutes; part 3, about 35–50 minutes. Auditory, visual, and learning rate scores.

Scholastic Reading Readiness Test. STS. Grades kgn–1. One form. Readiness.

Van Wagenen Reading Readiness Scales. Van Wagenen. Grades kgn–1. One form. Part I: Listening vocabulary; Part II: Range of information, perception of relations, opposites, memory span for ideas, word discrimination. Part I and Part II may be obtained separately.

V. REPRESENTATIVE READING AND STUDY SKILL TESTS

American School Achievement Tests. Bobbs-Merrill. Grades 2–3, 4–6, 7–9. Three forms. Reading and arithmetic; reading vocabulary, arithmetic and spelling; paragraph meaning and vocabulary, respectively, at successive levels.

Botel Reading Inventory. Follett Publishing. Grades 1–12. Two forms. Phonics mastery, word recognition, word comprehension, reading, listening. Group test.

California Phonics Survey. McGraw-Hill. Grades 7–College. One form. Time: one class period. Group testing of phonic accuracy.

California Reading Test. McGraw-Hill. Grades 1, 2, 3, lower 4, 4–6, 7–9, 9–14. Time: 20–50 minutes. Vocabulary, comprehension, total score.

Diagnostic Reading Scales (Spache). McGraw-Hill. Grades 1–6 and retarded readers in high school. Two forms. Time: less than 45 minutes. Materials for individual diagnosis of difficulties.

Diagnostic Reading Tests. Committee on Diagnostic Reading Tests. Grades kgn–4, 4–6, 7–13. Two to 8 forms. Time: 15–60 minutes on different parts. Survey test: rate, narrative comprehension, vocabulary and textbook-type comprehension. Diagnostic tests: vocabulary, comprehension, rate, word attack.

Diagnostic Reading Test: Pupil Progress Series. Scholastic Testing Service. Grades 1–8. One form. Word recognition, rate, specific comprehension, vocabulary, study skills.

Dolch Basic Sight Word Test. Garrard Publishing. Assigned to no specific grade. Untimed. Recognition of the 220 words in the Dolch Basic Word List.

Doren Diagnostic Reading Test. American Guidance Service. Any grade for analysis of word-recognition difficulties. One form.

Durrell Analysis of Reading Difficulty. Harcourt Brace Jovanovich. Grades 1–6. Time: 30–90 minutes. Materials for individual diagnosis of reading difficulties.

Durrell Reading-Listening Series. Harcourt Brace Jovanovich. Grades 1–3.5, 3.5–6, 7–9. Two forms. Listening and reading (vocabulary and sentences).

Gates Reading Survey. Teachers College Press. Grades 3–10. Three forms. Time: 45–60 minutes. Vocabulary and comprehension plus measures of rate and accuracy.

Gates-MacGinitie Reading Tests. Teachers College Press. Grades 1, 2, 3. Two forms for grades 1 and 2. Vocabulary and comprehension. Speed and accuracy for grades 2 and 3 (Primary CS), three forms Group tests.

Gates-MacGinitie Reading Tests: Survey D. Teachers College Press. Grades 4–6. Three forms. Speed and accuracy, vocabulary, comprehension.

Gates-McKillop Reading Diagnostic Tests. Teachers College Press. Grades 1–8. Two forms. Time: 60 –90 minutes. Materials for individual diagnosis of difficulties.

Gilmore Oral Reading Test. Harcourt Brace Jovanovich. Grades 1–8. Two forms. Time: 15–20 minutes. Comprehension, rate, and accuracy of oral reading. Analysis of errors used to diagnose reading difficulties.

Gray Oral Reading Tests (edited by H. M. Robinson). Bobbs-Merrill. Grades 1–12. Four forms. Time: a few minutes. Thirteen passages to provide data for analysis of errors.

High School Reading Test. Psychometric Affiliates. Grades 7–12. Two forms. Time: 40 minutes. Vocabulary, word discrimination, sentence meaning, paragraph comprehension.

Iowa Silent Reading Test. Harcourt Brace Jovanovich. Grades 4–8, 9–13. Four forms. Time: 45–60 minutes. Directed reading, comprehension of words, sentences, paragraphs, rate of reading, skill in alphabetizing and indexing.

Iowa Tests of Basic Skills. Houghton Mifflin. Grades 3–9. Four forms. Vocabulary, comprehension, language skills, work-study skills.

Lee-Clark Reading Test—First Reader. McGraw-Hill. Grades 1–2. Two forms. Time: about 25 minutes. Auditory and visual stimuli, following directions, completion, inference.

McCullough Word Analysis Tests. Personnel Press. Grades 4 through college. One form. Untimed. Diagnosis 7 types of word-analysis skills, 210 items.

Metropolitan Achievement Tests: Reading. Harcourt Brace Jovanovich. Grades 1, 2, 3, 3–4, 5, 6, 7, 8. Three forms. Time: about 45 minutes. Paragraph comprehension and vocabulary.

Monroe Diagnostic Reading Examination. Stoelting Company. Grades 1–6. One form. Time: about 45 minutes. Materials for individual diagnosis of difficulties.

Monroe Revised Silent Reading Tests. Bobbs-Merrill. Grades 3–5, 6–8, high school. Three and two forms respectively. Time 4–5 minutes. Rate and comprehension.

Monroe-Sherman Group Diagnostic Reading and Achievement Tests. C. H. Nevins. Grade 3 and up. One form. Achievement tests: paragraph meaning, speed, word discrimination, arithmetic, and spelling; aptitude tests; visual memory, auditory memory and discrimination, motor speed. Vocabulary. Group test.

Nelson Reading Test, Revised. Houghton Mifflin. Grades 3–9. Two forms. Time: 30 minutes. Vocabulary and comprehension.

New Developmental Reading Tests—Bond-Balow-Hoyt. Rand McNally. Grades 4–6. Two forms. Time: 60 minutes. Vocabulary, reading for information, reading for relationships, literal comprehension, reading for interpretation, reading for appreciation. For preparation plus testing, if given in one sitting, allow 75 minutes, if in two sittings, 35 minutes each.

Reading Comprehension: Cooperative English Test. Cooperative Tests and Services. Grades 7–12, 11–16. Four forms. Time: 40 minutes. Vocabulary, speed, and level of comprehension.

Reading Miscue Inventory. Macmillan Publishing Company. Grades 1–7.

Comprehension, sound similarity, graphic similarity, grammatical function similarity.

Reading Test: National Achievement Tests. Psychometric Affiliates. Grades 3–6, 6–8. Two forms. Time: 33 minutes. Following directions, sentence and paragraph meaning, rate.

Roswell-Chall Auditory Blending Test. Essay Press. Grades 1–4. One form. Time: about 5 minutes. Auditory blending.

Roswell-Chall Diagnostic Reading Test of Word Analysis Skills. Essay Press. Grades 2–6. Two forms. Time: about 5 minutes. Word-recognition skills.

Silent Reading Diagnostic Tests. Rand McNally. Grades 2.5–6 and for retarded readers in junior and senior high school. Time: 20, 29, 30 minutes for the three periods of testing. Subtests: words in isolation, words in context, visual structural analysis, syllabication, word synthesis, beginning sounds, ending sounds, vowel and consonant sounds.

Sipay Word Analysis Tests. Educators Publishing Service. Measures oral reading decoding skills. Seventeen subtests are provided.

Spache Diagnostic Reading Scales. McGraw-Hill. Grade 1 and up. Graded word lists, reading passages, phonics tests. Used for diagnosing reading difficulties. Individual test.

SRA Achievement Series: Reading. Science Research Associates. Grades (reading) 1, 2; 2–4; (work-study skills) 4–6; 6–9. One form grades 1, 2; two forms other grades. Verbal-pictorial association, language perception, comprehension, vocabulary in grades 1, 2; comprehension and vocabulary in grades 2–9; work-study skills in grades 4–9.

SRA Reading Record. Science Research Associates. Grades 6–12. One form. Time: 40 minutes. Rate, comprehension, sentence and paragraph meaning, general and technical vocabulary, graph and other specialized reading.

Stanford Diagnostic Reading Test. Harcourt Brace Jovanovich. Grades 2.5–4.5;4.5–8.5. Comprehension, vocabulary, syllabication, auditory skills, phonic analysis, rate. Group test.

Stanford Reading Tests, Revision. Harcourt Brace Jovanovich. Grades 1.5–2.4; 2.5–3.4; 3.5–4.4; 4.5–5.4; 5.5–6.9; 7–9.5. Three forms. Word reading, comprehension, vocabulary.

Tests of Reading: Cooperative Inter-American Tests. Guidance Testing Associates. Grades 1–3, 4–7, 8–13. Two forms. Time: about 25–50 minutes. Vocabulary and comprehension.

Van Wagenen Analytical Reading Scales. Van Wagenen Psycho-Educational Laboratory. Grades 4–6, 7–9, 10–12. One form. Untimed. Comprehension; central thought, details, ideas spread over several sentences, and interpretation. Each division may be obtained separately.

Williams Reading Tests, Revised. Bobbs-Merrill. Two forms. Grades 2–3; 4–9. Vocabulary in paragraph context. Group test.

Wisconsin Tests of Reading Skill Development: Word Attack. NCS Interpretive Scoring Systems. Grades kgn–2, 1–3, 2–4, 3–6. Part of the Wisconsin Design for Reading Skill Development.

Woodcock Reading Mastery Tests. American Guidance Service. Grades kgn–12. Letter identification, word identification, word attack, word comprehension, passage comprehension, total.

Indexes

SUBJECT INDEX